教育部哲学社会科学研究重大课题攻关项目：
推动智库建设健康发展研究（17JZD009）

南大智库文丛　李刚　主编

CTTI智库报告（2018）

李刚　王斯敏　邹婧雅　主编

2018 Chinese Think Tank Index Report

南京大学出版社

中国特色新型智库建设的"下半场"

——南大智库文丛序

2013年4月,习近平总书记对中国特色新型智库建设工作做了重要批示。根据中共中央办公厅、国务院办公厅2015年1月公开印发的《关于加强中国特色新型智库建设的意见》提出的时间表——到2020年实现中国特色新型智库建设总体目标,那么自2013年以来的这五年应属于中国特色新型智库建设的"上半场",未来三年应该属于新型智库建设的"下半场"。

2016年5月,习近平总书记指出:"近年来,哲学社会科学领域建设智库热情很高,成果也不少,为各级党政部门决策提供了有益帮助。同时,有的智库研究存在重数量、轻质量问题,有的存在重形式传播、轻内容创新问题,还有的流于搭台子、请名人、办论坛等形式主义的做法。"(《在哲学社会科学工作座谈会上的讲话》)我们认为习近平总书记的总结仍然是对五年新型智库建设切中肯綮的评估。

经过这五年的实践,我们对新型智库建设的深远意义认识得更加清晰。

第一,新型智库建设成为推动国家治理体系和治理能力现代化的重要抓手和重要路径。什么样的国家治理体系才是现代化的?什么样的治理能力才是现代化的?现代化不光是工具层面的,也应当是价值层面的,现代化的治理体系和现代化的治理能力体现在国家治理的价值、理论、方法、工具所具备的现代性上。以人民为中心的法治化、规范化、科学化、协同化、效用化的治理体系才是现代化的治理体系。综合运用并发挥国家治理体系的最大效用,达到全民福祉的最大化,形成"良好治理",就是现代化的治理能力。新型智库无疑是观察国家治理体系和治理能力现代性的一个重要指标。加强新型智库建设实质上就是在促进国家治理的现代性成长。

第二,新型智库建设继承了儒家"学为政本"传统,促进了国家治理的科学理性和专业理性。儒家强调"学为政本",这和黑暗的中世纪欧洲形成了鲜明的对比。有思想家说,中国文明是"早熟"的文明,这是与西方传统对比后得出的结论。秦汉以后,中国就建立了高度理性的非世袭的郡县制和官员任期制。隋唐以后,科举制已经成为官员选拔的主要制度,这比近代欧洲文官制度要早数百年。可以这么说,中古以后,中国国家治理模式就是建立在知识基础之上的贤人政治。但是,近代以来,西方逐渐走向了"学为政本"的国家治理法治化和专业化的路向,中国反而陷入积贫积弱、四分五裂的境况,国家治理不再依赖学术和知识共同体,"学为政本"的传统被迫中断。现代智库虽然起源于西方,却是为数不多的可以嫁接到中国文化传统的一种现代西方国家治理架构。现代智库体现的"学为政本"的贤人政治精神契合中国文化的精神,这就很好地解释了中国知识界为何对建设新智库充满热情。

第三,新型智库建设本质是开放言路,建立制度化的"政—知""政—产""政—媒""政—社"意见交通渠道,调动各行业知识精英参与国家治理的积极性。根据我国宪法,人民在国家治理中处于中心地位,但是在国家治理的体系和实践中,决策体系相对封闭,人民参与国家治理的渠道和机会均有限。实际上,不要说普通群众了,即使是高级知识分子,提供给他们参与决策咨询的选项也不多。新型智库建设不仅给政府的内脑——各级各类研究室带来了专业化的决策咨询工作理念,而且通过外脑——高校研究机构、社科院、党校行政学院、主流媒体的智库化转型,使得理论界、社科界、高等教育界的专家获得了制度化的建言献策管道。如果说内脑是新型智库建设中的存量部分,那么外脑就是智库建设中的增量部分。如果说内脑是以往决策咨询的主体,那么现在外脑和内脑则获得了对等的主体地位,虽然它们的话语权并不相等。这种不相等并不是由于到决策中枢的距离远近,而是缘自内脑和外脑的分工和专业素养的不同。在短期和应急决策咨询上,内脑发言权较大,而在长期和基础的决策咨询中,也许外脑话语权更大。决策咨询体系增量主体的扩大促进了国家治理体系的开放性、协商性、民主性、包容性。

第四,新型智库建设促进了有利于开展政策辩论的理性第二公共政策空间的成长。互联网的兴起虽然极大地提升了政策辩论的参与度,但是有时候这种参与也是无序的和非理性的,这往往使得正常的政策辩论在网络空间中无法开展。这种情况一方面是由于长期以来民众接受的政策素养教育严重不足,的确不知道如何开展一项严肃的政策辩论;另一方面是因为一部分自媒体人和公众号的写手为吸引眼球无所不用其极,搅乱了正常的政策辩论。而在新型智库建设过程中,政策共同体的要素和边界逐渐明晰,形成了由党委政府、人大政协、政策研究机构、新型智库、主流媒体等部门的专家组成的第二公共政策讨论空间。在这个共同空间中,智库起到了连接器和催化器的作用,推动了理性的公共政策辩论和协商。

正是因为认识到新型智库建设是推动国家治理体系和治理能力现代化的难得机遇,以天下为己任的中国哲学社会科学界才怀着满腔热情和历史使命感积极响应中央的号召,努力推动新型智库建设。

如果从新型智库实体建设来说,我们取得了巨大的成绩。根据中国智库索引的统计,截至2018年底,我国已经有9大类706家智库,分布于50多个战略和政策领域。根据规模和研究能力,这些智库分为国家高端智库、省级重点智库和普通专业智库三个层次,其中还包括一些按照"民非"(民办非企业单位)、社团或者企业形式运行的社会智库。另外,在智库的制度建设和运营管理上也探索出不少有益的经验,涌现出很多可圈可点的案例。

2017年,南京大学中国智库研究与评价中心和光明日报智库研究与发布中心征集评选了一系列值得重视的新型智库建设案例。例如,"复旦发展研究院:始终坚持国际化路径促进传统论坛转型为智库论坛""同济大学财经研究所:智库研究要抓重大现实问题要突出前瞻性——《重新认识和准确定义新时期我国社会的主要矛盾》""北京市信访矛盾分析中心:智库实证研究的佳作——《社会矛盾指数研究》""华中师范大学中国农村研究院:三十年专注农村社会调查——从走村串户到构建大数据智库调查服务平台""浙江师范大学非洲研究院近年来立足中非合作实践需要,成功探索出了一条学科、智库、媒体三位一体的发展路径""江南大学食品安全风险治理研究院旨在打造小而专、小而精、小而强,国际化视野的高校专业智库""长江教育研究院:充分利用人大政协渠道,搭建一流专业论坛,十年如一日专注中国教育现代化",等等。

对照《关于加强中国特色新型智库建设的意见》提出的到 2020 年要实现的总体目标,我们认为新型智库建设"上半场"没有解决好的问题有以下几点。

第一,我国智库产业集中度和产业集群性很低。实体数量的增长并不意味着我国新型智库就形成了"党政部门、社科院、党校行政学院、高校、军队、科研院所和企业、社会智库协调发展"的局面,就形成了"定位明晰、特色鲜明、规模适度、布局合理的中国特色新型智库体系"。总体上说,我国智库机构"散""弱""小"的局面并未发生根本改变,其实由于数量增加了,智库类机构"散""弱""小"的总体情况可能反而更严重,这导致我国智库产业集中度和产业集群性很低。

相反,美国智库产业集中度和产业集群性很高。华盛顿智库街上的近 400 家美国智库中,三分之一以上的智库拥有的全职研究员和职员在百人左右。美国西海岸的兰德公司有员工 1850 人,芝加哥大学的全美舆情研究中心(NORC)有全职研究员和职员 800 余人。可以说,美国智库不仅多,而且单个规模大、研究咨询力量强、影响力大。反观我们的智库,虽然中国社科院全院总人数 4200 多人,有科研业务人员 3200 多人,但这些研究人员分属 31 个研究所、45 个研究中心和 120 个学科,每个研究所(中心)拥有的研究人员平均起来不过 42 人。更关键的在于,这些研究所和研究中心都是独立行政单元,跨所(中心)的协同合作非常困难。这种现象不仅存在于中国社科院,也存在于不少省级社科院。至于高校智库,"散""弱""小"的现象则更严重。C9 高校中的哲学社会科学研究机构动辄数百个,但是其中绝大多数都属非实体非法人的教授课题组,往往会因为教授转会或者退休而"人亡政息",形成大量"僵尸机构"。可以说,我国智库体系中杂牌军多、正规军少,业余选手多、专业选手少,新智库多、老牌智库少。因此,中央抓国家高端智库建设,省市抓重点智库建设是非常必要的。如果不能把有限的经费和专家资源集中到一起,还是分散发展,那就不可能迅速改变我国新型智库体系"散""弱""小"的局面。

我国的主要专家资源集中在高校系统,但是高校过于重视学科建设,把主要资源都投入学科建设。决定学科建设能否进入一流的主要指标主要包括纵向的项目、学位点、重点实验室、"戴帽子"的各类人才数量、高水平论文和各类奖项的数量等。遗憾的是，新型智库的质量和数量并不在其中，这就导致大部分高校对新型智库建设都不够重视，不愿意投入真金白银。国家在一流高校里认定了14家高端智库(含高端培育智库)，有些智库的确发挥了智库的功能，但也有一些智库还是以教学研究为主，转型脚步慢了半拍；还有的高校虽然拿到了国家高端智库建设的入场券，但是并未给予足够重视。

第二，新型智库建设未能有效突破体制上的"三明治瓶颈"。实体数量的增长并不意味着智库研究质量的同步提升和新型体制机制的落地生根，我国智库的治理体制难以突破"三明治瓶颈"。2018年3月，黄坤明同志在国家高端智库理事会扩大会议上的讲话中指出，试点工作以来，中央和有关部门在经费管理、人员出国、奖励激励、会议管理等方面出台了一系列含金量很高的政策，赋予试点单位很大的自主权和政策空间，但不少单位承接、落实还不到位，很多政策仍然悬置。人员管理、薪酬待遇、职称评定、财务管理等方面的掣肘比较突出。

产生这种现象的根本原因是我国大部分智库都是附属型智库。根据中国智库索引的数据，我国智库体系中95%的智库都是母体机构下属的非法人的实体智库和非法人挂靠性质的智库。这些智库外部治理结构类似三明治，三明治的上层是国家/省市部委智库管理部门，中间是母体单位(比如高校和社科院)，下层才是智库。之所以称之为智库治理的"三明治瓶颈"，是因为国家/省市部委智库管理部门根本无法直接管理这些母体单位下属的非独立智库，而是要通过母体单位(也可以叫平台单位)才能作用到智库。母体单位(平台单位)就像三明治的中间层隔绝了国家/省市部委智库管理部门和非独立智库之间的直接治理联系，国家/省市部委智库管理部门任何政策落地都需要母体单位(平台单位)制定实施细则，或者经过母体单位(平台单位)的认可同意配套相应的落地政策。比如，中央出台的增加经费中专家劳务费用支出比例的意见，如果未经母体单位(平台单位)认可并制定相应的实施细则和财务审批的流程，那么中央的含金量很高的意见就不可能作用于非独立智库(三明治下层)，非独立智库望眼欲穿的好政策由于三明治中间层的梗阻就无法落地，政策红利也就无法释放出来。

对于母体单位(平台单位)来说，下属智库只是众多业务单元之一，是否值得为中央/省市部委智库管理部门的政策落实制定配套的细则和流程，还有许多其他考量。以高校为例，学科建设是主要任务，不可或缺，而智库建设属于锦上添花，可有可无。如果要为中央/省市部委智库管理部门的政策落实制定细则、配套资源，就会存在是否会激怒主体院系的问题。如果同意智库增加经费中专家劳务费用支出比例，那么非智库单位要比照执行怎么办？不同意的话，非智库单位会援例争吵；如果同意的话，科研经费中学校分成势必减少，伤及自身利益。因此，大部分高校都会对中央出台的增加经费中专家劳务费用支出比例的文件采取置之不理的做法。三明治中间层对智库宏观治理影响巨大，可以说对非独立智库而言，母体单位（平台单位）的智库治理才是最直接最关键的，中央/省市部委智库管理部门的智库治理属于天高皇帝远、鞭长莫及。如何破解智库宏观治理中的"三明治瓶颈"呢？根本解决方法是把非独立智库变成独立法人实体机构。比如南京大学为化解智库治理的"三明治瓶颈"，就让下属的两家省级重点智库——长江产业经济研究院和紫金传媒智库在省民政厅注册为"民非"法人实体智库，这样一来"三明治瓶颈"的中间层就不存在了。独立的法人实体智库可以直接执行中央/省市部委智库管理部门的有关智库治理的政策文件。学校内部其他院系和研究中心也无法援引这两家智库享受的政策红利。同时，为了让这两家智库同时利用学校的资源，南京大学还发文成立了南京大学长江产经研究院和南京大学紫金传媒智库。南京大学通过一个法人实体两块牌子的方式成功化解了智库治理的"三明治瓶颈"。

第三，智库的研究咨询业务过于集中在政策过程的前端，业务模式头重脚轻。政策过程包含议程设置、政策辩论、决策与路演、政策教育、政策评估、政策反馈修正等，这是一个完整的政策环，每个环节都需要智库参加，但是每个环节需要不同层次不同专业的智库参加。如果从国家政策层面来说，在议程设置阶段和政策辩论阶段主要需要高层次高端智库参与，其他层次的智库由于缺乏全局性的视野和经验往往就不适合此项工作。可是在政策评估环节，即使是地方智库也可以从本地区出发对国家政策的执行情况开展评估和反馈。但是由于我们智库考核指标的设置往往给予高层次批示极高的权重，导致几乎所有智库都在思考全国性政策议程设置问题。这种定位错误,造成了大量的重复劳动和无效劳动,如雪片一样飞向北京的内参其实大多数是没有必要的。因此,绝大多数省级智库都不应该把业务重心放到全国性政策议程设置的决策咨询工作上。

相反,大量的专业智库应该把业务模式重心下移和后置,把主要精力放到政策教育、政策评估和政策反馈上来。专业智库角色定位主要不是当"国师"——为党委政府出思想、出概念和出思路,而是应该承担更多的技术性支援工作。专业智库的主要工作是调查研究、采集数据、数据分析、建模计算,是协助政府脚踏实地地落实政策,是用自己的数据、计算能力评估政策和项目的执行情况并及时反馈给政府。对于专业智库来说,可能核心能力并非思想力,而是调查、数据、计算、规划、评估等能力。没有这些核心能力,智库只能开展定性研究,靠拍脑袋为政府出主意,那样业务重心就浮于表面。

第四,智库和政府内部研究机构是"两张皮",供给与需求之间的信息不对称无法消除。智库是政府的外脑,政府内研究机构是内脑。习近平总书记指出,"要加强决策部门同智库的信息共享和互动交流,把党政部门政策研究同智库对策研究紧密结合起来,引导和推动智库建设健康发展、更好发挥作用"(《在哲学社会科学工作座谈会上的讲话》),强调的其实就是内脑和外脑的协同。内脑要指导、引导和推动外脑的对策研究,要解决政策研究和对策研究"两张皮"的问题,要消除需求和供给之间的信息不对称。这个问题之所以未得到有效解决,原因很多。首先,我国智库体系中高校智库比重过大。截至2017年底,CTTI来源604家智库中58%属于高校智库。这种情况得到中国社科院评价院的《中国智库综合评价AMI研究报告(2017)》核心智库目录的印证。该报告确定了166家核心智库,其中高校智库有79家,比重为47%。高校智库往往是由传统学术研究"翻牌"而来,更擅长的是学术研究而非对策研究。高校智库因为固有的师道尊严文化,往往缺乏"客户第一"的服务精神。智库是一种高端的决策咨询服务工作,不管是高端还是低端服务业,只要是服务业,没有"客户第一"的服务精神,那么服务工作就不可能做好。因此,让高校智库主动对接政府研究机构,心甘情愿地为政策研究部门做好技术支援性工作,心甘情愿地为政策研究部门做调查研究、采集数据、分析数据、撰写研究报告初稿，几乎是不可能的。其次，政府政策研究部门恐怕也未必看得上智库，更不愿意和智库共享数据和信息。坦率地说，二者之间也存在竞争关系，政策研究部门也有"教会徒弟饿死师傅"的忧虑。

解决这个问题的主要途径还是智库主动采用嵌入式决策咨询服务模式。嵌入式决策咨询服务模式是我们首次归纳的一个学术概念，指的是智库的对策研究通过嵌入政府政策研究过程解决外脑和内脑的协同问题。嵌入首先说明了智库和政府政策研究部门之间存在着一定距离，存在一定的区别；嵌入也意味着智库的对策研究有独立的价值，有自己独特的属性——和政府政策研究部门相比，智库研究可能更关心中长期问题，更关心基础问题，更关心前瞻性问题。嵌入式决策咨询服务包括政策过程的嵌入、决策咨询流程的嵌入、决策咨询场景的嵌入和政策共同体的圈层嵌入。政策过程的嵌入是指智库应该嵌入一个政策的完整过程，和内脑开展紧密合作，从议程设置、政策辩论、决策与推广、政策执行、政策教育、政策评估和政策反馈全过程的参与和发挥作用，不仅要关心政策文本的产生，还要促进政策文本的落地以及落地后的效果。决策咨询流程的嵌入是指要在调查研究、数据采集、数据分析、分析研判和撰写报告等过程中都和内脑紧密合作，充分发挥智库技术支援的优势，服务内脑的政策研究。决策咨询场景的嵌入是指积极参加领导的调研活动、决策咨询会议和政策路演活动，获得决策咨询活动的现场感与语境，如此才能了解政策产生的前因后果。政策共同体的圈层嵌入是指智库要和政府决策者、政策研究部门形成密切的联系，产生强烈的互信关系，这是其他三种嵌入的前提，也是结果。当然，政策共同体中并非只有决策者和政策研究者（内脑），还包含其他的要素，智库要和这些要素之间都形成密切的圈层嵌入。如果智库能实现四种形式的嵌入，那么就有可能解决对策研究脱离实际、不接地气、没有市场的困境，成为党委政府想得起、用得上、离不开的智库。

第五，智库成果认定与激励的指挥棒设计不合理。成果认定与激励制度是引导智库发展的指挥棒，但目前这个指挥棒设计不够合理，是制约智库健康发展的主要问题之一。我国智库成果认定标准非常单一，从我们收集到的各种认定奖励文本来看，各类智库都看重批示的行政级别，无论是折算成文章还是直接奖励金钱，都是行政级别越高的批示得奖越重。这种做法简单粗暴，必然导致智库只愿意为决策者服务而不是为决策过程服务，必然导致智库只愿意为高端决策者服务而不是为基层治理服务，必然导致智库只愿意着力揣摩领导意图的政策研究而不是基于客观事实基础的政策研究。其实，智库所承担的大量政策评估、政策宣传等工作都不会产生批示，但是这些技术支援性工作恰恰是政府更需要的。因此，这些工作都应该纳入智库成果的认定范围。政策评估等工作政府会以横向项目的形式交给智库，而在我们的智库考核体系中，横向项目恰恰是最不受重视的。我们认为，对于国家高端智库和省级重点智库而言，的确批示的权重应该大一些，因为这些智库的主要功能是咨政建言。可是对于大多数专业智库而言，用专业能力为党委政府提供技术性支援工作往往不会产生批示，对它们而言，批示就不应该是主要考核指标。

上述五大问题能否解决好，决定了新型智库建设"下半场"的成效。新型智库体系建设要解决智库产业的集中度和产业集群性问题，实体化和法人化是解决体制机制创新、克服"三明治瓶颈"的重要途径，业务重心下移和后置是解决智库浮于表面、注重形式传播问题的重要思路，而推行嵌入式决策咨询服务模式是解决政策研究与对策研究衔接、发挥内脑和外脑协同研究效应的重要选择，智库成果认定与激励措施的调整则始终是最重要的保障。

2017年，我被批准承担教育部哲学社会科学研究重大课题攻关项目——"推动智库建设健康发展研究"（项目编号：17JZD009）。此后，我带课题组调研了一些智库和智库管理部门，它们反映的情况引发了我上述思考。恰逢"南大智库文丛"又有新书出版，考虑到原来的丛书序已经和形势有所脱节，故以此文作为"南大智库文丛"的新序。"南大智库文丛"在南京大学出版社的大力支持下已经出满10种。其中4种已经重印，这对我们也是很大的鼓舞。《CTTI智库报告（2018）》是我们中心和光明智库共同推出的第三份报告，报告用中英双语种出版，目的是向海外宣传中国特色新型智库建设的成就，展示中国智库的群体风采。

南京大学中国智库研究与评价中心被智库界称为"智库的智库"，我们中心的使命就是研究中外智库发展的规律，促进中国智库共同体的发展，为智库交流搭建平台，为中国智库培养管理人才，为我国智库和公共政策研究机构提供管理咨询服务。

经过数年的努力，我们中心取得了一些成绩。

第一，我们和光明日报社共同开发了"中国智库索引"。CTTI系统是具有智库垂直搜索、智库数据管理和智库在线智能评价三位一体的具有自主知识产权智库信息系统。目前收录706家智库、12299名专家、19071次智库会议和咨询活动记录、120303项智库研究成果记录。CTTI成为我国找智库、找专家服务和找专家成果的第一平台。

第二，我们和光明日报社共同创立了"中国智库治理论坛"。2016年12月，第一届年会在南京大学召开，与会代表近700人。2017年12月，第二届年会在北京召开，与融媒体峰会一起进行，与会代表预计300人，实际到会700余人。2018年12月，第三届年会在南京召开，实际到会代表近800人。经过三届年会，论坛对促进我国新型智库共同体建设起到了积极作用。

第三，我们编撰了中英文对照的《CTTI智库报告》和工具书《中国智库索引》，这些书已经被国内数百所高校图书馆以及海外的不少东亚图书馆和著名智库，如华盛顿布鲁金斯学会、基辛格研究中心等采购收藏。

第四，南京大学中国智库研究与评价中心是我国最早在博士生招生目录上设立智库研究方向的博士生培养项目单位。我们智库中心已经培养了4名智库专业博士毕业生，为促进智库和公共政策研究机构管理成为一个专门的学术领域做出了应有的贡献。

李刚

2019年9月5日

各章节作者名单

子报告名称	姓名
《2018CTTI来源智库发展报告》	邹婧雅、冯雅
	英文版翻译：胡文琴、马雨溪、赵芳
《2018 CTTI高校智库暨百强榜报告》	于亮
	英文版翻译：李茹、孙羽
《2017"CTTI智库最佳实践奖"评选活动报告》	马雪雯
	英文版翻译：沙子杰

目 录

2018CTTI 来源智库发展报告 / 001

1 中国特色新型智库建设进展 / 001

  1.1 智库政策文件制定点面俱到 / 001

    1.1.1 国家政策引导智库发展方向 / 001

    1.1.2 省市政策层层跟进 / 002

    1.1.3 政策文件系统性增强 / 003

    1.1.4 为各类型智库发展提供政策保障 / 004

  1.2 智库体系和平台建设日渐成熟 / 005

    1.2.1 智库体系布局逐步合理完善 / 005

    1.2.2 智库平台丰富多样 / 007

  1.3 智库交流与传播日益深化 / 009

    1.3.1 智库会议促进智库思想的交流传播 / 009

    1.3.2 网络平台促进智库信息的交流传播 / 010

    1.3.3 参与国际交流，发出"中国智声" / 011

  1.4 智库研究与评价长足发展 / 012

    1.4.1 智库研究与评价机构如雨后春笋 / 013

    1.4.2 智库研究成果井喷式增长 / 014

  1.5 小结 / 016

2 "中国智库索引"CTTI 系统概述 / 017

  2.1 CTTI 系统开发与建设进展回顾 / 017

    2.1.1 CTTI 系统研发背景 / 017

2.1.2　CTTI 系统的总体架构 / 018

　　　2.1.3　CTTI 系统主要功能 / 022

　2.2　CTTI 数据收录情况概览 / 025

　2.3　CTTI 的作用与影响 / 029

3　2018 年度 CTTI 来源智库目录增补 / 032

　3.1　CTTI 来源智库增补原则 / 032

　3.2　2018CTTI 来源智库增补过程 / 034

　3.3　天津来源智库增补经验 / 036

　3.4　CTTI 来源智库数据分析 / 037

4　MRPAI 测评指标体系与排序规则 / 042

　4.1　评价基本原则 / 042

　4.2　MRPAI 测评指标的确定 / 043

　4.3　MRPAI 智库测评指标的赋值 / 048

5　MRPAI 排序规则 / 050

　5.1　MRPAI 排序规则的设计原理 / 050

　5.2　MRPAI 排序规则 / 051

　　　5.2.1　数量指标排序 / 051

　　　5.2.2　效能指标排序 / 052

　5.3　MRPAI 智库专家排序规则 / 052

　5.4　大学智库指数排序规则 / 054

　5.5　MRPAI 测评系统 / 055

6　来源智库测评结果分析 / 056

　6.1　社会智库测评数据示例 / 056

　6.2　各研究领域智库测评数据示例 / 058

　　　6.2.1　宏观经济与国际贸易领域 / 059

6.2.2 产业与金融领域 / 060

6.2.3 区域研究与国际关系领域 / 061

6.2.4 党的建设与国家治理领域 / 063

6.2.5 社会治理与公共事业领域 / 064

6.2.6 法律与公共安全领域 / 066

6.2.7 文化与教育领域 / 067

6.2.8 环境、能源与基础设施领域 / 069

6.2.9 信息与科技领域 / 070

6.2.10 "三农"领域 / 071

6.2.11 "一带一路"领域 / 072

6.2.12 综合型智库 / 073

7 加强中国特色新型智库建设的几点建议 / 074

7.1 创新智库体制机制,完善智库治理 / 074

7.2 改善智库服务模式,提供嵌入式服务 / 075

7.3 优化智库人力资源布局,充实人才队伍 / 076

7.4 增强国际交流合作,让世界理解中国 / 077

7.5 树立智库品牌意识,打造旗舰产品 / 077

7.6 促进智库协调发展,完善智库体系 / 078

附录:CTTI 来源智库目录(2018—2019) / 080

2018 Annual Report on the Development of CTTI Source Think Tanks / *110*

1   Progress in the Construction of New Types of Think Tanks with Chinese Characteristics / *110*

    1.1   Full Formulation for Think Tank Policies and Documents / *110*

        1.1.1   Guidance on the Direction of Think Tank Development by National Policies / *110*

        1.1.2   Provincial and Municipal Policies Followed Up Level by Level / *113*

        1.1.3   The Systematic Improvements of Policies and Documents / *114*

        1.1.4   Policy Support for the Development of Different Types of Think Tanks / *116*

    1.2   The Think Tank System and Platform Becoming Mature / *118*

        1.2.1   Gradual and Reasonable Improvement in the Configuration of Think Tank System / *118*

        1.2.2   Diverse Think Tank Platforms / *122*

    1.3   Deepening Communication and Dissemination of Think Tanks / *124*

        1.3.1   Think Tank Conferences Promoting the Communication and Dissemination of Think Tank Ideas / *125*

        1.3.2   Network Platforms Promoting the Communication and Dissemination of Think Tank Information / *127*

        1.3.3   Participating in International Exchange to Make "Voice of China's Think Tanks" / *129*

    1.4   Significant Progress in Think Tank Research and Evaluation / *131*

        1.4.1   Think Tank Research and Evaluation Institutions Spring Up / *132*

        1.4.2   A Massive Upsurge in Think Tank Research Findings / *133*

    1.5   Conclusion / *138*

2 An Overview of the CTTI System / *139*

　2.1 A Review of the Developing and Constructing Process of the CTTI System / *139*

　　2.1.1 Research and Development Background of the CTTI System / *139*

　　2.1.2 Overall Architecture of the CTTI System / *141*

　　2.1.3 Main Functions of CTTI System / *145*

　2.2 Overview of CTTI Data Inclusion / *150*

　2.3 The Role and Impact of CTTI / *155*

3 Addition to Catalogue of CTTI's Source Think Tanks in 2018 / *161*

　3.1 Principles of Source Think Tank Addition / *161*

　3.2 The Process of Adding Source Think Tanks in 2018 / *164*

　3.3 Tianjin Source Think Tanks Addition Experience / *166*

　3.4 Analysis of the CTTI Source Think Tank Data / *168*

4 The MRPAI Assessment Indicator System and Ranking Rule / *174*

　4.1 Basic Principles of Evaluation / *174*

　4.2 Selection of the MRPAI Assessment Indicators / *175*

　4.3 Value Assignment for MRPAI Indicators / *183*

5 The MRPAI Ranking Rules / *187*

　5.1 Principle for Designing MRPAI Ranking Rules / *187*

　5.2 MRPAI Ranking Rules / *188*

　　5.2.1 Ranking by Quantitative Indicators / *188*

　　5.2.2 Ranking by Effectiveness Indicators / *189*

　5.3 MRPAI Think Tank Expert Ranking Rules / *190*

　5.4 University Think Tank Index Ranking Rules / *193*

　5.5 MRPAI Assessment System / *194*

6　The Analysis of MRPAI Assessment Result Data / 195

　　6.1　Examples of Evaluation Data on Private Think Tanks / 196

　　6.2　Examples of Evaluation Data on Think Tanks in Various Research Areas / 199

　　　　6.2.1　Macro-Economy and International Trade / 200

　　　　6.2.2　Industry and Finance / 202

　　　　6.2.3　Regional Research and International Relations / 204

　　　　6.2.4　Party Building and National Governance / 207

　　　　6.2.5　Social Governance and Public Utilities / 209

　　　　6.2.6　Law and Public Security / 211

　　　　6.2.7　Culture and Education / 214

　　　　6.2.8　Environment, Energy and Infrastructure / 217

　　　　6.2.9　Information and Technology / 219

　　　　6.2.10　Three Rural Issues / 220

　　　　6.2.11　The Belt and Road Initiative / 222

　　　　6.2.12　Comprehensive Think Tank / 223

7　Suggestions on Strengthening the Construction of New Think Tanks with Chinese Characteristics / 225

　　7.1　Innovating the System and Mechanism of Think Tanks and Improving the Governance of Think Tanks / 225

　　7.2　Improving Think Tank Service Model and Providing Embedded Service / 227

　　7.3　Optimizing the Distribution of Human Resources in Think Tanks and Enriching the Talent Team / 228

7.4 Enhancing International Exchange and Cooperation to Make the World Understand China / *230*

7.5 Establishing Brand Awareness of Think Tanks and Building Flagship Products / *232*

7.6 Promoting the Coordinated Development and Improving the System of Think Tank / *233*

Appendix: CTTI Source Think Tanks (2018 - 2019) / *235*

2018 CTTI 高校智库暨百强榜报告 / 274

1 高校系统高度重视新型智库建设 / 274

2 高校在新型智库建设中的独特作用 / 275

  2.1 学科齐全，便于开展跨学科的问题导向研究 / 275

  2.2 人才富集，有利于开展大规模数据工程 / 275

  2.3 高校智库有开展公共外交的便捷通道 / 276

  2.4 高校智库舆论公信力较高 / 276

  2.5 高校智库专业特征明显 / 276

3 高校智库在新型智库体系中占据了重要地位 / 276

  3.1 高校智库的地域分布 / 277

  3.2 中国高校智库类型及研究领域分布 / 278

  3.3 高校智库的规模 / 278

  3.4 中国大学智库指数 / 278

4 CTTI 高校智库百强评价愿景与原则 / 281

  4.1 CTTI 高校智库百强评价的界定 / 281

  4.2 CTTI 高校智库百强评价的目的 / 282

  4.3 CTTI 高校智库百强评价的原则 / 283

5 CTTI 高校智库百强评价体系及算法 / 286

  5.1 CTTI 高校智库百强评价体系构建 / 286

  5.2 CTTI 高校智库百强榜遴选过程 / 293

  5.3 CTTI 高校智库百强榜名单 / 293

6 CTTI 高校智库百强榜数据分析 / 297

  6.1 CTTI 百强高校智库地域分布 / 297

  6.2 CTTI 百强高校智库大学分布 / 298

7 高校新型智库建设中的主要问题 / 300

7.1 缺乏明确的政策咨询信息，供求信息不对称 / 300

7.2 传播意识淡薄，忽视宣传工作 / 300

7.3 智库治理机制需要优化 / 300

8 加强高校新型智库建设的几点建议 / 302

附录：CTTI 高校智库百强机构小传 / 306

2018 Annual Report on CTTI University Think Tanks & Top 100 University Think Tanks / *351*

1 Great Importance Attached to the Construction of New Types of University Think Tanks / *351*

2 The Unique Role Played by Universities in the Construction of New Types of Think Tanks / *353*

    2.1 Comprehensive Disciplines Make It Easier to Conduct Interdisciplinary Problem-Oriented Researches / *353*

    2.2 Abundant Talents Are Conducive to the Implementation of Large-Scale Data Projects / *354*

    2.3 University Think Tanks Provide an Easy Approach to Developing Public Diplomacy / *355*

    2.4 University Think Tanks Have a High Level of Public Credibility / *355*

    2.5 University Think Tanks Have Distinct Specialized Characteristics / *355*

3 The Important Role Played by University Think Tanks in the System of New Types of Think Tanks / *356*

    3.1 Regional Distribution of University Think Tanks / *357*

    3.2 Distribution of University Think Tanks in China by Type and by Area of Research / *358*

    3.3 Scale of University Think Tanks / *359*

    3.4 University Think Tank Index in China / *359*

4 Visions and Principles of the CTTI Top 100 University Think Tanks Evaluation / *363*

    4.1 Definition of the CTTI Top 100 University Think Tanks Evaluation / *363*

    4.2 Purpose of the CTTI Top 100 University Think Tanks Evaluation / *364*

4.3　Principles of the CTTI Top 100 University Think Tanks Evaluation / 366

5　The CTTI Top 100 University Think Tanks Evaluation System and Algorithm / 370

　　5.1　Establishment of the CTTI Top 100 University Think Tanks Evaluation System / 370

　　5.2　Selection Process of the CTTI Top 100 University Think Tanks / 380

　　5.3　The CTTI Top 100 University Think Tanks / 381

6　Data Analysis of the CTTI Top 100 University Think Tanks / 386

　　6.1　Regional Distribution of the CTTI Top 100 University Think Tanks / 386

　　6.2　Distribution of the CTTI Top 100 University Think Tanks in Colleges or Universities / 388

7　Major Problems in the Construction of New Types of University Think Tanks / 390

　　7.1　Lack of Clear Information on Policy Consultation and Imbalance between Information Supply and Demand / 390

　　7.2　Weak Awareness of Communication and Publicity / 391

　　7.3　Management Mechanisms of Think Tanks Required to Be Improved / 391

8　Suggestions on How to Improve the Construction of New Types of University Think Tanks / 394

Appendix: Brief Biographies of the CTTI Top 100 University Think Tanks / 400

2017"CTTI 智库最佳实践奖"评选活动报告 / 474

前　言 / 474

1　智库最佳实践案例评选活动源起 / 474

　　1.1　最佳实践 / 474

　　1.2　智库最佳实践 / 476

　　　　1.2.1　OTT 智库最佳实践系列 / 476

　　　　1.2.2　智库最佳实践的内涵 / 477

　　　　1.2.3　智库最佳实践的要素 / 477

　　1.3　中国智库需要寻觅适合自身发展的"最佳实践" / 478

　　　　1.3.1　新型智库建设呼唤"最佳实践" / 478

　　　　1.3.2　新型智库建设过程中涌现"最佳实践" / 479

　　　　1.3.3　"最佳实践"为新型智库研究咨询赋能 / 479

　　1.4　智库最佳实践案例评选活动的意义 / 480

2　CTTI-BPA 最佳实践案例评选回顾 / 481

　　2.1　材料征集与审核 / 481

　　2.2　评选过程回顾 / 481

　　2.3　评选内容分析 / 482

　　　　2.3.1　申报主体类型多样、分布广泛 / 483

　　　　2.3.2　研究报告主题趋于多元化、专业化 / 484

　　　　2.3.3　智库活动蓬勃开展、品牌效应逐渐成形 / 485

　　　　2.3.4　智库体制机制建设有了新突破 / 486

　　2.4　评选结果 / 487

　　2.5　会议回顾 / 490

3　CTTI-BPA 最佳实践案例撷英 / 493

　　3.1　研究报告篇 / 493

3.1.1 北京市信访矛盾分析中心:《社会矛盾指数研究》——智库实证研究的佳作 / 493

3.1.2 同济大学财经研究所:《重新认识和准确定义新时期我国社会的主要矛盾》——智库研究要抓重大现实问题,突出前瞻性 / 494

3.1.3 江南大学食品安全风险治理研究院:《中国食品安全发展报告》——在专业理论研究上凝练品牌成果;打造小而专、小而精、小而强,国际化视野的高校专业智库 / 495

3.2 管理篇 / 496

3.2.1 山东社会科学院创新工程:以创新工程为抓手,加速传统社科院迈向一流新型智库 / 496

3.2.2 华中师范大学中国农村发展智库:三十年专注农村社会调查——从走村串户到构建大数据智库调查服务平台 / 497

3.3 活动篇 / 497

3.3.1 复旦发展研究院:上海论坛——始终坚持国际化路径,促进传统论坛转型为智库论坛 / 497

3.3.2 浙江师范大学非洲研究院:"学科、智库、媒体三位一体"的发展路径 / 498

3.3.3 长江教育研究院:教育智库与教育治理高峰论坛——充分利用人大政协渠道,搭建一流专业论坛,十年如一日专注中国教育现代化 / 499

结 语 / 500

2017 Report on the Best Practice Awards for CTTI Think Tanks / *501*

Preface / *501*

1   The Origin of Best Practice Awards for Think Tanks / *501*

    1.1   Best Practice / *501*

    1.2   Best Practice of Think Tanks / *504*

        1.2.1   OTT Best Practice Series / *504*

        1.2.2   Connotation of Think-Tank Best Practice / *505*

        1.2.3   Elements of Think-Tank Best Practice / *506*

    1.3   The Necessity of Chinese Think-Tank Development to Seek Best Practice / *507*

        1.3.1   Calling for Best Practice to Develop New-Type Think Tanks / *507*

        1.3.2   Best Practice Emerging in the Construction of New-Type Think Tanks / *509*

        1.3.3   "Best Practice" Empowering Consultation to New Think-Tank Research / *510*

    1.4   Significance of BPA Selection for Think Tanks / *511*

2   Process Review of CTTI-BPA Cases Selection / *512*

    2.1   Material Collection and Review / *512*

    2.2   Selection Process Review / *513*

    2.3   Analysis of the Selection / *514*

        2.3.1   Diverse and Widely Distributed Subjects of Application / *515*

        2.3.2   Topics of Research Reports toward Diversification and Specialization / *517*

        2.3.3   Think Tank Events Booming and Brand Effects Taking Shape / *518*

        2.3.4   New Breakthroughs in the Institutional Mechanisms of Think Tanks / *521*

2.4　Selection Results / 522

2.5　Conference Review / 527

3　Best Practice Examples of CTTI-BPA / 532

 3.1　Research report / 532

  3.1.1　Beijing Institution of Letters to Government: *Research on the Social Contradictions Index*—A Model Think-Tank Empirical Research / 532

  3.1.2　Institute of Finance and Economics of Tongji University: *Rethinking and Accurately Defining the New-Era Principal Contradiction in China's Society*—The Think Tanks Research Should Pay Attention to Major Practical Problems and Give Prominence to the Foresight / 533

  3.1.3　Institute for Food Safety Risk Administration of Jiangnan University: *Report on China Food Safety Development*—Making Brand Achievements in Professional Theoretical Research; Building Small but Specialized, Fine and Strong Think Tanks with International Vision in Colleges and Universities / 535

 3.2　Management / 537

  3.2.1　Innovation Project of Shandong Academy of Social Sciences: Speed Up Transforming the Traditional Academy of Social Sciences to a First-Class New Think Tank Based on Innovative Projects / 537

  3.2.2　Institute of China Rural Studies of Central China Normal University: Rural Social Survey in Thirty Years—Developing from Village-to-Village Survey to Building the Investigation and Service Platform of Big-Data Think Tank / 539

 3.3　Events / 540

3.3.1 Fudan Development Institute: Shanghai Forum—Adhere to the International Path and Promote the Transformation of the Traditional Forum into a Think-Tank Forum / 540

3.3.2 Institute of African Studies of Zhejiang Normal University: The Development Path as "Trinity of Disciplines, Think Tank and Media" / 542

3.3.3 Changjiang Education Research Institute: Summit Forum on Education Think Tanks and Education Governance—Make Full Use of the Channels of the CPPCC National People's Congress, Set Up the First-Class Professional Forum and Focus on the Modernization of China's Education All the Time / 543

Conclusion / 545

2018CTTI 来源智库发展报告

1 中国特色新型智库建设进展

1.1 智库政策文件制定点面俱到

1.1.1 国家政策引导智库发展方向

(1) 中央高度重视新型智库建设

中国特色新型智库建设是党和政府科学决策、民主决策、依法决策的重要支撑，对于坚持和发展中国特色社会主义道路，增强我国国际话语权，实现中华民族伟大复兴有重要意义，因此受到了以习近平同志为核心的党中央的高度重视。在党的十八大之后，多位党和国家领导人在多种场合多次强调建设中国特色新型智库的重要性和必要性，阐述新型智库建设的内涵意义、建设目标、建设路径以及智库的责任担当等。

2013年4月，习近平总书记对中国特色新型智库建设作出重要批示，这是中央最高领导专门就智库建设做出的最为明确、内涵最为丰富的一次重要批示。同年5月，时任中共中央政治局委员、国务院副总理刘延东在"繁荣发展高校哲学社会科学推动中国特色新型智库建设"座谈会上指出了建设中国特色新型智库的重要意义。2014年3月，习近平总书记在访问德国时将智库建设提上了国家外交层面，"智库外交"将会成为我国国际交流与合作的"第二轨道"。此后，习近平总书记多次在会见他国领导人、出席国际论坛时提出要发挥智库作用，推动国际合作交流。2016年5月，习近平总书记在哲学社会科学工作座谈会上指出智库建设的成就，提出了问题以及智库建设的重点。2017年10月，习近平总书记在十九大报告中明确指出："加快构建中国特色哲学社会科学，加强中国特色新型智库建设。"2018年3月，李克强总理在《政府工作报告》中提到"建好新型智库"。党和国家领导人有关新型智库建设重要讲话和指示促进了一系列政策文件的制定,极大推动了中国特色新型智库建设进程。布鲁金斯学会中国中心主任李成认为国家领导层亲自关心智库建设,这是全世界都没有过的现象,也是中国智库发展的最大利好。

(2) 智库政策顶层设计日趋完善

党的十八届三中全会提出要加强中国特色新型智库建设,建立健全决策咨询制度。党的十八届五中全会强调要实施哲学社会科学创新工程,建设中国特色新型智库。2015年1月,中共中央办公厅、国务院办公厅印发的《关于加强中国特色新型智库建设的意见》(以下简称《意见》)成为我国新型智库建设的纲领性文件,阐述了新型智库建设的一系列重大理论和实践问题,标志着我国智库建设开始迈入高速发展时代;2015年11月,中央深化改革领导小组会议通过了《国家高端智库建设试点工作方案》,此后相继印发《国家高端智库管理办法(试行)》和《国家高端智库专项经费管理办法(试行)》;2017年5月,中共中央印发《关于加快构建中国特色哲学社会科学的意见》,民政部、中宣部等9部门联合印发《关于社会智库健康发展的若干意见》等。这些政策文件阐述了中国特色新型智库建设的重大意义,规划了总体的建设蓝图,以顶层设计的形式将中国特色新型智库纳入国家治理体系,具有长期性、全局性、战略性,引导了中国特色新型智库的建设发展方向。

1.1.2 省市政策层层跟进

党和国家领导人关于中国特色新型智库建设的重要论述、国家层面的智库发展政策为中国特色新型智库建设做出了宏观指导,各省市出台的有关新型智库建设的政策,则是将顶层政策逐级落实的重要一步。随着省市政策层层跟进,我国新型智库的治理逐渐规范化、制度化、流程化和法治化,我国新型智库治理的制度体系进一步完善,智库发展环境进一步优化。

在《意见》出台之后,各个省市积极响应,出台了相应的实施意见,或是将新型智库实施意见列入提案议程。例如,湖南省、江苏省、广东省、上海市等二十多个省级行政区均出台了加强新型智库建设的实施意见。各个省份或直辖市出台的新型智库建设意见虽然不尽相同，但都是在认真学习《意见》的精神之后，根据当地智库发展的实际情况，提出的进一步加强当地新型智库建设，建立健全决策咨询制度的实施意见。《意见》具有宏观意义，具有全局性、战略性，省级新型智库建设实施意见将《意见》精神和省情相互融合，提炼出了对于一省而言既具有指导意义，又有具体可操作价值的实施纲领。与省级政策相比，市级有关中国特色新型智库建设的政策文件更加注重本市的智库体系的构建，例如深圳市、苏州市等市在梳理本地区智库发展的现状、特点、问题之后，结合相关经验，提出构建智库格局的方式途径以及相关智库管理体制改革的措施。

1.1.3 政策文件系统性增强

除了从中央到省市层层跟进落实的中国特色新型智库建设实施意见之外，近两年，我国还出台了一系列智库具体建设层面的政策文件，类型丰富多样，政策文件的系统性逐渐增强，智库政策体系进一步完善。例如，出台了《国家高端智库建设试点工作方案》，明确了高端智库建设的指导思想、基本要求，提出了试点智库入选条件、认定程序、运行管理的具体措施。与之相配套的《国家高端智库管理办法》和《国家高端智库专项经费管理办法（试行）》则为试点工作搭建了基本制度框架，初步形成了一套规范有效的工作机制和运行模式。

此外，政策文件内容涉及范围广，涵盖智库建设的方方面面。按照出台的政策内容可以分为以下几类：

一是与新型智库建设管理与考核评估相关。例如 2016 年 12 月，江苏省出台《江苏省新型智库管理与考核评估试行办法》，对于江苏省新型智库考核评价指标体系作出详细说明。2018 年 7 月，黑龙江新型智库建设工作会议审议了《黑龙江省新型智库管理办法》。浙江省在 2018 年新型智库建设工作会议上讨论了浙江省新型智库建设管理办法与新型智库考核评价指标体系的制定，从而加强和规范新型智库建设与管理。除政府文件之外，华东师范大学、上海师范大学、湖南师范大学、福州大学等众多高校也出台了相应的智库建设管理办法。

二是与智库经费管理相关。兵马未动,粮草先行。智库经费使用的自主性和灵活性将直接影响到智库的运营发展,以及智库人才的积极性。2015年出台的《国家高端智库专项经费管理办法(试行)》为中国特色新型智库建设经费管理做出了总体指导。2016年12月,财政部和全国哲学社会科学规划领导小组又对《专项经费管理办法》作出了补充。在此之后,宁夏回族自治区、安徽省、黑龙江省等省市陆续出台了与本地区相适应的经费管理办法,对于专项经费的开支范围、预算管理、监督检查等作出明确说明。

三是与智库成果认定及奖励相关。智库研究不同于学术研究,其成果形式也与传统的学术成果有较大差异。如何完善智库成果认定与奖励体系,关乎智库研究人员的积极性。《关于加强中国特色新型智库建设的意见》和各省市加强新型智库建设的实施意见都明确提出要建立和完善智库成果认定机制和激励机制。此后,安徽省、湖南省等省份和华东政法大学、西南大学、安徽财经大学等高校出台了单独的智库成果认定办法。

1.1.4 为各类型智库发展提供政策保障

为落实《意见》中提出的"统筹推进党政部门、社科院、党校行政学院、高校、军队、科研院所和企业、社会智库协调发展"的智库发展格局,我国出台了一系列促进各类型各行业各领域智库发展的政策文件,特别是扶持高校智库和社会智库的发展。

一是促进高校智库发展的政策文件。高校建设高端智库有着天然的优势。2013年5月,刘延东副总理在"繁荣发展高校哲学社会科学推动中国特色新型智库建设座谈会"上强调要发挥高校独特优势,为建设中国特色新型智库贡献力量。2014年2月,教育部关于印发《中国特色新型高校智库建设推进计划》,致力打造结构合理、形式多样的高校智库发展格局。此后,云南省、甘肃省、辽宁省、广东省、宁夏回族自治区、陕西省等众多省份均有出台推进高校智库建设发展的相关文件。

二是促进社会智库发展的政策文件。社会智库发展处在智库圈层的最外层,发展力量最为薄弱。若要形成党政军智库、高校智库、社会智库协调发展的局面，必须优化社会智库的发展环境，大力支持社会智库的健康发展。2017年5月，民政部、中央宣传部、中央组织部等9部门联合出台了《关于社会智库健康发展的若干意见》，对规范和引导社会智库健康发展作出了一系列部署安排，标志着我国社会智库发展进入了新阶段。此后，甘肃省、江苏省、山东省等省份也紧跟中央步伐，结合实际情况，出台促进社会智库发展的实施意见。

三是促进各行业智库发展的政策文件。随着新型智库建设浪潮的掀起，各行业、各领域也纷纷加入新型智库建设的大军，出台了众多政策文件，促进专业性智库的建设发展。各大部委，如水利部、公安部、农业部、交通部等均出台了相关促进专业智库建设发展的实施意见。此外，其他部门、行业也就新型智库建设提出了建设方案，要求促进行业性、专业性智库的发展，建立健全各行业领域决策咨询制度。例如，自2016年工信部下发《工业和信息化部办公厅关于加强工业和信息化领域新型智库建设的意见》文件后，工信部政法司组织建立工信领域智库名录，集聚智库资源，提高决策咨询水平，目前全国共有91家机构入选工信部智库名录，其中高校智库29家；2018年1月，国家测绘地理信息局党组制定印发了《关于加强测绘地理信息新型智库建设的实施意见》，对测绘地理信息领域新型智库体系建设布局进行了全面部署；3月，广东省科技厅起草了《广东省科学技术厅科技智库管理办法（试行）（征求意见稿）》，将科技智库建设提上日程；6月，杨传堂（交通运输部党组书记）和李小鹏（交通运输部党组副书记、部长）在《光明日报》发表《建设高质量的交通运输新型智库》；9月，民航局出台《关于加强民航局新型智库建设的实施办法》，标志着中国民航新型智库进入实施阶段。

1.2 智库体系和平台建设日渐成熟

1.2.1 智库体系布局逐步合理完善

据《全球智库报告2017》数据显示，我国智库总数位居世界第二。但是数量上的优势并不意味着质量上的优势，我国目前仍然缺乏具有较大国际影响力和知名度的智库。《意见》中阐述了建设新型智库体系的意义、目的、特征和路径。打造一批"国家亟需、特色鲜明、制度创新、引领发展的专业化高端智库"是构建中国特色新型智库体系的重要战略选择。重点建设一批高端智库，给予资金和政策上的支持，树立智库建设的标杆效应和典范效应，有助于引领我国新型智库的发展方向，丰富和充实我国新型智库体系。目前，我国形成了"国家高端智库为引领，省市级重点智库为支撑，其他新型智库为补充"，纵向层次分明，横向类型丰富的新型智库体系。

其一，国家高端智库引领发展。当前改革已进入攻坚期和深水区，面临问题更加复杂化。如何提高党和政府决策的民主性、科学性，啃下"硬骨头"是打好改革攻坚战的重要一环。国家高端智库的建设，瞄准国家亟须解决的重大战略问题，将更好服务于党和政府的重要战略决策。2015年12月，国家高端智库建设试点工作启动会在京举行，共有25家机构入选首批国家高端智库建设试点单位，并组建了国家高端智库理事会。总体来说，入选的首批高端智库类型多样，特色鲜明，涵盖研究领域范围广，具有典型性和代表性。2017年，中宣部公布了13家国家高端智库建设培育单位。此外，其他各部门，各行业领域的重点智库建设项目也逐步设立，并将智库项目与决策有待解决的选题对接。例如，教育部于2017年9月成立高校高端智库联盟，首批31家成员单位共同签署《高校高端智库联盟公约》，旨在打造党和政府"信得过、用得上"的智库，提升高校高端智库协同发展的示范集群效应。

其二，省市级重点智库支撑发展。省市级重点智库的培育发展作为我国特色新型智库体系的重要组成部分，属于国家级高端智库的后备力量，并为其发展起到了支撑的作用。截止到2018年10月份，我国共有24个省级行政区设立省级重点智库、重点培育智库或是重点智库研究项目。以江苏省为例，2015年11月江苏省委办公厅、省政府办公厅出台了《关于加强江苏新型智库建设的实施意见》，随后公布了首批9家重点高端智库，并制定《江苏省新型智库管理与考核评估试行办法》《江苏省新型智库考核评价指标体系》《重点高端智库考核评估与经费管理办法（讨论稿）》《重点高端智库考核评价指标体系（讨论稿）》等文件，为省级重点智库建设提供了良好的政策支持。此外,江苏省还设立了新型智库建设工作指导委员会,下设江苏省新型智库建设办公室负责新型智库建设事宜,并在2017年5月成立江苏省新型智库理事会,作为指导全省新型智库建设的议事机构和评估机构。2016年,江苏省委宣传部下发《关于设立江苏省重点培育智库的通知》,确立了15家省级重点培育智库名单。除了省级高端智库、重点培育智库,江苏省还设立了几十家决策研究基地。这些智库涵盖经济、法制、农业、历史、教育、气候等近百个研究领域。至此,江苏省初步形成了"高端智库＋重点培育智库＋决策研究基地"的三级金字塔形新型智库建设布局。

其三,其他新型智库补充发展。一方面,由于当前我国智库建设中"杂牌军多、正规军少,业余选手多、专业选手少,新智库多、老牌智库少",因此,中央抓国家高端智库建设、省市抓重点智库建设是非常必要的,可以将有限的经费和专家资源集中到一起,改变新型智库体系"小""弱""散"的特点。另一方面,由于我国智库数量众多,除了国家级、省市级重点智库之外,还有大量依托高校和科研院所的专业智库,研究基地,企业智库,社会智库等。这类智库分布在各行各业,研究领域、智库实力、智库规模各不相同,作为我国新型智库体系的重要补充力量,对于活跃智库思想市场有重要作用。

1.2.2 智库平台丰富多样

目前,我国智库发展还处于初级阶段,虽然近些年数量激增,但是总体实力不强,发展不均衡。在建设中国特色新型智库的宏伟工程中,智库联盟作为重要的智库平台,在开展合作研究与交流、信息资源共享方面有着不可替代的作用,也在一定程度上改变"小""弱""散"的智库发展局面,形成智库合力、扩大智库影响力。自从《意见》出台之后,我国智库平台建设日渐丰富,智库联盟日渐活跃。智库联盟按其研究领域、所涉及区域范围等有多种类型:

一是区域性智库联盟。区域性智库联盟集结所在区域的优势智库力量,聚焦区域发展亟须解决的问题,提供区域政策咨询服务。例如,2015年9月,江苏省内首家区域性智库联盟"宁镇扬智库联盟"在南京成立。该联盟是由南京、镇江、扬州三市社科联共同发起成立的智库创新协作平台,旨在凝聚三地人才智力,针对全面深化改革进程中遇到的各种难点问题,传达民情民意,为党委、政府决策提供依据,促进宁镇扬区域经济、政治、文化、社会、生态文明建设等各项事业一体化、可持续协调发展。2016年6月,由全国"一带一路"沿线32个支点城市社联等枢纽智库组建的非法人学术团体组成的"全国'一带一路'沿线城市智库联盟"成立。该联盟旨在积极响应"一带一路"的合作倡议,为相关城市和机构围绕"一带一路"建设开展联合研讨、合作研究、战略研判、政策评估,为政府提供咨询、为地区间发展战略对接提出建议,推动智库研究与政府决策良性互动提供了一个重要平台。

二是国际性智库联盟。近几年,我国智库界积极投身国际交流与合作,拓展和组建智库"朋友圈",在各类国际性智库论坛中发出中国声音。2017年10月,来自纽约、巴黎、新加坡、首尔、香港、北京、上海7个城市的智库研究机构作为发起人共同成立"全球城市智库联盟"。该联盟旨在成为全面推动城市治理学术和政策研究的平台、全球层面城市治理最佳实践的交流平台和促进城市之间各主体沟通合作的平台。2018年3月,由中国人民大学倡议并推动,与世界大学联盟携手合作组建的联盟组织"世界大学智库联盟"成立,该联盟将围绕中国"一带一路"绿色发展主题,对全球特别是"一带一路"倡议地区各国共同面临的热点问题进行深入交流与探讨,旨在加强智库建设、发挥智库影响力,合力将"知识交流"打造成"知识云端",将"智库对话"提升为"智库联盟",构筑一条"智力丝路",协力献计全球治理与发展。2018年5月,上海合作组织经济智库联盟成立,旨在建立稳定的交流与合作机制,为区域经济合作的持续健康发展搭建智库联盟平台。

三是行业(领域)性智库联盟。该类型智库由相关行业(领域)的智库组成,聚焦本行业(领域)的发展动态与存在问题,构建起行业(领域)内智库交流合作的平台。例如,2018年6月,工信智库联盟成立大会暨工信智库论坛在北京召开,工信智库网站正式开通。工信智库联盟应致力建设成为工业和信息化领域工作交流、理论研讨、服务政府、对外联络的重要平台,切实发挥好桥梁纽带和服务支撑作用。2018年7

月,国内20家知名研究机构发起成立"美国研究智库联盟",围绕美国政经形势、美国内外经济政策、中美关系等问题,开展基础性、政策性和前瞻性研究,积极开展国际交流合作。2018年11月,福建省生态文明智库联盟成立,旨在聚合省内智库资源,为福建生态文明建设提供更多智力支持。

1.3 智库交流与传播日益深化

随着我国新型智库的建设发展,智库实力增强,智库之间的交流互动也逐渐增加。一方面,国内智库之间的会议交流、人才交流、项目合作等逐渐频繁,日益深化;另一方面,自从习近平总书记将智库提到国家外交层面,"智库外交"成为国际交流的第二轨道。我国智库慢慢走出国门,融入国际智库发展的大环境,逐渐与国际智库展开对话交流。

1.3.1 智库会议促进智库思想的交流传播

各类不同主题的智库会议与论坛是智库思想、智库观点、智库研究交流碰撞的重要平台。自《意见》出台之后,我国智库进入了一个发展的黄金期,各种层次、类型、主题的智库会议或智库论坛也纷纷涌现,智库专家针对不同领域亟须解决的重大理论或实践问题,例如针对"一带一路""大数据""互联网+""人工智能""脱贫攻坚"等议题,展开深入交流,打造一批有一定影响力的会议论坛。例如,2014年12月,首届"中国大学智库论坛"年会在上海市举行,至今已举办4届。该论坛旨在探讨高校智库面对新形势新要求,如何重点围绕国家重大战略需求开展具有前瞻性、针对性的政策研究,提高研究质量、推动内容创新,从而引领和带动高校智库的发展,扩展高校智库影响力。第一届"中国智库治理论坛"于2016年12月17日在南京大学举行,会议由光明日报社、南京大学主办,会议集主旨报告、分类研讨、成果发布于一体,吸引了全国智库界、思想理论界数百位专家学者积极参与,在国内取得较大影响。时隔一年后,"2017中国智库治理暨思想理论传播高峰论坛"在北京隆重举办,来自智库界、思想理论界、省市自治区智库管理部门、高校科研管理部门等领域近800人参加会议。国家哲学社会科学规划办公室、教育部社科司相关负责人到会指导,主办双方主要负责人张政总编辑、陈骏校长发表致辞,分管领导李春林副总编、陆先高副总编、朱庆葆副书记等登台主持或发布研究成果。理论界和智库界名家魏礼群、张军扩、蔡昉、冯俊,年度智库代表刘鸿武等发表主旨演讲。在大会专设的两场专题会议、六个平行分论坛、多个成果发布环节中,更多与会者畅所欲言、深度交流。除了光明日报及光明新媒体矩阵的全面报道,人民日报、中央电视台新闻频道、新华社、中国社会科学报、《国家治理》期刊等数十家媒体纷纷报道此次论坛,充分体现了该活动的影响力。

随着各行业领域开始投身专业智库的建设,除了综合性的智库会议和论坛之外,不同主题、不同领域的专业智库论坛也逐渐增加。例如,创始于 2015 年 12 月的"环境与发展智库论坛"至今已举办 4 届,是西部资源环境与区域发展智库每年定期举办的精品学术交流活动,聚焦资源环境与区域发展热点前沿问题,致力于支撑环境与发展战略决策、推广和传播环境与发展科学技术与思想。2018 年 8 月,"2018 首届中国科技企业智库高端研讨会"在中国科学院文献情报中心顺利举办,旨在研究中国科技型企业智库发展中面临的问题,促进中国企业发展与科技创新深度融合,讨论企业智库在支撑企业发展、应对外部风险中的作用发挥与担当问题。

1.3.2 网络平台促进智库信息的交流传播

随着我国智库的飞速发展,智库信息呈现出指数增长,因此,各类型智库平台也不断涌现。智库网络平台对于智库信息的展示传播、智库信息共建共享等有着重要的作用。

智库网络平台根据不同的服务对象,可以分为不同类型:一是综合性智库网络平台。综合性智库网络平台重点聚焦区域智库研究,服务区域内智库的发展。"湖北新型智库平台"是湖北地区首个智库交流平台,其定位是立足湖北,服务全国,放眼世界,其目标是打造一个智库成果传播转化平台,各类智库借智引智平台,决策者与智库沟通平台。智库平台的建设对于推动智库专家成果的及时发布与广泛传播,进一步加强智库与决策机构的衔接,促进智库成果在决策机构中的转化与应用发挥了重要作用。由江苏省委宣传部主办的"江苏智库网"是江苏智库发展的重要展示窗口,对于江苏省的著名智库、智库专家、智库研究、智库活动等有全方位的呈现。

二是专题性智库网络平台。专题性智库网络平台侧重于展现某一领域、某一行业的智库相关信息。例如，2018年1月，"贵州大数据智库平台"正式发布，该平台汇聚了数据、知识、专家等资源，面向贵州各级政府提供科学决策，同时面向具体问题的全过程提供精确的知识服务和决策支撑，并基于决策模型和人工智能技术，按主题自动生成以数字为基础、有判断、有建议、可回溯的数字化报告，统筹规划政务数据资源和社会数据资源，快速推进大数据与政务、经济、社会、科技等方面深度融合应用。"青岛科技智库平台"于2017年4月上线运行，并于2018年11月正式开发运行。该平台可提供近年来青岛市科学技术信息研究院积累的产业技术路线等300余项智库研究成果、文献检索6200多万条，智库专家与社会公众经过注册认证后，即可获取全方位平台服务。这是青岛建设高水平科技智库，为全市科技创新决策提供智能化信息服务的又一重要举措，也是国内首家科技智库研究平台。该平台提供了科技创新动态监测服务、智库成果共享服务、专题知识服务、个性化定制服务等四项服务。

1.3.3　参与国际交流，发出"中国智声"

随着中国特色新型智库进程的深入，我国智库近些年逐渐走出国门，积极参与国际交流，参与全球性议题的合作研究，发出"中国智声"，传播中国理念。参与国际交流，既要"引进来"，又要"走出去"。建设"一批具有较大影响力和国际知名度的高端智库"，不仅需要借鉴西方发达国家的智库建设经验，引进国际智库人才，还需要国内智库拥有国际视野，积极投身国家的交流合作中，充分发挥国内智库在国际事务中的作用。我国近些年通过申办或承办国际性智库会议、积极参与国际智库论坛、主动打造智库国际交流平台等方式，推动中国智库走出国门，走向世界，会议的主题大都围绕国家重要战略方针，例如中非合作、"一带一路"等。

"中非智库论坛"于2011年由浙江师范大学创办，是经中国外交部、商务部批准设立的中非学术交流高端平台。论坛每年分别在中国和非洲举办，以"民间为主、政府参与、坦诚对话、凝聚共识"为宗旨，旨在促进对非研究，增进中非了解，扩大双方共识,为中非关系发展建言献策。中非智库论坛创立以来,形成了一系列重要成果,在国际上产生了广泛影响,被中国外交部纳入中非合作论坛框架内,成为中非学术交流与智库对话的机制化高端平台。2018年9月,习近平总书记在2018年中非合作论坛北京峰会上提出"要扩大文化艺术、教育体育、智库媒体、妇女青年等各界人员交往,拉紧中非人民的情感纽带"。这也是"智库外交"的体现。

"中国-中东欧国家智库交流与合作网络"(简称"16＋1智库网络")是由国务院总理李克强提议、中国和中东欧17国总理共同签署的《苏州纲要》明确提出"支持中国社会科学院牵头组建16＋1智库交流与合作网络"而建立的。"16＋1智库网络"将整合中国社会科学院、中国国内和中东欧16国智库的优势资源,积极贯彻新型智库建设、中欧伙伴关系、"一带一路"倡议等战略,积极配合与推动"16＋1合作",旨在提供一个中国与中东欧国家间国际性智库协调机制与高端交流平台。2018年4月,中国首家在欧洲独立注册的智库"中国-中东欧研究院"在匈牙利科学院揭牌成立,是中国-中东欧国家合作、智库交流进程中的一个重要标志,它的成立将积极推进中国与中东欧国家间的人文交流、学术交往和政策沟通。

丝路国际智库网络(Silk Road Think Tank Network,简称SiLKS)是由中国国务院发展研究中心(DRC)联合有关国际智库于2014年在土耳其伊斯坦布尔首届"丝路国际论坛"上倡议,并于2015年10月在西班牙马德里"丝路国际论坛2015"上,由33家智库、8家国际组织和1家企业正式发起成立的国际智库合作网络,旨在为推动共商共建"一带一路"提供高水平智力支撑。2016年6月,丝路国际智库网络首次年会在波兰华沙举行,会议通过《丝路国际智库网络指导原则》。目前,SiLKS共有55家成员和伙伴机构,其中,成员42个,伙伴13个,包括来自30个国家的36家权威智库以及联合国开发计划署、联合国工发组织等的12家国际机构和7家国际知名企业。

1.4 智库研究与评价长足发展

近年来,中国特色新型智库建设一派欣欣向荣之势,各地区各行业智库建设热火朝天,随着实践的深入,智库建设不断积累经验,也不断经受诸多现实问题的困扰。

智库相关研究是剖析智库运行发展机理、总结智库建设经验、提出智库发展方向的重要途径。智库评价则是对智库建设进行"问诊把脉",有利于校正智库发展方向,鞭策智库取长补短。中国特色新型智库建设、智库研究与评价之间鱼水交融,相辅相成。自 2015 年《意见》出台之后,智库研究与评价也迎来了春天,智库相关研究与评价出现了井喷式增长。

1.4.1 智库研究与评价机构如雨后春笋

智库研究与评价机构可以称作"智库的智库",主要以智库或整个智库产业为研究对象,是开展智库研究与评价的重要力量。

2014 年,上海大学智库与智库产业研究中心是为了对接国家及上海市加快智库建设的需求,根据中央领导有关指示精神,于 2014 年成立的校级智库研究机构。中心以国家发展、上海发展为中心议题,立足中国改革发展与现代化的实践,旨在打造一个中国综合性知识的学界思想库。

2015 年,是智库研究与评价机构建立的峰年,例如,2015 年 3 月,中国文化产业智库研究中心成立;4 月,南京大学中国智库研究与评价中心成立;5 月,浙江工业大学全球智库研究中心正式揭牌,光明日报智库研究与发布中心成立;6 月,上海市社会科学院智库研究中心开始进入实体化运营阶段;11 月,四川省社会科学院、中国科学院成都文献情报中心联合成立"中华智库研究中心"。2017 年 7 月 21 日,中国社会科学评价研究院在北京成立。

此后,智库研究与评价机构进入稳步发展阶段。一方面,已成立的智库研究与评价机构稳健运营,发布了众多具有影响力的智库发展报告、智库评价报告、期刊论文、学术著作等;另一方面,不断有新的机构加入智库研究与评价的阵营,例如武汉大学世界一流智库评价研究中心、长江教育研究院教育智库与教育治理研究评估中心、山东社会科学院智库研究中心、河北省社科院新型智库研究中心、清华大学公共管理学院智库研究中心等智库研究与评价机构相继成立。

1.4.2 智库研究成果井喷式增长

在习近平总书记关于智库的重要论述的指导下,我国新型智库建设研究如火如荼,智库研究成果也出现井喷式增长。逐渐形成了扎根中国智库本土实践的中国特色新型智库建设的知识体系和学术体系,为中国特色新型智库建设奠定了雄厚的知识基础和理论基础。

(1)智库研究专著纷纷出版

智库专著是反映智库研究的重要形式。在建设中国特色新型智库的浪潮中,各类智库专著的数量不断攀升。值得注意的是,除了部分智库专家学者以一己之力出版了专著之外,还有众多以一个智库机构或是研究团队合作编著或译著出版的智库系列丛书,这类专著兼具系统性、专业性、前沿性等多种特点,往往产生重大影响。

《南大智库文丛》是南京大学中国特色新型智库建设计划的重要组成部分,也是南京大学中国智库研究与评价中心和光明日报智库研究与发布中心的合作平台之一,旨在宣传推介国外智库建设的有关经验,为新形势下中国特色新型智库建设提供借鉴。该文丛由中心副主任、首席专家李刚担任主编,至今已策划、编辑、出版重点图书10部,主要包括《完善智库管理:智库、"研究与倡导型"非政府组织及其资助者的实践指南》《思想的掮客:智库与新政策精英的崛起》《国会的理念:智库和美国外交政策》《兰德公司(1989—2009):美国战略学知识的重构》《美国政治的转变:新华盛顿与智库的兴起》《中国智库索引》《智库、外交政策和地缘政治:实现影响力的路径》《思想产业:悲观主义者、党派分子及财阀如何改变思想市场》《智库评价理论与方法》《CTTI智库报告(2017)》等。

由浙江师范大学非洲研究院王珩教授所著的《高校智库建设的理论范式和实践创新》于2017年9月经世界知识出版社出版。该书属于《浙江师范大学非洲研究文库·非洲智库与思想研究系列》丛书,着力解决当前高校智库建设的三个基本问题:一是"为什么"的问题,即高校能不能建智库,为什么要建设高校智库;二是"是什么"的问题,即高校智库区别于其他智库的特质内涵是什么,优势功能有哪些;三是"怎么做"的问题,即如何推进高校智库建设,真正通过智库实现高校思想知识价值的转化、延伸,达到溢出效应。

由加拿大西安大略大学政治学教授唐纳德 E. 埃布尔森(Donald E. Abelson)著,复旦发展研究院译的《北部之光——加拿大智库概览》于 2017 年 11 月出版,属于上海社会科学院智库研究中心《当代国际智库译丛》系列图书。该书作为首部对加拿大智库进行综合性考察的著作,对于了解加拿大政策机构有重要意义。该书探讨了智库在加拿大的兴起,论述了许多智库领域常见的问题,即智库以何种方式、在何种情况下能够影响公共舆论和公共政策。作者分析了加拿大智库通常在哪些情形下会更加重视政治倡导而非政策研究本身,也力求说明为何智库机构适合且有能力进行有关重要政策议题的话语构建。《当代国际智库译丛》还有译著,如詹姆斯·麦甘著、谢华育等译《智库的催化作用:转型国家的改革之路》,库必来·亚多·阿林著、王成至译《新保守主义智库与美国外交政策》等。

(2)智库论文数量与日俱增

光明日报《智库》版(周刊)于 2014 年 12 月 25 日创刊,至今已推出 200 余期。作为全国平面媒体中首个以"智库"命名的专刊,以展示中国智库尖端研究成果、助推中国特色新型智库建设为宗旨,以刊登专家文章、专访等为主要形式,内容涵盖智库研究成果发布、智库专家对策建议、智库自身建设研究、智库成功经验介绍等诸多方面,为建设中国特色新型智库发出主流媒体应有的声音,引起社会强烈关注。

2016 年 2 月,中国科学院文献情报中心和南京大学联合主办了我国第一份智库专业期刊《智库理论与实践》,为学术化的智库研究提供了专业的发表平台,旨在探索智库理论、支撑智库建设、指导智库实践、传播智库成果,主要栏目有特稿/专稿、理论研究、智库建设、专家访谈、案例剖析、智库评价、智库报告、智库扫描等。该期刊为双月刊至今已出版 16 期,发表文献 300 余篇。

此后,众多报纸、杂志开始纷纷建立智库专栏,接受智库相关研究的论文。《图书馆论坛》《智库理论与实践》《图书情报知识》《图书与情报》《图书馆杂志》《图书馆》《新世纪图书馆》《情报探索》《农业图书情报学刊》等图情类学术期刊发表了大量智库研究论文，使我们图情档学科成为支持新型智库研究的又一重要学科。中国特色新型智库事业的高速发展、专业发表平台纷纷建立、智库研究人员的研究热情等都极大促进了智库研究论文数量的增长。截至2018年11月，在中国知网上，仅以"智库"或"智囊团"或"思想库"为篇名的论文就有10000余篇，且绝大部分发表于2013年之后。正是这些数量繁多、涉及领域宽广的专业论文给予了中国特色新型智库建设极大的理论支撑。

（3）智库评价报告种类繁多

部分智库研究与评价机构依托自身优势研究资源，建立不同的评价指标，在不同维度对我国特色新型智库建设进程进行阶段性的总结与呈现，形成相应的智库报告。任何评价指标都可能存在不足，但多元化的评价指标对于构建中国特色新型智库评价体系有重要的意义，换言之，智库评价有助于总结智库建设经验，发现智库建设短板，校正智库建设方向。目前国内已出版的智库报告有：上海社会科学院智库研究中心的《中国智库报告》系列、中国社科院的《中国智库综合评价 AMI 研究报告》、零点国际发展研究院与中国网联合推出的《中国智库影响力报告》、浙江工业大学全球智库研究中心的《中国大学智库发展报告》、南京大学中国智库研究与评价中心推出的《CTTI智库报告》系列、四川省社科院与中国科学院成都文献情报中心联合推出的《中华智库影响力报告》系列、中国社科院中国社会科学评价中心推出的《全球智库评价报告》等。总体而言，我国各智库研究与评价机构推出了种类繁多、指标多元的智库报告，初步形成了客观数据与主观评价相结合的评价方式，完善了我国智库评价体系。

1.5 小　结

中国特色新型智库是国家软实力的重要组成部分，新型智库建设是构建现代治理体系、增强现代治理能力、推动政策共同体更加开放化的重要抓手和重要路径。2013年4月15日，习近平总书记就中国特色新型智库建设作出了高瞻远瞩、细致入微的批示,将智库发展视为国家软实力的重要组成部分,并提升到国家战略的高度。自此至今6年多的时间里,从中央到地方,促进智库建设的政策文件频频出台;国家级、省市级智库体系和平台逐渐完善;智库对外交流传播逐渐深化;智库相关研究蓬勃开展;中国特色新型智库建设的外部环境不断改良,内生动力不断增强,我国智库的建设与发展进入了一个黄金时代,掀起一轮高潮。围绕着建设一批"国家亟需、特色鲜明、制度创新、引领发展的专业化高端智库"的建设目标,中国特色新型智库建设取得了令人瞩目的成就,逐步形成了以"高端智库为引领,省市级重点智库为支撑,其他新型智库为补充,纵向层次分明,横向类型丰富"的新型智库体系。我国智库在实践发展中不断聚焦中国问题,提炼中国经验,发出中国声音,传递中国思想,展示中国风采,智库在服务国家战略、社会公共政策方面的作用日益凸显。

2 "中国智库索引"CTTI系统概述

2.1 CTTI系统开发与建设进展回顾

2.1.1 CTTI系统研发背景

2013年4月15日,习近平总书记在一份批示中指出,要建设可以匹敌西方著名智库的具有中国特色、中国风格和中国气派的中国特色新型智库,启动了智库建设的国家战略。然而,直到2015年我国还没有建立起一套完整的智库情况统计分析方法,关于中国究竟有多少家智库这一问题的回答众说纷纭,缺乏智库统计指标体系则是导致我国没有完整系统的智库统计数据的主要原因。

为解决全面描述、全面收集智库数据的问题,提供数据整理、数据检索、数据分析、数据应用的功能,南京大学中国智库研究与评价中心与光明日报智库研究与发布中心开展了"中国智库索引"(简称CTTI)的研究开发工作,并于2015年6月成立了以李刚为主持人的课题组。截至目前,CTTI系统研发主要经历了四个阶段:第一阶段为2015年6月至10月,该阶段完成了系统需求分析、字段设计,确定了系统设计的基本思想,明确了系统架构设计。同年10月18日,在由光明日报理论部和南京大学共同主办的"新型智库机构评估与治理创新专题研讨会"上发布了CTTI的中期研究成果,这一成果也被评为2015年智库界十大事件之一。随后,2015年11月至2016年6月进入系统开发的第二阶段,这一阶段完成了CTTI的整体系统的开发。2016年7月至9月进入第三阶段,主要完成了系统环境部署,上线内测,以及委托第三方测试系统安全性等工作。系统最终于2016年9月28日正式上线发布,开放给被收录的所有来源智库录入数据。

经过前三个阶段的系统开发,CTTI已经拥有较为完备的数据字段,并在2016年收录与发布了首批来源智库名录。经过一年多的运营,CTTI收集到了大量来自各类智库和管理部门的实际需求,发现面向智库的信息管理工具的缺乏已严重制约智库机构的日常管理。对此,2017年5月,南京大学中国智库研究与评价中心与光明日报智库研究与发布中心课题组决定进一步完善CTTI的数据字段及优化系统功能,以支撑应对上述需求的解决方案。在此基础上,两个中心提出合力打造一款面向智库IT治理的增强型数据信息工具,CTTI Plus版本应运而生。为了维护系统的稳定性和现有数据的可靠性,CTTI Plus版本的核心功能将延续CTTI的设计,但同时是对原有CTTI的一次全面升级。而且,其与CTTI产品定位的区别在于,CTTI Plus版不仅仅聚焦于智库的定量评价,也着眼于满足智库信息管理的业务需要。

在课题组的共同努力下,CTTI Plus于2017年底完成更新与上线测试工作,并从2018年起投入使用。同年5月,由光明日报智库研究与发布中心和南京大学中国智库研究与评价中心联合主办"2017CTTI智库最佳实践案例(BPA)发布暨智库评价系统研讨会"在南京召开,会上专门举行了CTTI Plus系统发布及上线仪式,再次获得了国内智库同行及专家学者的热切关注,新版系统也得到更广范围的推广和利用。

2.1.2 CTTI系统的总体架构

目前,CTTI的总架构除了本地主系统外,还包含智库云管理功能和智库共同体机制两个方面。其中,用户权限分配采用多级叠加的星型结构,用户身份和权限描述拓扑结构如图1所示。

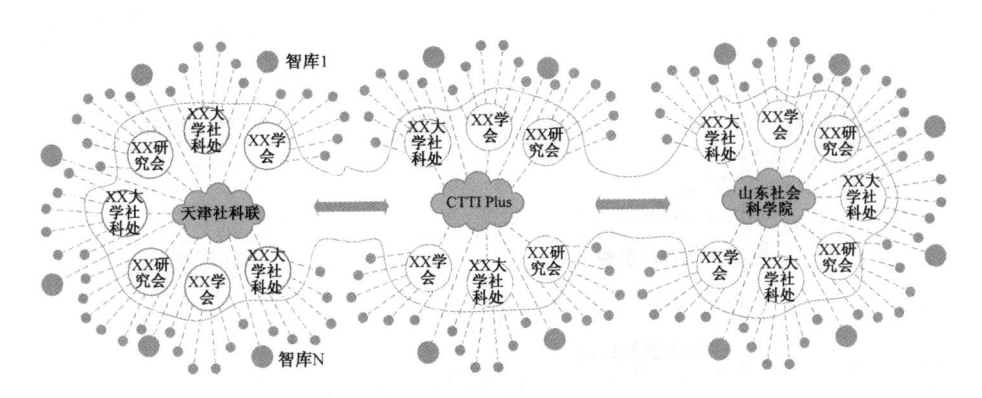

图 1　CTTI Plus 功能架构拓扑图

曲线所标定的核心区域为智库共同体用户和智库云用户，曲线外部的点代表云智库。CTTI 将为中国智库共同体提供网络化的线上信息共享平台，并通过智库云功能进一步描述智库管理的层级。

（1）智库共同体——为了打造中国新型智库线上联盟，共享智库建设成果，CTTI 引入了智库共同体机制。智库共同体旨在为有志于推进我国新型智库交流合作的智库机构和智库管理部门提供一个实体化的网络资源平台。智库共同体成员将以政府管理部门、事业单位和非营利单位法人为主。成员机构将享有系统所有数据和功能的使用权，同时 CTTI 将协助其在本地部署系统、建立本地智库云，并保证系统内数据的日刷新，如图 2 所示。

对于共同体成员自行增加的智库，可通过系统内流程推荐到 CTTI 来源增补资源池，并赋予适当权重。共同体成员的本地数据分为两部分：CTTI 系统收录的机构和专家数据将由 CTTI 向共同体成员日刷新；共同体成员自建机构和专家数据在本地进行维护，以保障数据安全性和私密性。当共同体用户推荐的智库被纳入 CTTI 来源智库名录时，CTTI 将一次性收录该智库所有数据，并与其他来源智库统一管理日刷新到共同体本地系统。

为与共同体成员现有管理信息系统兼容，我们还支持成员单位前台界面的风格

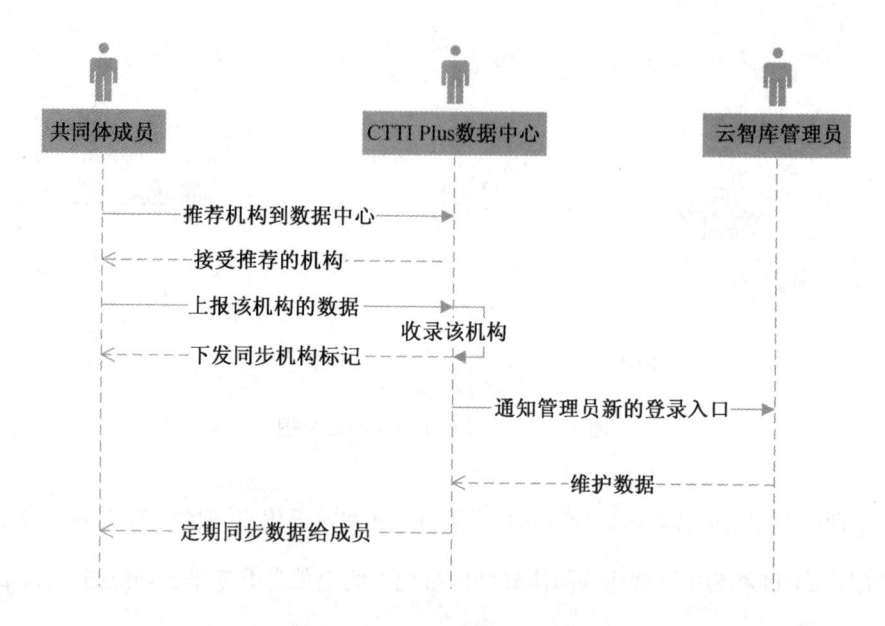

```
共同体成员              CTTI Plus 数据中心          云智库管理员
    |─── 推荐机构到数据中心 ───>|                          |
    |<─── 接受推荐的机构 ──────|                          |
    |─── 上报该机构的数据 ────>|                          |
    |                        | 收录该机构                |
    |<── 下发同步机构标记 ─────|                          |
    |                        |─ 通知管理员新的登录入口 ──>|
    |                        |<──── 维护数据 ───────────|
    |<── 定期同步数据给成员 ───|                          |
```

图 2　CTTI Plus 数据交互机制

定制,并提供数据交换接口,以便与现有系统对接和交换数据,同时将以单点登录的方式实现所有共同体成员管辖下的前台用户统一登录。

(2)智库云——为了满足广大智库管理部门在实际工作中的业务需求,经过对大量智库机构和智库管理单位的实地走访调研以及前期经验沉淀总结,CTTI 二期增设了智库云功能。智库云功能是将 CTTI 系统完善的智库数据字段、先进的数据库架构以及科学的智库评价算法面向广大有数据管理需求的机构或部门开放,以线上大数据资源托管平台的方式为广大智库机构和管理部门提供数据管理服务,旨在为不具备智库数据管理系统设计和研发能力的用户提供成熟的智库管理和索引服务,通过开通智库云,可以让普通机构、单位同样拥有中国智库索引系统的数据管理和检索能力(如图 3 所示)。

智库云用户可以自行添加机构用户和专家用户从而实现对管辖对象的管理,同时,云用户享有 CTTI 的高可信资源而无须单独部署,不占用本地硬件资源。但需要强调的一点是,为保证数据安全,所有智库云之间的数据都是相对独立的,即智库云

开通智库云等于在本地拥有了一套CTTI Plus系统

CTTI智库云用户为不具备本地化部署条件的智库管理机构和大型智库提供的一种服务

智库云用户享有CTTI的高可信资源而无须单独部署，不占用本地硬件资源

图 3　智库云管理系统

用户的所有数据只对该智库云框架内的所有云智库账号开放，并不面向公众开放。智库云管理员可以通过创建云智库的方式将下属智库单位和专家纳入智库云中统一管理（如图 4 所示）。

图 4　智库云管理界面

随着智库云的全面铺开，智库界将逐渐形成统一的数据管理标准，该标准与 CTTI 测评算法无缝对接，使智库评价切实作用于智库日常管理，从而达到评价与管

理的相互促进,以及评价方法与管理水平的双螺旋上升。

2.1.3 CTTI系统主要功能

(1) 前台检索与浏览

CTTI系统前台主要实现检索和新闻浏览功能。就检索功能而言,检索流程包括机构检索、专家检索、产品检索、活动检索、需求检索以及综合检索等六类任务。CTTI支持模糊查询和多条件查询。多条件查询只需以空格分隔条件即可,与常见搜索引擎使用方法一样。其中,综合检索是前五类检索的"或"操作。对于这五类检索任务,CTTI均提供对检索结果的二次筛选功能。每项筛选项下设若干个条件,可通过勾选进行筛选。对于机构和专家的检索,CTTI提供按字母索引,便于快速查找。CTTI最终检索结果包括结果列表和相关结果两部分,结果列表是指符合检索条件的所有条目的列表,结果条目按照命中权重即检索字段匹配率从高到低排序(图5)。

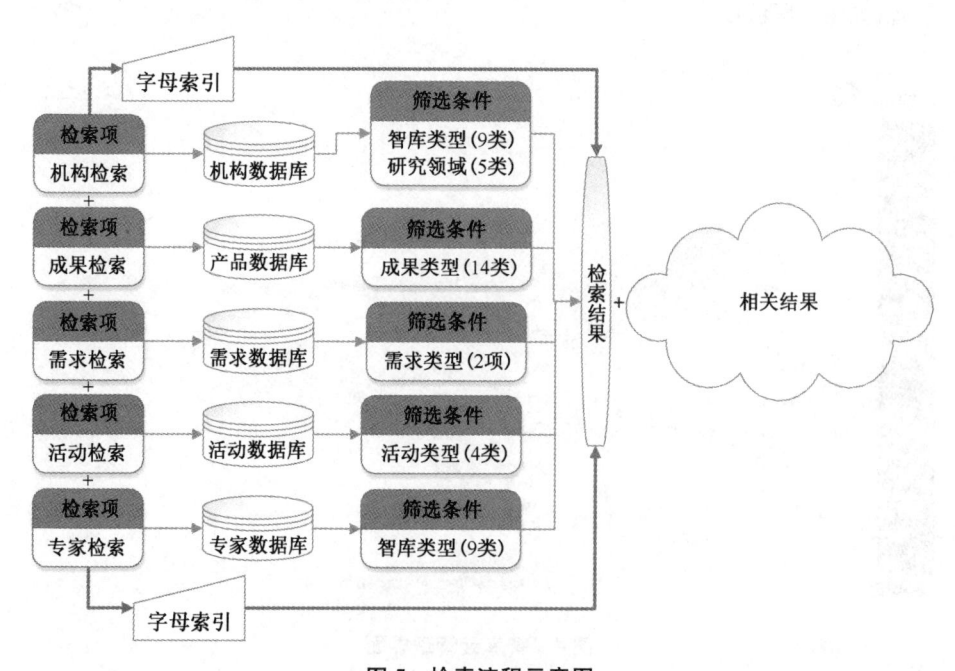

图 5　检索流程示意图

与此同时,CTTI系统前台还设有新闻浏览功能,系统会定期推送系统站内最新要闻与公告,以及点击次数较多的热门机构与不同类型的成果,便于用户及时获取相关信息。

(2) 后台数据处理与用户管理

基于强大的数据库支撑,CTTI 后台具体包含数据处理与用户管理两个任务流程。数据处理流程主要实现的功能包括数据的录入、修改、审核、发布和维护(如图 6 所示)。其中"数据"不仅包括机构、专家、产品和活动数据,也包括新闻、需求信息等周边数据。数据均来自手工收集的网络或纸质信息源。在数据处理流程中,机构用户和专家用户可通过不同的入口登录系统,录入对应字段的数据。这些数据经系统管理员审核后发布或开放检索。系统管理员拥有审核权和数据管理的最高权限。对于审核后的数据,所有系统用户和访客都可以直接检索查询。

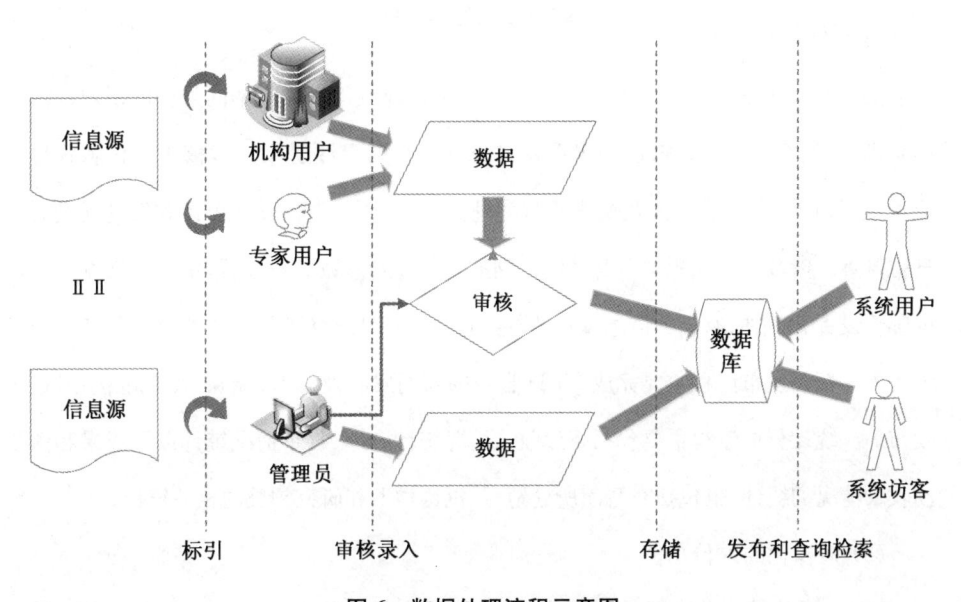

图 6 数据处理流程示意图

另一方面,后台管理流程只对系统管理员开放,包括用户注册和身份管理、日志管理、参数设置、新闻发布、统计分析、数据管理和审核等(如图 7 所示)。

其中,虚线所示的流程为用户注册流程,包括机构用户注册和专家用户注册。专

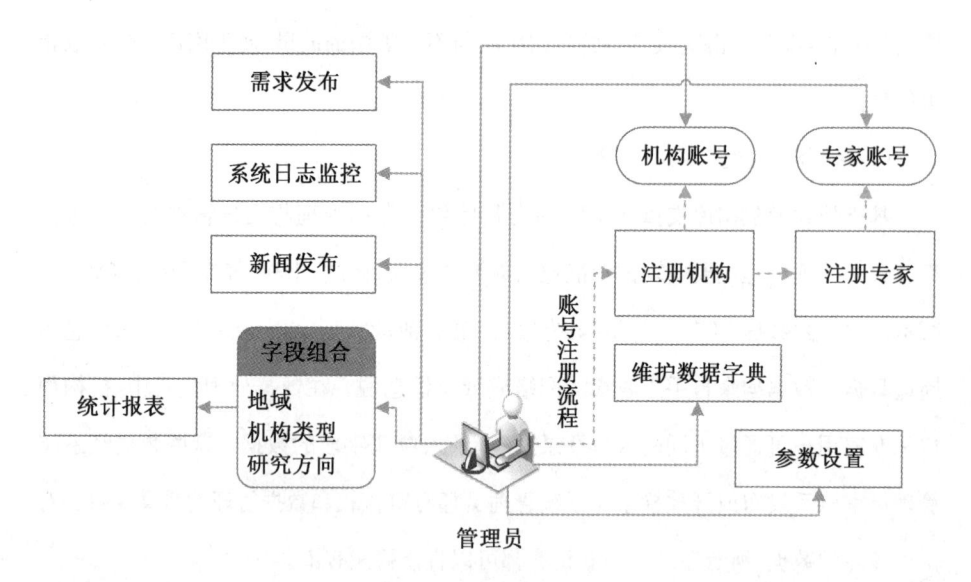

图 7 后台管理流程

家需要与智库关联才能注册为系统用户。身份管理流程完成对不同身份的用户账户的管理，包括增、删、改、查询、密码重置、权限设置、前台注册用户审核等。日志管理流程主要对前、后台所有涉及操作的行为进行记录，便于进行操作审计和发现问题后进行排查。参数设置流程主要对系统用到的一些控制参数进行设置，主要包括发邮件的邮箱设置、网站抓取相关信息设置（频度、时间等）、日志管理的日志留存时间和日志大小等。新闻发布流程主要完成 CTTI 自身的新闻发布及修改、删除、发布审核、撤销发布等。统计分析流程主要包括智库收录情况统计、专家收录情况统计以及成果和活动收录情况的统计，也包括对智库所处地域、机构类型和研究领域的相关统计。

(3) 多样化的评价功能

CTTI 评价是一种多因子的评价模型，其评价包含几十个，甚至上百个因子，尽可能最大限度地提升智库评价的真实性。在 MRPAI 算法的基础上，CTTI 系统将灵活可配的定制化评价和专家主观评价相结合。一方面，系统设有可配置字段的统计功能，允许提供多种不同类型、不同维度的统计结果展现方式，便于用户更加直观地观察数据状态，将用户从烦琐的报表中解放出来，快速便捷地完成日常管理工作。高级用户在登录系统后,可依据评价目标和侧重点自行选择数据维度,调用不同的算法,并根据偏好配置权重,最终得到定制化的评价排序结果。另一方面,就智库评价而言,专家对于智库的主观印象是一个不可或缺的维度。CTTI系统现已收录近万名专家,并把这些专家都纳入智库主观评价资源池中。系统将以邮件通知的方式将待评价智库列表以链接的形式发送至专家,由专家登录系统对智库打分,再由高级用户或系统管理员将主观评价结果与定量评价结果作综合计算。

值得一提的是,CTTI系统采用主流的大数据分析技术,已实现对智库数据进行离线数据统计、分析和挖掘功能,力争从不同角度对智库机构和专家进行客观评价和排序,主要包括智库间的横向对比、专家间的横向对比,以及智库和专家自身的在各个领域的发展趋势,旨在为党和政府提供决策服务,为指定领域内的政策咨询提供数据支撑。

所有智库云用户基本享有与CTTI主系统功能一一映射的各项检索、浏览、管理、数据处理及评价等功能。

2.2 CTTI数据收录情况概览

截至目前,CTTI共收录机构706家、专家11 992位、活动17 878场、成果115 421项。可以说,CTTI已经涵盖了类型丰富、体量较大的智库数据,能够在一定程度满足智库信息检索的不同需求。

以收录专家信息为例,通过后台统计,在已填报学历信息的专家中,四分之三以上的专家都接受过博士阶段的教育,有15%的专家接受过硕士教育,而本科、专科及其他学历仅占不到10%(图8)。这说明新型智库拥有较多的高层次智力资源,大部分专家都接受过专业的学术研究培训与教育,在某一领域较为精通。因此,我们对新型智库建设的人力资本还是要持有信心的。

与此同时,我们也统计了专家所在学科的分布情况。依据"专家所在学科分布图"可知,这些专家分布在13个学科领域(图9)。其中,近四分之三的专家都是来自经济学、法学和管理学学科,经济学领域专家最多,占26%,法学和管理学专家分别

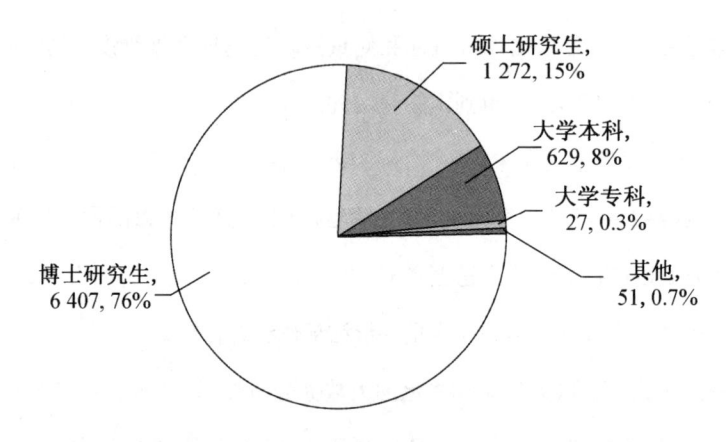

图 8　专家学历分布图

占到 23% 和 20%。除这三类学科外,工学专家占 9%,文学和哲学专家各占 5%,历史学专家占 4%,理学和教育学各占 3%,艺术学、医学、军事学及农学这几个学科专家都不足 1%。可见,我国新型智库专家主要集中在社会科学领域,自然科学和人文学科领域专家较少,专家学科结构有待进一步优化。

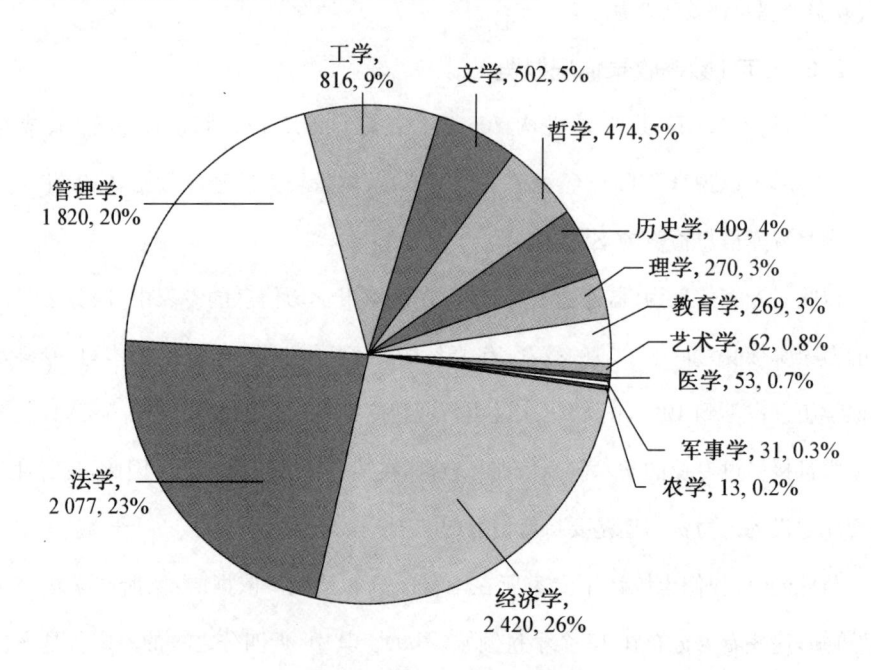

图 9　专家所在学科分布图

通过对CTTI各子数据库的数据进行统计,我们发现成果数据库收录的信息量最多,而且智库成果的种类也十分丰富。其中,内参是我国智库最具特色且最为重要的决策咨询成果,来源智库累计贡献单篇内参近8 000篇。但根据来源智库的内参成果统计显示,76%的内参上报后未能得到回应,当然其中不排除保密因素,有些内参被批示了没有反馈。而在被批示的内参中,17%的智库内参获省部级批示,3%的内参获厅(司/局)级批示,约2%的内参获副国级或正国级批示(图10)。这从某种程度也反映出,新型智库的政策研究供给与决策需求之间存在一定错位,智库在研究咨询的针对性和及时性方面还有待加强。

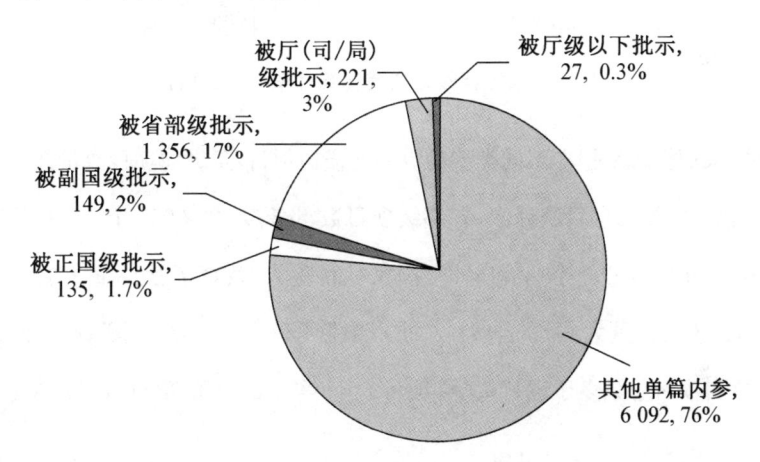

图10 来源智库内参批示情况统计图

其次,从数量统计上看,论文一直都是来源智库主要的一项成果。在"来源智库论文情况统计图"中,我们按论文所在期刊被核心期刊目录收录情况进行统计得出如下结果(图11)。由于一篇论文可能同时会被多个核心期刊目录收录,因此我们只统计各核心期刊目录收录的来源智库论文的篇次。显然,CSSCI收录的论文最多,有2万篇次的论文来自CSSCI刊物;SCI和SSCI收录的论文数均在1 000~2 000篇这个范围;"三报一刊"发表的论文有213篇,仅占CSSCI收录篇次的1%。需要肯定的是,来源智库大多具有深厚的学术研究功底。但智库研究不同于一般意义上的学术研究和基础理论研究,必须强调服务意识和开拓创新能力。以高校智库为主体的新型智库体系要注重提升智库属性,在学术研究与决策服务之间实现合理的资源配置。

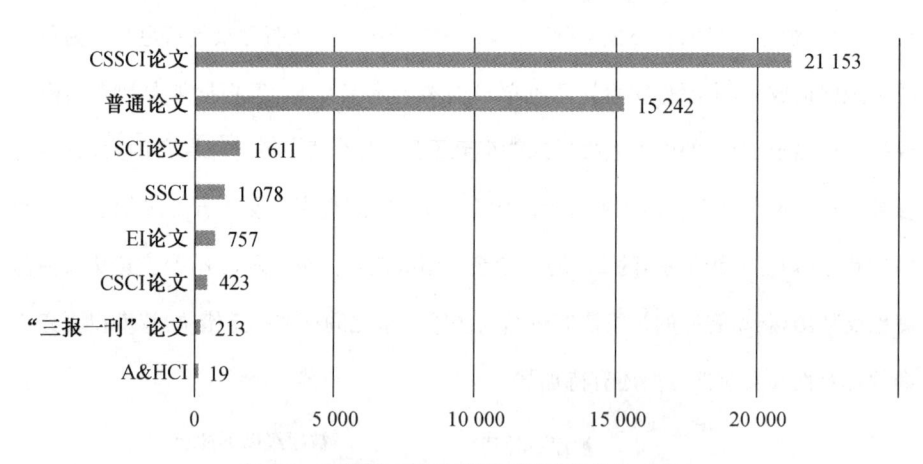

类型	数量
CSSCI论文	21 153
普通论文	15 242
SCI论文	1 611
SSCI	1 078
EI论文	757
CSCI论文	423
"三报一刊"论文	213
A&HCI	19

图11　来源智库论文情况统计图(单位:篇)

此外,来源智库承担有不同类型的纵向与横向项目,且纵向项目数量几乎是横向项目的两倍。在纵向项目统计中,省部级项目数量最多,共 2 051 个(占 47%),国家社科一般/青年项目 685 个(占 16%),国家社科重大/教育部社科重大项目 306 个(占 7%),国家社科重大/国家自然科学重点项目 235 个(占 5%)(图 12)。而在横向项目中,文科项目总数多于理科;文科项目大于(等于)5 万的项目数量最多,理科项

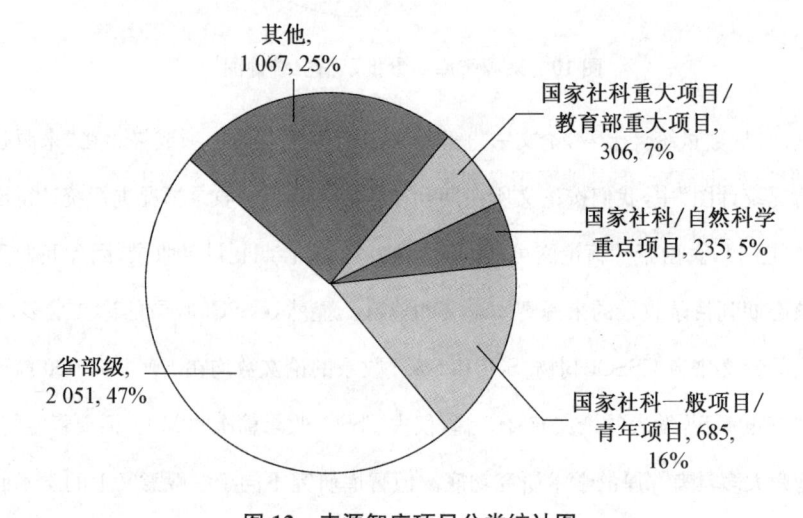

图12　来源智库项目分类统计图

目大于(等于)10万的项目数量最多(图13)。平均来看,每个来源智库承担各类项目7个,但如何更有效地将其转化为政策研究成果,是新型智库应该去思考的问题。

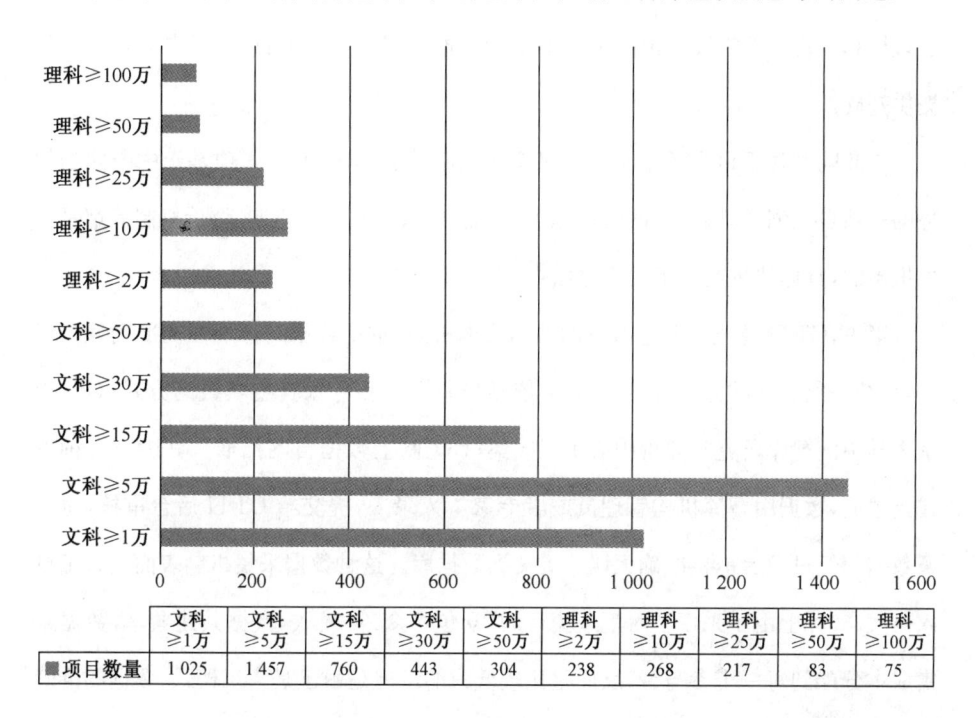

	文科≥1万	文科≥5万	文科≥15万	文科≥30万	文科≥50万	理科≥2万	理科≥10万	理科≥25万	理科≥50万	理科≥100万
项目数量	1 025	1 457	760	443	304	238	268	217	83	75

图13 来源智库项目分类统计图(文科/理科)

2.3 CTTI的作用与影响

CTTI的用户群体包括政府、企业事业单位、社会团体等,由于这些用户有大量的政策研究、咨询需求,但是他们未必知道谁是最恰当的解决方案提供者。而智库也经常处于任务不足,不知道客户在哪里的情景。CTTI设计目标之一就是解决这种信息不对称情况。CTTI作为一个智库的"垂直搜索引擎"(专业搜索),以完备的字段作为支撑,以多角度查询的方式全方位展示查询结果,实现对智库机构从内部架构到外部活动、从人员组成到成果发布的立体式展示,实现对智库各种信息的智能分析,快速准确检索到目标信息,如为课题找专家和为专家找课题,从而消除智库和用户之间的"信息不对称"。CTTI的成功上线填补了我国智库数据管理和在线评价工具的空白，为我国智库评价工作提供了基础数据，厘清了新型智库评价这项集机构评价、成果评价、人员评价以及活动评价于一体的复杂工作的头绪，并引导这项工作趋于理性和客观。但需要指出的是，CTTI 的数据以智库评价为目的，旨在为各种评价提供基础。

与此同时，CTTI 并不是对西方某个成熟产品的模仿，而是一项基于中国体制优势的一项自主创新，因为它的设计理念、功能布局、数据采集机制、评价机制等都是自主提出的，具体体现在以下几个方面：

第一，CTTI 建立了共建共享的数据采集机制，重视数据的客观性和准确性。目前，系统采集数据的方式有三种：(1) 依靠来源智库和专家自主填报的方式；(2) 南京大学中国智库研究与评价中心手工收集；(3) 网上数据自动抓取。其中第一种方式是主流，数据由智库机构管理员或者专家本人录入，提交给 CTTI 后台审核，每一条数据都经过后台审核准确无误才提交到数据库。这种数据采集机制表面上人工投入巨大，实际上由于采用了时下最流行的"众包"(众筹)模式，数据共建共享，数据采集成本分摊到每一个参与者，反而是比较低廉的。但是由于是人工模式，数据的准确性和客观性大大增强。为减少人为干扰影响力数据的情况，CTTI 每个智库每个专家的影响力数值除后台管理员填报的少数字段外，都是根据填报的数据自动计算出影响力数值的。

第二，CTTI 的 UI 设计和用户体验达到了同类产品的前沿水平。比如，CTTI 允许几百上千人同时录入数据，由于现代科研中合作研究是一种常态，那么一定会出现同一篇文献不同专家不同智库先后录入各自名下这种场景。因此，在 CTTI 中录入数据时，只要出现关联数据，系统就会自动拉取原来存在的数据，让最近的录入者修改补充。这样不仅杜绝了雷同数据，而且节省了数据录入量。另外，为使数据录入人员无须查阅系统说明书就可以知道如何准确地录入数据，CTTI 几乎为每个字段都提供了数据录入提示语，提示语不仅解释了字段的含义，而且给出了示例。

第三，CTTI 系统和数据安全性达到了准金融数据安全级别。在部署方案上，

CTTI将应用服务器与数据服务器分开部署,采用内外网隔离的方案,公网用户只能访问应用服务器,无法直接访问到数据服务器,保证了数据的安全性;在通讯协议方面,CTTI使用https的SSL加密协议,保证所有请求数据在传输的过程中都是加密的,防止攻击者通过拦截篡改请求内容来非法访问系统。由于CTTI收录的数据众多,为了防止系统数据被轻易地窃取,CTTI在反扒网方面也做了应对设计,采用了B/S架构并以科学的权限设置和角色分配,保障信息的可用性和可控性,一般访客访问系统只能查询到最基本的数据,无法看到系统的全貌。

第四,CTTI创新了用户分层服务模式。CTTI的用户除了有需要利用智库的党和政府的政策研究机构,负责智库注册、指导的民政局、宣传部等部门,智库管理员和专家等机构内部用户,还有大学、媒体、科研院所等学术宣传单位,各种企业等营利部门,以及一般的公众。CTTI针对不同层次的用户,设计了分层服务方案,给予针对性的服务,不同层次用户访问到的数据层次和类型有所不同。例如,各种统计图标、统计工具在设计时就充分考虑了行政管理部门的需要。在数据的呈现与导出方面,充分考虑了智库的需要,智库和专家可以方便地在CTTI中进行数据管理与导出。

第五,CTTI在一定意义上建立了中国特色新型智库的统计指标体系和元数据标准。系统涵盖的900多个字段实现了对智库基本信息、专家信息、成果信息、活动信息的各种属性的全面覆盖,给出了立体的智库各要素画像。这些数据字段可以成为今后其他智库系统开发的元数据。

整体来看,自系统上线以来,CTTI已经被60余家高校图书馆免费试用,如北京大学、中国人民大学、复旦大学、南京大学、东南大学等。在线访问量近200万次,成为我国找智库、找智库专家的重要平台,影响力与日俱增。

与此同时,已有山东省社会科学院和天津社科联两家单位成为CTTI智库共同体成员,完成本地的系统部署。其中,"中国智库索引"天津版(CTTI-TJ)于2018年最早建成并正式投入运行,与之深度融合的社科联综合业务管理系统也已投入使用。目前纳入CTTI-TJ的云智库20多家、智库机构240多家,智库专家2000余人。天津市社科联的会议管理、课题管理、社科评奖、期刊编审、年会论文申报等业务将直接调用CTTI-TJ数据资源,业务新数据也将直接写入CTTI-TJ数据库,真正实现了"让CTTI数据活起来、用起来"。随着CTTI-TJ上线运行,天津市社科联还探索建立了CTTI来源智库动态管理机制,每年为天津地区的CTTI来源智库排名,后10%的智库机构将面临淘汰。

2018年1月,南京大学中国智库研究与评价中心和光明日报智库研究与发布中心联合编辑出版了《中国智库索引》工具书,该书已经被国内智库和高校图书馆广泛收藏,同时也被布鲁金斯学会和基辛格研究中心等世界著名智库图书馆收藏。2018年5月,基于CTTI来源智库数据撰写的《CTTI智库报告(2017)》(双语版)成功发行,且英文版已被国际著名的智库研究专业网站 ON THINK TANK 全文发表。此后,许多海外智库研究者予以高度关注。2018年12月6日晚八点,该网站主任 Enrique Mendizabal、华盛顿都市城市研究所研究员米尔顿博士等数十位专家学者同时在线,邀请南京大学中国智库研究与评价中心李刚教授作为《CTTI智库报告(2017)》作者代表,共同就中国新型智库建设和《CTTI智库报告(2017)》等议题展开热烈讨论。《中国智库索引》和《CTTI智库报告(2017)》宣传推介对CTTI来源智库起到了积极作用。

随着CTTI在国内外取得的影响力日益显著,以及智库共同体成员和智库云的不断增加,系统数据增量必将迎来一个快速发展的阶段。届时,凭借近万名专家组成的学术共同体资源,结合灵活可定制的客观定量评价功能,CTTI将成为智库界兼具管理与评价功能的重要工具,助力我国新型智库建设向前推进。

3 2018年度CTTI来源智库目录增补

3.1 CTTI来源智库增补原则

党的十九大以来,中国特色新型智库建设进入稳定发展的新时期,中央有关部委和有关省市都遴选了本地本系统的重点和重点培育智库,为了使CTTI来源智库目标能够比较准确地反映特色新型智库发展的形势,在充分研究讨论并征求专家意见的基础上,CTTI团队决定启动2018年CTTI来源智库增补工作,仍然沿用智库主动申请、数据填报、专家评审、摸底调研相结合的方式,对增补智库执行严格的遴选程序与要求。

(1)增补智库资质要求

坚持首批来源智库入围标准不变,参照以下七方面考量(表1),尤其注重是否实体化运行,是否有良好的政策研究咨询能力与成果。凡是被各省市和中央部委认定为省部级重点和重点培育智库(政策研究基地)者优先考虑。

表1 来源智库遴选参考指标

	具体内容	量化指标
政治要求	遵守国家法律法规	
学术基础	近2年来,智库专职研究人员在学术刊物上发表过学术论文	近2年内,专职研究人员在CSSCI来源期刊或者人民日报、光明日报理论版发表文章人均1篇以上
领域要求	有特色鲜明、长期关注的决策咨询研究领域	
组织形式	相对稳定、运作规范的实体性研究机构	有机构成立批文或其他证明文件
	健全的治理结构	有组织章程,设立理事会、学术委员会等组织
资源保障	一定数量的专职和兼职研究人员与行政人员	有1~2名领军人物,5人以上的全职研究员和5人以上的兼职研究员与研究助理
	有保障、可持续的资金来源	年度经费30万元以上
	固定的办公场所与基本设备	50平方米以上独立办公室
运行与成果	正常开展研究、咨询、会议活动	每年举办的活动不少于3场
	提交研究成果	每年至少正式发布(或向用户提交)3份以上研究报告和3篇以上报刊文章
	网站和新媒体	有独立的网站,微信(或者微博)等新媒体账号

(续表)

	具体内容	量化指标
	智库连续出版物	有期刊、内参等印本或电子版简报等出版物
国际合作与交流	有开展国际合作交流的条件,有望产生一定的国际影响	

(2) 增补规则

高校智库由各高校科研管理部门推荐或智库机构自荐,若由高校下属智库机构自荐,须该校科研管理部门同意。为确保对来源智库及大学智库指数评价的公平性,我们对每家高校的CTTI来源智库的数量做了一些规定,但那些实力雄厚、特色鲜明、成果丰硕、活跃度高、机制灵活的高校智库不受此限制。此外,针对入选智库数量较少的地域、类型、政策领域,我们在增补时对其进行充分考量,并给予适当倾斜。

(3) 增补程序

申请增补智库填写附件表—资格审查—为符合标准的智库建立账号—初选智库填写数据—数据审核—筛选出数据质量和数量达到CTTI来源智库标准的智库—CTTI来源智库增补专家组审核—公布增补名单,颁发来源智库证书。

3.2 2018CTTI来源智库增补过程

2018年7月17日,CTTI团队发出《2018CTTI来源智库增补启事》,本年度增补工作正式启动。拟申请增补智库须填写《2018CTTI来源智库增补申请表》,提供机构基本信息及主管/直属单位科研管理部门意见以备资格审查。来源智库增补工作得到了智库界和各级科研管理部门的大力支持。截止到2018年9月30日,CTTI增补工作组共收到各类申请材料近200份,其中绝大部分都是省部级重点(培育)智库,也有部分是教育部重点(或国别)研究基地,以及个别国家高端培育智库。经南京大学中国智库研究与评价中心与光明日报智库研究与发布中心联合调研、讨论、审定,工作组初步遴选出87家合格智库。

初选工作完成后，增补工作组立即发函邀请初选智库进行数据采集工作。在多方努力下，自2017年10月11日至11月20日，历时一个多月时间，初选智库积极踊跃、严谨细致地录入了机构基本信息、专家、活动、成果等多种类型的大量珍贵数据，有力地支持了CTTI增补工作的展开。

数据采集截止之后，工作组随即组织专家团队以数据填报情况、增补申请表和调研结果为依据，以数据的科学性、完整性和相应竞争力为标准，对初选合格的智库进行二次评估。针对未履行初选通知义务的，或未提供足够有效数据以供专家评审的智库，工作组将其排除在增补名单之外。

经过以上各环节的工作，最终确定本年度CTTI增补智库共84家，其中党政部门智库1家、社科院智库2家、党校行政学院智库1家、高校智库79家、科研院所智库1家。

另一方面，由于天津市社科联与南京大学、光明日报自2016年建立战略合作关系。按照三方战略合作协议，2018年天津地区CTTI来源智库增补工作由天津市社科联负责组织实施，按数据填报、增补申报和增补评审三个阶段组织开展来源智库增补，得到了天津各智库机构及上级主管单位的积极响应。天津市社科联于2018年下半年启动了CTTI-TJ数据填报工作。截至11月下旬，天津市二百余家智库，尤其是各申请增补的智库严谨细致录入了机构基本信息、专家、活动、成果等多种类型的大量数据，有力支持了后续增补评审工作。在此基础上。天津市社科联确定了兼顾全国智库要求及天津智库特点的增补申报原则，开展智库增补申报工作。至申报截止，共收到14家单位的32份申请书，基本涵盖了天津市主要高校、社会智库机构。经形式审查、退修、审定后，遴选出30家候选智库参与增补评审。为确保增补评审公平公正，天津市社科联反复推敲，制定了详细增补评审方案。通过资质评审、量化评分、MRPA计分三个环节，将总得分排于前21位的智库推荐为CTTI来源智库。

最终，通过对CTTI已有来源智库名单的调整、勘误，加上本年度新增补的84家来源智库，以及天津地区推荐的21家智库，CTTI现有正式来源智库706家。

3.3 天津来源智库增补经验

本年度智库增补工作中,天津地区增补智库数量较多。自2016年CTTI首批来源智库名单发布以来,由省(市、自治区)级单位负责组织本地区来源智库增补工作,尚属首次,天津市社科联之所以能够圆满完成本次增补,有以下三点原因:

第一,天津市社科联领导的高度重视确保了天津首开地区自主增补先河。为建设CTTI-TJ、做好天津地区CTTI来源智库增补,天津市社科联领导多次赴京赴宁,商讨三方合作战略具体内容和细节。增补工作开始后,天津市社科联党组高度重视,多次研商,保证了增补工作标准规范、过程严肃、结果公正。

第二,天津智库工作的前期基础确保了增补工作高质量高水平完成。2015年以来,天津市社科联陆续开展了系列智库工作,不仅组建了各级各类智库组织,还建立了以CTTI-TJ为数据库的智库信息化平台。截至目前,天津智库联盟已有上百家成员智库,智库信息化平台已实现20多个云智库、200多家智库机构、2000多位智库专家在线共享信息、协同工作。这些前期工作为高质量高水平完成本次增补工作奠定了坚实基础。

第三,各智库机构及其上级单位的支持确保本次增补工作按时保质完成。自增补通知发布,天津市社科界表现出了极大的参与热情和认真的参与态度。尽管数据填报工作量极大、增补申报及汇报的准备时间相对较短,各智库机构及其上级单位密切配合、周密组织,仍在规定时间内按时保质完成了相应工作,确保天津地区的CTTI来源智库增补工作圆满完成。

天津地区的CTTI来源智库增补工作是首年尝试,借鉴了全国经验,也摸索了适合地方特点的方式,综合起来有以下几方面的特点:

一是对标全国,注重地方。在申报阶段,天津制定了与全国申报指标项目一一对应的地方申报标准,并根据地方智库建设实际,对部分申报指标数值进行了调整。同时,为突出"天津智库服务天津"的地方智库特色,在申报和评审阶段,还专门设置了考察智库服务地方经济社会发展的相关指标。

二是参与面广,认可度高。申请参与本次增补的智库基本覆盖了天津市主要高等院校、科研院所和重点社会智库。各智库机构及其上级主管单位高度认可和重视,不仅反复向社科联咨询增补要求细节,更有单位组织所属参评智库提前就会议评审汇报环节进行演练。

三是标准明确,评审科学。市社科联先后制定了明确的增补申报标准、资质审查标准、会议评审打分标准,并使用 CTTI-TJ 自动计算了 MRPA 分数。考虑到智库工作不同于传统科研工作,天津市社科联聘请了决策咨询管理和需求部门、智库管理部门、智库专家等各方面专家组成会议评审专家组,避免了高校教授做评审专家带来的"既当裁判员又当运动员"问题,保证了评审的科学性公正性。

四是动态管理,系统规划。今年增补工作结束后,天津地区共有 50 家 CTTI 来源智库。天津市社科联将充分借助库中海量数据资源,对 50 家 CTTI 来源智库实行动态管理、末位淘汰机制,让数据库"活"起来、把数据"用"起来、带智库"动"起来。同时,CTTI 来源智库增补和 CTTI-TJ 数据填报两项工作,也将与天津市社科联开展的智库分类评价、重点智库扶持、社会智库管理等工作有机结合,共同构成天津市社科界智库建设工作体系,形成重点突出、层次分明的智库工作格局。

3.4 CTTI 来源智库数据分析

(1) CTTI 来源智库地区分布

首先,按照中国行政区划标准,CTTI 来源智库地区分布情况如图 14 所示。就整体情况而言,华北地区、华东地区在数量方面优势较为明显,仅这两个地区的来源智库共占据入选智库总量的一半以上。其中,华北地区共有 269 家机构被 CTTI 系统收录,占所有入选机构数量的 38.10%;华东地区以 190 家紧随其后;其余几个地区来源智库分布相对均衡。

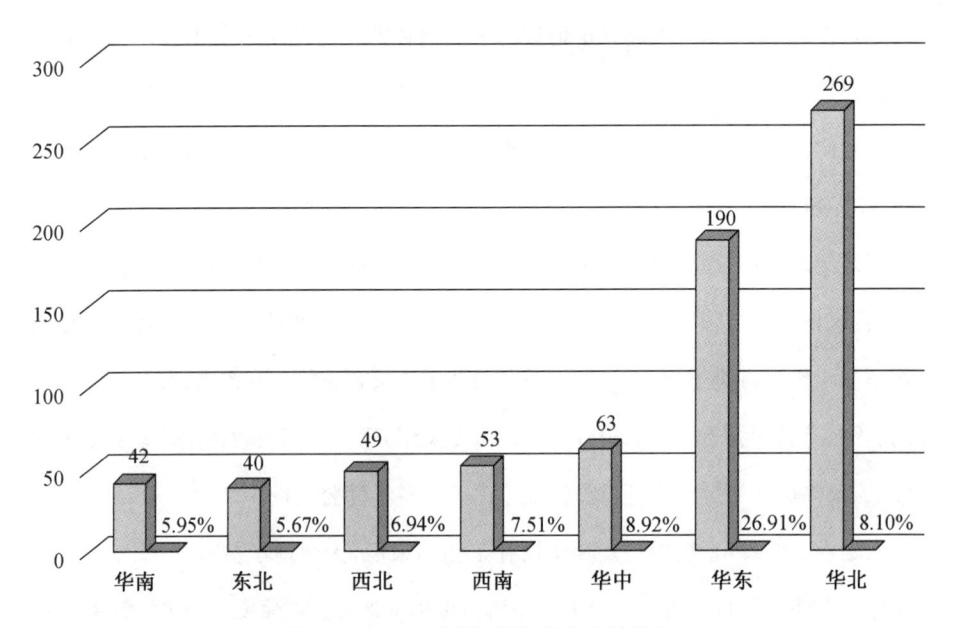

图 14　CTTI 来源智库地区分布统计图

其次,和往年相比,来源智库排名前五的地域分布情况基本没有变化,仍是北京、上海、天津、江苏和湖南。其中,北京地区共有 197 家智库入选,来源智库总量稳居榜首。这与北京特殊的政治、经济和文化地位密不可分。上海、天津和江苏入围智库地区排名紧随其后。湖南作为社会科学发展大省,近年来充分整合省内资源优势,新型智库建设成效显著。与此同时,广东、湖北及陕西等地也不断壮大自己的智库队伍,入选智库数均达到 20 家以上。此外,像重庆市、山东省、浙江省、四川省、河北省、甘肃省、江西省、辽宁省等地智库数量也有一定程度的提升,智库建设呈现出一派"百花齐放"的景象(图 15)。

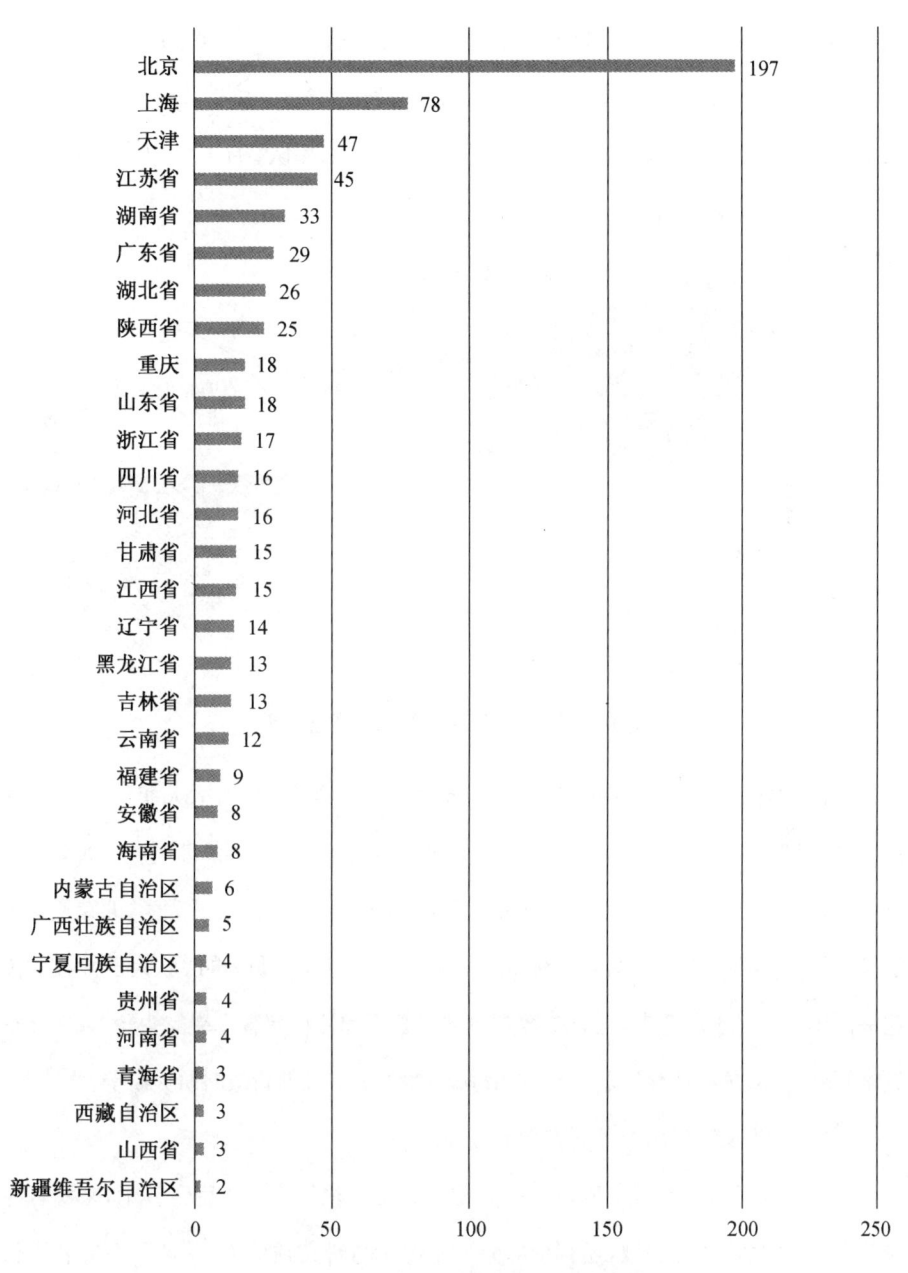

地区	数量
北京	197
上海	78
天津	47
江苏省	45
湖南省	33
广东省	29
湖北省	26
陕西省	25
重庆	18
山东省	18
浙江省	17
四川省	16
河北省	16
甘肃省	15
江西省	15
辽宁省	14
黑龙江省	13
吉林省	13
云南省	12
福建省	9
安徽省	8
海南省	8
内蒙古自治区	6
广西壮族自治区	5
宁夏回族自治区	4
贵州省	4
河南省	4
青海省	3
西藏自治区	3
山西省	3
新疆维吾尔自治区	2

图 15 CTTI 来源智库地域分布统计图

(2) CTTI 来源智库类型

根据 CTTI 来源智库类型分布统计图可知,高校智库依旧是来源智库最主要的类型,共441家,占各类智库总量的62%;党政部门智库69家,占10%;社科院智库51家,占7%;党校行政学院智库48家,占7%;社会智库36家,占5%;科研院所智库34家,占5%;传媒智库13家,占2%;企业智库8家,占1%;军队智库6家,占1%(图16)。

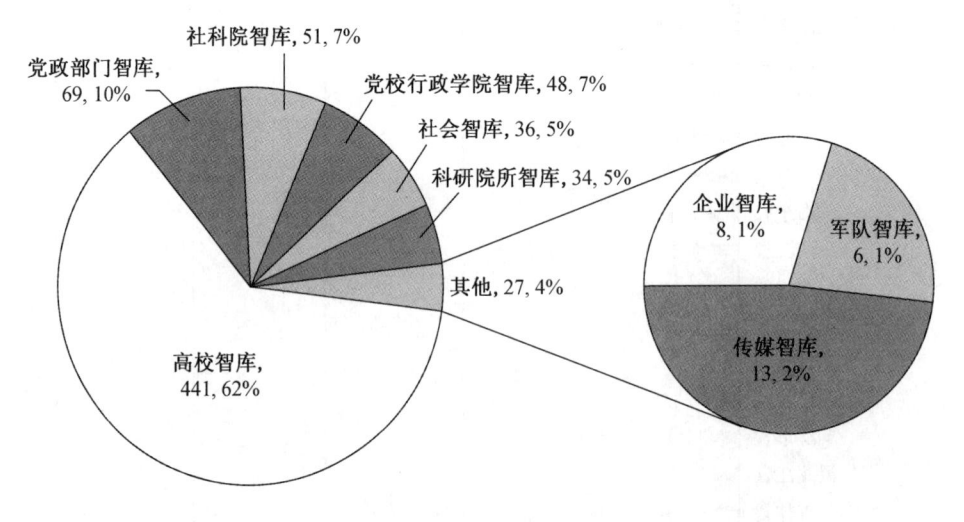

图16 CTTI来源智库类型分布统计图

从智库类型分布的整体情况看,各类智库所占比例几乎没有太大变化,较去年相比,高校智库、党政部门智库和社科院智库均有不同幅度的增加。其中,正如前文所述,新增来源智库的主体也是高校智库,以西安交通大学、上海交通大学、北京交通大学等众多一流高校为代表的大学纷纷增加了自身的智库力量,再次壮大了高校智库这一群体。而对于后两者,也有少数党政部门智库和社科院智库崭露头角,如东北亚战略研究院、黑龙江社会发展与地方治理研究院、山东省创新战略研究院等。

(3) CTTI来源智库主要研究领域分布

专业化分工是现代新型智库的一大重要特征。根据CTTI后台显示,来源智库涉及有54个具体研究领域,还有少部分智库选择的研究领域为"其他",在此暂不做统计。需要说明的是,这些来源智库既存在只研究特定领域的,即一家智库专攻某个特定研究政策;也存在部分智库有多个研究领域,即一家智库涉猎多种研究政策。从CTTI来源智库研究领域分布统计图(图17)可以看出,来源智库的研究领域相对较

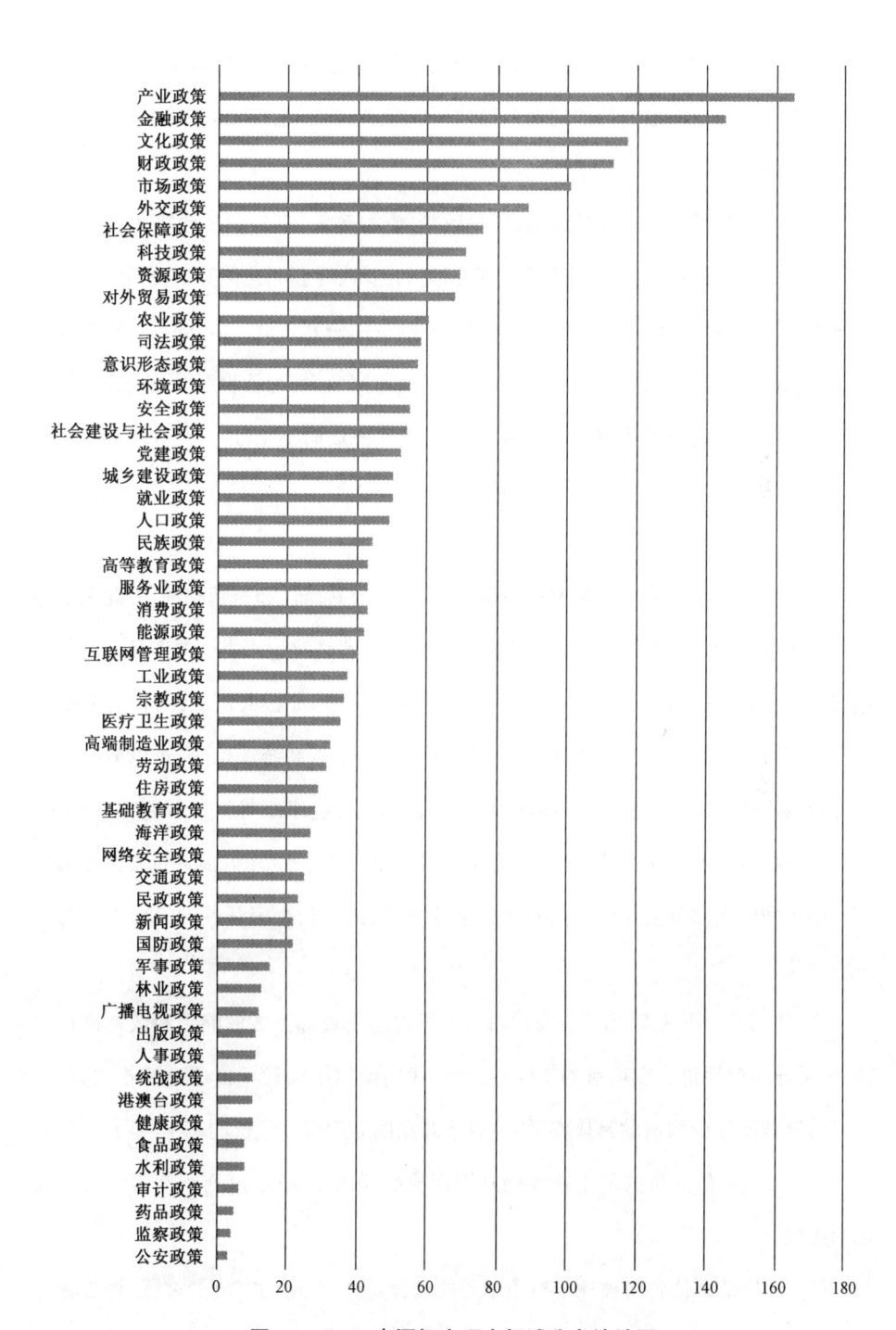

图 17　CTTI 来源智库研究领域分布统计图

为分散，聚焦的政策领域多元化。其中，产业政策、金融政策、文化政策、财政政策和市场政策是来源智库最为关注的 5 个具体研究领域，均有超过 100 家智库从事相关领域的研究。

此外，外交政策、社会保障政策、科技政策、资源政策、对外贸易政策的智库研究主体也较多。由此可见，与现实生活息息相关的经济、社会和文化等重要问题仍是智库最为关注的领域，且每一领域都体现出不同的智库研究力量。但同时，针对人事政策、统战政策、港澳台政策、水利政策、审计政策、监察政策、药品政策以及公安政策等特定领域展开研究的专业型智库不多，行业的智库发展尚不充分。

4 MRPAI 测评指标体系与排序规则

4.1 评价基本原则

智库旨在提供公共政策研究和咨询产品，具有公共属性和非营利性，因此无法完全按照市场机制来衡量智库以及智库产品的价值。那么对这一类公共产品的价值测量，最常用的方法就是公共评价。公共评价的类型众多，如公共产品评价、公共服务评价、公共机构评价、公共治理评价、公共环境评价、公共系统评价等，难以穷举。公共评价的主体也具有多样性，包括政府、个人、企业、社会组织等。一般而言，如果把公共资源投入者看成是评价的甲方（委托方），被评价者是乙方，开展评价者则是第三方。由于我国大部分公共资源的投入方是政府，因此社会组织开展的评价可称为第三方评价。

CTTI 智库测评是以第三方身份对智库机构运用资源方式的能力和效益进行过程-结果导向型评价。在项目的实施过程中，我们借鉴第四代评价理论的相关方法，同时结合智库评价领域的具体实际，将以下几点确立为智库评价的基本原则。

（1）实施评价的目的是为智库提升管理质量提供专业服务，而不是生产治理权和话语权。

（2）评价是评估者向被评价对象学习的过程，是一个对话交流的过程，评价者与被评价对象需要共同参与评价过程，而不是单方面的训导与规范。

（3）评价是基于数据的系统分析，无数据则无法测量，无法获得数据的智库，不在评价范围之内。对评价中数据的解读要客观、准确，不能歪曲评价分析的结果。

（4）评价过程必须公正公开，结果可核查可重复，及时回应社会问责。同时，评价者具备核心的业务能力。

（5）尊重机构的商业秘密、保护人的隐私、严守国家秘密的安全底线。

（6）一切为了公共福祉，以非营利的形式在一定范围内公开共享评价结果。

4.2 MRPAI 测评指标的确定

CTTI 数据库字段是对智库机构、专家、成果、活动、媒体影响力的"画像"，是描述智库的元数据格式和标准"词汇"，从理论上说词汇越丰富，"画像"越准确。基于这些数据字段，我们希望运用数据科学的专业技能，结合现代智库管理的专门知识，对 CTTI 来源智库的数据开展定量和定性相结合的分析，把结果提供给智库共同体。对此，本年度报告在已有的 MRPA 测评体系的基础上进行完善和补充，确立了新的测评指标体系——MRPAI。需要注意的是，在选择和确定测评指标时，我们并不是涵盖数据库每一个数据字段，而是有所选择。具体而言，我们在确定测评指标时主要关注以下几项原则：

（1）指标数据颗粒度与可获得性相适应。我国新型智库建设虽已取得一定成效，但各智库工作差异性极大，原始数据形式多样。另外，我国智库数据累积性不强，数据管理意识欠缺，除了教育部重点基地有规范的数据填报制度外，大部分机构并无长期的数据积累。针对这种情况，为了鼓励智库填报 CTTI，降低填写数据的难度，大部分数据库字段都专门设置了合理数量范围的必填数据项。因此，在确定 MRPAI 指标时必须结合 CTTI 字段的实际数据情况，考虑数据的可获得性，具体遵循以下流程（图18）：

图 18　MRPAI 指标选择流程

最初,将提出的指标逐一输入系统进行匹配,如果数据的可获得性不足 80%,则舍弃或者降低指标的颗粒度。比如关于智库专家指标,原本希望对智库专家的职称和年龄结构进行评价,但是经过数据匹配发现,该字段数据的获取量未能达标,而 90% 的智库都填写了专家数量和年度预算,所以这两个值就被确定为衡量智库资源(R 值)的基本指标。

(2) 指标数据的关键性、代表性和表达性要显著。选取的指标必须是体现智库属性的关键性、代表性的字段。智库的属性主要体现在完善的治理结构、强烈的政策影响倾向、积极主动地运用论坛和会议等形式扩大公共影响力、深入调研深入实际,因此从反映这些属性的内参、批示、研究报告、项目、会议、调研等字段中,选取了较多的指标,体现了指标突出智库属性的倾向性。

(3) 指标要具备客观性与系统性。指标的客观性有两层含义,一是指标和 CTTI 数据字段一样,是对智库真实属性的揭示,是由最具客观性的字段综合而来;二是指标取值的客观性,这些值不是估值等主观性强的数值。指标的系统性是指各种指标之间存在严密的逻辑关系。比如 MRPAI 五个一级指标体现了投入产出的绩效逻辑,这样的指标才能称为指标体系。

(4) 指标体系必须能起到以评促建的作用,要符合当下新型智库建设的现状。如果说 2013 年以来的这五年中国特色新型智库建设取得了一定成效,那么未来三年将是新型智库建设的"攻坚"阶段,是实现新型智库建设的高质量发展的关键阶段。

但同时我们也要承认,仍存在对智库建设规律认识不到位,运行不够规范化、不够流程化等诸多问题。因此,我们不能依据国际标准或者不符合我国智库实际建设情况的标准来测评智库,否则容易挫伤被测评智库的积极性,难以起到以评促建的鼓励性和肯定性作用。

依据以上原则,我们确定了5个一级指标,24个二级指标。5个一级指标分别是M(治理结构)、R(智库资源)、P(智库成果)、A(智库活动)、I(智库媒体影响力),命名为智库MRPAI测评指标(表2)。MRPAI属于结果导向的智库效能测评体系,它可以从两大维度来测评智库,一是资源占用量,二是资源的运用效果,也就是效能。它既能测量智库的体量、产量,也能测评智库的效能,还可以测量智库属性的强弱。因此,MRPAI体系符合指标选择的诸多原则,可以对CTTI来源智库进行有效测量。

从二级指标看,当我们单纯关注R指标时,可以测量智库预算的大小和人员的多寡,毫无疑问资金雄厚,专家和行政人员多的智库是体量大的智库。当我们单独关注P指标时,可以测量智库研究成果的多少,显然成果多的智库是好智库。当我们单独关注A指标时,可以测量智库开展活动的多少,不能说活动多的智库就是好智库,但是活动少的智库一定是智库特征不明显的智库,这样的智库更像大学里的研究中心,或者政府的政策研究室,虽然有一定的学术和政策影响力,但智库属性可能比较弱。当我们单独关注I指标时,可以测量智库受到媒体报道的数量多少和社会影响力大小,媒体影响力是智库发挥咨政启民作用的途径之一,也是衡量智库水平的重要指标。

当P类的$P1$、$P2$、$P5$加上A类和I类指标之总值比较高时,我们一般认为该智库的智库属性比较强。当我们将智库的产出除以资源后,得到的结果就是智库的效能。因此,MRPAI也可以测量智库的效能。

表 2　MRPAI 智库测评指标及其赋值

一级指标	代码	二级指标	代码	计分规则	分值
治理结构	M	理事会(董事会)	M1	有则赋值	15
		学术委员会	M2	有则赋值	10
		咨询/顾问委员会	M3	有则赋值	10
		管理团队/首席专家	M4	有则赋值	10
		国家高端智库	M5	是则赋值	100
智库资源	R	年度预算	R1	≤100 万	20
				每增加 10 万赋值	1
		科研人员	R2	≤10 人	40
				每增加 1 人赋值	2
		行政人员	R3	≤5 人	20
				每增加 1 人赋值	1
		网络资源	R4	有中文门户	20
				有英文门户	8
				有微信公号	8
				有官方微博	5
				有专门数据采集平台	10
智库成果	P	单篇内参(无论是否被批示)	P1	按篇赋值	2
		被批示内参	P2	正国级/每条	30
				副国级/每条	20
				省部级/每条	10
				副省部级/每条	5
		智库主办/承办期刊	P3	每种 CSSCI 来源刊	20
				每种普通期刊	10
				每种通讯/内参集	8
		图书(正式出版)	P4	每种赋值	2
		研究报告	P5	每份赋值	4

（续表）

一级指标	代码	二级指标	代码	计分规则	分值
		人民日报理论版、求是、光明日报	P6	每篇赋值	5
		论文	P7	CSSCI来源刊论文/每篇	1
				SSCI/A&HCI收录/每篇	2
				CSCI/EI 收录/每篇	1
				其他普通论文/每篇	0.5
		纵向项目	P8	纵向-国家社科重大/教育部社科重大	10
				纵向-国家社科重点/国家自科重点	6
				纵向-国家社科一般项目/青年项目	4
				纵向-省部级项目	2
				纵向-其他	0.5
		横向项目	P9	每项基本分2＋每10万赋值1分	
智库活动	A	会议	A1	主办承办全国性会议/每次	10
				省市自治区一级会议/每次	5
				国际性会议/每次	10
				其他会议/每次	3
		培训	A2	全国性培训活动/每次	8
				其他层次培训	2
		调研考察	A3	接受副国级领导以上调研活动/每次	15
				接受省部级领导/专家调研/每次	5
				接受其他层次领导/专家调研/每次	2
				外出调研考察	1

(续表)

一级指标	代码	二级指标	代码	计分规则	分值
智库媒体影响力	I	报纸新闻报道	I1	中央级	5
				省部级	4
				地方级	3
				境外媒体	2
				其他媒体	1
		电视新闻报道	I2	中央级	5
				省部级	4
				地方级	3
				境外媒体	2
				其他媒体	1
		网络新闻报道	I3	中央级	5
				省部级	4
				地方级	3
				境外媒体	2
				其他媒体	1

4.3 MRPAI智库测评指标的赋值

指标权重的分配有多种方式，MRPAI采取的是直接赋值法，这样的好处是易于理解，直观公开，可复核。被评价者可以根据既定的算法直接复核所得数值是否准确，评价主客体之间的对话性好。但是对评价的要求比较高，不仅赋值要比较合理，而且测评系统也要保证精确，否则就无法及时回应被评价者的质疑。

表2指标赋值采取了德尔菲法，先后进行了4轮专家调查，合计98位领导和专家接受了问卷调查。以下是对赋值的说明。

表2中MRPAI二级指标赋值考虑了以下几点情况：

（1）$M1 \sim M4$对智库结构的测评只考察是否有内部管理机构，而没有考察这些机构运转是否正常。这符合我国新型智库建设的现状，先看有没有这些内部机构，以后测量时再看运转是否规范。因此分值并不高,满分仅45分。M5则是对已经被列为国家高端智库的特别赋值,是对这种地位的一种肯定。

(2) $R1$ 考察的是年度预算。考虑到我们智库普遍规模偏小,年度经费100万元是常态,因此没有再区别年度预算100万以下的智库。小于等于100万的,统一赋值20分,每增加10万元增加1分。

(3) $R2 \sim R3$ 是人员指标及其赋值。我们没有区别全职和兼职,原因是人事制度改革,兼职的人也可能是全职员工,加上智库专家大部分属于弹性工作制度,连全职还是兼职都很难区分。因此,小于等于10位科研人员的机构统一赋值40分,然后每增加1人赋值2分。行政团队小于等于5人规模的为20分,每增加1人赋值1分。随着系统数据的日益规范,日后这部分数据在填报时可能需要提供相应的证明材料,各智库还应尽快完善员工聘任合同。

(4) $R4$ 网络资源其实也可以看成是智库的建设成效。我们把网站等看作是跟办公场所一样的基础设置。现代智库对办公室场所要求不高,如果智库不填这个数据,真实性也无从复核,因此,对于人、财、物、网,$R4$ 舍弃了对有形物质办公条件的测量,而是把重点放在网络条件上。这几个指标都是可核查的,具有可操作性。鉴于我国大多数智库对网站建设的关注不够,对社交媒体运用更是非常陌生,所以这个指标也只是根据"有/无"进行赋值,没有考虑质量之高下。

(5) P 指标中,内参、批示和研究报告的赋值比较高。被询问的专家普遍认为这是反映智库决策影响力的主要指标,分值应该加大。这也是建智库的主要目的。目前这个数值是根据专家的意见调高的。对于大部分省级智库而言,拿到国家级领导人的批示并不容易,所以正国级领导批示的分值反而对普通智库的总分影响不大,因为大多数智库都拿不到。由于MRPAI测评侧重的是分类排序,是把相同层次的智库放在一起比较,那么这样的赋值相对公平。为了鼓励写内参,凡是发表在省部级以上内参集(内部报送性连续出版物),如《光明内参》等,无论是否被批示都予以赋值。给予P6指标较高的分值体现了《人民日报》《光明日报》《求是》在我国政策话语体系中的特殊地位，如果能在这些报刊上发文章，也意味着政策影响力和公众影响力的扩大。

（6）MRPAI测评指标体系给予了智库活动成果比较重要的地位。高层次高水平的论坛和会议是智库发挥影响力的重要途径，这也是智库区别于传统研究机构的重要特征。世界著名智库几乎都是会议中心，几乎都是重大政策路演的主要平台。因此对于智库举办的全国性会议和国际性会议赋值比较高。虽然"搭台子、请名人"这种不良风气确实存在，但这只是少数现象。会议不仅可以传播信息，而且是智库拓展研究网络、政策网络的主要渠道之一。

调研考察是具有中国特色的智库研究方法。没有调查研究就没有发言权，大数据分析也无法替代亲身实地调查。因此，MRPAI测评指标对此类活动也给予较高的分值。

（7）I指标考察的重点在于智库的媒体影响力。无论在国内外，媒体影响力一直是智库界关注的重点，计算全国性或国际性的重要报纸、杂志、电视等传媒的引用率也是最为常见的公开评价。这是因为智库不同于传统的学术研究机构，传播与研究对智库而言同等重要，因而在电视、报纸、网络上露面或发表看法被认为是智库影响力的重要体现。目前，我们暂时仅将报纸、电视及网络上传播的新闻报道纳入评价范围，这三种媒介在智库传播上的应用及影响范围更为广泛，有一定质量保障。其中，对不同级别的报道给予了不同分值，中央级是最具权威性的，因此赋予最高分值，分值随报道级别降低依次递减。今年是首次尝试引入I指标，后续我们也考虑将更多不同形式的新媒体指标纳入媒体影响力评价中。

5 MRPAI排序规则

5.1 MRPAI排序规则的设计原理

排序是一种重要的评价方法，也是评价结果的一种重要展示形式。它是按照一个或者n个指标，对评价客体的主要的、普遍的、规律性的、稳定的、客观性的特征或者要素进行比较，并对结果予以一定形式展示的评价方法。排序评价可以有效和直观地揭示同类事物总体特征和个体差异,但是这种方法也不可避免地会忽略个体的细节,尤其是排序指标过少的情况下,运用这种评价方法要防止出现"只见森林,不见树木"的偏差。

运用排序评价法需要注意:1)同类比较。评价客体之间共性越大,评价结果越准确。因此,我们设计 MRPAI 排序算法时,坚持先分类后排序的方式,这样可以减少误差。2)多维度展示。如果只从单一维度展示排序结果,往往会用评价客体的一种特征掩盖评价客体的另外几种特征,不利于揭示客体的多元特征。这样不仅不利于客体信息的多维度表达,对于评价客体而言也是一种不公平评价。因此,MRPAI 排序注意到从多个维度来展示评价结果。

5.2 MRPAI 排序规则

MRPAI 智库排序共 13 项,分数量指标排序和效能指标排序两类。

5.2.1 数量指标排序

(1) 智库资源(R 值)排序,依据是智库年度预算($R1$)、研究人员($R2$)、行政人员($R3$)、网络资源($R4$)4 个指标赋值的算术和。

(2) 智库成果(P 值)排序,依据是单篇内参($P1$)、被批示内参($P2$)、智库主办/承办期刊($P3$)、图书($P4$)、研究报告($P5$)、人民日报理论版、求是、光明日报文章($P6$)、论文($P7$)、纵向项目($P8$)、横向项目($P9$)9 个指标赋值的算术和。

(3) 智库活动(A 值)排序,依据是会议($A1$)、培训($A2$)、调研考察($A3$)3 个指标赋值的算术和。

(4) 智库产出(PAI 值)排序,以产出影响力为导向,排序规则是 $PAI=P+A+I$,即成果、活动与媒体影响力这 3 个指标赋值的算术和。

(5) 智库综合测评 $T(n)$ 排序,排序规则是 $T(n)=R+M+P+A+I$,即资源、管理、成果、活动和媒体影响力 5 个指标赋值的算术和。

以上 5 种排序反映了智库的资源总量和产出总量,描述了每个智库资源和产出在 CTTI 来源智库中的相对位置。智库在 5 类排序中的位置肯定不会是一样的,其差异性恰恰反映了智库的个体性特征,体现智库的特色。

除了上述 5 种数量指标排序外,今后我们还会具体引入 E 值(专家评分),进行 $PAI-E$ 的排序,即 PAI 值与 E 值的算术和。PAI 值能够有效衡量智库的产出与社会影响力,但由于 CTTI 系统对数据采集主要以数据众包模式为主,可能导致各家智库填报数据的不均衡,例如有些智库填报的数据量过多,而有些过少。为了解决这一弊端,系统将在客观数据基础上引入专家主观分值,按照一定比例将两项分值相加进行排序。

5.2.2 效能指标排序

效能指的是智库的能力(competence)和效率(efficiency),智库能力是对智库的资源配置策略是否合理、管理能力是否具备,以及智库的组织制度和组织文化的发育程度的综合反映。而智库效率则是指智库用最节约的时间、资本、人力使产出最大化的能力。在给定资源总量的情况下,智库的成果和活动产出越大,说明智库效能越高。由于在本报告中,资源包含了专家、行政、预算、网络四类,智库产出并不是这四类资源简单组合的结果,而是这四类资源复杂整合运用的结果(表 3)。

表 3　智库效能指标排序规则

排序名称	规则	说明
资源总效能	$(P+A)/R$	产出值/资源值
专家效能	$(P+A)/R2$	产出值/专家资源值
行政团队效能	$(P+A)/R3$	产出值/行政团队资源值
资本贡献率	$(P+A)/R1$	产出值/资本投入值
专家成果贡献率	$P/R2$	成果值/专家资源值
行政团队活动贡献	$A/R3$	活动值/行政团队资源值

5.3　MRPAI 智库专家排序规则

建设具有高影响力和知名度的智库,需要拥有一流的高层次的智库专家,他们是智库思想创新的核心人物。通过测评发现高绩效的专家是非常有意义的,因为高绩效、高水平和高知名是呈正相关的。倘若智库人才管理不好,其他更是无从谈起。

MRPAI智库专家测评的原理简单明了，其指标分三类，分别是专家个人研究成果（P 值）、专家个人活动（A 值）和荣誉奖励（H 值）。具体测评指标和赋值参见表4。MRPAI智库专家绩效用 E_p 表示，绩效是三类指标赋值的算术和。

$$E_p = P1 + P2 + P4 + P5 + P6 + P7 + P8 + P9 + A1 + A2 + A3 + H1$$

表4　MRPAI智库专家测评指标及赋值表

一级指标	代码	二级指标	代码	计分规则	分值
专家成果	P	单篇内参（无论是否被批示）	P1	按篇赋值	2
		被批示内参	P2	正国级/每条	30
				副国级/每条	20
				省部级/每条	10
				副省部级/每条	5
		图书（正式出版）	P4	每种赋值	2
		研究报告	P5	每份赋值	4
		人民日报理论版、求是、光明日报文章	P6	每篇赋值	5
		论文	P7	CSSCI来源刊论文/每篇	1
				SSCI/A&HCI收录/每篇	2
				CSCI/EI 收录/每篇	1
				其他普通论文/每篇	0.5
		纵向项目	P8	纵向-国家社科重大/教育部社科重大	10
				纵向-国家社科重点/国家自科重点	6
				纵向-国家社科一般项目/青年项目	4
				纵向-省部级项目	2
				纵向-其他	0.5
		横向项目	P9	每项基本分2+每增加10万赋值1	

（续表）

一级指标	代码	二级指标	代码	计分规则	分值
专家活动	A	专家参加国际或者全国性会议/次	A1	主持/致辞/主题发言	4
				普通代表	1
		专家参加其他层次会议		主持/致辞/主题发言	2
				普通代表	0.5
		全国性培训活动	A2	讲师	3
		其他层次培训		讲师	1
		参与接待副国级领导以上考察调研活动		每次	4
		参与接待省部级领导/专家考察调研	A3	每次	1
		参与接待其他层次领导/专家考察调研		每次	0.5
专家获奖	H	省部级以上奖励	H1	每次	2

由于专家效能分值及其名次属于专家个人隐私，因此不予公开，如果有专家需要了解有关情况，可以发邮件到 ctti@nju.edu.cn 索取。

5.4 大学智库指数排序规则

智库作为现代社会从事战略和政策研究、咨询的专业机构，是现代政治运作、行政管理和社会治理综合需求的产物，是知识社会分工进一步细化的产物。高校和智库是两类性质完全不同的社会机构。一般而言，大学历史要比智库悠久得多，大学的体量要比智库大很多，大学的结构和功能要比智库复杂得多。高校智库大多是高校的一部分，智库功能是高校多种功能中的一种。一般而言，如果一个大学从事战略研究和政策研究的院系和科研机构越多，它的智库能力就越强。不难发现，经济学院、政府管理学院、国际关系学院、法学院等特色院系实力比较强的大学，它的智库能力就越强，它办的智库影响力也就越大。哈佛大学并不在政治中心，但是由于肯尼迪政府学院的影响力，哈佛大学的智库能力在美国大学中名列前茅。大学智库指数就是对大学的智库能力和智库影响力的描述和评价。

CTTI 大学智库指数是把来源智库中直属于同一个大学智库的各个智库的综合测评分值进行求和,这个值就是该大学的智库总值,定义该值为 U^{ts}。这样必然会有一个大学的 U^{ts} 值最大,标记为 $\max U^{ts}$。然后利用统计学中归一化的方法将数据转化为纯量,以便于比较和更直观地体现数据特征,即用其他大学的 U^{ts} 值去除以 $\max U^{ts}$,得到的比值一定小于等于 1,然后把比值乘以 100,得到的就是该大学智库指数,定义为 index^{UT}。具体公式如下:

$$\mathrm{index}^{UT} = U^{ts} / \max U^{ts} \times 100$$

本年度有关高校智库的详细测评分析可查阅《2018 CTTI 高校智库暨百强榜报告》。

5.5 MRPAI 测评系统

MRPAI 测评系统是 CTTI 系统后台的一个系统,它包含智库排序、专家排序、大学智库指数排序 3 个子系统。智库排序既可以综合排序,也可以分不同类型排序。专家排序和大学智库指数排序也是如此。

MRPAI 测评系统深刻理解了 MRPA 指标体系、赋值和排序规则,运用了先进的排序算法,也包含了一些基本的机器学习功能,能够做到对来源智库进行即时测评。

另外,MRPAI 测评系统还有查询功能和数据统计分析功能,不仅能够准确定位智库和专家,而且可以统计出每个智库 MRPA 指标 74 个得分点的得分情况,每位专家 MRPAI 指标 48 个得分点的得分情况。这样就可以清楚地分析来源智库各分值之间的比例,也就可以揭示智库在管理、资源、成果、活动等具体方面的强弱,对改善智库管理有极大帮助。

其次,MRPAI 测评系统指标项分值做成了可调整的参数形式,这样评价主体(可能是智库管理部门、研究者、有特定需求的用户)可以根据不同的目的调整指标赋值,从而得出不同的个性化的排序结果。这体现了 MRPAI 测评系统的灵活性。

需要说明的是,目前 MRPAI 测评系统布置在后台,前台暂时无法查阅,这样可以比较好地保护机构和专家测评数据安全,尊重专家个人隐私。未经机构和专家本人同意,CTTI项目组不会向任何第三方透露详细测评结果。本次发布的数据只是一级指标数值,不涉及二级指标得分的具体数值。各智库如果需要具体得分详情,可以以机构名义发正式函件到邮箱 ctti@nju.edu.cn,南京大学中国智库研究与评价中心会导出相关测评结果给来函机构。

6　来源智库测评结果分析

本年度测评依旧延续往年原则,不仅基于科学合理的评价体系,还要结合完善的智库填报数据情况。通过对 706 家 CTTI 来源智库的数据填报情况进行分析,其中有 520 家智库填写了较为充分、准确的数据。因此,我们的测评排序的对象也主要以这 520 家智库为主。基于历年累积的数据,本年度测评分为三类:一是对社会智库的测评,二是对高校智库的测评(详见《2018 CTTI 高校智库暨百强榜报告》),三是对各研究领域智库的测评。为保护智库的隐私,我们仅公布各类测评中排名前列的智库测评分析结果,若来源智库想了解自己的具体排名,请邮件联系南京大学中国智库研究与评价中心(ctti@edu.nju.cn),我们将一对一提供相关信息。

6.1　社会智库测评数据示例

通过对社会智库数据进行审核,其中有 26 家数据填写较为完整,将依据其产出影响力分值,即所谓的 PAI 值(成果、活动与媒体影响力这 3 项指标赋值的算术和)进行排序,最终选取公布排名前 15 的社会智库测评结果,如表 5 所示。

表 5　社会智库 PAI 值评分 Top15

(按智库名称首字母音序排列)

智库名称	PAI	P 值	A 值	I 值
察哈尔学会	132	108	24	0
长江教育研究院	1 182.5	1 086.5	96	0
重庆智库	486	366	120	0

(续表)

智库名称	PAI	P值	A值	I值
东中西部区域发展和改革研究院	127	52	75	0
广东财经大学华南商业智库	179	128	49	2
广东中策知识产权研究院	322	237	76	9
国观智库	503	193	253	57
海国图智研究院	583.5	321.5	257	5
盘古智库	698.5	412.5	286	0
上海新金融研究院	103	58	45	0
深圳创新发展研究院	332	272	60	0
中国国际经济交流中心	121.5	1.5	120	0
中国丝路智谷研究院	783.5	783.5	0	0
中国与全球化智库	4 217.5	3 354.5	836	27
中智科学技术评价研究中心	241	208	33	0

和往年相比，社会智库的测评结果一直比较稳定，需要说明的是，大部分社会智库没有录入媒体报道，所以I值相对较低。但实际上，他们输出了大量的智力成果，在国内社会乃至国际上均产生了重要的影响。例如，中国与全球化智库每年出版10余部研究著作，包括与社科文献出版社合作出版发布的《中国企业国际化报告》《中国留学发展报告》《中国区域人才竞争力报告》等，承担国家多个部委的课题和举办多个论坛及智库研讨会，向中国政府有关部委提交过百余份建言献策报告，拥有大量的品牌成果和较高的媒体曝光度，是国内领先的社会智库型全球化研究机构。中国国际经济交流中心开展的中日、中美、中韩、中欧等对话对于促进中国与其他国家的对话交流有着重要意义，其举办的"全球智库峰会"是思想的盛宴，亦是全球智库交流合作的重要平台。盘古智库倡议成立了由来自中国、美国、德国、意大利、印度、新加坡、加拿大等国的海内外近二十家一流智库组成的全球治理智库连线，大大提高了中国智库在全球治理中的话语权。中国丝路智谷研究院为致力实现"中国梦"、推动"一带一

路"建设，推进国家参与完善和制定国际经济组织、国际金融组织治理和顶层设计的新型智库，已被中央政府推进"一带一路"建设工作领导小组办公室、国家信息中心"一带一路"大数据中心推出的"一带一路"大数据报告列为国内"一带一路"研究最佳智库之一。察哈尔学会自创立以来，目前已成为中国公共外交研究领域的核心机构之一，有力地推动了中国公共外交理论与实践的发展及国际关系社会智库的完善。

还有部分社会智库在某些特色领域表现卓越。如长江教育研究院聚集了一批国内外知名教育专家，自2009年开始每年"两会"前在北京举办"北京·长江教育论坛"，邀请全国人大代表、全国政协委员、知名教育专家和教育部有关司局领导共同探讨教育改革与发展问题；并从2015年起发布年度教育指数——《中国教育指数》及年度《中国教育十大关键词》，产生了广泛的社会影响。海国图智研究院长期为中国公众及政策制定者提供科学、公正及客观的政策分析、研究报告及学术向导，扎实推进"中美关系""风险预测""东南亚政治经济""一带一路"等领域的研究，为政府、企业以及个人客户提供一流智力支持和决策咨询服务。广东中策知识产权研究院是广东首个引进的侧重于知识产权政策研究、战略制定、产业运营等方面的国家级知识产权高端专业服务机构，在知识产权领域贡献了重要力量。中智科学技术评价研究中心近年来形成了一系列国家级蓝皮书，在评价指标体系构建和进行竞争力评价方面具有权威性影响，例如《世界创新竞争力报告》《全球环境竞争力报告》《中国茶产业发展报告》等。

此外，东中西部区域发展和改革研究院、重庆智库、国观智库等社会智库也各具特色，他们为政府决策提供了有力的决策支持。广东财经大学华南商业智库作为今年新晋智库也具有一定潜力。

6.2 各研究领域智库测评数据示例

我们把来源智库分为12个政策研究领域，分别是宏观经济与国际贸易领域；产业与金融领域；区域研究与国际关系领域；党的建设与国家治理领域；社会治理与公共事业；法律与公共安全领域；文化与教育领域；环境、能源与基础设施领域；信息与科技领域;"三农"领域;"一带一路"领域;综合型智库。在每一研究领域内,我们同样依据来源智库的产出影响力(PAI值)进行测评分析,并选取公布每一领域排名前列的智库测评结果。需要注意的是,每类结果排名不分先后,皆按智库名称首字母音序排列。

6.2.1 宏观经济与国际贸易领域

从事宏观经济与国际贸易政策领域研究的来源智库有62家,他们大多聚焦于国民经济、地区经济发展、国际或区域贸易等问题,表6则选取公布其中排名前15智库的测评结果。高校智库依托经济学相关学科领域的资源优势,为这一领域贡献了众多成果。如复旦大学中国经济研究中心定位于前瞻性地为中国未来中长期经济增长与发展提供政策咨询和建议,重点关注未来20年中国经济增长与发展中的重大战略问题,据此撰写了大量的内参和智库报告。吉林大学数量经济研究中心则擅于利用定量分析的方法研究我国经济领域的前沿问题,开发了"经济与社会指数研究数据库"智库信息平台,并且其网站建设较为完善,访问量近6万次。南开大学经济与社会发展研究院借助自身独特的学科优势,提高科研成果的社会转化能力,围绕经济和社会发展的热点问题发出南开声音。另外,也有部分党政部门智库表现突出,如内蒙古自治区发展研究中心和河北省发展和改革委员会宏观经济研究所,二者都围绕地方经济社会运行中热点、难点问题开展大量调研,为当地政府在经济领域的决策做好智囊保障。

表6 宏观经济与国际贸易领域智库 *PAI* 值评分 Top15

(按名称首字母音序排列)

智库名称	PAI	P值	A值	I值
安徽财经大学安徽经济发展研究院	2 635.5	2 057.5	575	3
对外经济贸易大学国际经济研究院	1 376.5	1 376.5	0	0
复旦大学中国经济研究中心	1 212	1 020	192	0
河北省发展和改革委员会宏观经济研究所	792	747	45	0
淮阴工学院苏北发展研究院	755.5	753.5	2	0

(续表)

智库名称	PAI	P值	A值	I值
吉林大学数量经济研究中心	1 351.5	1 141.5	179	31
暨南大学广州南沙自由贸易试验区研究基地	734	650	84	0
南开大学经济与社会发展研究院	1 500.5	1 083.5	380	37
南通大学江苏长江经济带研究院	760.5	485.5	58	217
内蒙古自治区发展研究中心	2 333	2 292	41	0
上海对外经贸大学国际经贸治理与中国改革开放联合研究中心	1 164	1 120	44	0
首都经济贸易大学北京市经济社会发展政策研究基地	889.5	868.5	21	0
天津财经大学天津市自由贸易区研究院	776.5	649.5	127	0
中国财政科学研究院	802	792	10	0
中南财经政法大学中国收入分配研究中心	753.5	548.5	205	0

6.2.2 产业与金融领域

同样有62家来源智库从事产业与金融领域研究，他们大多聚焦于金融政策、各类产业政策、企业管理、市场消费、创新发展等问题，表7选取公布其中排名前15智库的测评结果。在金融领域，中国人民大学重阳金融研究院被中国官方认定为中国金融学会绿色金融专业委员会秘书处，且研究院聘请了来自10多个国家的96名前政要、银行家、知名学者为高级研究员，在国际上享有较高的知名度，被大量媒体所报道，在多个领域发挥了重要影响力。苏宁金融研究院作为一流的企业智库代表，也是该领域重要的智力来源，该智库曾在30余家主流财经媒体和自媒体平台开设专栏，月均发布专栏文章400余篇、接受媒体访问100余次，在主流财经论坛积极发声，塑造了自身的广泛影响力。并且，苏宁金融研究院专门设立了数据管理的日常工作岗，安排专人负责更新和维护其在CTTI系统里的数据，实现了智库现代化管理。在企业营运方面，中国企业营运资金管理研究中心可谓业界翘楚，建立了多个智库信息平台、专题数据库和综合数据库,开发了"全球企业资金管理案例库",无论是其成果还是媒体报道都显示出自身独特的优势。

表7 产业与金融领域智库 *PAI* 值评分 Top15

(按名称首字母音序排列)

智库名称	PAI	P值	A值	I值
安徽大学创新发展研究院	2 370.5	2 279.5	91	0
北京工业大学北京现代制造业发展研究基地	659	614	45	0
福建师范大学竞争力研究中心	576.5	517.5	59	0
国观智库	503	193	253	57
河北工业大学京津冀发展研究中心	5 093	4 177	916	0
河北金融学院德融研究院	636	280	356	0
黄河科技学院中国(河南)创新发展研究院	1 117	309	477	331
机械工业经济管理研究院	1 696	1 598	98	0
南京大学江苏长江产业经济研究院	3 284.5	817.5	2 344	123
苏宁金融研究院	1 926.5	1 561.5	365	0
天津商业大学现代服务业发展研究中心	515.5	515.5	0	0
西南财经大学中国家庭金融调查与研究中心	678.5	367.5	188	123
中国海洋大学中国企业营运资金管理研究中心	9 297	9 235	62	0
中国人民大学重阳金融研究院	1 280	801	479	0
中南财经政法大学产业升级与区域金融湖北省协同创新中心	2 171	1 108	1 060	3

6.2.3 区域研究与国际关系领域

为进一步推动和加强我国高校的区域和国别研究,教育部于2012年3月召开了"区域和国别研究第一次工作会议",随后几年全国100多所高校近400家研究机构成为教育部国别区域研究备案中心,高校国别和区域研究呈现迅速发展的良好势头,高校智库成为区域研究的主力队伍。其中，华东师范大学周边合作与发展协同创新中心将区域国别研究建立在国际政治经济学、地缘政治学和历史学的跨学科协同研究基础上，推出了一系列有影响力的重要学术与咨政成果，并设立海外工作室，创造智库海外推进的新模式。而浙江师范大学非洲研究院则是在教育部、外交部支持下于 2007 年成立的中国高校首个综合性、实体性非洲研究院，经 10 年多发展已成为有广泛影响力的中国非洲研究机构与国家对非事务智库。该智库向国家各部委提交各类咨询报告 40 余篇，多篇报告获国家领导人批示或被《教育部高校智库专刊》录用，同时还在国际上主办了"中非智库论坛""中非媒体智库研讨会"等一系列影响广泛的重要学术会议，获得了国内外媒体的大量报道。

除高校智库的努力外，也有少部分社会智库和社科院智库在该领域贡献了重要的力量。2018 年 8 月，联合国经济与社会理事会（ECOSOC）正式批准授予全球化智库（CCG）联合国经社理事会非政府组织"特别咨商地位"，CCG 成为获此资质的为数不多的中国机构之一，也是第一个正式取得该地位的中国智库。CCG 获得该"咨商地位"，标志着中国智库正积极走出去，充分发挥民间组织的国际影响力，深度参与全球治理。11 月 11 日—13 日，旨在通过创新全球治理以实现世界和平、推动多边合作的"巴黎和平论坛"在巴黎举办，CCG 提出的两项倡议——成立国际人才组织联合会和国际电商联盟 D50 从近 900 个项目中成功突围，获得了主办方的高度认可。同时，CCG 理事长王辉耀入选巴黎和平论坛执委会，作为执委会成员指导并参与论坛工作。这标志着中国智库有更多机会深度参与全球治理。

盘古智库聚焦全球治理、一带一路、创新驱动、宏观经济等领域的研究，尤其在中韩关系和中印关系领域的研究咨询取得了业界公认的影响力。中国社会科学院欧洲研究所是专门从事欧洲综合领域研究及国别研究的国家级科研机构，产出了丰硕的研究成果，同时搭建了"中国中东欧国家智库交流与合作网络"，在促进与加强中国对中东欧国家的"二轨外交"上扮演了重要角色（表 8）。

表8 区域研究与国际关系领域智库 *PAI* 值评分 Top15

（按名称首字母音序排列）

智库名称	*PAI*	*P* 值	*A* 值	*I* 值
复旦大学美国研究中心	885	207	609	69
广东外语外贸大学广东国际战略研究院	1 941.5	1 622.5	290	29
广西大学中国-东盟研究院	646.5	401.5	245	0
华东师范大学周边合作与发展协同创新中心	5 965	4 546	1 419	0
暨南大学华侨华人研究院	800	604	187	9
盘古智库	698.5	412.5	286	0
上海外国语大学中东研究所	1 932.5	773.5	622	537
上海外国语大学中国国际舆情研究中心	1 155.5	1 155.5	0	0
四川大学南亚研究所	732.5	360.5	372	0
同济大学德国研究中心	767.5	367.5	400	0
延边大学朝鲜半岛研究院	918	637	281	0
云南大学周边外交研究中心	2 004.5	1 801.5	184	19
浙江师范大学非洲研究院	3 316.5	2 029.5	1 187	100
中国社会科学院欧洲研究所	1 168	1 142	26	0
中国与全球化智库	4 228.5	3 365.5	836	27

6.2.4 党的建设与国家治理领域

有26家来源智库从事党的建设与国家治理领域研究，这些智库主要围绕党建、政府、社会体制等方面问题，表9选取公布其中排名前10智库的测评结果。在党建方面，东南大学中国特色社会主义发展研究院表现不俗，其围绕对党的创新理论进行跟踪研究和阐释，以及对中国特色社会主义发展展开实践和对策研究两大主要工作，取得了丰硕的理论成果，曾先后在《人民日报》《光明日报》《红旗文稿》等中央媒体发表近10篇重要理论文章，举办了若干相关会议和培训，并积极打造自身的国际影响力。在国家治理方面，北京市信访矛盾分析研究中心以大量翔实的信访数据和资料为基础,提交内参 200 份以上,并获得大量批示,对政府在信访政策领域的相关决策提供了重要的支持和参考。与此同时,北京大学国家治理研究院也为这一领域做出了一定贡献,该研究院是集科学研究、学科建设、人才培养和社会服务于一体的综合性新型智库,研究院拥有较为完善的管理制度,每年举办有多场重要会议活动,且多篇内参曾获正国级领导批示,为国家治理现代化决策提供支持。

表 9 党的建设与国家治理领域智库 *PAI* 值评分 Top10

(按名称首字母音序排列)

智库名称	PAI	P 值	A 值	I 值
北京大学国家治理研究院	1 557.5	751.5	806	0
北京市信访矛盾分析研究中心	3 049.5	2 503.5	546	0
东南大学中国特色社会主义发展研究院	2 135	2 014	121	0
华中科技大学国家治理研究院	503.5	233.5	270	0
江苏党的建设理论与实践创新研究院	444	444	0	0
江西师范大学管理决策评价研究中心	705	550	116	39
南开大学中国政府与政策联合研究中心	296.5	135.5	82	79
西安交通大学中国改革试点探索与评估协同创新中心	345.5	265.5	80	0
中国社会科学院上海市人民政府上海研究院	1 900.5	739.5	971	190
中国行政体制改革研究会	523.5	145.5	42	336

6.2.5 社会治理与公共事业领域

在本报告所划分的 12 大智库领域中,社会治理与公共事业研究领域的来源智库数量最多,共计 72 家。表 10 选取公布其中排名前 20 智库的测评结果。这一领域来源智库主要聚焦地方治理、医疗、卫生、社会保障、区域规划等各方面公共政策,具体领域各有特色。如城乡社区社会管理湖北省协同创新中心立足于国家建设和湖北省跨越式发展的重大需求,开展政、学、研、企、用五位一体协同攻关,构建城乡社区社会管理创新的"智库""人才库""思想库""信息库"。中心建有城乡社区社会管理的专业化智库信息平台,以及多种专题数据库和综合数据库,成果数量颇丰,内参也多次获得不同级别的领导批示,整体实力较强。江西师范大学苏区振兴研究院系江西省重点新型智库试点建设单位,在整合校内资源优势的基础上,开展苏区振兴的基础理论与应用对策研究,为原中央苏区的振兴发展提供智力支持和社会服务。现已向中央、国家部委(办)、省委、省政府提供咨询报告、政策建议40多份,已有30余份获得党和国家领导、部委领导、省委、省政府领导批示。华东师范大学城市中心依托学校人文地理学国家重点学科以及社会学、经济学等主要学科,开展城市地理、城市社会等方面的研究,承担有多项国家重点项目,每年举办有大量的相关会议,并开展多样化的接待和考察活动,产生了一定范围的影响力。

表10 社会治理与公共事业领域智库 PAI 值评分 Top20

(按名称首字母音序排列)

智库名称	PAI	P 值	A 值	I 值
创新型城市发展与评估研究院	476.5	425.5	51	0
广州大学广州发展研究院	581.5	405.5	133	43
华东师范大学中国现代城市研究中心	2 449	1 364	870	215
华南理工大学社会治理研究中心	872	571	301	0
江苏省社会科学院区域现代化研究院	742.5	674.5	60	8
江西省情研究中心	1 258.5	1 218.5	40	0
江西师范大学苏区振兴研究院	1 963	1 760	167	36
江西师范大学中国社会转型研究协同创新中心	1 220.5	1 162.5	28	30
民政部-华东师大中国行政区划研究院	542.5	276.5	112	154
南京医科大学健康江苏研究院	420.5	358.5	50	12
山东大学卫生管理与政策研究中心	486	231	255	0
上海大学基层治理创新研究中心	686	472	214	0

(续表)

智库名称	PAI	P值	A值	I值
上海交通大学中国城市治理研究院	646	214	416	16
四川大学中国西部边疆安全与发展协同创新中心	998	992	6	0
武汉大学社会保障研究中心	708.5	627.5	76	5
燕山大学河北省公共政策评估研究中心	1 699.5	1 658.5	41	0
盐城师范学院沿海发展智库	636	602	33	1
云南大学边疆民族问题智库	929.5	910.5	19	0
浙江大学中国西部发展研究院	1 654.5	1 022.5	632	0
中南财经政法大学城乡社区社会管理湖北省协同创新中心	26 574.5	20 974.5	5 034	566

6.2.6 法律与公共安全领域

有42家来源智库从事法律与公共安全领域研究，这些智库多为高校智库，他们依托相关专业学科开展不同的专业研究方向，表11选取公布其中排名前15智库的测评结果。其中，武汉大学国际法研究所是我国国际法研究领域的学术重镇，同时也是首批国家高端智库之一，拥有丰硕的成果，过去一年共出版著作15部，在国内外学界和实务界产生了较大反响；还在 Chinese Journal of International Law、Hong Kong Law Journal、人民日报、中国法学等国内外知名期刊和报纸上发表各类学术论文60余篇，提交咨询报告50余篇，承担了横向、纵向各类科研项目近30项。江南大学食品安全风险治理研究院依托学科优势与主管机构支持，在专注于食品安全风险治理的基础上不断扩大研究领域，树立了《中国食品安全发展报告》《中国食品安全网络舆情发展报告》等一系列品牌成果，服务政府决策，并开发了食品安全事件大数据挖掘与监测平台，为中国食品安全治理提供数据支撑，在国内外均树立了一定的影响力。

在公共安全领域，江苏省公共安全研究院充分发挥政府主管部门职能优势、高校研究优势,构建政府机关、高校、科研院所深度融合的协同创新体制机制,牵头承担全省公共安全重大需求项目的研究任务,撰写的多篇内参曾获省部级领导批示,为推进江苏公共安全治理体系和治理能力现代化建设提供理论支撑和智力支持。

表 11　法律与公共安全领域智库 PAI 值评分 Top15

（按名称首字母音序排列）

智库名称	PAI	P 值	A 值	I 值
公安部现代警务改革研究所	1 438.5	978.5	433	27
广西民族大学广西知识产权发展研究院	436	168	268	0
江南大学食品安全风险治理研究院	2 460	2 009	273	178
江苏警官学院江苏省公共安全研究院	2 010.5	1 434.5	481	95
南京理工大学江苏省知识产权发展研究中心	385.5	182.5	192	11
南京师范大学中国法治现代化研究院	2 312.5	2 136.5	176	0
深圳大学港澳基本法研究中心	1 498.5	345.5	703	450
天津大学国家知识产权战略实施研究基地	552.5	188.5	360	4
武汉大学国际法研究所	4 738	4 624	114	0
武汉大学环境法研究所	808.5	635.5	173	0
中国人民公安大学首都社会安全研究基地	478	356	119	3
中南财经政法大学法治发展与司法改革研究中心	2 676.5	1 169.5	672	835
中南财经政法大学知识产权研究中心	2 700	1 677	888	135
中南大学知识产权研究院	811.5	406.5	404	1
中南大学中国文化法研究中心	579	323	229	27

6.2.7　文化与教育领域

共有 70 家来源智库从事文化与教育领域的研究,涉及语言文化、民族文化、传媒、教育、历史等方向,表 12 选取了 PAI 值排名前 20 的智库名单。在该领域,近 80% 的智库是高校智库,这主要是因为高校拥有的丰富的人文社科研究资源,因此在开展文化教育领域的决策咨询服务时,与其他智库相比拥有天然的学术优势。特别是在教育领域,师范类大学智库表现突出。华东师范大学课程与教学研究所聚焦课程理论国际化、课程评价与政策、学科课程、教师专业发展与学习科学等研究领域和方向,主办了《全球教育展望》《课程研究前沿》等刊物,相继领衔研制起草了《国家基础教育课程改革纲要》《教师教育课程标准》等重要政策性文本,开发了"中小学课程实施过程质量监测智库平台",为我国新一轮基础教育课程改革和教师教育课程改革做出杰出贡献,被誉为课程与教学研究领域的"国家队"。湖南师范大学道德文化研究院建立了"中国道德状况测评数据中心",动态掌握中国道德状况,为政府决策提供智力支持。武汉大学传媒发展研究中心是中国传播创新研究的重要平台,定期出版《中国传播创新研究蓝皮书》《中国媒体发展研究报告》,并于2015年、2016年连续荣获中国传媒学科杰出贡献奖(机构类),为中国传媒与社会发展提供了理论支撑与咨询服务。除了高校智库之外,还有少数社会智库、党政智库和传媒智库。例如,长江教育研究院、南京大屠杀史与国际和平研究院、中国青少年研究中心等。

表12 文化与教育领域智库 PAI 值评分 Top20

(按名称首字母排序)

智库名称	PAI	P 值	A 值	I 值
北京联合大学北京学研究基地	663	553	102	8
北京师范大学国际与比较教育研究院	966.5	719.5	247	0
北京师范大学中国教育与社会发展研究院	4 030.5	3 741.5	289	0
北京外国语大学国际中国文化研究院	3 157.5	2 439.5	718	0
北京外国语大学国家语言能力发展研究中心	616.5	478.5	138	0
长江教育研究院	1 182.5	1 086.5	96	0
东南大学道德发展智库	1 672.5	1 386.5	286	0
湖南师范大学道德文化研究院	1 551	1 333	180	38
华东师范大学国家教育宏观政策研究院	1 061.5	887.5	0	174
华东师范大学课程与教学研究所	1 923	1 222	701	0
华东师范大学中国现代思想文化研究所	1 255	1 150	105	0

(续表)

智库名称	PAI	P值	A值	I值
南京大屠杀史与国际和平研究院	862.5	538.5	298	26
南京大学紫金传媒智库	1 702	1 245	427	30
南京理工大学江苏人才发展战略研究院	732	678	54	0
南京艺术学院紫金文创研究院	850.5	248.5	602	0
苏州大学东吴智库文化与社会发展研究院	1 401.5	1 295.5	106	0
武汉大学媒体发展研究中心	2 001	914	1 012	75
西藏民族大学西藏文化传承发展协同创新中心	611	553	42	16
厦门大学高等教育发展研究中心	2 766.5	2 575.5	161	30
浙江大学中国科教战略研究院	649	491	135	23

6.2.8 环境、能源与基础设施领域

环境、能源与基础设施领域主要包括生态环境开发与保护、气候气象问题、能源开发、可持续发展问题和交通、航运等基础设施建设等方面，主要以高校智库为主。共有30家来源智库从事该领域研究，表13选取了PAI值评分排名前10的智库。北京交通发展研究基地紧紧围绕城市交通运输体系建设进行理论与实证研究，累计发表900多篇学术论文，出版著作80余部，完成300多项科研项目，为推动北京交通建设发展提供强大的学术和智力支持。西南石油大学四川石油天然气发展研究中心成功打造了"西部油气论坛""中国天然气行业景气指数"等知名学术品牌，提交的多份智库成果为地方政府、能源企业制定中长期发展战略提供了科学咨询与政策建议，为社会公众和研究人员正确研判油气行业发展形势提供了重要参考。成都理工大学创立的自然灾害防治与地质环境保护研究智库，在地质灾害评估、环境保护等领域开展研究，研究成果累计获得近70项奖项，经济效益达数十亿元，出版专著、教材50余部，国内外发表论文近3 000篇，获授权发明专利近50项。上海海事大学成立的上海国际航运研究中心主要为政府和国内外企业与航运机构等提供决策咨询和信息服

务,中心全力建设的"中国航运数据库"是一个整合中国港航领域统计数据、信息资源的公共服务平台,旨在为政府机关、航运企业、科研院校等各类用户提供具有便捷的查询和数据分析等功能的一站式数据服务。

表 13　环境、能源与基础设施领域智库 PAI 值评分 Top10

(按名称首字母排序)

智库名称	PAI	P 值	A 值	I 值
北京交通大学北京交通发展研究基地	7 897	6 172	1 725	0
北京交通大学北京物流信息化研究基地	771.5	391.5	380	0
成都理工大学自然灾害防治与地质环境保护研究智库	1 964	1 668	296	0
电力规划设计总院	1 785.5	1 365.5	420	0
国网能源研究院	1 558	1 184	374	0
华北电力大学北京能源发展研究基地	514	481	33	0
南京信息工程大学气候与环境治理研究院	762	637	125	0
上海海事大学上海国际航运研究中心	1 700	1 312	327	61
天津大学亚太经合组织可持续能源中心	603	186	415	2
西南石油大学四川石油天然气发展研究中心	430	310	85	35

6.2.9　信息与科技领域

信息与科技领域涵盖互联网、信息技术、科学技术等政策问题,有 19 家来源智库主要从事该领域研究,表 14 选取了 PAI 值排名前 3 的智库名单。此类智库大多来自科研院所。例如,江西省科学院科技战略研究所是江西省"高端科技智库",围绕江西科技经济社会发展的重大问题开展全局性、前瞻性的研究,建有"世界生命湖泊科学应用与信息共享平台",撰写了数十篇内参报告,为江西省科技发展提供了决策帮助。暨南大学广州市舆情大数据研究中心建立了传播大数据实验室,拥有完善的境内外舆情数据挖掘系统与案例库平台,促进了大数据的跨学科的交流和跨界共享。除了科研院所智库和高校智库,还有部分社会智库,如深圳创新发展研究院、中智科学技术评价研究中心和阿里研究院等。深圳创新发展研究院举办了"大梅沙中国创新论坛""深圳改革30人论坛",设立"金鹏改革创新奖"等一系列品牌项目,从2014年起每年发布《中国改革创新年度报告》,促进国内外智库交流,有助于提高中国社会智库的国际化水平。

表14 信息与科技领域智库 *PAI* 值评分 Top3

(按名称首字母排序)

智库名称	PAI	P值	A值	I值
暨南大学广州市舆情大数据研究中心	557.5	220.5	242	95
江西省科学院科技战略研究所	1 165.5	1 072.5	93	0
深圳创新发展研究院	332	272	60	0

6.2.10 "三农"领域

"三农"领域是指涉及农业、农村、农民等三个方面研究。从事"三农"问题研究的共有10家来源智库,涉及农村教育、新农村建设、农业现代化、农村经济等多个研究方向,表15选取了 *PAI* 值排名前5的智库名单。华中师范大学中国农村研究院创建历史可上溯至20世纪80年代,长期以来,以田野调查为基础,实证研究为导向,产出了一大批高质量研究成果,建立了中国农村智库发展平台,以"一库知农"为建设目标,汇集农村调查、研究多维度数据,实现农村形态、变迁与实态的立体展示。浙江大学中国农村发展研究院形成了一批具有一定国际认可度和政策影响力的优秀研究成果,如《城市化进程中的土地问题》获得了首届中国农村发展研究著作奖;主办了多种高层次的国际和国内学术研讨会,如与国家自然科学基金委员会联合举办的"农业经济管理学科前沿与发展战略国际学术研讨会",与中国留美经济学会联合举办的"中国'三农'问题国际研讨会"等,在国内外产生了重要影响。除了关注我国三农问题,南京农业大学金善宝农业现代化研究院重点研究南美洲与非洲国家的农业发展,总结日本和韩国等东亚地区的农业现代化经验,每年出版一套"金善宝蓝皮书",内容包括金善宝农业现代化研究院一年来在农业经济与农村发展领域的研究成果,每年举办一次金善宝农业峰会以及江苏农村发展高层论坛,就当年我国农业经济与农村发展中的重要事件、问题进行研讨,为江苏省乃至我国农业现代化建设以及实施农业"走出去"战略提供政策参考。

表 15 "三农"领域智库 PAI 值评分 Top5

(按名称首字母排序)

智库名称	PAI	P 值	A 值	I 值
东北农业大学现代农业发展研究中心	607.5	486.5	81	40
东北师范大学中国农村教育发展研究院	786.5	741.5	45	0
华中师范大学中国农村研究院	8 870.5	8 125.5	737	8
南京农业大学金善宝农业现代化研究院	701	691	10	0
浙江大学中国农村发展研究院	1 552.5	656.5	534	362

6.2.11 "一带一路"领域

自从我国提出"一带一路"倡议之后,与"一带一路"倡议相关的领域研究一直是智库研究的热点。据 CTTI 来源智库数据显示,共有 17 家智库从事"一带一路"领域研究,涉及国际旅游资源开发、高端人才培养、中外经贸与文化交流、国际商务合作、区域与国别社会发展研究等多个研究方向,表 16 选取了 PAI 值排名前 5 的智库。在这 17 家智库中,有 15 家智库是高校智库,依托了所属高校丰富的研究资源,或是地理优势。例如,内蒙古财经大学充分利用了区位优势,建立了"中蒙俄经贸合作与草原丝绸之路经济带构建研究协同创新中心",紧密围绕着"中蒙俄经济走廊"和"草原丝绸之路经济带"建设展开研究,组建了"中蒙合作发展研究院"、中蒙商学院等多个国际合作平台与研究中心。西安交通大学成立的"一带一路"自由贸易试验区研究院成立标志着西部自贸试验区研究工作进入国际化、市场化、开放式的新阶段,成为陕西自贸区快速发展的新引擎,为陕西实现追赶超越发展目标提供强有力的智库支撑。除了 15 家高校智库,还有中国丝路智谷研究院和一带一路百人论坛两家社会智库。这两家社会智库汇集国内外著名的专家学者、政府官员、企业家、媒体从业者等各界精英,为推动"一带一路"的建设提供智力支持。

表 16　"一带一路"领域智库 PAI 值评分 Top5

（按名称首字母排序）

智库名称	PAI	P 值	A 值	I 值
北京第二外国语学院中国"一带一路"战略研究院	482.5	298.5	120	64
江苏师范大学"一带一路"研究院	504	400	104	0
内蒙古财经大学中蒙俄经贸合作与草原丝绸之路经济带构建研究协同创新中心	1 503	1 043	460	0
西安交通大学"一带一路"自由贸易试验区研究院	841.5	597.5	142	102
中国丝路智谷研究院	783.5	783.5	0	0

6.2.12　综合型智库

除了上文提及的 11 大主要研究领域之外,还有一类综合型的智库,主要由各个地方党校/行政学院、社会科学院等组成。综合型智库与其他领域智库不同,往往展开的是跨学科、多领域、综合性的研究。CTTI 来源智库共有 46 家综合型智库,各省社科院在 46 家综合型智库中占近 60%。综合型智库借助自身的体制和资源优势开展了大量智库研究工作。例如,山东省社会科学院作为山东省首批重点新型智库建设试点单位,倡导成立了"山东智库联盟",开通在线网站与微信公众号,并通过举办泰山智库论坛、创办《山东社会科学报道》等措施,紧紧围绕省委省政府中心工作和经济文化强省建设,重点推出智库精品成果。中共湖南省委党校(湖南行政学院)不仅开展了大量的培训与会议,而且其创办的《决策咨询要报》《智库通讯》《决策咨询成果选集》在省内产生较大影响。中共浙江省委党校(浙江行政学院)着力提升学术影响力和科研咨政工作水平,高水平建设红色学府示范党校取得积极有效进展,智库高被引论文的数量在党政智库中稳居前茅。此外,部分社科院还积极参与智库的研究与评价工作。例如,中国社会科学院、上海社会科学院、四川社会科学院、山东社会科学院等,相继发布了有关智库的专题评估报告。

7　加强中国特色新型智库建设的几点建议

根据《意见》中提及的 2020 年实现中国特色新型智库总体目标,从 2013 年 4 月习近平总书记提出了建设中国特色新型智库的倡议到现在,时间已逾大半。在 5 年多的中国特色新型智库建设"上半场"中,取得了令人瞩目的成就。但是,在"上半场"建设进程中,中国特色新型智库建设中存在的一些问题也逐渐显现出来,正如习近平总书记指出"有的智库研究存在重数量、轻质量问题,有的存在重形式传播、轻内容创新问题,还有的流于搭台子、请名人、办论坛等形式主义的做法"。因此,在中国特色新型智库建设的"下半场"中,既要认真汲取"上半场"的建设经验,更要着力解决"上半场"遗留的问题。

7.1　创新智库体制机制，完善智库治理

自从党的十八大提出"健全决策机制,发挥思想库的作用"开始,我国从中央到地方出台了一系列促进智库发展的政策文件,从宏观的规划指导到具体的实施意见,层层跟进、点面俱到。但是,在建设中国特色新型智库的具体实践中,智库发展仍然受到现有机制体制的限制。究其原因,主要是因为我国智库大都是体制内智库,包括各党校、行政学院、社科院系统、高校智库等,大部分有主管单位,并没有完全独立的法人资格。因此,智库的运营易受到主管单位的限制,导致智库建设陷入"三明治"陷阱,即三明治上层是国家/省市部委智库的管理部门,中间是母体单位(如高校、社科院),下层才是智库,国家/省市部委需要通过母体单位才能作用到智库,这在一定程度上造成了政策落地困难,限制了智库的发展。此外,还存在着智库自身运行机制不够完善、智库成果认定与激励制度不合理等问题。

中国特色新型智库建设不是速决战,而是场持久战。只有破除机制体制的禁锢,完善智库治理体系,才能优化智库发展的外部环境,增强智库发展的内生动力。一方面,要改善智库管理体制,促进中央省市的智库发展政策落地,使智库充分享受政策

红利。在5年多的发展历程中，部分智库的发展经验值得借鉴。例如，南京大学成立南京大学长江产经研究院和南京大学紫金传媒智库，同时这两家智库在省民政厅注册了"民非"法人实体智库，从而通过"一个实体，两块牌子"的方式，化解了智库发展的"三明治陷阱"，让两家智库既享受了国家政策红利，同时又可便捷利用学校资源。另一方面，要改善智库运行机制，优化智库内部生态，促进智库良性发展；制定科学合理的智库成果认定和激励制度。一是重视智库内部"基本法"——智库章程的确立，使智库的运行制度化、标准化。二是改变以往以核心期刊论英雄的学术评价模式，灵活认定智库成果，提高智库研究人员的积极性，为智库研究提供保障。

7.2 改善智库服务模式，提供嵌入式服务

除了与决策部门关系密切的政府内部研究室之外，大部分智库与决策部门之间存在着供给与需求信息不对称。一方面，由于政府信息公开程度不够，或是信息公开受限，智库获得政府信息的渠道单一，无法获取详细可靠的信息数据作为研究支撑；另一方面，决策部门与智库的互动不够深入，智库难以有机会参与政府政策研讨，便会出现"文件数据得不到、政策信息得不到、批示反馈看不到"的问题。其次，目前智库的研究咨询业务过于集中政策过程的前端，业务模式头重脚轻，即智库提供的政策咨询服务集中在政策的起草拟定环节，较少关注政策的评估、反馈和政策教育，业务重心浮于表面。

建设中国特色新型智库是完善决策机制的重要途径，而改善智库服务模式是提供科学决策咨询服务的重要前提。一是注重需求侧改革。决策部门要重视、信任、依靠、支持智库提供决策咨询服务，给予智库发展政策支持、财力支持、信息支持、平台支持，促进政府大院里的政策研究室与智库的协同合作。二是智库需要改变以往咨询服务模式，以政策过程的嵌入、决策咨询流程的嵌入、决策咨询场景的嵌入和政策共同体的圈层嵌入等方式，为决策部门提供"嵌入式决策咨询服务"。具体而言，智库通过政策过程的嵌入，从政策的讨论、制定到政策的实施，再到政策的评估反馈，为决策部门提供全链条式的服务；通过决策咨询流程的嵌入，从数据采集到最终报告撰

写,充分发挥智库的技术支持;通过决策场景的嵌入,了解政策产生的前因后果;通过政策共同体的圈层嵌入,与决策部门、政策研究部门产生强烈互信。

7.3 优化智库人力资源布局,充实人才队伍

人才是智库发展之基。近几年来,我国智库实体数量飞速增长,仅 CTTI 收录的就有 700 多家智库,分布于 50 多个战略和政策领域。但是值得注意的是,智库人才队伍建设并没有跟上智库机构数量的增长步伐。目前,我国智库的人才队伍存在着"兼职人员多,全职人员少;研究人员多,辅助人员少;研究团队多,领军专家少"的问题。因此,必须优化智库人力资源布局,充实智库人才队伍,才能为智库发展提供源源不断的动力,保障智库研究成果的高质量与高水平。智库人才队伍建设必须重视以下几点:

第一,注重辅助人员与研究人员的比例。合理的辅助人员与研究人员比例是提高研究效率的重要保障。辅助人员包括行政人员、研究秘书、研究助理等。例如,兰德公司的经验是"两个研究员不如一个研究员加半个秘书的效率高"。除了大量行政事务之外,智库研究工作同样具有琐碎性、长期性、日常性。辅助人员可以为研究人员做好研究的后勤保障。第二,增加全职研究人员的比例。外聘研究人员或是兼职研究人员可以促进智库思想的交流,扩大智库的研究领域,树立智库的品牌效应。但是如果兼职研究人员数量过多,则不易形成稳定高效的智库研究团队。但是目前来看,部分智库的兼职研究人员数量远远超过全职研究人员,需要吸纳更多全职研究人员,建立自身的核心研究团队。第三,需要智库领军人物。一方面,智库发展需要学术领军人物。在智库起步阶段和智库品牌创立阶段,需要有影响力的专家提升智库知名度。另一方面,智库的运营管理需要"懂智库、精学术、通管理"的掌舵人才。学术明星型的智库管理者对智库发展而言,往往如虎添翼。第四,吸纳和培养"T"型人才,优化人才结构。智库研究具有多学科、宽领域、复杂性、综合性的特点。博中有专的"T"型人才开展智库研究具有天然的专业优势。总之,培养智库领军人才、聚集一流智库专家、合理配置人力资源,形成以领军人才为统领,以高级专家为核心,以研究

员为骨干，以研究助理为辅助，具备一定规模的智库研究队伍布局，才能为中国特色新型智库建设提供人才保障。

7.4 增强国际交流合作，让世界理解中国

我国新型智库建设作为实现我国治理能力和治理体系现代化的重要途径，不能完全闭门造车，而要以积极姿态投身国际交流合作中。一方面，是中国特色新型智库建设的需求。西方智库发展较早，运行机制较为成熟。我国新型智库建设还处于起步阶段，需要破解大量机制体制难题。因此，中国特色新型智库建设要与国际接轨，加强智库的国际交流，了解西方智库界动态，借鉴西方智库发展经验，才能知己知彼。当然，借鉴并不等于"照抄"，中国特色新型智库建设还需要牢牢把握"特""新"二字。

另一方面，增强智库国际交流是我国外交战略的需要。"智库外交"已逐渐成为官方外交和民间交流之外的"第二轨道"，其核心是信息与思想的交流。智库在对外交流中，凭借着与官方决策的特殊关系和专业政策研究者的特殊身份，相比于官方外交和民间交流有着更大的灵活性和专业性，往往发挥着重要作用。当前，我国国家综合实力不断上升，同国际社会的互联互动变得空前紧密，积极参与全球治理、推动全球命运共同体的构建。但是随着世界格局的不断变化，政治经济全球化不断加强，我国参与全球事务面临着更加复杂的挑战，需要更强大、更专业、更深入的理论支撑和决策支持。以中国特色新型智库服务中国特色大国外交，在全球治理中打出"组合拳"，为发展中国特色大国外交提供理论基础、政策咨询、交流平台。因此，我国智库要围绕着我国战略需求，直击全球热点问题，在全球治理中发出"中国智声"，提高我国智库国际影响力，让世界理解中国。例如，围绕着"一带一路"倡议，我国打造了一批智库与国际论坛。这些智库与论坛在宣传"一带一路"政策，树立中国国际话语权方面起了不可忽视的重要作用。

7.5 树立智库品牌意识，打造旗舰产品

专业性是智库的基本属性，失去专业性，智库研究将会成为"无源之水，无本之木"。但是目前仅国内智库有数千家之多，涉及专业领域极其广泛，如何在众多智库

中一枝独秀,是智库在建设发展过程中必须要思考的问题。智库与纯学术研究机构不同,智库还具有媒体性,肩负着政策教育、引导舆论的作用,而智库的公信力是智库发挥上述职能的保障。因此,智库必须树立品牌意识,用心打造智库的旗舰产品,提高智库辨识度和公信力。首先,智库研究要体现"专、精、特、优",这是智库的立身之本。例如,浙江师范大学非洲研究院长期聚焦非洲研究,开展了系统全面的研究工作,积累了大量研究成果,现在是国内非洲研究的翘楚。

其次,着力打造智库的旗舰产品。智库与智库的旗舰产品相辅相成,即智库通过旗舰产品推广和传播智库研究成果,而优秀的智库产品反过来有助于树立智库的品牌形象。一是打造知名论坛或会议。例如,复旦发展研究院承办的上海论坛是国际大型学术论坛,旨在搭建中外政商学界人士共同交流沟通的平台,为区域发展及国家大计建言献策。自 2005 年创办以来,出席论坛的国内外演讲嘉宾近 4 000 人次。论坛始终坚持创新引领,以求更好地为人类进步、国家发展和民生改善服务,已逐渐成为国内外知名的论坛品牌。二是打造旗舰刊物。例如国际著名智库兰德公司出版的旗舰杂志《兰德评论》(*Rand Review*);中国国际经济交流中心创办的刊物《全球化》,重点针对国际国内经济社会发展的重大战略问题研究,注重反映国际社会所关心的中国问题,国内所关心的国际问题,在国内有较大影响。三是出版明星产品。例如上文提及的南京大学中国智库研究与评价中心编写的《南大智库文丛》,浙江师范大学非洲研究院拍摄的大型纪录片《我从非洲来》。

7.6 促进智库协调发展,完善智库体系

《意见》中提出要"统筹推进党政部门、社科院、党校行政学院、高校、军队、科研院所和企业、社会智库协调发展",但从目前发展现状看,我国各类智库还存在着不协调的问题。据 CTTI 来源数据显示,高校智库占据我国智库总数的半壁江山,而企业智库和社会智库却不到十分之一。其他的,诸如党政军智库、社科院等虽然在数量上位居第二,但是这类智库凭借着与决策部门的密切关系,在提供决策咨询服务时有天然的优势。此外,智库的地域分布不均,例如华东和华北地区的智库数量占据总数的近

75%，具体来看，主要集中在北京和上海两地。当然，智库产业的集中性和集群性与北京、上海两地的政治、经济、文化地位相关。不可否认的是，我国的中西部地区虽然经济发展较为落后，但是同样需要专业的智库机构为当地经济社会发展提供政策咨询服务，在全面建成小康社会的宏伟目标下，这种需求甚至更为迫切。但是目前我国中西部地区智库发展较为滞后。

因此，促进智库协调发展，一方面，要促进各类型智库的协调发展，特别是社会智库、企业智库。其他类型的智库或多或少易受到体制影响，社会智库则具有独特的优势，更具客观性、独立性、灵活性。因此，必须大力支持社会智库的发展，充分发挥社会智库的优势，形成"鲶鱼效应"，繁荣政策市场。另一方面，要支持中西部地区的地方智库发展。只有立足当地，才会知根知底，才能为当地社会经济发展提供强大的智力支持。

附录：CTTI 来源智库目录（2018—2019）

（按照机构首字母拼音顺序排列，不分先后）

（一）党政部门智库（69家）

北京市信访矛盾分析研究中心

财政部关税政策研究中心

财政部国际财经中心

重庆市经济信息中心（重庆市综合经济研究院）

当代世界研究中心

福建省人民政府发展研究中心

公安部公安发展战略研究所

公安部现代警务改革研究所

国家发展和改革委员会国际合作中心

国家发展和改革委员会宏观经济研究院

国家海洋局海洋发展战略研究所

国家教育发展研究中心

国家税务总局税收科学研究所

国家体育总局体育科学研究所

国家卫生计生委卫生发展研究中心

国家卫生计生委医院管理研究所

国家新闻出版广电总局广播影视发展研究中心

国家应对气候变化战略研究和国际合作中心

国家知识产权局知识产权发展研究中心

国土资源部油气资源战略研究中心

国网能源研究院

国务院发展研究中心

河北省财政科学与政策研究所

河北省发展和改革委员会宏观经济研究所

环境保护部环境与经济政策研究中心

机械工业经济管理研究院

吉林省人民政府发展研究中心

江苏省人民政府研究室

江西省情研究中心

教育部高等学校社会科学发展研究中心

辽宁省人民政府发展研究中心

南京大屠杀史与国际和平研究院

内蒙古自治区发展研究中心

农业部农村经济研究中心

全国党的建设研究会

山东省创新战略研究院

山东省宏观经济研究院

商务部国际贸易经济合作研究院

上海市发展改革研究院

上海市教育科学研究院

上海市浦东改革与发展研究院(中国(上海)自由贸易试验区研究院)

上海市人民政府发展研究中心

司法部预防犯罪研究所

天津滨海综合发展研究院

天津市科学学研究所

统一战线高端智库

浙江省发展规划研究院

中共中央编译局

中共中央编译局马克思主义研究部

中共中央编译局世界发展战略研究部

中国财政科学研究院

中国城市和小城镇改革发展中心

中国国际问题研究院

中国国土资源经济研究院

中国教育科学研究院

中国劳动保障科学研究院

中国老龄科学研究中心

中国旅游研究院

中国浦东干部学院长江三角洲研究院

中国浦东干部学院领导研究院

中国浦东干部学院中国特色社会主义研究院

中国青少年研究中心

中国人民银行金融研究所

中国人事科学研究院

中国统计学会/国家统计局统计科学研究所

中国文化遗产研究院

中国现代国际关系研究院

中国新闻出版研究院

中华人民共和国民政部政策研究中心

（二）社科院智库（51家）

安徽省社会科学院

北京市社会科学院

重庆社会科学院

重庆市生产力发展中心

创新型城市发展与评估研究院

福建省社会科学院

甘肃省社会科学院

广东省社会科学院

广西社会科学院

贵州省社会科学院

海南省社会科学院

河北省社会科学院

河南省社会科学院

黑龙江省社会科学院

黑龙江省社会科学院　东北亚战略研究院

黑龙江省社会科学院　黑龙江社会发展与地方治理研究院

湖北省社会科学院

湖南省社会科学院

吉林省社会科学院

江苏省社会科学院

江苏省社会科学院　区域现代化研究院

江西省社会科学院

辽宁社会科学院

南京市社会科学院

内蒙古自治区社会科学院

宁夏社会科学院

青海省社会科学院

区域现代化研究院

山东社会科学院

陕西省社会科学院

上海社会科学院

四川省社会科学院

天津社会科学院

西藏自治区社会科学院

新疆社会科学院

云南省社会科学院

浙江省社会科学院

中国社会科学院

中国社会科学院财经战略研究院

中国社会科学院当代中国马克思主义政治经济学创新智库

中国社会科学院当代中国研究所

中国社会科学院国家金融与发展实验室

中国社会科学院国家全球战略智库

中国社会科学院欧洲研究所

中国社会科学院上海市人民政府上海研究院

中国社会科学院社会发展战略研究院

中国社会科学院世界经济与政治研究所

中国社会科学院台湾研究所

中国社会科学院意识形态研究智库

中国社会科学院中国文化研究中心

中国社会科学院中国-中东欧国家智库交流与合作网络

（三）党校行政学院智库（48家）

安徽行政学院安徽省公共政策研究评估中心

甘肃行政学院

国家行政学院

国家行政学院电子政务研究中心

国家行政学院发展战略与公共政策研究中心

国家行政学院决策咨询部

河北行政学院

江苏党的建设理论与实践创新研究院

山东行政学院

陕西省行政学院

上海市委党校　上海行政学院

云南跨越式发展研究院

中共安徽省委党校

中共北京市委党校　北京行政学院

中共重庆市委党校　重庆市行政学院

中共福建省委党校　福建行政学院

中共甘肃省委党校

中共广东省委党校　广东行政学院

中共广西区委党校　广西行政学院

中共贵州省委党校　贵州行政学院

中共海南省委党校　海南省行政学院

中共河北省委党校

中共河南省委党校　河南行政学院

中共黑龙江省委党校　黑龙江省行政学院

中共湖北省委党校　湖北省行政学院

中共湖南省委党校　湖南行政学院

中共吉林省委党校　吉林省行政学院

中共江苏省委党校

中共江西省委党校　江西行政学院

中共辽宁省委党校

中共内蒙古自治区委员会党校　内蒙古自治区行政学院

中共宁夏区委党校　宁夏行政学院

中共青海省委党校　青海省行政学院

中共山东省委党校

中共陕西省委党校

中共四川省委党校

中共天津市委党校　天津行政学院

中共天津市委党校　新时代创新型与服务型政府建设研究中心

中共天津市委党校　新时代天津党的建设决策研究中心

中共天津市委党校　新时代现代化经济体系研究中心

中共西藏自治区委党校　西藏自治区行政学院

中共新疆维吾尔自治区委党校　新疆维吾尔自治区行政学院

中共浙江省委党校　浙江行政学院

中共中央党校

中共中央党校党的建设教研部

中共中央党校国际战略研究院

中国行政体制改革研究会

中央社会主义学院中国政党制度研究中心

（四）高校智库（441家）

安徽财经大学安徽经济发展研究院

安徽大学创新发展研究院

北京大学国际战略研究院

北京大学国家发展研究院

北京大学国家治理研究院

北京大学文化产业研究院

北京大学宪法与行政法研究中心

北京大学中国都市经济研究基地

北京第二外国语学院北京对外文化传播研究基地

北京第二外国语学院北京旅游发展研究基地

北京第二外国语学院首都对外文化贸易研究基地

北京第二外国语学院中国"一带一路"战略研究院

北京服装学院首都服饰文化与服装产业研究基地

北京工业大学北京社会管理研究基地

北京工业大学北京现代制造业发展研究基地

北京航空航天大学中国航空工程科技发展战略研究院

北京交通大学北京交通发展研究基地

北京交通大学北京物流信息化研究基地

北京交通大学国家经济安全研究院

北京交通大学中国马克思主义与文化发展研究院

北京理工大学北京经济社会可持续发展研究基地

北京联合大学北京学研究基地

北京农学院北京新农村建设研究基地

北京师范大学国际与比较教育研究院

北京师范大学首都教育经济研究基地

北京师范大学首都文化创新与文化传播工程研究院

北京师范大学智慧学习研究院

北京师范大学中国基础教育质量监测协同创新中心

北京师范大学中国教育与社会发展研究院

北京师范大学中国收入分配研究院

北京体育大学冬奥文化研究中心

北京外国语大学国际中国文化研究院

北京外国语大学国家语言能力发展研究中心

北京外国语大学海湾阿拉伯国家研究中心

北京外国语大学加拿大研究中心

北京外国语大学日本研究中心

北京外国语大学英国研究中心

北京外国语大学中德人文交流研究中心

北京外国语大学中东欧研究中心

北京信息科技大学北京市知识管理研究基地

北京语言大学北京文献语言与文化传承研究基地

成都理工大学四川矿产资源研究中心

成都理工大学自然灾害防治与地质环境保护研究智库

重庆大学城乡建设与发展研究院

重庆大学公共经济与公共政策研究中心

重庆大学国家网络空间安全与大数据法治战略研究院

重庆大学经略研究院

重庆大学可持续发展研究院

重庆大学中国公共服务评测与研究中心

重庆工商大学长江上游经济研究中心

大理大学云南宗教治理与民族团结进步智库

大连海事大学"一带一路"研究院

大连外国语大学东北亚研究中心

东北财经大学经济与社会发展研究院

东北大学中国东北振兴研究院

东北农业大学现代农业发展研究中心

东北师范大学东亚研究院

东北师范大学中国农村教育发展研究院

东南大学道德发展智库

东南大学反腐败法治研究中心

东南大学交通法治与发展研究中心

东南大学人民法院司法大数据研究基地

东南大学现代管理会计创新研究中心

东南大学中国高质量发展综合评价研究院

东南大学中国特色社会主义发展研究院

对外经济贸易大学国际经济研究院

对外经济贸易大学全球价值链研究院

对外经济贸易大学中国世界贸易组织研究院

福建师范大学竞争力研究中心

复旦大学复旦发展研究院

复旦大学美国研究中心

复旦大学人口与发展政策研究中心

复旦大学上海市高校智库研究和管理中心

复旦大学亚太区域合作与治理研究中心

复旦大学政党建设与国家发展研究中心

复旦大学中国经济研究中心

复旦大学中国研究院

甘肃政法学院西北民族地区侦查理论与实务研究中心

广东财经大学国民经济研究中心

广东外语外贸大学广东国际战略研究院

广西大学广西创新发展研究院

广西大学中国-东盟研究院

广西民族大学广西知识产权发展研究院

广州大学广州发展研究院

贵州大学贵州省大数据产业发展应用研究院

贵州大学中国-东盟研究中心

国际关系学院公共市场与政府采购研究所

国际关系学院国际战略与安全研究中心

哈尔滨工程大学黑龙江区域创新驱动发展研究中心

哈尔滨工业大学黑龙江省双创智库

哈尔滨工业大学"一带一路"人才战略智库

哈尔滨医科大学黑龙江省公共健康安全及医改策略研究智库

海南大学海南低碳经济政策与产业技术研究院

海南大学海南国际旅游岛发展研究院

海南大学海南省南海政策与法律研究中心

河北大学河北省生态与环境发展研究中心

河北大学伊斯兰国家社会发展研究中心

河北工业大学京津冀发展研究中心

河北金融学院德融研究院

河北经贸大学河北省道德文化与社会发展研究中心

河北经贸大学京津冀一体化发展协同创新中心

河北经贸大学社会管理德治与法治协同创新中心

河北师范大学长城文化安全研究中心

河北师范大学现代服务与公共政策研究基地

河南大学中原发展研究院

黑龙江大学黑龙江省文化发展战略研究中心

黑龙江大学龙江振兴发展研究中心

黑龙江大学文化发展战略协同创新高等研究院

黑龙江大学中俄全面战略协作协同创新中心

湖北经济学院碳排放权交易湖北省协同创新中心

湖南大学国际贸易研究智库

湖南大学金融发展与信用管理研究中心

湖南大学廉政研究中心

湖南大学岳麓书院国学研究与传播智库

湖南大学中国产业金融协同创新中心

湖南大学中国文化软实力研究中心

湖南师范大学道德文化研究院

湖南师范大学湖南省汉语国际推广研究院

湖南师范大学社会主义核心价值观研究院

湖南师范大学生态文明研究院

华北电力大学北京能源发展研究基地

华东交通大学高铁与区域发展研究中心

华东理工大学能源经济与环境管理研究中心

华东理工大学社会工作与社会管理研究中心

华东师范大学长三角区域一体化研究中心

华东师范大学俄罗斯研究中心

华东师范大学国家教育宏观政策研究院

华东师范大学基础教育改革与发展研究所

华东师范大学课程与教学研究所

华东师范大学上海人口结构与发展趋势创新研究基地

华东师范大学中国文字研究与应用中心

华东师范大学中国现代城市研究中心

华东师范大学中国现代思想文化研究所

华东师范大学周边合作与发展协同创新中心

华东政法大学华东检察研究院

华东政法大学中国法治战略研究中心

华南理工大学公共政策研究院

华南理工大学广州市金融服务创新与风险管理研究基地

华南理工大学社会治理研究中心

华南理工大学政府绩效评价中心

华中科技大学非传统安全研究中心

华中科技大学国家治理研究院

华中科技大学健康政策与管理研究院

华中科技大学张培刚发展研究院

华中师范大学中国农村研究院

淮阴工学院苏北发展研究院

黄河科技学院中国（河南）创新发展研究院

吉林大学创新创业研究院

吉林大学东北亚研究中心

吉林大学社会公正与政府治理研究中心

吉林大学数量经济研究中心

吉林大学中国国有经济研究中心

吉林大学中国人口老龄化与经济社会发展研究中心

吉林大学中国文化研究所

暨南大学产业经济研究院

暨南大学广州南沙自由贸易试验区研究基地

暨南大学广州市舆情大数据研究中心

暨南大学华侨华人研究院

江南大学食品安全风险治理研究院

江苏第二师范学院教育现代化研究院

江苏海事职业技术学院"一带一路"应用型海事人才研究院

江苏警官学院江苏省公共安全研究院

江苏师范大学"一带一路"研究院

江西财经大学江西全面建成小康社会决策支持协同创新中心

江西财经大学江西省战略性新兴产业发展监测、预警与决策支持协同创新中心

江西理工大学有色金属产业发展研究中心

江西师范大学管理决策评价研究中心

江西师范大学江西产业转型升级发展研究中心

江西师范大学苏区振兴研究院

江西师范大学中国社会转型研究协同创新中心

昆明理工大学云南综合交通发展与区域物流管理智库

昆明学院昆明科学发展智库

兰州财经大学丝绸之路经济研究院

兰州大学阿富汗研究中心

兰州大学丝绸之路经济带建设研究中心

兰州大学西北少数民族研究中心

兰州大学循证社会科学研究中心

兰州大学中国政府绩效管理研究中心

兰州大学中亚研究所

辽宁大学东北地区面向东北亚区域开放协同创新中心

辽宁大学东北振兴研究中心

辽宁大学转型国家经济政治研究中心

民政部-华东师大中国行政区划研究院

南昌大学江西发展研究院

南昌大学旅游规划与研究中心

南昌大学中国中部经济社会发展研究中心

南京财经大学现代服务业智库

南京大学长江产业经济研究院

南京大学长江三角洲经济社会发展研究中心

南京大学非洲研究所

南京大学社会风险与公共危机管理研究中心

南京大学中国南海研究协同创新中心

南京大学紫金传媒智库

南京理工大学江苏人才发展战略研究院

南京理工大学江苏省知识产权发展研究中心

南京农业大学金善宝农业现代化研究院

南京师范大学中国法治现代化研究院

南京信息工程大学气候与环境治理研究院

南京医科大学健康江苏研究院

南京艺术学院紫金文创研究院

南开大学滨海开发研究院

南开大学当代中国问题研究院

南开大学经济与社会发展研究院

南开大学日本研究中心

南开大学亚太经济合作组织（APEC）研究中心

南开大学政治经济学研究中心

南开大学中国公司治理研究院

南开大学中国特色社会主义经济建设协同创新中心

南开大学中国政府与政策联合研究中心

南通大学江苏长江经济带研究院

内蒙古财经大学中蒙俄经贸合作与草原丝绸之路经济带构建研究协同创新中心

内蒙古大学蒙古国研究中心

内蒙古大学蒙古学研究中心

宁波大学东海研究院

宁夏大学回族研究院

宁夏大学中国阿拉伯国家研究院

青海大学青海省情研究中心

清华大学布鲁金斯公共政策研究中心

清华大学国际关系研究院

清华大学国情研究院

清华大学技术创新研究中心

清华大学卡内基全球政策中心

清华大学现代管理研究中心

清华大学中国应急管理研究基地

清华大学中国与世界经济研究中心

山东大学当代社会主义研究所

山东大学孔子学院研究中心

山东大学山东发展研究院

山东大学山东区域金融改革与发展研究中心

山东大学卫生管理与政策研究中心

山东大学县域发展研究院

山东大学犹太教与跨宗教研究中心

山东大学政党研究所

山西财经大学资源型经济转型协同创新中心

山西大学管理与决策研究所

山西大学晋商学研究所

陕西师范大学教育实验经济研究所

陕西师范大学西北国土资源研究中心

陕西师范大学西北历史环境与经济社会发展研究院

陕西师范大学"一带一路"建设与中亚研究协同创新研究中心

陕西师范大学语言资源开发研究中心

陕西师范大学中国西部边疆研究院

上海财经大学公共政策与治理研究院

上海财经大学上海国际金融中心研究院

上海财经大学中国产业经济研究中心

上海财经大学中国公共财政研究院

上海财经大学中国自由贸易试验区协同创新中心

上海大学毒品与国家安全研究中心

上海大学基层治理创新研究中心

上海大学拉丁美洲研究中心

上海大学土耳其研究中心

上海大学智库产业研究中心

上海对外经贸大学国际经贸治理与中国改革开放联合研究中心

上海对外经贸大学上海WTO事务咨询中心

上海海事大学上海国际航运研究中心

上海海事大学中国（上海）自贸区供应链研究院

上海交通大学城市科学研究院

上海交通大学第三部门研究中心

上海交通大学改革创新与治理现代化研究中心

上海交通大学国家海洋战略与权益研究基地

上海交通大学国家文化产业创新与发展研究基地

上海交通大学人文艺术研究院

上海交通大学世界一流大学研究中心

上海交通大学舆论学研究院

上海交通大学中国城市治理研究院

上海交通大学中国海洋装备工程科技发展战略研究院

上海外国语大学丝路战略研究所

上海外国语大学英国研究中心

上海外国语大学中东研究所

上海外国语大学中国国际舆情研究中心

上海外国语大学中国外语战略研究中心

上海政法学院上海合作组织研究院

上海政法学院"一带一路"安全研究院

深圳大学城市治理研究院

深圳大学港澳基本法研究中心

深圳大学中国海外利益研究院

沈阳师范大学人力资源开发与管理研究所

首都经济贸易大学北京市经济社会发展政策研究基地

首都师范大学北京基础教育研究基地

四川大学南亚研究所

四川大学社会发展与西部开发研究院

四川大学中国西部边疆安全与发展协同创新中心

四川大学中国藏学研究所

苏州大学东吴智库文化与社会发展研究院

苏州科技大学城市发展智库

天津财经大学法律经济分析与政策评价中心

天津财经大学工商管理研究中心

天津财经大学金融与保险研究中心

天津财经大学天津市自由贸易区研究院

天津财经大学中国滨海金融协同创新中心

天津财经大学中国经济统计研究中心

天津城建大学天津城镇化与新农村建设研究中心

天津大学国家知识产权战略实施研究基地

天津大学教育科学研究中心

天津大学生物安全战略研究中心

天津大学亚太经合组织可持续能源中心

天津大学中国传统村落与建筑文化传承协同创新中心

天津大学中国绿色发展研究院

天津大学中国文化遗产保护国际研究中心

天津工业大学天津法治信访研究中心

天津科技大学能源环境与绿色发展研究中心

天津科技大学食品安全战略与管理研究中心

天津理工大学循环经济与绿色发展研究中心

天津理工大学中国重大工程技术"走出去"投资模式与管控智库

天津商业大学现代服务业发展研究中心

天津师范大学国家治理研究中心

天津师范大学区域发展战略与改革研究中心

天津师范大学应急管理研究中心

天津师范大学自由经济区研究所

天津体育学院全民健身研究智库

天津外国语大学东北亚研究中心

天津外国语大学"一带一路"天津战略研究院

同济大学财经研究所

同济大学德国研究中心

同济大学可持续发展与新型城镇化智库

同济大学中国战略研究院

武汉大学国际法研究所

武汉大学国家文化发展研究院

武汉大学环境法研究所

武汉大学经济发展研究中心

武汉大学经济外交研究中心

武汉大学媒体发展研究中心

武汉大学社会保障研究中心

武汉大学信息资源研究中心

武汉大学质量发展战略研究院

武汉大学中国边界与海洋研究院

武汉大学中国语情与社会发展研究中心

武汉大学中国中部发展研究院

西安交通大学欧亚经济（论坛）与全球发展研究院

西安交通大学社会治理和社会政策协同创新研究中心

西安交通大学丝绸之路国际法与比较法研究所

西安交通大学丝绸之路经济带研究协同创新中心

西安交通大学中国改革试点探索与评估协同创新中心

西安交通大学中国管理问题研究中心

西安交通大学中国（西安）数字经济发展监测预警基地

西安交通大学"一带一路"自由贸易试验区研究院

西北大学丝绸之路文化遗产保护与考古学研究中心

西北大学中东研究所

西北大学中国西部经济发展研究中心

西北工业大学西部国防科技工业发展研究中心

西北师范大学甘肃省文化资源与华夏文明建设研究中心

西北师范大学精准扶贫与区域发展研究中心

西北师范大学"一带一路"战略与教育发展研究中心

西北政法大学反恐怖主义研究院

西北政法大学民族宗教研究院

西南财经大学金融安全协同创新中心

西南财经大学中国家庭金融调查与研究中心

西南财经大学中国金融研究中心

西南财经大学中国西部经济研究中心

西南大学公共文化研究中心

西南大学统筹城乡教育发展研究中心

西南大学希腊研究中心

西南大学西南民族教育与心理研究中心

西南大学伊朗研究中心

西南交通大学西部交通战略与区域发展研究中心

西南科技大学四川循环经济研究中心

西南石油大学四川石油天然气发展研究中心

西南政法大学人权研究院

西藏大学西藏可持续发展研究所

西藏民族大学西藏文化传承发展协同创新中心

厦门大学东南亚研究中心

厦门大学高等教育发展研究中心

厦门大学宏观经济研究中心

厦门大学台湾研究院

厦门大学中国能源政策研究院

湘潭大学地方立法与区域社会治理研究中心

湘潭大学公共管理与区域经济发展研究中心

湘潭大学毛泽东思想研究中心

湘潭大学政府绩效评估与管理创新研究中心

湘潭大学中国共产党革命精神与文化资源研究中心

燕山大学河北省公共政策评估研究中心

燕山大学河北省设计创新及产业发展研究中心

延边大学朝鲜半岛研究院

盐城师范学院沿海发展智库

云南财经大学公共政策研究中心

云南财经大学印度洋地区研究中心

云南财经大学云南省防灾减灾智库

云南大学边疆民族问题智库

云南大学缅甸研究院

云南大学文化发展研究院

云南大学周边外交研究中心

浙江大学创新管理与持续竞争力研究中心

浙江大学非传统安全与和平发展研究中心

浙江大学公共政策研究中心

浙江大学民营经济研究中心

浙江大学中国科教战略研究院

浙江大学中国农村发展研究院

浙江大学中国西部发展研究院

浙江大学"一带一路"合作与发展协同创新中心

浙江农林大学中国农民发展研究中心

浙江师范大学非洲研究院

浙江万里学院宁波海上丝绸之路研究院

中国传媒大学国家传播创新研究中心

中国传媒大学首都传媒经济研究基地

中国海洋大学海洋发展研究院

中国海洋大学日本研究中心

中国海洋大学中国企业营运资金管理研究中心

中国科学技术大学安徽大数据应用协同创新中心

中国科学技术大学安徽省科技创新与区域发展研究中心

中国矿业大学中国城市公共安全管理智库

中国民航大学临空经济研究中心

中国民航大学中国民航环境与可持续发展研究中心（智库）

中国农业大学国际发展研究中心

中国农业大学国家农业农村发展研究院

中国农业大学中国土地政策与法律研究中心

中国人民大学重阳金融研究院

中国人民大学国家发展与战略研究院

中国人民大学民商事法律科学研究中心

中国人民大学人口与发展研究中心

中国人民大学社会转型与社会治理协同创新中心

中国人民大学刑事法律科学研究中心

中国人民大学中国财政金融政策研究中心

中国人民公安大学首都社会安全研究基地

中国政法大学法治政府研究院

中国政法大学人权研究院

中国政法大学司法文明协同创新中心

中国政法大学中国行政体制改革研究会

中南财经政法大学产业升级与区域金融湖北省协同创新中心

中南财经政法大学城乡社区社会管理湖北省协同创新中心

中南财经政法大学法治发展与司法改革研究中心

中南财经政法大学知识产权研究中心

中南财经政法大学中国收入分配研究中心

中南大学地方治理研究院

中南大学教育立法研究基地

中南大学金属资源战略研究院

中南大学两型社会与生态文明协同创新中心

中南大学社会稳定风险研究评估中心

中南大学统一战线参政议政工作室

中南大学医疗卫生法研究中心

中南大学应用伦理学研究中心

中南大学知识产权研究院

中南大学中国村落文化研究中心

中南大学中国文化法研究中心

中山大学国家治理研究院

中山大学南海战略研究院

中山大学粤港澳发展研究院

中央财经大学公共采购研究所

中央财经大学绿色金融国际研究院

中央财经大学首都互联网经济发展研究基地

中央财经大学中国财政发展协同创新中心

中央财经大学中国银行业研究中心

（五）军队智库（6家）

北京系统工程研究所

国防科学技术大学国防科技与军民融合研究中心

国防科学技术大学国防科技战略研究中心

国防科学技术大学国际问题研究中心

中国人民解放军国防大学

中国人民解放军军事科学院

（六）科研院所智库（34家）

北京科学学研究中心

国家测绘地理信息局测绘发展研究中心

湖南省农村发展研究院

江苏省科学技术情报研究所（江苏省科学技术发展战略研究院）

江苏省苏科创新战略研究院

江西省科学院科技战略研究所

联合国教科文组织国际工程教育中心

辽宁省科学技术情报研究所科技发展战略研究中心

青岛市科技发展战略研究院

山东省科技发展战略研究所

上海国际问题研究院

上海科学技术政策研究所

上海市科学学研究所

首都科技发展战略研究院

水利部发展研究中心

天津市经济发展研究院

西部资源环境与区域发展智库

冶金工业经济发展研究中心

浙江省科技信息研究院（浙江省科技发展战略研究院）

中国电子信息产业发展研究院

中国工程院

中国航天工程科技发展战略研究院

中国环境科学研究院

中国科协创新战略研究院

中国科学技术发展战略研究院

中国科学技术信息研究所

中国科学院

中国科学院科技战略咨询研究院

中国科学院预测科学研究中心

中国石油经济技术研究院

中国信息通信研究院

中国信息与电子工程科技发展战略研究中心

中国艺术研究院文化发展战略研究中心

中国中医药信息研究会中医药智库分会

（七）企业智库（8家）

阿里研究院

北京市长城企业战略研究所

电力规划设计总院

国家开发银行研究院（金融研究发展中心）

苏宁金融研究院

腾云智库

中国管理科学研究院专家咨询委员会

中信改革发展研究基金会

（八）社会智库（36家）

北京国际城市发展研究院

察哈尔学会

长江教育研究院

长沙市现代产业发展研究会

重庆智库

东中西部区域发展和改革研究院

广东财经大学华南商业智库

广东亚太创新经济研究院

广东中策知识产权研究院

国观智库

海国图智研究院

海南亚太观察研究院

蓝迪国际智库

辽宁省软科学研究会

盘古智库

上海春秋发展战略研究院

上海福卡经济预测研究所有限公司

上海华夏社会发展研究院

上海金融与法律研究院

上海新金融研究院

深圳创新发展研究院

万博新经济研究院

新丝绸之路经济研究院

知远战略与防务研究所

中国国际经济交流中心

中国金融四十人论坛

中国经济体制改革研究会

中国领导科学研究会

中国南海研究院

中国企业改革与发展研究会

中国丝路智谷研究院

中国与全球化智库

中国(海南)改革发展研究院

中智科学技术评价研究中心

综合开发研究院(中国·深圳)

"一带一路"百人论坛

(九)传媒智库(13家)

第一财经研究院

封面智库

凤凰国际智库

光明日报文化产业研究中心

光明智库

广州日报数据和数字化研究院

经济日报社中国经济趋势研究院

瞭望智库

南方舆情数据研究院

南风窗传媒智库

盛京汇智库

人民网新媒体智库

新华通讯社

2018 Annual Report on the Development of CTTI Source Think Tanks

1 Progress in the Construction of New Types of Think Tanks with Chinese Characteristics

1.1 Full Formulation for Think Tank Policies and Documents

1.1.1 Guidance on the Direction of Think Tank Development by National Policies

(1) The Construction of New-Type Think Tanks Highly Valued by the Party Central Committee

The construction of new types of think tanks with Chinese characteristics is highly valued by the CPC Central Committee with Comrade Xi Jinping at its core, for serving as an important support for making decisions in a sound, democratic way on the basis of law by the Party and the government, and having great significance to stay on and develop the path of socialism with Chinese characteristics, enhance China's global voice and achieve national rejuvenation. Since the 18th CPC National Congress, the Party and state leaders have repeatedly emphasized the importance and necessity of building new types of think tanks with Chinese characteristics on many occasions, and expounded the connotations, goals, ways and the responsibilities of think tanks.

In April, 2013, President Xi Jinping made an important instruction for the construction of new types of think tanks with Chinese characteristics, which was the clearest and richest comment from the central highest leadership of it; in May of that year, the significance of constructing such think tanks was pointed out by Liu Yandong, member of the Political Bureau of the CPC Central Committee and Vice Premier of the State Council then, in the forum "Developing the Philosophy and Social Sciences of University, Promoting the Construction of New Types of Think Tanks with Chinese Characteristics". President Xi made the development of think tanks as a national diplomacy when visiting Germany in March, 2014, after which "Think Tank Diplomacy" would become the "second track diplomacy" in our international exchanges and cooperation. Since then, President Xi repeatedly put forward that we should make use of think tanks to promote international exchanges and cooperation when he met other state leaders or attended international forums. In a forum on work in philosophy and social sciences in May, 2016, President Xi mentioned the achievements made in think tank's development, and pointed out its problem and focus. In the report at the 19th CPC National Congress of the CPC in October, 2017, President Xi made clear that, "we will work faster to develop philosophy and social sciences with Chinese characteristics, and develop new types of think tanks with distinctive Chinese features". In the *Report on the Work of the Government* in March, 2018, Premier Li Keqiang referred that "we will see China's new-type think tanks are well run". Such important speeches and instructions about the development of new-type think tanks made by the Party and state leaders, facilitated the formulation of policies and documents and greatly developed the construction of new types of think tanks with Chinese characteristics. Li Cheng, director of Brookings Institution China Center, thought it has never happened around the world that national leaders are concerned about the development of think tanks in person, but it also the biggest advantage for it.

(2) The Top-Level Design of Think Tank Policies Being Perfected

The Third Plenary Session of the 18th CPC Central Committee proposed to enhance the construction of new types of think tanks with Chinese characteristics while creating and improving a system of decision-making consultation. The development of such think tanks, along with the need for a campaign of innovation in philosophy and social science, was highlighted again at the Fifth Plenary Session of the 18th CPC Central Committee. "Opinions on Strengthening the Construction of New Types of Think Tanks with Chinese Characteristics" ("The Opinions") was issued as a guiding document for the development of new-type think tanks, by the General Office of the CPC Central Committee and the General Office of the State Council in January, 2015. "The Opinions" expounded the theoretic and practical problems in developing new-type think tanks, which marked the rapid development stage of the construction of think tanks. In November, 2015, "The Plan of Pilot Projects for China Top Think Tanks" was adopted at the session of the Central Leading Group for Deepening Reforms (CLGDR); thereafter, "Tentative Measures for the Administration of China Top Think Tanks" and "Tentative Measures for the Management of Special Funds for China Top Think Tanks" were also successively issued. In May, 2017, the CPC Central Committee issued "Opinions on Accelerating the Construction of Philosophy and Social Sciences with Chinese Characteristics". The nine ministries and departments including the Ministry of Civil Affairs and the Publicity Department of CPC Central Committee, issued "Opinions on Sound Development of Private Think Tanks" and so on. These policies and documents clarified the significance of building new types of think tanks with Chinese characteristics while planning the overall blueprint and making such think tanks into the national governance system based on the top-level design, which is a long-term endeavor of holistic and strategic importance, guiding the direction of developing the think tanks.

1.1.2 Provincial and Municipal Policies Followed Up Level by Level

The Party and state leadership's remarks on think tanks and the national development policies of think tanks gave general guidance to the construction of new types of think tanks with Chinese characteristics, and the policies of think tank's development from all provinces and cities are an important step toward implementing the top-level design. As the provincial and municipal policies followed up level by level, the management for new-type think tanks becomes standardization, institutionalization, proceduralization and legalization so that both the management system and the development environment have been further improved.

Provinces and cities responded well to "The Opinions" and introduced corresponding recommendations, or placed these recommendations into their proposal agendas. For example, recommendations on how to build new-type think tanks have been released by more than twenty provincial level administrative regions, including Hunan, Jiangsu, Guangdong and Shanghai. Despite the differences among provinces or municipalities, these recommendations were presented according to the actual situation of the development of local think tanks, in order to strengthen their construction, to establish and improve the system of decision-making consultation. On a macroscale, "The Opinions" is the one with overall and strategic importance, so that these recommendations combine its spirit into the provincial conditions, and extract principles that have guiding and practical values for the province. Compared with provincial policies, the municipal policies and documents of building new-type think tanks with Chinese characteristics are focused more on developing their own system of think tanks. For example, some cities like Shenzhen, Suzhou, came up with ways to shape a pattern of think tanks and to reform relevant management system with their experience, after reviewing their current situations, features and problems about the local development of think tanks.

1.1.3 The Systematic Improvements of Policies and Documents

For the past two years, the recommendations on how to build new-type think tanks have been followed up and implemented from the Party Central Committee to provinces and cities. In addition, the diverse policies and documents of the concrete construction in think tanks continued to be published, from which we can see policies and documents gradually became systematic and the system of think tank policies have been improved. "The Plan of Pilot Projects for China Top Think Tanks", for example, identifies the guidelines and basic requirements of developing top think tanks, and puts forward the specific measures on how to be selected, qualified and managed as pilot projects for think tanks. The fundamental institutional framework for the pilot projects is built by the corresponding "Measures for the Administration of China Top Think Tanks" and "Tentative Measures for the Management of Special Funds for China Top Think Tanks", which have initially formed a standard, effective working mechanism and operation model.

In addition, every aspect of think tank development has been covered by the wide-ranging policies and documents that can be divided as follows:

First are policies and documents associated with the development and management of new-type think tanks and their assessment and appraisal. Jiangsu, for example, has released "Tentative Methods for the Assessment and Appraisal of New-Type Think Tanks in Jiangsu" in December 2016 to explain the assessment and evaluation index system of its new-type think tanks. "Measures for the Administration of New-Type Think Tanks in Heilongjiang" was under deliberation at the work conference of developing new-type think tanks in Heilongjiang in July, 2018. In the same year, Zhejiang Province discussed the making of measures to develop and manage its new-type think tanks, and the assessment and appraisal index system of the new-type think tanks at its work conference of developing new-type think tanks, strengthening and standardizing the development and management of such think tanks. Besides these government documents, many universities, such as East China Normal University, Shanghai Normal University, Hunan Normal University and Fuzhou University, have also introduced some measures for the administration of new-type think tanks.

Second are policies and documents concerned with the fund management of think tanks. As an old Chinese saying goes, food and provisions should go ahead of troops. The autonomy and flexibility in the use of think tank funds directly affect the operation and development of think tanks, and the motivation of talents. "Tentative Measures for the Management of Special Funds for China Top Think Tanks" ("The Special Funds Management Measures"), issued in 2015, made a general guidance to manage the funds for new-type think tanks with Chinese characteristics. "The Special Funds Management Measures" was supplemented by the Ministry of Finance and the National Planning and Leading Group for Philosophy and Social Sciences in December, 2016. After that, some provinces, including Ningxia Autonomous Region, Anhui and Heilongjiang, released measures for funds management one after another, appropriate to themselves, and explained the expense range, budget management, supervision and inspection of special funds.

Third are policies and documents connected with the accreditation and reward for think tank's findings. The research of think tanks are different from academic research, so there are large differences in the form of their findings. Improving the system of accreditation and reward for think tank's findings is related to the motivation of researchers. Establishing and enhancing the accreditation and incentive mechanisms for think tank's findings have been set out in the "Opinions on Strengthening the Construction of New Types of Think Tanks with Chinese Characteristics" and recommendations on how to build new-type think tanks by provinces and cities. Thereafter, provinces like Anhui and Hunan, and universities like East China University of Political Science and Law, Southwest University, Anhui University of Finance and Economics, introduced independent measures for the accreditation of think tank's findings.

1.1.4 Policy Support for the Development of Different Types of Think Tanks

A series of policies and documents have been published to develop different types of think tanks in various industries and fields, especially ones to support the development of university and private think tanks, in order to implement the construction pattern of "coordinately promoting the development of Party or government organizations, Academy of Social Sciences, Party schools or administrative colleges, universities, armed forces, research institutions and private think tanks" in "The Opinions".

First are policies and documents to promote the development of university think tanks. Universities possess natural advantages to build top think tanks. The Vice Premier, Liu Yandong, emphasized the unique role of universities in constructing new types of think tanks with Chinese characteristics in the forum "Developing the Philosophy and Social Sciences of Universities, Promoting the Construction of New Types of Think Tanks with Chinese Characteristics" in May, 2013. "Plan to the Construction of New-Type University Think Tanks with Chinese Characteristics", issued by the Ministry of Education in February, 2014, devoted to forging a development pattern of various university think tanks with rational structure. After that, Yunnan, Gansu, Liaoning, Guangdong, Ningxia Autonomous Region, Shaanxi and other provinces all released relevant documents to develop university think tanks.

Second are policies and documents to promote the development of private think tanks. On the edge of the think tank circle, the development of private think tanks is weakest in capacity. To make coordination with Party or government organizations, universities and private think tanks, the development environment of private think tanks must be made to soundly support the construction of private think tanks. The nine ministries and departments including the Ministry of Civil Affairs, the Publicity Department of CPC Central Committee, the Organization Department of CPC Central Committee, issued "Opinions on Sound Development of Private Think Tanks" in May, 2017, making arrangements to standardize and guide the healthy development of private think tanks, which marks a new stage of China's development of private think tanks. Keeping up with the Party Central Committee, provinces like Gansu, Jiangsu and Shandong introduced recommendations on how to promote private think tanks based on the practical situation.

Third are policies and documents to promote the development of think tanks in various fields. With the rising of building new-type think tanks, the development of think tanks has been gradually involved in various industries and fields, and relevant policies and documents to promote the specialization of think tanks have been published. Ministries, such as Ministry of Water Resources, Ministry of Public Security, Ministry of Agriculture and Ministry of Transport, have announced recommendations on how to specialize think tanks. Moreover, projects for the construction of new-type think tanks proposed by other departments and industries, claimed for boosting industrial and specialized think tanks, setting up and improving the system of decision-making consultation in various fields. Since "Opinions on

Improving New-Type Think Tanks in the Industry and Information Technology" issued by the General Office of the Ministry of Industry and Information Technology (MIIT) in 2016, the think tank list in the field of industry and information technology was established by the Policies and Regulations Department of MIIT to gather resources of think tanks and enhance the level of decision-making consultation. At present, 91 institutions in China have been selected in the think tank list of MIIT, including 29 university think tanks. "Opinions on Improving New-Type Think Tanks in Surveying, Mapping and Geoinformation" was issued by the Leading Party Members' Group of National Administration of Surveying, Mapping and Geoinformation in January, 2018 to fully deploy the system of new-type think tanks in surveying, mapping and geoinformation; in March, Department of Science and Technology of Guangdong Province presented a draft, "Tentative Measures for the Administration of New-Type Think Tanks in Science and Technology", planning to build think tanks in science and technology; in June, Yang Chuantang (Secretary of the Leading Party Members' Group of Ministry of Transport) and Li Xiaopeng (Deputy Secretary and Minister of the Leading Party Members' Group of Ministry of Transport) published the article, "The Construction of High-Quality, New-Type Think Tanks in Transport" in *Guangming Daily*; in September, Civil Aviation of Administration issued "Implementation of Improving New-Type Think Tanks of Civil Aviation of Administration", which meant the new-type think tanks of CAAC (Civil Aviation Administration of China) entered the implementation phase.

1.2 The Think Tank System and Platform Becoming Mature

1.2.1 Gradual and Reasonable Improvement in the Configuration of Think Tank System

According to "2017 Global Go To Think Tank Index Report", China ranks the second in terms of total number of think tanks. Clearly, advantage in numbers is not same as fine quality. In fact, China still lacks think tanks with better international influence and reputation. "The Opinions" expounds the significance, aims, characteristics and ways to build the system of new-type think tanks. The important, strategic choice to develop new types of think tanks with Chinese characteristics is to build "specialized and top think tanks that the state is in urgent need of, each being unique in its own way for institutional innovation and leadership in development". Focusing on building top think tanks, giving funds and policy supports, as well as making examples and models in think tank construction all contribute to leading the direction of new-type think tanks, and enriching the system of them. Nowadays, China has formed a system of new-type think tanks "led by national top think tanks, supported by provincial and municipal key think tanks and supplemented by other new-type think tanks" which is clear in the portrait level and abundant in the landscape level.

First, China top think tanks lead the development. As the reform entered a critical stage and a more difficult phase, the problems we confront are more complicated. How to make more democratic and scientific decisions for the Party and government and solve the tough issues are the major part of the battle to reform. The development of China top think tanks aims at strategic problems that urgently need to be solved, for better serving to make strategic decisions of the Party and government. The experimental construction of China Top Think Tanks (CTTT) was officially launched when the conference on this endeavor was held in Beijing in December, 2015. Since then, 25 institutions have been selected as experimental units for CTTT construction and a CTTT Council was established. Overall, with varied types and distinctive features, the first batch of CTTT are typical and representative, covering a wide range of research. Publicity Department of CPC Central Committee announced 13 CTTT units for priority development in 2017. In addition, programs of key think tanks in other departments and industries have been gradually set up, and topics about think tank programs and decisions have been connected to solve. Ministry of Education, for example, established a university alliance of top think tanks in September, 2017, and 31 first member units jointly signed "University Alliance Convention on Top Think Tanks", aiming to build useful think tanks trusted by the Party and government and make better demonstrated cluster effect in joint development of top think tanks of universities.

Second, provincial and municipal key think tanks support the development. The cultivation and development of provincial and municipal key think tanks is an important part of the system of new-type think tanks with Chinese characteristics, serving as the reserve force for national top think tanks to support their development. 24 provincial administrative regions in China have set up provincial key think tanks, think tanks for priority development or research projects of key think tanks by October, 2018. Take Jiangsu for example, the General Office of CPC Jiangsu Provincial Committee and the General Office of Jiangsu Provincial Government released "Opinions on How to Strengthen the Building of New Types of Think Tanks in Jiangsu", and then announced the first nine key top think tanks and developed a series of documents, including "Tentative Measures for the Assessment and Appraisal of New-Type Think Tanks in Jiangsu", "Assessment and Appraisal Index System of New-Type Think Tanks in Jiangsu", "Methods for the Appraisal of Key High-Level Think Tanks and Fund Management (the Draft)" and "Assessment and Appraisal Index System of Key Top Think Tanks (the Draft)", providing effective policy support for the construction of key provincial think tanks. What's more, Jiangsu established the Committee for Guiding the Construction of New-Type Think Tanks, and founded the New-Type Think Tank Council of Jiangsu Province in May, 2017 to discuss the construction of CTTT and evaluation of this endeavor. In 2016, Publicity Department of CPC Jiangsu Provincial Committee released "Notice on Establishing Think Tanks for Priority Development in Jiangsu" and made a list of 15 provincial key think tanks for priority development. Besides these provincial high-level think tanks and think tanks for priority development, Jiangsu also established dozens of research centers for decision-making. Such think tanks spread in nearly one hundred research areas, such as economy, law, agriculture, history, education and climate. So far, Jiangsu has initially formed the configuration of three-level pyramidal new-type think tanks that is "top think tanks + think tanks for priority development + research centers for decision-making".

Third, other new-type think tanks supplement the development. On the one hand, there are "more mixed think tanks than standard ones, more amateur think tanks than specialized ones, more new think tanks than old ones" in China. So the Central Committee should focus on the development of CTTT and provinces and cities should focus on the development of key think tanks, so as to put the limited funds and expert resources together to change the characteristics of new-type think tank system of "smallness, weakness and looseness". On the other hand, due to a large number of think tanks in China, besides the national, provincial and municipal key think tanks, there are many specialized think tanks, research centers, corporate think tanks, private think tanks and so on, which depend on universities and research institutes. Those think tanks can be found in all walks of life, but they are different from each other in research areas, strength and scale. At the same time, such think tanks play an important role in motivating the marketplace of think tank ideas.

1.2.2 Diverse Think Tank Platforms

At present, China's development of think tanks is still at an early stage, with a sharp rise in number, but still weak in strength and imbalanced in development. As an important platform in the magnificent project of building new-type think tanks with Chinese characteristics, think tank alliances play a unique role in carrying out research cooperation and communication, and sharing information resources, as well as partly changing the situation of "smallness, weakness and looseness" of think tank development so as to make think tanks work as a unit and expand their influence. After the announcement of "The Opinions", China's think tank platforms gradually become diverse while think tank alliances are increasingly dynamic. These alliances can be divided into many types by research areas, regions and scales as follows:

First, regional think tank alliances. Combining their own superior strength, regional think tank alliances focus on problems to be solved in development and provide the service for policy consultation. Jiangsu, for example, the first regional think tank alliance, "Think Tank Alliance among Nanjing, Zhenjiang and Yangzhou", was founded in Nanjing in September, 2015. The alliance is an innovative collaboration platform of think tanks, jointly launched by Federations of Social Science in Nanjing, Zhenjiang and Yangzhou, and aims to gather talents and intellectual resources of these places to overcome various difficulties and problems in comprehensively deepening reform. It can also convey people's feelings and opinions, feed into advice for the decision-making of the Party committee and government and promote the integration and sustainable, coordinated development of economic, political, cultural social, ecological and civilized construction in the region of Nanjing, Zhenjiang and Yangzhou. In June, 2016, "National Think Tank Alliance among Cities along the 'Belt and Road'" was set up by unincorporated academic groups that were constituted with key think tanks including Federations of Social Science in 32 pivot cities along the " Belt and Road". The alliance is intended to positively respond to the "Belt and Road" Initiative and create a great platform making joint discussion, cooperation and research, strategic study and judgement, and policy evaluation for cities and institutions in the development of "Belt and Road", offering consultation to the government, suggestions to synergize development strategies in areas, and promoting benigs between think tank research and government decision-making.

Second, international think tank alliances. In recent years, the think tank community in China is devoted to international communication and cooperation, and expanding the network of think tanks to make China's voice heard on various international think tank forums. In October, 2017, "Think Tank Alliance of Global Cities" was jointly founded by research institutes of think tanks in New York, Paris, Singapore, Seoul, Hongkong, Beijing and Shanghai. The alliance aims to be a platform that promotes academic and policy research of urban management in an all-round way, a communication platform of best practices for urban management at the global level, and a platform to boost communication and cooperation of the bodies among cities. Working together with Worldwide Universities Network (WUN), Renmin University of China proposed and advanced to set up "Think Tank Alliance of Worldwide Universities" which focuses on the theme of green development of the "Belt and Road" to deeply communicate and discuss hot issues for all countries in the world, especially the region of the "Belt and Road" Initiative in March, 2018. The alliance aims to strengthen the development of think tanks, wield their influence and work together to make "knowledge exchange" into "knowledge cloud", promote "think tank dialogue" as "think tank alliance" and build an "intellectual silk road", contributing to global governance and development. Shanghai Cooperation

Organization Economic Think Tank Alliance was established in May, 2018 in order to build a stable exchange and cooperation mechanism and a platform of think tank alliance to make sustainable and sound development for regional economic cooperation.

Third, industrial (domanial) think tank alliances. Such think tanks are constituted with think tanks in the relevant industries (domains), focusing on trends and problems of their industries (domains) and constructing platforms for exchange and cooperation of think tanks. For example, the Conference on the Establishment of MIIT Think Tank Alliance & MIIT Think Tank Forum were held in Beijing in June, 2018, when the website of MIIT Think Tanks was officially launched. MIIT Think Tank Alliance should aim to become a platform for work exchange, theoretical discussions, government services and foreign liaison in the area of industry and information technology, giving full play to the role as a bridge of linking and supporting. Twenty famous research institutes in China founded "Think Tank Alliance of American Studies" in July, 2018 to carry out basic, policy-oriented and prospective researches on such issues as economic and political situation of the United States, domestic and foreign policies of the United States and the relation between China and the United States, so as to actively conduct international exchange and cooperation. Think Tank Alliance of Ecological Civilization in Fujian was established in November, 2018, which aimed to pool provincial think tank resources together to provide more intellectual support for the development of ecological civilization of Fujian.

1.3 Deepening Communication and Dissemination of Think Tanks

With the development of China's new-type think tanks, their strength and interaction are gradually growing. On the one hand, exchanges among think tanks in terms of conferences, talents and programs are more frequent and increasingly deepening; on the other hand, since President Xi made the development of think tanks as a national diplomacy, the "Think Tank Diplomacy" has become the second track in our international exchanges. Our think tanks are steadily going abroad to join in the international think tank development and gradually make dialogues and exchanges with international think tanks.

1.3.1 Think Tank Conferences Promoting the Communication and Dissemination of Think Tank Ideas

Different think tank conferences or forums on different themes serve as an important platform for think tanks' exchanges of ideas, opinions and researches. After "The Opinions" was released, the development of China's think tanks entered a golden period when think tank conferences or forums at various levels with different types or themes were emerging. Think tank experts could carry out deep discussion on important theoretical or practical issues that need to be solved in different areas, such as the "Belt and Road", "big data", "Internet plus", "Artificial Intelligence" and "poverty alleviation", so as to hold conferences or forums with some influence. "China's University Think Tank Forum" has been held for four years since its first annual meeting held in Shanghai in December, 2014. This forum aims to discuss how university think tanks conduct prospective, well-targeted policy researches in reserve for the state's major strategic needs, improve research quality and promote content innovation in face of new situation and requirements, so as to lead and drive the development of university think tanks, and expand their influence. Hosted by Guangming Daily Press and Nanjing University, the first "Conference on Chinese Think Tank Governance" was launched in Nanjing University on December 17th, 2016, combining keynote reports, discussion in categories and the releasing of works, and attracting hundreds of experts and scholars in think tank community and ideological and theoretic circles, and making great influence in China. One year later, "Chinese Think Tank Governance &. the Spreading of Thoughts and Theories Summit Forum 2017" was grandly held in Beijing, with nearly 800 participants from think tank community, ideological and theoretic circles, administrative departments of provinces, cities and autonomous regions, and university departments of scientific research. Officials of National Philosophy and Social Sciences Planning Office and Social Sciences Department of Ministry of Education made guidance in this conference; Zhang Zheng, chief editor of Guangming Daily Press, and Chen Jun, ex-president of Nanjing University, delivered speeches there; leading officials in charge, such as the deputy chief editor Li Chunlin, the deputy chief editor Lu Xiangao, and the deputy secretary of Party committee of Nanjing University Zhu Qingbao, hosted the conference or published research findings. Notables from the theoretic circles and think tank community, like Wei Liqun, Zhang Junkuo, Cai Fang, Feng Jun, and Liu Hongwu (the representative of annual think tanks) gave keynote speeches. More and more participants shared their opinions and made in-depth communication in the two special sessions, six paralleled sub-conferences and several occasions to publish results for the Summit Forum. Besides extensive coverage of *Guangming Daily* and its media matrixes, more than ten media, including *China Daily*, CCTV News Channel, Xinhua News Agency, Chinese Social Sciences Today, and the journal *National Governance*, reported this forum, so that we can see its great influence.

With the development of specialized think tanks from all walks of life, the number of specialized think tank forums with different themes in various areas is also gradually growing, in addition to comprehensive think tank conferences and forums. "Forum on Environment and Development", for example, has been held for four times since December, 2015. It is an annual activity of excellent academic exchanges to build think tanks based on resources and environment in the western area of China, concentrating on hot and prospective issues on resources, environment and regional development, supporting strategic decisions on environment and development, and spreading relevant thoughts and scientific technologies. "2018 First China High-Level Seminar for Technology Incorporate Think Tanks" was successfully held at the National Science Library of Chinese Academy of Sciences in August, 2018, which aimed to study problems for technology incorporate think tanks, promote the deep combination between the incorporate development and technological innovation, and discuss the role of incorporate think tanks to play and the responsibilities to take in supporting the development of incorporates and dealing with outside risks.

1.3.2 Network Platforms Promoting the Communication and Dissemination of Think Tank Information

As think tanks developing rapidly in China, the think tank information is growing exponentially; so the think tank platforms of different types are constantly springing up. Think tank network platforms are crucial in displaying, disseminating, building and sharing think tank information.

The think tank network platforms can be divided into different types for various clients. First, comprehensive think tank network platforms. Comprehensive think tank network platforms focus on studying regional think tanks and serving their development. As the first think tank platform to exchange in Hubei, "A New-Type Think Tank Platform in Hubei" is positioned to serve the whole country and embrace the world based in Hubei, and aims to build a platform to disseminate and transform think tank results, exchange and attract talents, and facilitate communication between decision-makers and think tanks. The building of think tank platforms gives an impetus to timely issues and widely disseminate the achievements of think tank experts, further strengthens the connection between think tanks and decision-making bodies, and motivates think tank achievements to give full play in transforming and applying in the decision-making bodies. "Think Tanks in Jiangsu" in the host of Publicity Department of the CPC Jiangsu Provincial Committee, is an important showcase for the think tank development in Jiangsu, and completely presents prestigious think tanks, think tank experts, researches and activities.

Second, specialized think tank network platforms. The specialized think tank network platforms focus on revealing relevant information about think tanks in a field or industry. "A Think Tank Platform of Big Data in Guizhou" was officially launched in January, 2018, which pooled resources like data, knowledge and experts together to provide scientific decision-making for all levels of government in Guizhou and precise intellectual service and decision-making support for the whole process of solving specific problems. On the basis of decision-making model and AI technology, it can also automatically generate sensible, advisable and traceable reports by subject based on digital characteristics, as well as make overall plans for governmental and social data resources to rapidly promote deep integration and application of big data into aspects like government affairs, economy, society and technology. "Qingdao Think Tank Platform of Science and Technology" came online in April, 2017 and was officially run in November, 2018. What it can share is more than 300 think tank research findings and more than 62 million literature search references, including industrial technology roadmaps, which have been accumulated by Qingdao Institute of Science and Technology Information in recent years. After registration and certification, think tank experts and the public can be fully served on this platform. This is a new important action of Qingdao to develop high-level technology think tanks and provide intelligent information services for its scientific and innovative decision-making. The platform offers four services, including dynamic monitoring of technology and innovation, think tank result sharing, knowledge of special subjects and personalized and customized services.

1.3.3 Participating in International Exchange to Make "Voice of China's Think Tanks"

With further developing new types of think tanks with Chinese characteristics, our think tanks began to go abroad and actively participated in international exchange and took part in cooperation and research on global issues in recent years to make "voice of China's think tanks" and deliver Chinese values. Participating in international exchange we not only need to "bring in", but also to "go abroad". To build "influential and international top think tanks", we should draw on experience of developed countries and attract international think tank talents, as well as embrace an international perspective to energetically engage in exchanges and cooperation among countries and give full play to China's think tanks in international affairs. In the past few years, China has bid for or hosted international think tank conferences, vigorously participated in international think tank forums and actively built think tank platforms for international exchanges so as to promote China think tanks to go abroad, which were reflected in themes of these conferences focusing on important strategies in China, like China-Africa Cooperation, the "Belt and Road" Initiative.

"China-Africa Think Tank Forum" (CATTF) was launched by Zhejiang Normal University in 2011, as a high-level platform for academic communication between China and Africa, which was approved by Ministry of Foreign Affairs and Ministry of Commerce of the People's Republic of China. With the tenets of "NGO Initiative, Government Support, Frank Dialogue and Consensus Building", it is held in China and Africa every year. CATTF aims to promote African and Chinese studies, enhance mutual understanding, work for consensus, and offer constructive advice on cooperation. Since its founding, CATTF has scored a series of important achievements and brought great influence all over the world so that it was incorporated into the framework of Forum on China-Africa Cooperation (FOCAC) by Ministry of Foreign Affairs of the People's Republic of China and became a high-level institutional platform for China-Africa academic exchanges and think tank dialogues. President Xi Jinping said, "With more people-to-people exchanges in culture and art, education, sports, and among our think tanks, the media, and women and young people, we will strengthen the bond between the people of China and Africa" in 2018 Beijing Summit of the FOCAC in September, 2018, which also reflected "Think Tank Diplomacy".

"China-CEEC Think Tanks Network" (16＋1 Think Tanks Network) was proposed by Li Keqiang, Premier of the State Council, and based on "the building of a 16＋1 think tank network developed under the leadership of Chinese Academy of Social Sciences" which was presented in the "Suzhou Guidelines" signed by 17 premiers of China and Central East and European Countries. "16＋1 Think Tanks Network" will integrate dominant resources of Chinese Academy of Social Sciences and think tanks in China and 16 Central East and European countries to carry out strategies, such as the construction of new-type think tanks, China-European Partnership and the "Belt and Road" Initiative, and to support and promote "16＋1 cooperation", whose aim is to build a coordination mechanism and top exchange platform of international think tanks between China and Central East and European countries. The first think tank of China, "China-CEE Institute", registered independently in Europe and it was established at Hungarian Academy of Sciences in

April, 2018, whose founding would boost China-CEEC cultural communication, academic exchange and policy dialogue, playing an important role in China-CEEC cooperation and think tank exchanges.

Silk Road Think Tank Network (SiLKS) was proposed by Development Research Center of the State Council (DRC) together with relevant international think tanks on the first "Silk Road Forum" in Istanbul, Turkey in 2014, and was officially established as an international think tank network by 33 think tanks, 8 international organizations and 1 incorporate on the "Silk Road Forum" in Madrid, Spain in October, 2015, whose aim is to provide high-level intellectual support for the "Belt and Road" through discussion and collaboration. "Silk Road Think Tank Network Guidelines" was approved on the first annual meeting of SiLKS in Warsaw, Poland in June, 2016. Now, there are 42 members and 13 partners in SiLKS, including 36 authorized think tanks in 30 countries, 12 international organizations such as the United Nations Development Programme, the United Nations Industrial Development Organization, and 7 international incorporates.

1.4 Significant Progress in Think Tank Research and Evaluation

In the past few years, the construction of new types of think tanks with Chinese characteristics has been thriving in industries of different regions. With the advancement of practices, the think tank development has been suffering from many realistic problems while gaining experience. The think tank research is an important way to analyze the working and development mechanism of think tanks, sum up the experience about think tank development and propose the developmental direction. With the diagnosis of think tank development, think tank evaluation will help correct its direction and urge think tanks to learn from each other. The construction of new types of think tanks with Chinese characteristics and think tank research and evaluation cannot be separated from each other. Since "The Opinions" was released in 2015, the think tank research and evaluation have been witnessing a massive upsurge.

1.4.1 Think Tank Research and Evaluation Institutions Spring Up

As "the brain trust of think tanks", think tank research and evaluation institutions mainly study think tanks or the whole think tank industry and play an important role in think tank research and evaluation.

According to the guiding principles from central leadership's instruction, Think Tank Industry Research Center of Shanghai University was set up as a school-level research institution in 2014 in order to speed up the development of think tanks in Shanghai and the whole country. The center takes national development and Shanghai's development as its core issue, based on the practice of reform, development and modernization, so as to build a comprehensively academic think tank in China.

The peak year for the building of think tank research and evaluation institutions was in 2015. Chinese Cultural Industry Think – Tank Research Center was established in March, 2015; in April, China Think Tank Research and Evaluation Center of Nanjing University was set up; in May, Zhejiang University of Technology's Global Think Tank Research Center was inaugurated and Think Tank Research and Release Center of *Guangming Daily* was founded; in June, CTTS of Shanghai Academy of Social Sciences began to operate as materialization; in November, Sichuan Academy of Social Sciences and Chengdu Library and Information Center of Chinese Academy of Sciences co-founded "Chinese Think Tank Research Center". China Institute of Social Science Evaluation was set up in Beijing on July 21st, 2017.

Since then, think tank research and evaluation institutions have come into a stage of steady development. On the one hand, with sustainable development, such established institutions published a lot of influential think tank development reports, think tank evaluation reports, journals, papers and academic works. On the other hand, there were more new think tank research and evaluation institutions founded, such as Wuhan University's World-Class Think Tank Research and Evaluation Center, Education Think Tank and Education Governance Research and Evaluation Center of Changjiang Education Research Institute, Think Tank Research Center of Shandong Academy of Social Sciences, New-Type Think Tank Research Center of Hebei Academy of Social Sciences and Think Tank Research Center of Tsinghua University's School of Public Policy and Management.

1.4.2 A Massive Upsurge in Think Tank Research Findings

The construction and research of new-type think tanks is booming in China with a massive upsurge in findings, which is guided by President Xi's thought. A system of knowledge and academic studies on the construction of new types of think tanks with Chinese characteristics has taken initial shape—a system rooted in China's own think-tank-related practice, which has laid a strong informational and theoretical foundation for building new types of think tanks with Chinese characteristics.

(1) Abundant Publications of Books About Think Tank Research

Think tank books are an important form of think tank research. In the wave of building new-type think tanks with Chinese characteristics, the number of all kinds of think tank books is increasing. Remarkably, in addition to books of some think tank experts or scholars published by themselves, many book series are compiled or translated by a think tank institution or research team, with characteristics of systematicness, professionalism and advancement tending to make a significant impact.

As an important part of the plan of Nanjing University for building new-type think tanks with Chinese characteristics, *Nanjing University Think Tank Collection* is one of the platforms for the cooperation between China Think Tank Research and Evaluation Center of Nanjing University and Think Tank Research and Release Center of *Guangming Daily*, which aims to disseminate and introduce experience about the construction of foreign think tanks to offer us some advice in the new situation. The collection was edited by Li Gang, deputy director of the center and top expert, who has edited and published ten key books, including *Improving Think Tank Management: Practical Guidance for Think Tanks*, *Research Advocacy NGOs, and Their Funders*; *The Idea Brokers: Think Tanks and the Rise of the New Policy Elite*; *A Capitol Idea: Think Tanks and US Foreign Policy*; *La RAND Corporation (1989 - 2009): La reconfiguration des saviors stratégiques aux États-Unis*; *The Transformation of American Politics: The New Washington and the Rise of Think Tanks*; *Chinese Think Tank Index(CTTI)*, *Think Tanks, Foreign Policy and Geo-Politics: Pathways to Influence*; *The Ideas Industry: How Pessimists, Partisans, and Plutocrats Are Transforming the Marketplace of Ideas*; *Theory and Methodology of Think Tank Evaluation*; *2017 Chinese Think Tank Index Report*.

Theoretical Paradigm and Practical Innovation on the Development of University Think Tanks, written by Wang Heng, the professor of Institute of African Studies of Zhejiang Normal University (ZNU), has been published by World Affairs Press in September, 2017. As one of a series of books about African think tanks and thought studies under the library of Institute of African Studies of ZNU, the book focuses on solving three fundamental questions on the current development of university think tanks: firstly, "why"—whether universities develop think tanks or not and the reasons why universities develop think tanks; secondly, "what"—what connotations and particularities that make university think tanks different from other think tanks are and what their advantages are; thirdly, "how"—how to promote the development of university think tanks, transform and extend the value of university ideology and knowledge to make spillover effects by think tanks.

Northern Lights: Exploring Canada's Think Tank Landscape, written by Donald E. Abelson, the political science professor of University of Western Ontario, and translated by Fudan Development Institute, was published in November, 2017 and belonged to *Contemporary International Think Tank Translations Series* released by CTTS of Shanghai Academy of Social Sciences. As the first book to comprehensively explore Canada's think tanks, this book is of importance to know Canada's policy institutions. It discusses how think tanks rise in Canada, and expounds many common problems about think tanks—how or in which circumstances think tanks will influence public opinions and policies. The writer analyzes the circumstances in which the think tanks will pay more attention to advocating politics instead of policy research, and strives to explain why think tank institutions are suitable and capable to construct the discourse on important policy issues. There are other wonderful series like *Contemporary International Think Tank Translations*, for example, *Think Tanks as Catalysts: Democratization and Market Reform in Developing Transitional Countries*, whose writer is James G. MacGann and translators include Xie Huayu, *Think Tanks: The Brain Trusts of US Foreign Policy*, written by Kubilay Yado Arin and translated by Wang Chengzhi.

(2) Increasingly Growing Think Tank Papers

Think Tanks of *Guangming Daily* (Weekly), established on December 25th, 2014, has released more than 200 issues. As the first issue named after "Think

Tanks" in national print media, it aims to present top research findings of think tanks and boost the development of new types of think tanks with Chinese characteristics by publishing articles of experts, conducting exclusive interviews and so on. It mainly releases think tank research findings, offers strategies and suggestions of think tank experts, develops and researches themselves and introduces experience of successful think tanks to give out due voice from mainstream media and attach the society's great attention to the construction of such think tanks.

As a platform to publish findings of academic think tank research, *Think Tank Theory and Practice* is the first professional journal of think tanks in China, jointly established by National Science Library of Chinese Academy of Sciences and Nanjing University in February, 2016, aiming to explore think tank theories, support think tank construction, guide think tank practice and spread think tank findings. It is constituted with different columns, such as features/feature stories, theoretical research, think tank development, expert interview, case analysis, think tank evaluation, think tank report and think tank scan. This journal is published every two month and has published 16 issues with a total of more than 300 papers so far.

Since then, newspapers, journals and magazines started to launch think tank columns and accept papers about think tank studies. Many library and information academic journals, such as *Library Tribune*, *Think Tank Theory and Practice*, *Document, Information & Knowledge*, *Library and Information*, *Library Journal*, *Library*, *New Century Library*, *Information Research* and *Journal of Library and Information Sciences in Agriculture*, have published a large number of papers on think tank for academic research, making library, information and archives science become an important subject which supports new-type think tank research. The increasing of papers on thank tank studies is mainly due to the rapid development of new-type think tanks with Chinese characteristics, the building of publication platforms for papers and the enthusiasm of think tank researchers. By November, 2018, CNKI has collected over 10,000 papers with "think tank", "brain trust" or "thinking bank" in the title alone, mostly published after 2013. Because of these numerous papers involved in many fields, the construction of new-type think tanks with Chinese characteristics is greatly supported by theories.

(3) Different Types of Think Tank Evaluation Reports

Depending on their own research resources, some think tank research and evaluation institutions set up different evaluation indexes to periodically conclude and present the construction of new types of think tanks with Chinese characteristics in different dimensions, which produces corresponding think tank reports. Limitations may exist in any evaluation index, but diversified evaluation indexes are of great importance to build the think tank evaluation system with Chinese characteristics. In other words, think tank evaluation will help to summarize experiences, find shortcomings and adjust direction while developing think tanks. At present, the published think tank reports in China include series of *Chinese Think Tank Report* of CTTS of Shanghai Academy of Social Sciences, *Comprehensive Evaluation AMI Research Report on Chinese Think Tank* of Chinese Academy of Social Sciences (CASS), *Chinese Think Tank Influence Report* issued jointly by the Horizon Institute of Global Development Power and state-run news website China.org.cn, *Chinese University Think Tank Development Report* of Zhejiang University of Technology's Global Think Tank Research Center, series of *Chinese Think Tank Index Report* of China Think Tank Research and Evaluation Center of Nanjing University, series of *Impact Report of Chinese Think Tank* issued by Sichuan Academy of Social Sciences and Chengdu Library and Information Center of Chinese

Academy of Sciences, *Global Think Tank Evaluation Report* of China Social Sciences Evaluation Center of CASS. Overall, such various think tank reports with diversified indexes released by think tank research and evaluation institutions, have initially formed an evaluation method combining objective data with subjective assessment, and have improved China's think tank evaluation system.

1.5 Conclusion

As an essential part of national soft power, the construction of new types of think tanks with Chinese characteristics is an important means to build modern governance system, strengthen modern governance capability and drive a more open policy-oriented community. President Xi made far-sighted, detailed instructions on this construction on April 15th, 2013 that we should regard think tank development as an important part of national soft power and make it a national strategy. Since then, documents and policies to promote think tank development have been successively issued at all levels from central to local for more than five years; national, provincial and municipal think tank systems have been gradually improved; the international communication of think tanks has been more frequent; with the vigorous development of think tank researches, the external environment has also been improved and the endogenous dynamics has been strengthened, bringing the construction and development of China's think tanks into golden age and reaching new heights. Towards the goal to build "specialized top think tanks that the state is in urgent need of, each being unique in its own way for institutional innovation and leadership in development", we have gained outstanding achievements and gradually formed a new-type think tank system which is "led by national top think tanks, supported by provincial and municipal key think tanks and supplemented by other new-type think tanks, clear in the portrait level and abundant in the landscape level". China think tanks always focus on issues in China, summarize experience of China, give out China's voice, deliver China's ideas and display Chinese style in development, coming to play an important role in serving national strategies and social public policies.

2 An Overview of the CTTI System

2.1 A Review of the Developing and Constructing Process of the CTTI System

2.1.1 Research and Development Background of the CTTI System

On April 15, 2013, President Xi Jinping pointed out in an instruction that we should build new types of think tanks with Chinese characteristics, Chinese style and Chinese manner that can rival famous western think tanks, and a state strategy of think tank constructing was launched. However, China failed establishing a complete statistical analysis method for think tanks until 2015. Opinions varied on how many think tanks were there in China. The reason why China did not have complete and systematical think tank statistics was that we lacked think tank statistical indicator system.

In order to comprehensively describe and collect think tank data and to equip it with the function of data collection, data search, data analysis and data application, China Think Tank Research and Evaluation Center (CTTREC) of Nanjing University, in collaboration with Think Tank Research and Release Center (TTRRC) of *Guangming Daily*, started to research and develop China Think Tank Index (CTTI) and formed a research group hosted by Li Gang in June, 2015. By now, the research and development of CTTI System have experienced four phases. The first phase was from June to October in 2015. During this period, researchers completed the system requirement analysis and field design. They determined the basic idea of system design and clarified the system architecture design. On October 18th of the same year, CTTI's mid-term research results were released at the "Symposium on Think Tank Evaluation and Governance" jointly sponsored by *Guangming Daily* Theory Department and Nanjing University. The achievement was also selected as one of the top ten think tank events of 2015. Subsequently, from November 2015 to June 2016 was the second phase of the system development when researchers completed the development of CTTI's overall system. From July to September 2016, it entered the third phase, when system environment deployment, online test, and commissioning a third-party to test system security were completed. The system was finally released online on September 28, 2016 and was accessible to all sourced think tanks to input data.

After the first three phases of system development, CTTI had a relatively complete data field and a list of the first group of source think tanks was included and released in 2016. After more than a year of operation, CTTI had collected a large number of actual needs from various think tanks and management departments. They found that the lack of information management tools for think tanks had seriously restricted the daily management of think tanks. In this regard, in May 2017, the Chinese Think Tank Research and Assessment Center of Nanjing University and the research team of Think Tank Research and Release Center of *Guangming Daily* decided to further improve the CTTI data fields and optimize system functions to support solutions to these needs. On this basis, the two centers proposed to jointly create an enhanced data information tool for IT management of think tanks, and the CTTI Plus version came into being. In order to maintain the stability of the system and the reliability of existing data, the core functions of the CTTI Plus version would resemble those of CTTI, but the new version would be a comprehensive upgrade of the original one. Moreover, the difference between its positioning and CTTI product positioning is that the CTTI Plus focuses not only on the quantitative evaluation of think tanks, but also on the business needs of think tank information management.

With the joint efforts of the research team, CTTI Plus had been updated and tested online by the end of 2017 and put into use since 2018. In May of the same year, the "2017 CTTI Think Tank Best Practice Awards (BPA) Release and Think Tank Evaluation System Seminar" was held in Nanjing by Think Tank Research and Release Center of *Guangming Daily* and China Think Tank Research and Evaluation Center of Nanjing University. The release and launching ceremony of CTTI Plus system in this event attracted eager attention of domestic think tank peers, experts and scholars. The new version of the system has also been widely promoted and utilized.

2.1.2 Overall Architecture of the CTTI System

At present, apart from local main system, the overall architecture of CTTI also includes two other aspects: cloud management of think tanks and the think tank community mechanism. It features a multi-level star topology for user rights assignment. The topology of user ID and rights description is shown in Fig. 1.

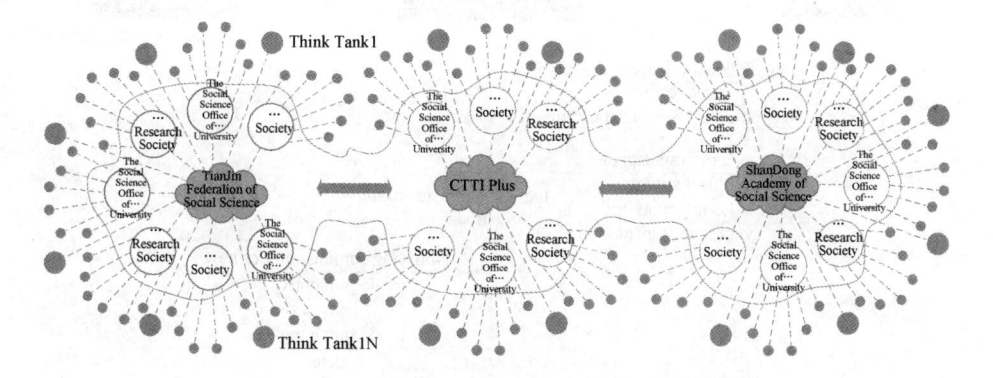

Fig. 1 Topology of CTTI Plus' Functional Architecture

The central area demarcated by the curved line represents the think tank community users and the think tank cloud users; the dots beyond the curved line stand for the cloud think tanks. CTTI will provide an online information sharing platform for the Chinese Think Tank Community, as well as further description of the levels of think tank management through the think tank cloud function.

(1) The Think Tank Community (TTC) has been incorporated as a new mechanism into CTTI for the construction of an online alliance of new types of Chinese think tanks and the sharing of achievements in think tank development. The TTC is meant to offer a substantiated network resource platform for think tanks and administrative authorities that are committed to promoting exchange and cooperation among new Chinese think tanks. The TTC membership will mainly consist of government authorities, public institutions, and non-profit legal persons. The members will have access to all the data and functions of the system. Meanwhile, CTTI will assist them in deploying local systems, creating local think tank clouds, and ensuring the daily refreshing of intra-system data, as shown in Fig. 2.

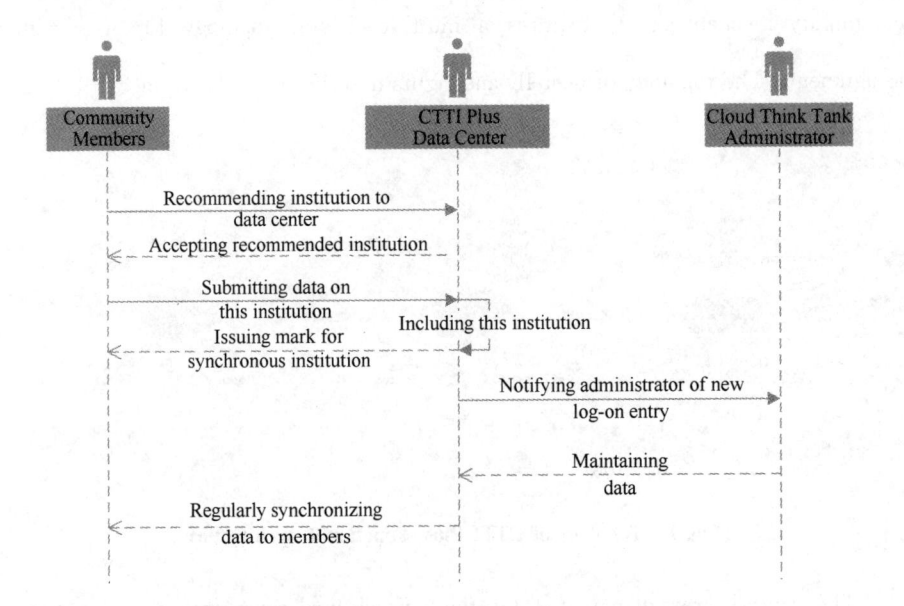

Fig. 2　CTTI Plus' Data Interchange Mechanism

Think tanks added by TTC members can be recommended to CTTI's pool of supplementary resource and properly weighed via an intra-system process. The local data of TTC members will be divided into two parts: the data on institutions and experts included in the CTTI system will be refreshed on a daily basis to TTC members by CTTI; the data on institutions and experts created by TTC members themselves will be locally maintained for security and privacy. When a TTC user-recommended think tank is included in the CTTI source think tank list, CTTI will incorporate all its data at one go and refresh such data on a daily basis, together with those of other source think tanks, to the TTC's local system.

For compatibility with TTC members' existing information management systems, it will support customized front interfaces for member units and provide data exchange interfaces to facilitate connection and data exchange with existing systems. In addition, single sign-on will be adopted for log-on by foreground users under the control of all TTC members.

(2) The Think Tank Cloud function has been developed for CTTI II to meet the think tank supervisory authorities' needs in practical work, after visits to a large number of think tanks and think tank supervision units as well as a summary of previous experience. CTTI has developed the think tank cloud function, which provides institutions or authorities with data management needs with access to the CTTI system's well-developed think tank data fields, advanced database schema, and scientific assessment algorithm. It offers data management service to think tanks and supervisory authorities by means of an online big data resource trusteeship platform. Think tank clouds are meant to provide well-developed think tank management and index service to users that are incapable of designing and developing think tank data management systems. Access to think tank clouds can endow common institutions

and units with the same capacity for data management and retrieval as those of the CTTI system. (As shown in Fig. 3.)

Create Think Tank Cloud
To establish a CTTI Plus system locally

Think Tank Cloud User
Have access to CTTI's highly trustworthy resources without separate deployment or use of local hardware resources

CTTI Think Tank Cloud User
A service for think tank management organizations and large think tanks that do not have localized deployment conditions

Fig. 3　Think Tank Cloud Management System

Think tank cloud users can add institution and expert users by themselves for supervision of what is under their control. Meanwhile, they will have access to CTTI's highly trustworthy resources without separate deployment or use of local hardware resources. It is necessary to emphasize that, in order to maintain data security, all data among think tank clouds are independent of each other. All data belonging to the users of any think tank cloud are only accessible to the think tank accounts within the framework of that particular cloud rather than to the public. Think tank cloud managers can incorporate think tanks and experts into think tank clouds for centralized management by creating cloud think tanks. (As shown in Fig. 4).

With the integrated development of think tank clouds, the think tank community will develop a unified data management standard. Seamlessly combined with CTTI assessmemt algorithm, this standard will ensure that think tank assessment has a real effect on the daily management of think tanks, which enables mutual promotion of assessment and management and enhances both the assessment method and the effectiveness of management.

Fig. 4　Think Tank Cloud Management Interface

2.1.3　Main Functions of CTTI System

(1) Foreground Retrieve and Browse

Main functions of the front end of CTTI system are retrieval and news browsing. In terms of retrieval, the process includes six types of tasks: institution retrieval, expert retrieval, product retrieval, activity retrieval, demand retrieval and comprehensive retrieval. CTTI supports fuzzy queries and multi-condition queries. Multi-condition queries can be achieved by separating key words by spaces, just like common search engines. Among them, comprehensive retrieval is the "OR" operation of the first five types of retrievals. And as for these five tasks, CTTI provides a secondary screening function for the search results. There are several conditions for each screening item, which can be selected by checking. For institution and expert retrievals, CTTI provides an alphabetical index for quick searching. Final retrieval results of CTTI include two parts: a result list and a related result. The result list refers to a list of all the items that meet the search condition, and the result items are sorted according to the hit weight, which means that the matching rate of retrieval field is ranked from high to low (Fig. 5).

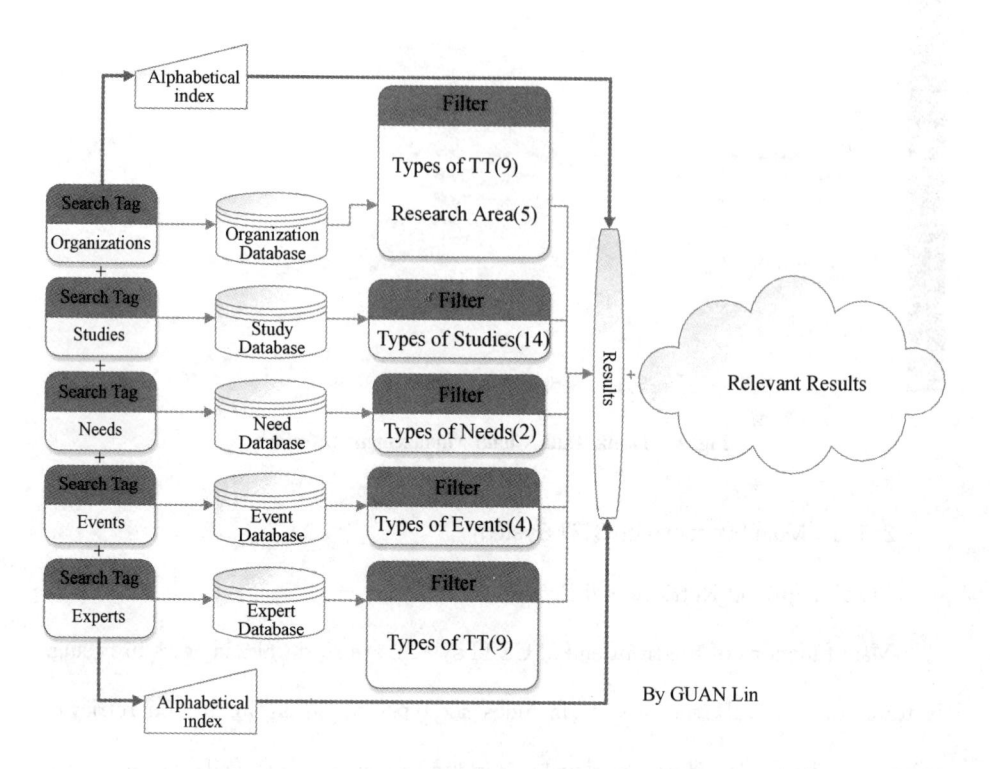

Fig. 5 Retrieval Task Process

At the same time, the CTTI system also has a news browsing function in the foreground. The system will regularly push the latest news and announcements into the system station, as well as popular organizations and different types of achievements with large number of hits, so that users can obtain relevant information in time.

(2) Background Data Processing and User Management

Based on a powerful database, the CTTI background includes two task processes: data processing and user management. The main functions of the data processing include data entry, modification, review, release and maintenance (as shown in Fig. 6). The "data" includes not only organization, expert, product and activity data, but also peripheral data such as news and demand information. Data comes from network or paper sources collected manually. In the data processing flow, institutional and expert users can log in to the system through different portals and enter the data of corresponding fields. These data will be released or open for retrieval after reviewed by the system administrator. System administrators have the highest authority for auditing and data management. For audited data, all system users and visitors can retrieve directly.

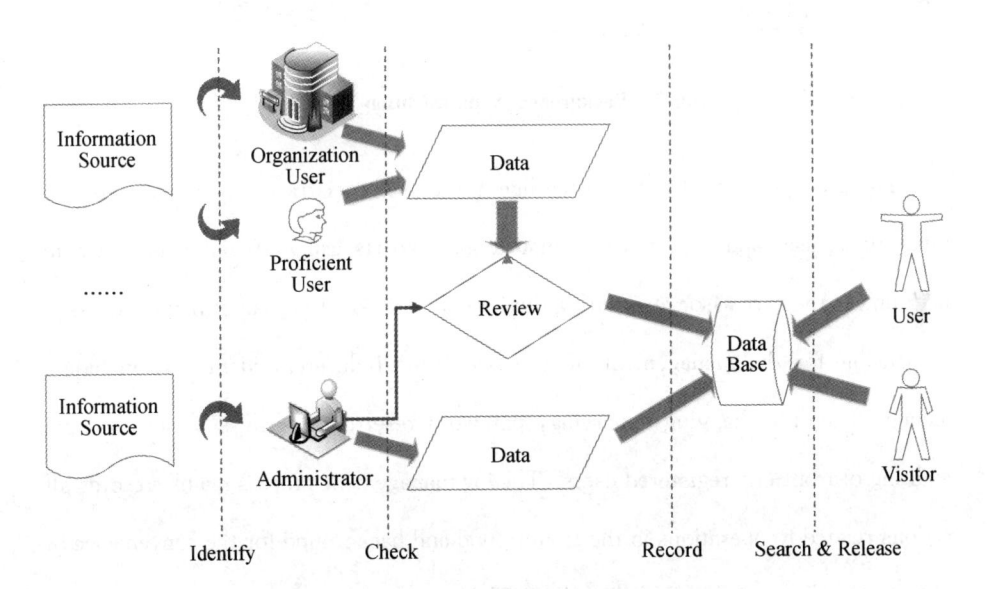

Fig. 6 Data Processing flow

On the other hand, the background management process including user registration and identity management, log management, parameter settings, news release, statistical analysis, data management, and auditing, is only open to system administrators (as shown in Fig. 7).

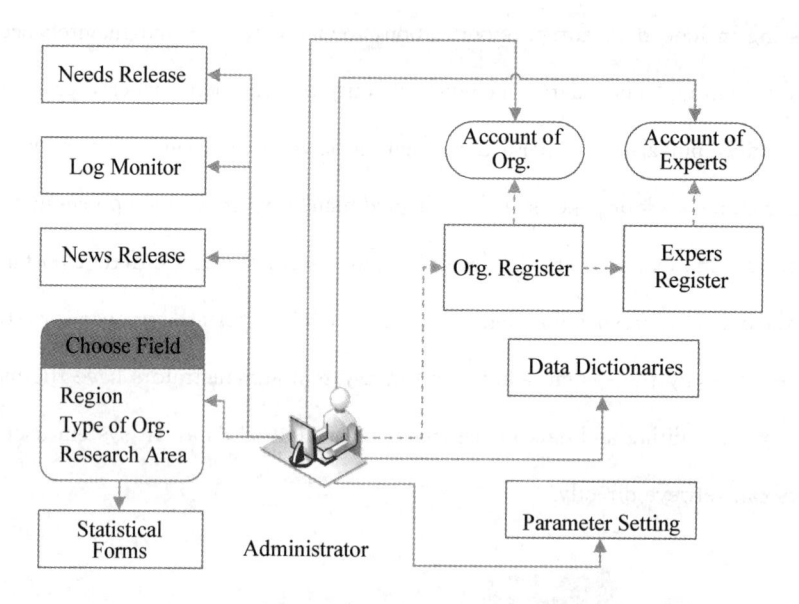

Fig. 7 Background Administration Process

The process shown by the dotted line is the user registration process, including institutional user and expert user registration. Experts cannot register as a system user unless they are associated with a think tank. The identity management process is responsible for the management of user accounts of different identities, including adding, deleting, changing, querying, password resetting, permission setting, and auditing of front-end registered users. The log management process mainly records all actions related to operations in the frontground and background for the convenience of operation auditing and troubleshooting. The parameter setting process mainly sets some control parameters of the system, including the email setting of sending emails, setting of information related to website crawling (frequency, time, etc.), log retention time of log management, and log size. The news release process mainly means CTTI's own news release, modification, deletion, review release, and revocation. The statistical analysis process mainly includes the statistics of the think tanks, experts, achievements and activities embodied, as well as the statistics of the region, organization type and research area of think tanks.

(3) Diversified Assessment Functions

The CTTI assessment is a multi-factor assessment model, which includes dozens or even hundreds of factors to maximize the authenticity of the think tank assessment. Based on the MRPAI algorithm, the CTTI system introduces customized assessment function that can be flexibly configured and subject assessment by experts. On the one hand, the system has statistic function of configurable fields, which allows different types and different dimensions of statistical results to be displayed, so that users can more intuitively observe the state of the data, freeing users from cumbersome reports and helping them deal with their daily management tasks quickly and easily. After logging in to the system, advanced users are free to choose data dimensions according to the target and focus of assessment. Then they can configure these dimensions according to their preferences and eventually obtain a customized ranking as a result of the assessment. On the other hand, in terms of think tank assessment, experts' impression makes an essential dimension. The CTTI system has now included nearly 10,000 experts, who will be incorporated into the pool of subjective assessment resources for think tanks. The system will send a list of think tanks to be assessed as a link in an email to experts, who will log into the system to grade them. Then advanced users or system administrators will make an integrated calculation of both the results of subjective assessment and those of quantitative assessment.

It is worth mentioning that the CTTI system adopts the mainstream big data analysis technology, and has realized the offline data statistics, analysis and mining functions of the think tank data. It aims to objectively evaluate and sort the think tank institutions and experts from different perspectives, mainly including parallel comparison among think tanks and that among experts, as well as how think tanks and experts are likely to develop in their particular fields. It is intended to provide the Party and the government with decision-making service and give statistical support for policy consultation in the designated areas.

All think tank users have access to basic functions corresponding to CTTI main system such as searching, browsing, managing, data processing and assessment.

2.2 Overview of CTTI Data Inclusion

Up to now, CTTI has included 706 institutions, 11,992 experts, 17,878 events, and 115,421 achievements. It means that CTTI has covered various types and large volume of think tank data, which can meet the different needs of think tank information retrieval to a certain extent.

Take expert information for example, through the background statistics, more than three-quarters of the experts who have filled in the academic information have received doctoral education, and 15% of the experts have received master's education, while undergraduates, junior college students and experts with other qualifications account for less than 10% (Fig. 8). It shows that the new think tank has more high-level intellectual resources, and most of the experts have received professional academic research training and education, and they are proficient in a certain field. Therefore, we still have confidence in the human capital of the construction of new think tank.

At the same time, we also have explored the distribution of experts in the discipline. According to Fig. 9, these experts are distributed in 13 subject areas. Among them, nearly three-quarters of the experts are from Economics, Law or Management, with the largest number of experts in Economics, accounting for 26%, and experts in Law and Management accounting for 23% and 20% respectively. In

addition to these three

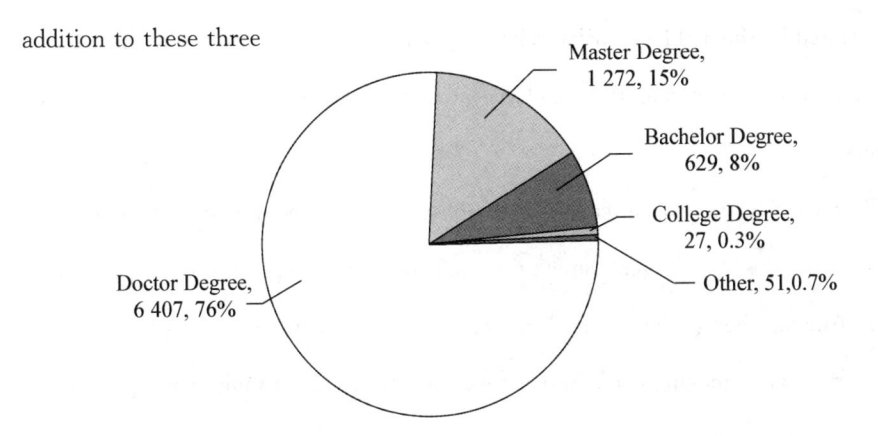

Fig. 8　Distribution of Experts' Education Background

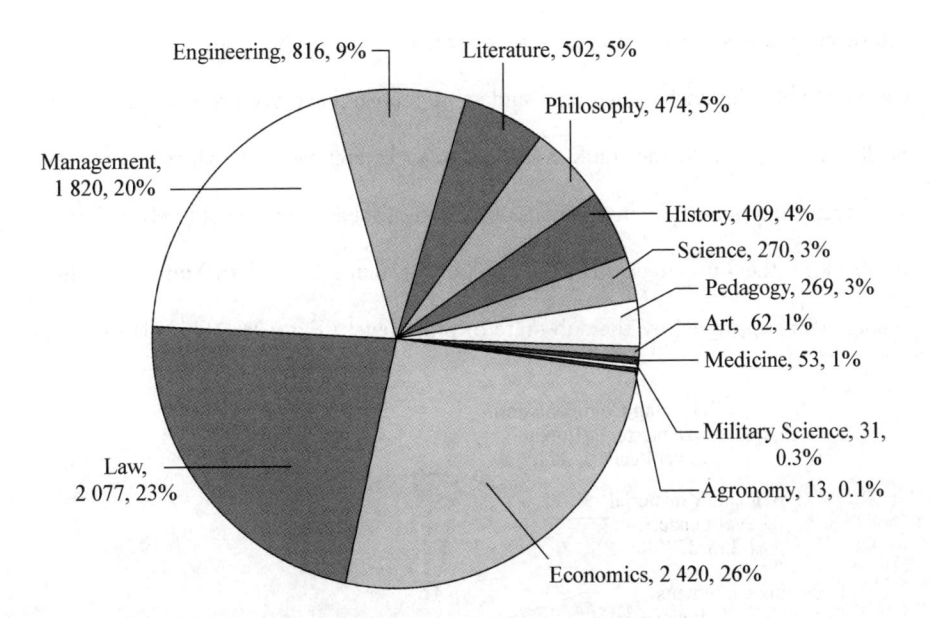

Fig. 9　Distribution of Experts' Specialized Fields

types of disciplines, Engineering experts account for 9%, experts in Literary and Philosophy each account for 5%, History experts account for 4%, Science and Education each account for 3%, and Art, Medicine, Military and Agronomy experts are less than 1%. It can be concluded that China's new think tank experts are mainly concentrated in the field of social sciences. There are few experts in the field of natural sciences and humanities, and the structure of experts is still to be further optimized.

By reviewing the data of each sub-database of CTTI, we found that the product database contains the largest amount of information, covering products of many fields. Among them, the internal reference is the most characteristic and most important decision-making consultation result in China's think tank, and source think tanks have contributed nearly 8,000 articles by now. However, according to the statistics of the internal reference results of source think tanks, 76% of the internal reference reports failed to get a response after submission. The factor of confidentiality cannot be ruled out, and some reports have been commented on but no feedback was given to the think tanks. Among the approved internal reference reports, 17% received comments or instructions at the provincial and ministerial level, 3% received feedback at the bureau/department level, and about 2% of the internal reference reports were approved by the sub-state or state level (Fig. 10). This also reflects to

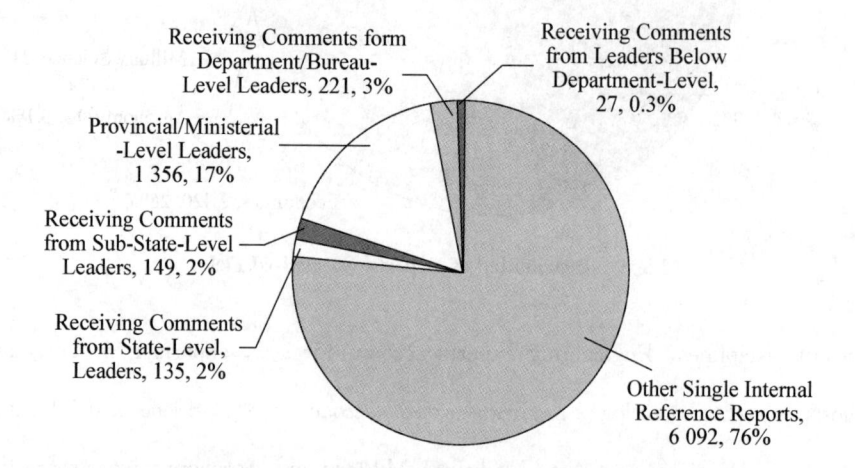

Fig. 10   Comments Received by Internal Reference Reports of Source Think Tanks

some extent that there is a certain mismatch between the supply of policy research and the decision-making needs of the new think tanks, and the current think tanks need to offer better-targeted and more timely research and consultation service.

Secondly, from the quantitative statistics, the paper has always been the main product of the source think tank. In the chart of "Papers Published by Source Think Tanks", we conclude the following results according to the journals in which the papers were included in the core journal catalogues (Fig. 11). Since a paper may be included in different core journal catalogues at the same time, we only count the number of source think tank papers included in each core journal catalog. Obviously, CSSCI has the largest number of papers, and 20,000 papers are from CSSCI source journals; SCI and SSCI have the number of papers ranging from 1,000 to 2,000; and

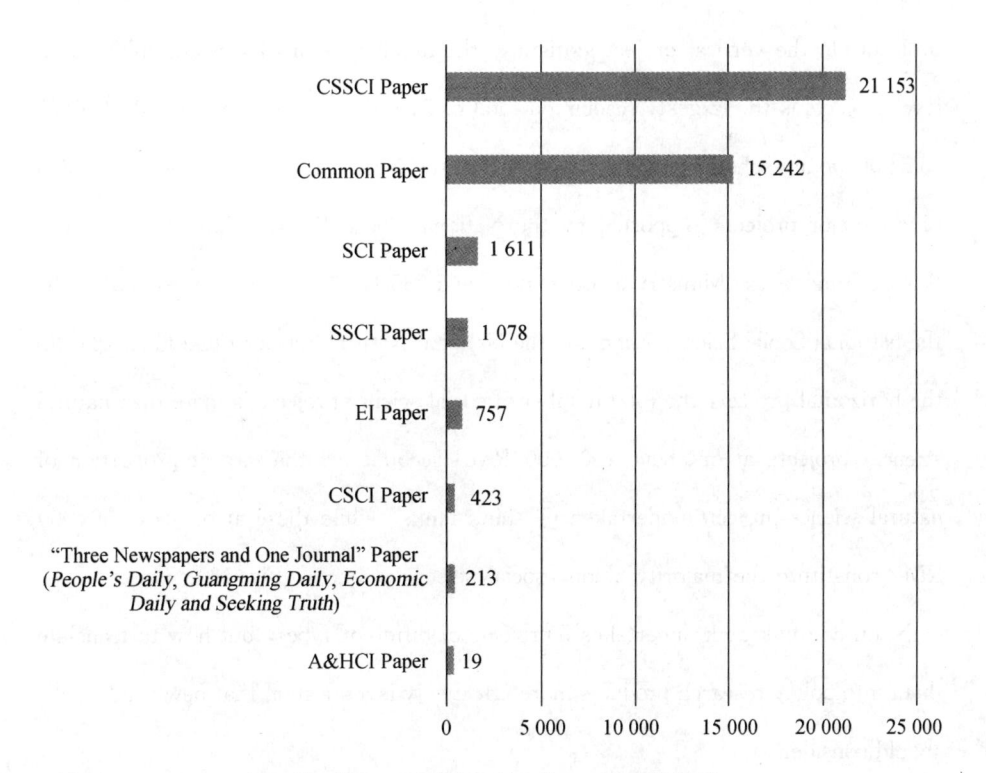

Category	Count
CSSCI Paper	21 153
Common Paper	15 242
SCI Paper	1 611
SSCI Paper	1 078
EI Paper	757
CSCI Paper	423
"Three Newspapers and One Journal" Paper (*People's Daily, Guangming Daily, Economic Daily and Seeking Truth*)	213
A&HCI Paper	19

Fig. 11　Papers Published by Source Think Tanks

the "Three Newspapers and One Journal" (*People's Daily*, *Guangming Daily*, *Economic Daily* and *Seeking Truth*) have published 213 papers, only accounting for 1% of the CSSCI inclusions. What needs to be affirmed is that most of the source think tanks have sound academic research foundation. However, think tank research is different from academic research and basic theoretical research in the general sense. It must emphasize service consciousness and pioneering and innovative ability. The new think tank system with college and university think tank as main body should focus on improving the attributes of think tank and realize reasonable resource allocation between academic research and decision-making services.

In addition, source think tanks have different types of vertical and horizontal projects, and the number of vertical projects is almost twice that of horizontal projects. In the vertical project statistics, the number of provincial and ministerial-level projects is the largest, reaching a total of 2,051 (47%); there are 685 (16%) common/young scholar projects supported by the National Social Science Fund, 306 (7%) major projects supported by the National Social Science Fund or the Social Science Fund of the Ministry of Education, and 235 (5%) key projects supported by the National Social Science Fund and the National Natural Science Fund (Fig. 12). In the horizontal project, the total number of social science projects is more than natural science; projects at or above 100,000 RMB account for the largest proportion of natural science projects undertaken by think tanks, while those at or above 50,000 RMB constitute the majority among social science projects (Fig. 13). On average, each source think tank undertakes 7 projects of different types, but how to translate them into policy research products more effectively is a question that new think tanks should consider.

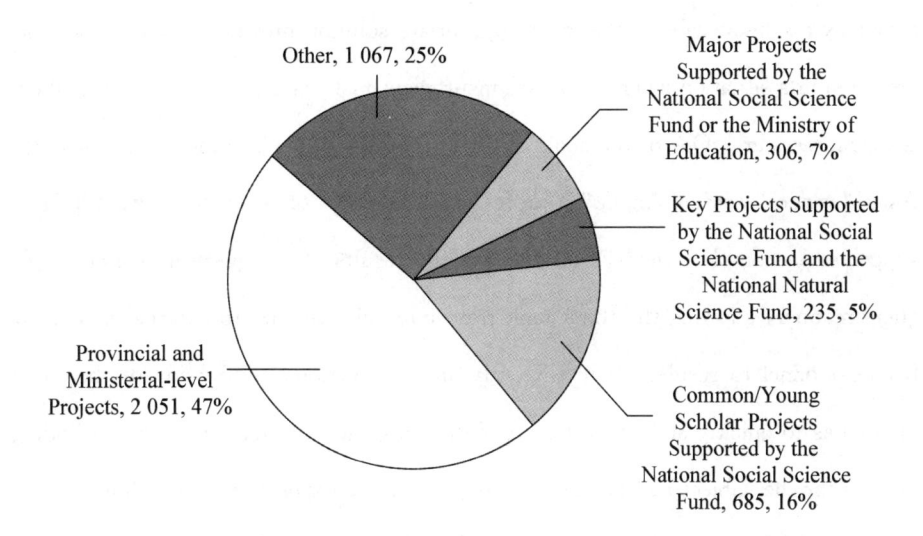

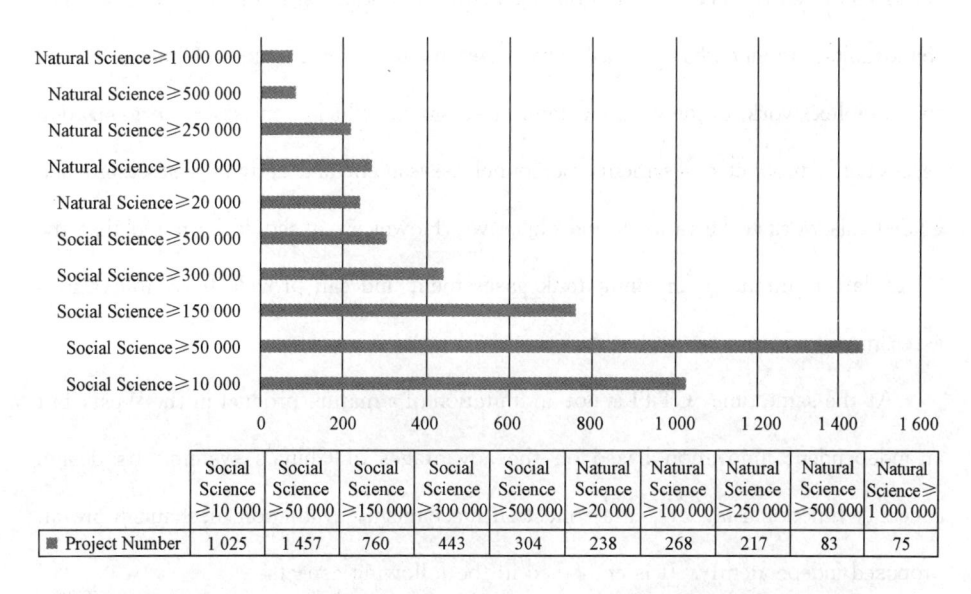

Fig. 12 Source Think Tank Projects by Type

	Social Science ≥10 000	Social Science ≥50 000	Social Science ≥150 000	Social Science ≥300 000	Social Science ≥500 000	Natural Science ≥20 000	Natural Science ≥100 000	Natural Science ≥250 000	Natural Science ≥500 000	Natural Science ≥1 000 000
Project Number	1 025	1 457	760	443	304	238	268	217	83	75

Fig. 13 Source Think Tank Projects by Type (Social Science/Natural Science)

2.3 The Role and Impact of CTTI

CTTI's user base includes governments, enterprises and social organizations, etc. These users have a large number of policy research and consulting needs, but they may not know who is the most appropriate solution provider. And think tanks are often in a situation where there are insufficient tasks and they have no idea where the customers are. One of the goals of CTTI is to solve this information asymmetry. As a "vertical search engine" (professional search) of a think tank, CTTI is supported by complete fields, and displays the results of the query in a multi-angle query manner, showing the think tank from internal structure to external activities, from personnel to results. It intelligently analyses various information of the think tank so as to quickly and accurately retrieve the target information, such as finding experts for the subject and finding the subject for the experts, thereby eliminate the "information asymmetry" between the think tank and users. The successful launch of CTTI has filled the blank of data management and online assessment tools in China's think tanks, provided basic data for the assessment of think tanks in China, clarified the complex work of new think tank assessment which consists of organization assessment, product assessment, personnel assessment and activity assessment and guided this work to be rational and objective. However, it should be noted that the CTTI data is intended for think tank assessment and can provide basis for various assessment.

At the same time, CTTI is not an imitation of a mature product in the West, but an independent innovation based on the advantages of China's system. Its design concept, functional layout, data collection mechanism, evaluation mechanism are all proposed independently. It is embodied in the following aspects:

First, CTTI establishes a data collection mechanism for co-construction and sharing, and attaches importance to the objectivity and accuracy of the data. At present, there are three ways to collect data in the system: (1) report by source think tanks and experts; (2) manual collection by China Think Tank Research and

Evaluation Center of Nanjing University; (3) automatic grab of online data. The first method is the mainstream. The data is input by think-tank administrators or experts and submitted to the CTTI background for review. Each piece of data can not be submitted to the database until it is verified by the background. This kind of data collection mechanism looks labor-intensive. However, thanks to the most popular "crowdsourcing" (crowdfunding) model, data is constructed and shared by users and the data collection costs are afforded by each participant, making them relatively low. The manual mode greatly improved the accuracy and objectivity of the data. In order to reduce the situation in which the data is interfered, the numerical value of impact of each expert in each think tank of the CTTI is automatically calculated according to the reported data, except for a few fields filled out by the background administrator.

Second, CTTI's UI design and user experience have reached the forefront of similar products. For example, CTTI allows hundreds of people to enter data at the same time. Since collaborative research is a normal state in modern scientific research, there must be such a scene where different experts and different think tanks have entered the same literature under their own names. Therefore, when data is entered in the CTTI, as long as the associated data appears, the system automatically pulls the existing data and allows the nearest entrant to modify it, which not only eliminates the same data, but also saves data entry. In addition, in order to help data entry personnel to accurately enter data without consulting the system manual, CTTI provides data entry prompts for almost every field. The prompts give explanation as well as examples of the field.

Third, system and data security of CTTI have reached the level of quasi-financial data security. On the deployment solution, CTTI deploys the application server separating from the data server and adopts the internal and external network isolation scheme. Public network users can only access the application server and cannot directly access the data server, which ensures data security. In terms of communication protocols, CTTI uses https SSL encryption protocol to ensure that all request data is encrypted during transmission, preventing an attacker from illegally accessing the system by intercepting the tampering request content. Due to the large amount of data collected by CTTI, in order to prevent the system data from being easily stolen, CTTI also make the design of anti-smashing network, adopting the B/S architecture and scientific permission setting and role allocation to ensure the availability and controllability of information. When general visitors access system, they can only query the most basic data and can not see the full picture of the system.

Fourth, CTTI has innovated a user tiered service model. In addition to the policy research institutions of the Party and government that need to use think tanks, the CTTI users also cover civil affairs bureaus and propaganda departments that are responsible for the registration and guidance of the think tank, internal users such as think tank administrators and experts, academic propaganda units like universities, media, and research institutes, companies and other profit-making organ as well as the general public. CTTI designed a layered service solution for different levels of users and provided targeted services. Different levels of users have access to different levels and types of data. For example, various statistical icons and statistical tools are designed in consideration of the needs of the administration departments. In the aspect of data presentation and export, the needs of think tanks are fully taken into consideration, and think tanks and experts can easily manage and export data in CTTI.

Fifth, CTTI has established a statistical indicator system and metadata standards for new types of think tanks with Chinese characteristics in a certain sense. More than 900 fields included by the system realize a comprehensive coverage of various attributes of think tank basic information, expert information, product information, and activity information, and give three-dimensional portraits of various elements of the think tank. These data fields can be used as metadata for future development of other think tank systems.

Overall, since the system was launched, CTTI has been freely tested by more than 60 university libraries, such as Peking University, Renmin University of China, Fudan University, Nanjing University, Southeast University, etc. ; online visits have reached nearly 2 million times, and it becomes an important platform to find think tank and think tank experts in China and its influence is increasing day by day.

At the same time, Shandong Academy of Social Sciences (SASS) and Tianjin Federation of Social Science (TFSS) have become members of the CTTI think tank community, having completed their local system deployment. "China Think Tank Index" Tianjin Edition (CTTI - TJ) was first established and officially put into operation in 2018, and the integrated business management system of social science federation which was integrated with it has also been put into use. At present, there are more than 20 cloud think tanks, over 240 think tanks, and more than 2,000 think tank experts in CTTI-TJ. The conference management, project management, social science awards, journal editors, annual conference papers and other services of Tianjin Federation of Social Science will directly deploy CTTI-TJ data resources. Its new business data will also be directly written into the database, making the CTTI data alive and useful. With the online launch of CTTI - TJ, Tianjin Federation of Social Science also explored to establish a dynamic management mechanism of CTTI source think tank, ranking the CTTI source think tanks in Tianjin every year and the latter 10% will face elimination.

In January 2018, China Think Tank Research and Evaluation Center of Nanjing

University and the Think Tank Research and Release Center of *Guangming Daily* jointly edited and published the reference book named *China Think Tank Index*, which has been widely collected by domestic think tanks and university libraries, and also has been collected by some world-renowned think tank libraries such as Brookings Institution and Kissinger Research Center. In May 2018, the 2017 *CTTI Think Tank Report* (Bilingual Edition) based on CTTI source think tank data was successfully published, and the English version was published in full text by ON THINK TANK, an internationally famous think tank research website. Since then, many overseas think tank researchers have paid high attention to it. At 8:00 pm on December 6, 2018, the website director Enrique Mendizabal and the Washington Metropolitan Institute researcher Dr. Milton and other dozens of experts and scholars were online at the same time, and they invited Professor Li Gang from China Think Tank Research and Evaluation Center of Nanjing University as the author representative of *CTTI Think Tank Report* (2017). They had a heated discussion on topics such as China's new think tank construction and *CTTI Think Tank Report* (2017). The promotion of *China Think Tank Index* and *CTTI Think Tank Report* (2017) has played a positive role in the CTTI source think tanks.

With the increasing influence of CTTI at home and abroad, and the steady increase in the number of think tank community members and think tank clouds, a period of fast development will surely come for the growth of system data. When that happens, by virtue of an academic community made up of nearly 10,000 experts and the capacity for customized, objective and quantitative assessment, CTTI will become a crucial tool for the think tank community, capable of both management and assessment—a tool that can help push ahead with the construction of new types of Chinese think tanks.

3 Addition to Catalogue of CTTI's Source Think Tanks in 2018

3.1 Principles of Source Think Tank Addition

Since the 19th National Congress of the Communist Party of China, the construction of new types of think tanks with Chinese characteristics has entered a new era of stable development. Relevant central ministries and commissions and relevant provinces and cities have selected their key think tanks and think tanks for priority development. In order to enable the CTTI source think tank objectives to more accurately reflect the development trend of new think tanks, the CTTI team decided to start the 2018 CTTI source think tank supplementation work on the basis of the full discussion and asking for experts' advice. They will continue the combination of voluntary application by think tanks, data submission, expert review and diagnostic research and there will be high requirements for the selection of the second batch.

(1) Requirements for Addition

We should adhere to the same standards that were applied to the selection of the first batch of think tanks. Think tanks that expect to be added will be considered in terms of the following seven steps, with particular focus on whether they operate as substantial entities and whether they are highly capable of policy research and advice as indicated by successful products. Those who have been identified by provinces, cities, ministries and commissions as provincial and ministerial-level key think tanks and think tanks for priority development (policy research bases) are preferred.

Table 1 Benchmarks for the Selection of Source Think Tanks

	Details	Quantitative Indicator
Political Requirement	Compliance with state laws and regulations	

Continued

	Details	**Quantitative Indicator**
Academic Foundation	Full-time think tank researchers have published papers in academic journals in the past two years	In the past two years, each full-time researcher has published at least one paper in any CSSCI source journal, *People Daily*, or the theoretical edition of *Guangming Daily*
Area of Research	Having a long-studied area for decision-making consultation with distinct characteristic	
Form of Organization	A relatively stable and well-regulated research entity	Having official document of approval for establishment or other documentary evidence
Form of Organization	A sound management structure	Having article of association and organizations like a board of directors and an academic committee
Support in Resources	A certain number of full-time/part-time researchers and administrators	Having one or two pacesetters, at least five full-time researchers, and at least five part-time researchers and research assistants
Support in Resources	Guaranteed and sustainable source of funds	At least 300,000 yuan of annual funds
Support in Resources	Fixed work place and basic equipment	An independent office with a size of at least 50 square meters
Operation and Products	Regular research, consultation and meetings	Holding at least three events per year
Operation and Products	Submission of research products	Officially releasing (or submitting to users) at least three research reports and three journal articles per year
Operation and Products	Website and new media	Having an independent website and a new media public account in WeChat or Weibo
Operation and Products	Serial publications	Having such printed or electronic publications as periodicals and internal references

Continued

	Details	Quantitative Indicator
International Cooperation and Exchange	Qualified for international cooperation and exchange with certain international impact	

(2) Rules of Addition

The think tanks of a university can be recommended by the university's research supervision department or by themselves. In the latter case, they should still obtain approval from that department. We have limited the number of CTTI source think tanks from each college or university in order to ensure fairness in the assessment of source think tanks and the university think tank index. However, such restrictions are not applicable to strong and highly active university think tanks that have distinct characteristics, abundant products, and flexible mechanisms. Besides, as for regions, categories and policy areas in which smaller numbers of think tanks have been selected, we will give them full consideration and an appropriate measure of preference during the adding process.

(3) Addition Procedures

i) Think tanks expecting to be added should fill out the attached form

ii) Qualification review

iii) Create accounts for think tanks that are up to the standard

iv) Think tanks that have passed the primary selection fill in the data

v) Data review

vi) Screen out the think tanks up to the CTTI criteria for the quality and quantity of data

vii) CTTI expert panel review

viii) Announce the addition list and issue the CTTI source think tank certificate.

3.2 The Process of Adding Source Think Tanks in 2018

The adding process was officially launched when the CTTI issued "2018 Notice on the Addition of CTTI Source Think Tanks" on July 17, 2018. Think tanks expecting to be added were required to fill out "2018 CTTI Source Think Tank Addition Application Form" and provide their basic information as well as opinions from the research supervision departments of the organizations in charge of them or the organizations they are directly affliated to for qualification review. The adding received strong support from think tanks and research management departments. By September 30, 2018, the CTTI Addition Work Group had received nearly 200 application materials of various types, most of which are provincial or ministerial-level key (nurturing) think tanks, and some are Ministry of Education (or state) key research bases, as well as several high-end cultivation think tanks of a country. The CTTREC of Nanjing University and the TTRRC of *Guangming Daily* made an initial selection of 87 qualified think tanks after joint surveys, discussions and reviews.

After the primary selection was completed, the Addition Work Group sent letters to the selected think tanks for data collection. Thanks to efforts from all quarters, these think tanks entered large amounts of precious data, including their basic information, experts, activities and products, in a responsive and meticulous manner between October 11 and November 20, 2017, which gave a strong support to the CTTI addition efforts.

As soon as data collection was over, the Work Group organized a team of experts for a second evaluation of the think tanks that had passed the primary selection, based on the data they filled in, their application forms and the survey results, by the standard of scientificity completeness and the corresponding competitiveness of data.

Think tanks which had not fulfilled the obligations they had been notified of during the primary selection, or which had failed to provide adequate and valid data for expert review, would be excluded from the addition list by the Wok Group.

After above procedures, it was finally decided that 84 think tanks would be added to CTTI this time. These include 1 think tank of Party/government organization, 2 think tanks of academy of social sciences, 1 think tank of the Party school or administrative college, 79 university think tanks and 1 think tank of the research institution.

On the other hand, Tianjin Federation of Social Science (TFSS), Nanjing University and *Guangming Daily* have established strategic cooperation since 2016. In accordance with the three-party strategic cooperation agreement, the 2018 addition of CTTI source think tanks in Tianjin was organized and implemented by TFSS. The three phases of data reporting, addition reporting and addition review got positive response from think tanks and superior supervisory units in Tianjin. TFSS launched the work of CTTI - TJ data reporting in the second half of 2018. By the end of November, more than 200 think tanks in Tianjin, especially those who expected to be added rigorously and meticulously entered a large amount of data of their basic information, experts, activities, products, etc., strongly supporting the follow-up addition review work. Based on it, TFSS clarified the addition reporting principle, which took both the requirements of the national think tank and the characteristics of the Tianjin think tank into consideration, and carried out the work of addition reporting. By the end of the application, a total of 32 applications from 14 units had been received, covering the major universities and private think tanks in Tianjin. After formal review, 30 candidate think tanks were selected to participate in the addition review. In order to ensure the fairness and impartiality of the addition review, TFSS repeatedly deliberated and formulated a detailed review plan. Through the qualification review, quantitative scoring, and MRPA scoring, the top 21 think tanks were recommended as CTTI source think tanks.

Finally, having modified and corrected CTTI's existing source think tank list, plus 84 new think tanks added this year, and 21 think tanks recommended by Tianjin, CTTI has 706 official source think tanks.

3.3 Tianjin Source Think Tanks Addition Experience

Tianjin takes a big proportion in this year's think tank addition work. Since the publication of CTTI's first batch of source think tanks in 2016, it is the first time that provincial (city, autonomous region) units have taken the responsibility of organizing the addition of source think tanks in the region. The reason why TFSS can successfully complete this work can be listed as follow:

First, the leaders of TFSS attached great importance to the addition, which ensured that Tianjin became the first area to organize the work. In order to construct CTTI - TJ and improve the CTTI source think tank addition in Tianjin, TFSS leaders went to Beijing and Nanjing several times to discuss the specific content and details of the cooperation strategy among the three parties. When the addition began, TFSS Party Group paid high attention to it and conducted many researches to ensure that the standard was supplemented, the process was serious, and the results were fair.

Second, the foundation of Tianjin think tank work ensured that the addition was completed with high quality. Since 2015, TFSS has successively launched a series of think tank work. They not only established think tank organizations of different types and levels, but also constructed a think tank information platform with CTTI - TJ as the database. Up to now, Tianjin Think Tank Alliance has nearly a hundred member think tanks, and the think tank information platform has more than 20 cloud think tanks, more than 200 think tank institutions, and over 2,000 think tank experts to share information and work collaboratively online. The preliminary work has laid a solid foundation for this addition with high quality and at a high level.

Third, support from think tanks and their superiors ensured the addition completed on time and in good quality. Since the release of the addition notice, Tianjin social science community has shown great enthusiasm and serious attitude. Despite the heavy workload of data reporting and the relatively short preparation time for addition declaration and report, think tanks and their superiors worked closely together and carefully organized the work to finish it on time.

The CTTI source think tank addition in Tianjin is the first year of the attempt. It has drawn on national experience and explored methods suitable for local characteristics. Features can be listed as follow:

The first is to comply benchmark of the country and pay attention to the locality. In the reporting stage, Tianjin with the formulated local reporting standards that correspond to national reporting indicators, and adjusted the values of some reporting indicators according to the construction situation of local think tanks. At the same time, in order to highlight the characteristic of the local think tank that "Tianjin Think Tank Serves for Tianjin", it also designed indicators that investigate how the think tank serve local economy and society development in the reporting and review stage.

Second, it has wide participation and high degree of recognition. Think tanks applying for participation in this addition basically covered Tianjin's major colleges and universities, research institutes and key social think tanks. Each think tank and its superior supervisory department highly recognized and valued it. They repeatedly consult TFSS for details of this addition. Some even organized the think tanks to manoeuvre the presentation in advance.

Third, the standards are clear and the assessment is scientific. The TFSS successively formulated clear addition reporting standards, qualification review standards, meeting evaluation and scoring standards, and used CTTI - TJ to automatically calculated MRPA scores. Considering that think tank work is different from traditional scientific research work, TFSS hired experts from different fields such as decision-making consulting management and demand departments and think tank management departments, think tank experts and other experts to form an assessment expert group. It can avoid the problems brought by appointing university professors who are the review experts and applicants at the same time, and can guarantee the scientificity and impartiality of the review.

The fourth characteristic is dynamic management and systematic planning. There are 50 CTTI source think tanks in Tianjin after the 2018 addition. TFSS will make full use of the massive data resources in the database to implement dynamic management and last place elimination mechanism to the 50 CTTI source think tanks, so that the database can be "alive" and "efficient" and the think tank can be "active". At the same time, the two tasks of CTTI source think tank addition and CTTI - TJ data report will also be combined with other measures held by TFSS, such as think tank classification evaluation, supporting key think tanks and social think tank management. They will together shape a think tank construction system in Tianjin social science community and form a think tank work structure with outstanding emphasis and hierarchy.

3.4 Analysis of the CTTI Source Think Tank Data

(1) Regional Distribution of CTTI Source Think Tanks

First, the regional distribution of the CTTI source think tanks is shown in Fig. 14, according to the administrative division of China. Overall, North China and East

China show a noticeable superiority in number. Source think tanks in these two regions account for more than a half of all the selected think tanks. There are 269 selected think tanks, or 38.22% of all the selected organizations in North China, closely followed by East China, which is 190. The distribution of source think tanks is relatively even in other regions.

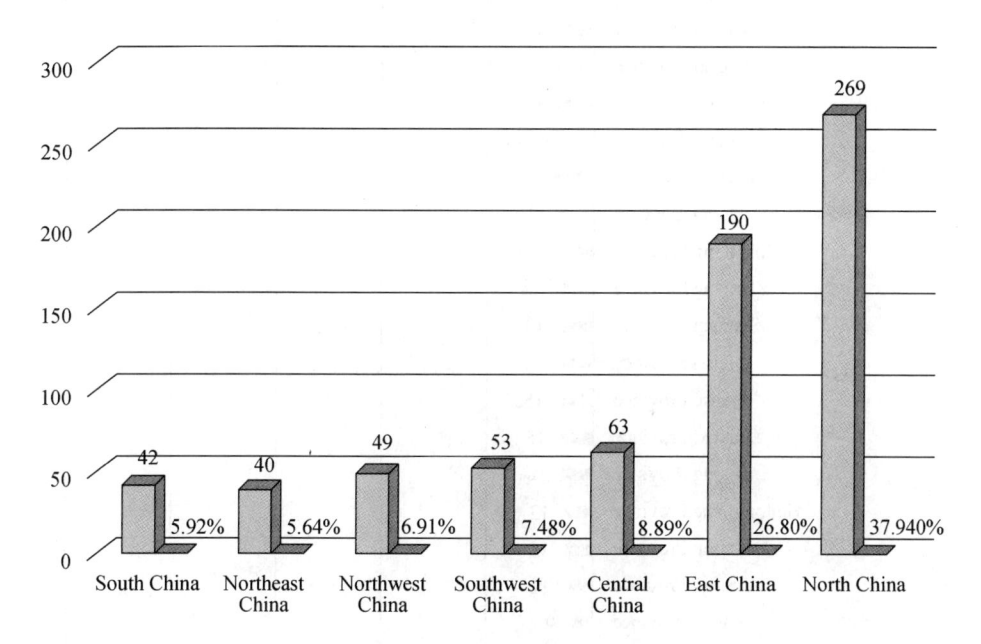

Fig. 14 Regional Distribution of the CTTI Source Think Tanks

Secondly, compared with previous years, the regional distribution of the top five source think tanks is basically unchanged, still in Beijing, Shanghai, Tianjin, Jiangsu and Hunan. Among them, a total of 197 think tanks are selected in Beijing, and the total number of source think tanks ranks first, which is inseparable from Beijing's special political, economic and cultural status. The rankings of Shanghai, Tianjin and Jiangsu closely followed. As a major province for the development of social sciences, Hunan has fully integrated the advantages of resources within the province in recent years, and the construction of new think tanks has achieved remarkable results. At the same time, Guangdong, Hubei and Shaanxi also continues to expand their think tanks, with the number of selected think tanks reaching more than 20. In addition,

Province (Region/City)	Number
Beijing City	197
Shanghai City	78
Tianjin City	47
Jiangsu Province	45
Hunan Province	33
Guangdong Province	29
Hubei Province	26
Shaanxi Province	25
Chongqing City	18
Shandong Province	18
Zhejiang Province	17
Sichuan Province	16
Hebei Province	16
Gansu Province	15
Jiangxi Province	15
Liaoning Province	14
Heilongjiang Province	13
Jilin Province	13
Yunnan Province	12
Fujian Province	9
Anhui Province	8
Hainan Province	8
Inner Mongolia Autonomous Region	6
Guanxi Province	5
Ningxia Hui Autonomous Region	4
Guizhou Province	4
Henan Province	4
Qinghai Province	3
Tibet Autonomous Region	3
Shanxi Province	3
Xinjiang Uyghur Autonomous Region	2

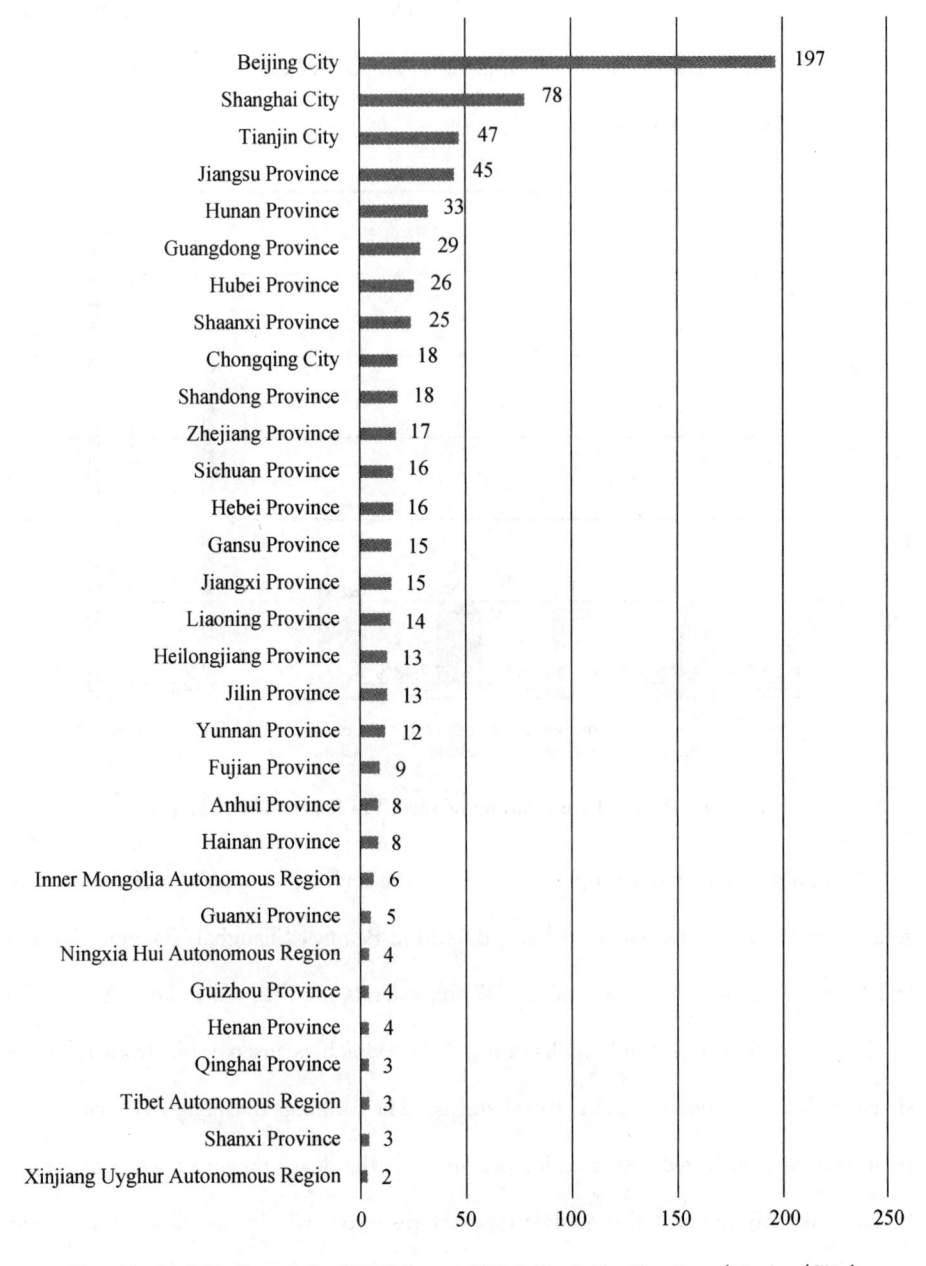

Fig. 15 Distribution of the CTTI Source Think Tanks by Province (Region/City)

the numbers of think tanks in Chongqing, Shandong, Zhejiang, Sichuan, Hebei, Gansu, Jiangxi, and Liaoning provinces have also been improved to some extent, and the construction of think tanks has presented a scene of "hundred flowers blooming".

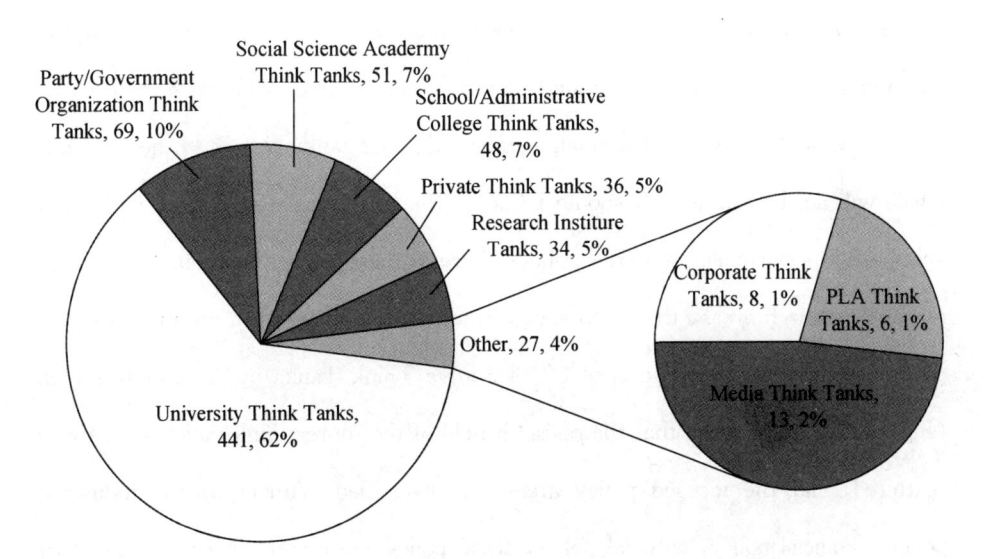

(2) Distribution of CTTI Source Think Tanks by Type

The statistical chart on the distribution of the CTTI source think tanks by type shows that, university think tank is still the most important type in source think tank with a total number of 441 and accounts for 62%. There are 69 (10%) think tanks in Party or government organizations, 51 (7%) in academies of social sciences, 48 (7%) in Party schools or administrative colleges, 36 (5%) private think tanks, 34 (5%) in research institutions, 13 (2%) media think tanks, 8 (1%) corporate think tanks, and 6 (1%) in the armed forces (Fig. 16).

Fig. 16 Distribution of CTTI Source Think Tanks by Type

From the overall distribution of think tank type, it is seen that the proportion of all kinds of think tanks has hardly changed much. Compared with last year, the numbers of think tanks of colleges and universities, Party and government departments, and the academies of social sciences have increased in different degrees. Among them, as mentioned above, the main body of the newly-added source think tanks is also think tanks of colleges and universities. Universities represented by Xi'an Jiaotong University, Shanghai Jiao Tong University, Beijing Jiaotong University and many other top-ranking universities have improved their own think tank strength and once again strengthened think tanks in colleges and univesities. For the latter two parts, there is also a small number of Party and government think tanks and academies of social sciences think tanks emerging, such as Northeast Asia Strategic Research Institute, Heilongjiang Social Development and Local Governance Research Institute, Shandong Academy of Innovation Strategy.

(3) CTTI Source Think Tank Distribution of Main Research Areas

Specialized division of labor is an important feature of modern new think tanks. According to the CTTI's background statistics, the source think tank involves 54 specific research fields, and a small number of think tanks choose "other" fields, which will not be counted. It should be noted that there are source think tanks that specialize in a particular research policy; there are also some think tanks that have multiple research areas, that is to say, a think tank is involved in multiple research policies. From the Distribution of CTTI Source Think Tanks by Area of Research (Fig. 17), it can be seen that the research field of the source think tanks is relatively scattered, and the focused policy areas are diversified. Among them, industrial policy, financial policy, cultural policy, fiscal policy and market policy are the most concerned five specific research areas of the source think tanks, and more than 100 think tanks are engaged in related fields.

In addition, there are many research focusing on think tanks that study diplomacy policy, social security policy, science and technology policy, resource policy,

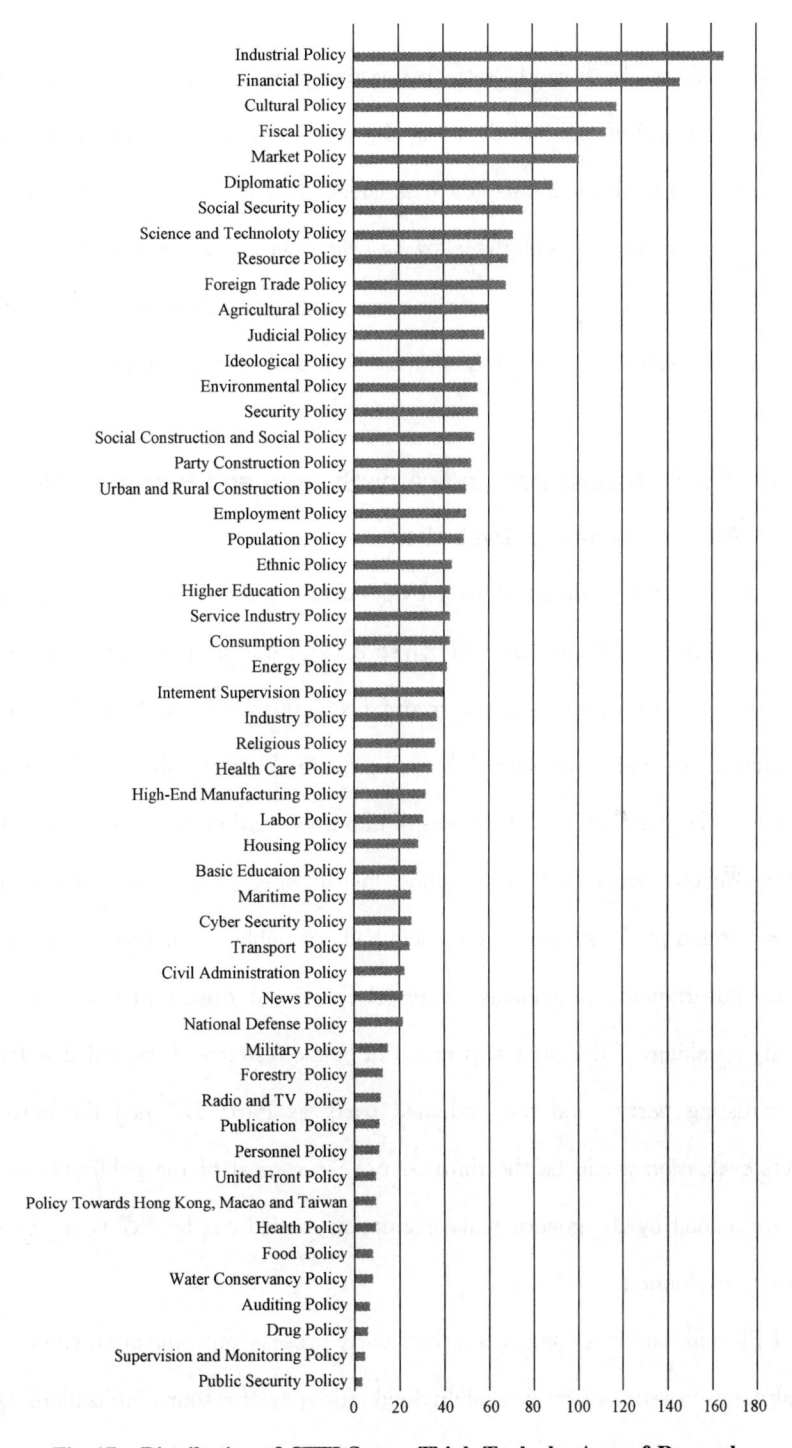

Fig. 17 Distribution of CTTI Source Think Tanks by Area of Research

and foreign trade policy. It can be seen that economic, social and cultural issues that are closely related to real life are still the areas of greatest concern for think tanks, and each area reflects different research forces of think tanks. In contrast, there are few specialized think tanks that study policies on the following fields: personnel; the United Front; Hong Kong, Macao and Taiwan; water conservancy; auditing; supervision and monitoring; drugs and public security. Think tanks in those industries are undeveloped.

4 The MRPAI Assessment Indicator System and Ranking Rule

4.1 Basic Principles of Evaluation

The think tank is designed to provide public policy research and consulting products, which is public and non-profit, so it is impossible to measure the value of think tanks and their products in full accordance with market mechanisms. Then the most common method of measuring the value of this kind of public product is public evaluation. There are innumerable types of public evaluation, which can be applied to public products, public services, public institutions, public governance, public environment and public systems. The main body of public evaluation is also diverse, including government, individuals, enterprises, social organizations, and so on. Generally speaking, if the party that invest in public resources is regarded as Party A (the entrusting party) and the evaluated party as Party B, then the party that conducts evaluation would be the third party. Since most of the public resources in China are funded by the government, evaluation carried out by NGOs can be called third-party evaluation.

CTTI think tank assessment is a third-party process/outcome-oriented evaluation of think tanks in terms of their capability and efficiency of resource utilization. During the process, we draw on relevant methods of the fourth-generation evaluation theory, combine with the specific reality of the field of think tank evaluation, and establish the following points as the basic principles of think tank evaluation.

(1) The purpose of evaluation is to professionally enhance the management of think tanks rather than generate power of governance or speech.

(2) Evaluation is the process of dialogue and exchange by which the evaluator learns from the evaluated. The evaluator and the evaluated need to participate in the evaluation process together, rather than unilateral disciplinary process.

(3) Evaluation involves systematic analysis based on data, the lack of which would make measurement impossible. Think ranks whose data are not available cannot be evaluated. The interpretation of the data in evaluation should be objective and accurate, and the results of the evaluation and analysis should not be distorted.

(4) The evaluation process must be fair and open, with verifiable and repeatable results and timely response to accountability demands from the public. The evaluator must have the essential professional qualifications.

(5) Business secrets must be respected, individuals' privacy protected, and basic security requirements be strictly complied with for state secrets.

(6) All for public benefit, the evaluation outcome is to be publicly shared in non-profit ways within a certain range.

4.2 Selection of the MRPAI Assessment Indicators

The fields in the CTTI database serve to portray think tanks, experts, products and activities. They are the metadata format and standard vocabulary for describing think tanks. Theoretically speaking, a richer vocabulary will make for a more accurate portrait. Based on these data fields, we hope to make quantitative and qualitative analysis of data from CTTI source think tanks with a combination of expertise in data science and specialized knowledge about modern think tank management, and offer the result to a think tank community. In this regard, this year's report is an improvement and supplementation on the basis of the existing MRPA evaluation system, and has established a new evaluation indicator system, MRPAI. It should be noted that when selecting and determining the measurement indicators, we do not cover every data field of the database, but make some choice. Specifically, we focus on the following principles when selecting those indicators:

(1) The granularity of the indicator data must be suited to their availability. Although China's new think tank construction has achieved certain results, think tanks differ enormously in their way of doing things, with a great variety in the form of raw data. Besides, China's think tanks have low data cumulativeness, and the awareness of data management is lacking. Most think tanks do not have long-term data archives except for the key centers under the Ministry of Education, which have standard data filling procedures. Such being the case, in order to encourage think tanks to apply for inclusion in CTTI and make it less difficult to fill in data, most of the database fields are specifically set up a reasonable number of required data items. As a result, when selecting MRPAI indicators, we must consider the availability of the actual data of CTTI field. Therefore, the MRPAI indicators were selected according to the following procedures:

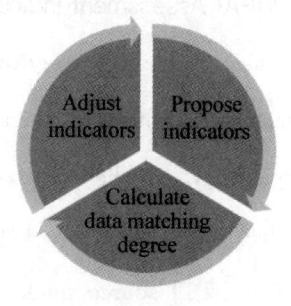

Fig. 18 MRPAI Indicator Selection Procedure

At the beginning, the proposed indicators are entered into the system one by one to match the data. If data availability is below 80%, the granularity of indicators is abandoned or lowered. Take the "think tank expert" indicator for example. Though we had expected to evaluate experts' professional titles and age structure, data matching showed that we have not acquired enough data in this field. However, the number of experts and the annual budget had been reported by 90% of the think tanks. So these two values were selected as basic indicators for measuring a think tank's resource (R).

(2) Indicator data must be highly essential, typical and expressive. The selected indicators must be essential and typical fields that can represent the attributes of think tanks. Such attributes are mainly reflected in a well-developed structure of governance, a strong tendency towards policy impact, proactive use of forums and meetings for greater public influence, and in-depth and pragmatic research and survey. Therefore, more indicators were selected from fields that can reflect such attributes (e. g. internal reference, written instructions or comments, research reports, projects, meetings, and research and survey) in order to highlight the attributes of think tanks.

(3) Indicators should be objective and systematic. The objectivity of indicators has two meanings: i) like CTTI data fields, indicators reveal the true attributes of think tanks as an integration of the most objective fields; ii) objective values instead of highly subjective estimates should be assigned to indicators. That indicators should be systematic refers to the existence of rigorously logical relationship between them. For instance, the five primary indicators of MRPAI reflect the performance logic of input and output. Only such indicators can make up what is called an indicator system.

(4) The indicator system must be conductive to the development of think tanks and suited to the status quo in this respect. If the construction of new types of think tanks with Chinese characteristics has achieved certain results in the past five years since 2013, then the next three years will be the crucial stage of the construction. It is a key stage for achieving high-quality development of new think tank construction. But we must also admit that there are still many problems such as inadequate understanding of how things work and the lack of standard procedures in operation. Therefore, we cannot measure the think tank according to international standards or standards that do not match to the present construction of China's think tanks. Otherwise, it would be easy to dampen the enthusiasm of the evaluated think tanks, and it would hardly help to develop think tanks by encouraging them and recognizing their performance.

According to these principles, we have selected 5 primary indicators and 24 secondary ones. The 5 primary indicators are M (management structure), R (resources), P (products), A (activities) and I (impact)—known as the MRPAI assessment indicators. As a result-oriented system for assessing the effectiveness of think tanks, MRPAI can evaluate a think tank from two dimensions—the quantity of resources used and the effect or effectiveness of resource utilization. It can measure a think tanks's size and output, its effectiveness, and the intensity of its attributes. Therefore, the MRPAI system is in accordance with the principles for indicator selection and suitable for effective measurement of CTTI source think tanks.

In terms of secondary indicators, when we are solely interested in R, we can measure the size of a think tank's budget and personnel. There is no doubt that a well-funded think tank with a large staff of experts and administrators is a big one. When we focus on P, we can measure the number of a think tank's research fundings. Obviously, a think tank with fruitful findings is a good one. When we only look at A, we can measure the number of events organized by a think tank. Though a think tank cannot be considered a good one just because it has held many events, one that rarely does so can never be a typical think tank. Such think tanks tend to be research centers in universities or the government's policy research offices. Although there is certain academic and policy influence, the think tank attributes may be weak. When we focus on I, we can measure the number of media reports and social impact. Media impact is one of the ways for think tanks to play the role in providing consultation for governments and educating the public, and it is also an important indicator to evaluate the level of think tanks.

An institution is usually considered to have strong think tank attributes when it has high values in $P1$, $P2$ and $P5$ and a high total value in the A and I category. MRPAI can also measure the effectiveness of a think tank, for its output divided by its resources equals its effectiveness.

Table 2 MRPAI Think Tank Assessment Indicators and Their Assigned Values

Primary Indicator	Code	Secondary Indicator	Code	Scoring Rule	Points
Management Structure	M	Board of Directors	$M1$	Assign value if yes	15
		Academic Committee	$M2$	Assign value if yes	10
		Advisory Committee	$M3$	Assign value if yes	10
		Management Team/Chief Expert	$M4$	Assign value if yes	10
		China Top Think Tank	$M5$	Assign value if yes	100
Resources	R	Annual Budget	$R1$	⩽1 million	20
				Assign value for each additional sum of 100,000 yuan	1

Continued

Primary Indicator	Code	Secondary Indicator	Code	Scoring Rule	Points
		Scientific Research Staff	R2	≤10 persons	40
				Multiplied by value for each additional person	2
		Administrative Staff	R3	≤5 persons	20
				Multiplied by value for each additional person	1
		Cyber Resources	R4	Has a portal in Chinese	20
				Has a portal in English	8
				Has a WeChat public account	8
				Has an official Weibo account	5
				Has a dedicated data acquisition platform	10
Products	P	Single internal reference reports with or without leaders' comments	P1	Assign value for each title	2
		Internal reference reports commented by leaders	P2	State level/per comment	30
				Sub-state level/per comment	20
				Provincial or ministerial level/per comment	10
				Sub-provincial or ministerial level/per comment	5
		Journals sponsored/run by Think Tanks	P3	Each CSSCI source journal	20
				Each common journal	10
				Each bulletin/collection of internal reference reports	8

Continued

Primary Indicator	Code	Secondary Indicator	Code	Scoring Rule	Points
		Books (officially published)	P4	Assign value for each report	2
		Research reports	P5	Assign value for each report	4
		Articles published in the theoretical edition of *People's Daily*, *Seeking Truth*, or *Guangming Daily*	P6	Assign value for each article	5
		Academic papers	P7	Each paper in CSSCI source journal	1
				Each paper included in SSCI/A&HCI	2
				Each paper included in CSCI/EI	1
				Each of other papers	0.5
		Vertical projects	P8	Vertical: major projects supported by National Social Science Fund or Social Science Fund of Ministry of Education	10
				Vertical: key projects supported by National Social Science Fund or National Natural Science Fund	6
				Vertical: common/young scholar projects supported by National Social Science Fund	4
				Vertical: provincial/ministerial level projects	2
				Vertical: others	0.5

Continued

Primary Indicator	Code	Secondary Indicator	Code	Scoring Rule	Points
		Horizontal projects	P9	Basic points for each project+1 mark point for every 100,000 *yuan*	
Activities	A	Conferences and meetings	A1	Each national conference sponsored or organized	10
				Each conference at the level of province, municipalities or Autonomous Region	5
				Each international conference	10
				Other meetings	3
		Training	A2	Each national training program	8
				Training on other levels	2
		Surveys and observations	A3	Each survey by leaders/experts at or above the sub-state level	15
				Each survey by leaders at or above the provincial/ministerial level	5
				Each survey by leaders/experts at other levels	2
				Outbound visits for survey or observation	1
Impact	I	Newspaper coverage	I1	Central level	5
				Provincial or ministerial level	4
				Local level	3
				Overseas media	2
				Other media	1

Continued

Primary Indicator	Code	Secondary Indicator	Code	Scoring Rule	Points
		Television coverage	I2	Central level	5
				Provincial or ministerial level	4
				Local level	3
				Overseas media	2
				Other media	1
		Internet coverage	I3	Central level	5
				Provincial or ministerial level	4
				Local level	3
				Overseas media	2
				Other media	1

4.3 Value Assignment for MRPAI Indicators

The weight of indicators can be distributed in many ways. The direct assignment method has been adopted for MRPAI because it is easy to understand, intuitive, open, and verifiable. The evaluated party can directly verify the accuracy of the values according to an established algorithm, which makes for effective dialogue between the evaluator and evaluated. However, this method entails a high demand for assessment; the values assigned should be reasonable and the assessment system must guarantee precision. Otherwise it would be impossible to give timely response to questioning from the evaluated party.

The Delphi Method has been adopted for value assignment in Table 2. Four rounds of questionnaire survey were conducted among 98 leaders and experts. The value assignment method is explained as follows.

The following circumstances have been taken into consideration when the values were assigned to the secondary MRPAI indicators in Table 2:

(1) The structural assessment of think tanks from $M1$ to $M4$ is only interested in the presence or absence of an internal management structure, without examining whether it works properly. This is compatible with the status quo of new think tanks in China; first we check if this internal structure exists, and we will not see if it works properly until we do measurements later. As a result, the value assigned is not high, with the full score being only 45 points. $M5$ is a special value assigned to what has been listed among China Top Think Tanks in recognition of such prestige.

(2) $R1$ looks at the annual budget. Considering the generally small size of Chinese think tanks, with an annual budget of one million yuan being the norm, there is no need differentiating think tanks with an annual budget below one million. Twenty points are assigned to each of such think tanks, with one extra point for each additional sum of 100,000 yuan.

(3) $R2$ and $R3$ consist of staff indicators and their values. We do not distinguish between full-time and part-time personnel. As a result of reforms in the personnel system, a part-time employee can also be a full-time one; moreover, it would be hard to say if think tank experts are full-time or part-time since most of them have flexible work hours. In view of this, 40 points are assigned to each institution that has 10 or fewer researchers, with 2 extra points for each additional person. There will be 20 points for each administrative team with 5 or fewer persons, with one extra point for each additional person. With the increasing standardization of system data, this part of the data may need to provide corresponding certification materials in the future, and each think tank should prepare the recruitment contracts as soon as possible.

(4) $R4$, or cyber resources, can actually be considered as outcomes of think tank

development. We see websites and other cyber resources as basic settings, just like work places. Since today's think tanks are not demanding when it comes to work places, there would be no way to verify whether they really have offices if they choose not to enter any data on this feature. Therefore, with respect to staff, funds, equipment and cyber resources, $R4$ focuses on cyber conditions while omitting the measurement of physical working conditions. All the indicators it involves are verifiable and feasible. Since most Chinese think tanks have paid inadequate attention to website construction and are quite unfamiliar with the use of social media, value assignment to this indicator is only based on presence or absence, without consideration of quality.

(5) Among the P indicators, high values are assigned to internal reference reports, leaders' instructions and comments, and research reports. The questioned experts commonly believed that these are major indicators of think tanks' influence on decision making and should carry more points. In fact, they also reflect the main purpose of building think tanks. The current points have been heightened according to experts' opinions. Since it is not easy for most provincial-level think tanks to obtain comments from state leaders, points for such comments do not make much difference for the total points of common think tanks. Such value assignment is relatively fair since MRPAI assessment focuses on comparing and ranking think tanks on the same levels. In order to encourage the writing of internal reference reports, values are assigned to any piece published in collections of such reports at or above the provincial or ministerial level (internally submitted serial publications), such as *Guangming Internal References*, with or without leaders' comments. The assignment of high values to the $P6$ indicator shows the special prestige of *People's Daily*, *Guangming Daily and Seeking Truth* in the Chinese system of policy discourse. Publishing

articles in any of them means expansion of influence on policy and the public.

(6) The MRPAI indicator system has accorded a relatively high status to think tanks' activities. High-level and high-caliber forums and conferences are important means by which think tanks can exert their influence. This is also a crucial feature that sets think tanks apart from traditional research institutions. Almost all of the world's famous think tanks are conference centers and major platforms for road shows of significant policies. As a result, high values are assigned to national or international conferences held by think tanks. There might be the undesirable practice of "erecting platforms and inviting celebrities", but this is only true for a very small number of think tanks. In addition to spreading information, conferences make one of the major channels by which think tanks can extend their research and policy networks.

Survey and observation is a method of research with Chinese characteristics for think tanks. "Without investigation, there is no right to speak", big data analysis cannot replace field survey. High values, therefore, are assigned to this type of activity in the MRPAI indicators.

(7) The focus of the *I* indicator is on the media impact of a think tank. At home and abroad, media impact has always been the focus of the think tank community. The citation rate of national or international newspapers, magazines, television and other media is also the most common public evaluation. This is because think tanks are different from traditional academic research institutions, and communication is as important as research for think tanks. Therefore, appearances or expressing opinions on television, newspapers, and the Internet are considered to be important manifestations of think tanks' influence. At present, we only include the coverage disseminated in newspapers, television and on the Internet since the application and influence of these three media in think tank communication are more extensive and

have certain quality guarantees. Different values are assigned to different levels of reports, and the central level is the most authoritative, so it is assigned with the highest value, and the values are successively decreased as the level of the report decreases. This year is the first time to introduce the I indicator. We will also consider incorporating more forms of new media indicators into the media influence evaluation.

5 The MRPAI Ranking Rules

5.1 Principle for Designing MRPAI Ranking Rules

Ranking is a crucial method of assessment and an important way to present the outcomes. In this method, the principal, universal, regular, stable and objective characteristics or elements of the object of assessment are compared according to one or a number of indicators, and the outcomes are presented in a particular form. The ranking method can effectively and visibly reveal the overall features of things in the same category and differences among them. However, details of individuals are likely to be overlooked, especially when there are too few indicators for ranking. Therefore, one must avoid the tendency of seeing the forest instead of the trees when using this method.

One needs to pay attention to the following things when using the ranking method:

1) Comparison within the same category. The accuracy of evaluation increases in proportion to similarity between the objects of evaluation. Therefore, when designing the MRPAI ranking algorithm, we always procede ranking with categorization to reduce error.

2) Multi-dimensional presentation. If the ranking result is presented in a single

dimension, one feature of the object of evaluation is likely to eclipse other features, which would make it difficult to reveal the diversity of its attributes. This would not only impede the repetitive expression of its information, but also lead to unfair evaluation. Therefore, MRPAI ranking makes a point of presenting the outcome in multiple dimensions.

5.2 MRPAI Ranking Rules

MRPAI offers thirteen kinds of think tank ranking, which fall into two categories—quantitative indicator ranking and effectiveness indicator ranking.

5.2.1 Ranking by Quantitative Indicators

1) The resource (R) ranking is based on the arithmetic sum of think tanks' annual budge ($R1$), research staff ($R2$), administrative staff ($R3$), and cyber resources ($R4$).

2) The product (P) ranking is based on the arithmetic sum of single internal reference reports ($P1$), leader-commented internal reference reports ($P2$), journals sponsored/run by think tanks ($P3$), books ($P4$), research reports ($P5$), articles published in the theoretical edition of *People's Daily*, *Seeking Truth*, or *Guangming Daily* ($P6$), academic papers ($P7$), vertical projects ($P8$), and horizontal projects ($P9$).

3) The activity (A) ranking is based on the arithmetic sum of conference and meetings ($A1$), training ($A2$), and survey and observations ($A3$).

4) The output (PAI) ranking, guided by output impact, is based on the formula $PAI=P+A+I$, i.e. the arithmetic sum of the value assigned to the three categories of indicators—product, activity and impact of media.

5) The integrated ($T(n)$) ranking is based on the formula $T(n)=R+M+P+A$, i.e. the arithmetic sum of the values assigned to the five categories of indicators—

resources, management, products, activity and impact of media.

These five kinds of ranking reflect think tanks' total resource and total product, describing the relative position of each CTTI source think tank in terms of resources and products. A think tank is bound to have different positions in the five types of ranking. Such difference reflects its individual attributes, and showcases its unique features.

Besides these five ranking rules, in the future we will specifically introduce E (Expert Score) to carry out $PAI\text{-}E$ ranking, i.e. the arithmetic sum of PAI and E. PAI can effectively evaluate the output and social impact of think tanks. However, the CTTI system mainly adopts the data crowdsourcing mode for data collection, which may lead to unbalanced data filling of various think tanks. For example, some think tanks input too much data to CTTI, while some input too little data. In order to solve this problem, the system will introduce the subjective score of experts on the basis of objective data, and rank think tanks by adding two scores together according to a certain proportion.

5.2.2 Ranking by Effectiveness Indicators

Effectiveness refers to a think tank's competence and efficiency. Competence is a comprehensive reflection of its strategy for resource allocation, its capacity for management, and the development of its organizational system and culture. The efficiency of a think tank means its ability to maximize its output with the most economical use of time, capital and manpower. Given the same total amount of resources, the more products and activities a think tank can offer, the more effective it will be. In this report, resources encompass four categories—experts, administration, budget and cyber resources. The output of a think tank is not the result of a simple combination of these resources, but that of a complex and integrated utilization of them.

Table 3 Rules for Think Tank Ranking by Effectiveness Indicator

Type of Ranking	Rule	Explanation
Total Resource Utilization Efficiency	$(P+A)/R$	Output value/resource value
Expert Effectiveness	$(P+A)/R2$	Output value/expert resource value
Efficiency of Administrative Team	$(P+A)/R3$	Output value/administration resource value
Capital Contribution Ratio	$(P+A)/R1$	Output value/capital investment value
Expert Product Contribution Ratio	$P/R2$	Product value/expert resource value
Administrative Team Activity Contribution	$A/R3$	Activity value/administration resource value

5.3 MRPAI Think Tank Expert Ranking Rules

To build a think tank with high impact and prestige, it is necessary to possess first-rate and high-level experts who are the core figures of thought innovation in the think tank. Our assessments have revealed that high performance experts are highly meaningful because there is a positive correlation between high performance, high competence and high prestige. If think tanks cannot manage talents well, anything else is not worth mentioning.

The principles for MRPAI assessment of think tank experts are straightforward. The indicators involved fall into three categories: experts' personal research products (P), their personal activities (A), and honors and awards (H). Specific assessment indicators and value assignment are shown in Table 4. The performance of think tank experts, symbolized by Ep, is the arithmetic sum of the values assigned to the indicators in the three categories.

$$Ep = P1 + P2 + P4 + P5 + P6 + P7 + P8 + P9 + A1 + A2 + A3 + H1$$

Table 4 Indicators and Value Assignment for MRPAI Think Tank Expert Assessment

Primary Indicator	Code	Secondary Indicator	Code	Scoring Rule	Points
Expert Products	P	Single interal reference reports (with or without leaders' comments)	P1	Value assigned to each report	2
		Leader-commented internal reference reports	P2	State level/per report	30
				Sub-state level/per report	20
				Provincial or ministerial level/per report	10
				Sub-provincial or ministerial level/per report	5
		Books (officially published)	P4	Value assigned to each title	2
		Research Reports	P5	Value assigned to each report	4
		Articles published in the theoretical edition of *People's Daily*, *Seeking Truth*, and *Guangming Daily*	P6	Value assigned to each article	5
		Academic Papers	P7	Each paper in a CSSCI source journal	1
				Each paper included in SSCI/A&HCI	2
				Each paper included in CSCI/EI	1
				Each common paper of other types	0.5
		Vertical Projects	P8	Vertical: major project supported by National Social Science Fund or Social Science Fund of Ministry of Education	10
				Vertical: key project supported by National Social Science Fund or National Natural Science Fund	6

Continued

Primary Indicator	Code	Secondary Indicator	Code	Scoring Rule	Points
				Vertical: common/young scholar project supported by National Social Science Fund	4
				Vertical: provincial/ministerial-level project	2
				Vertical: Other	0.5
		Horizontal Projects	P9	2 basic points for each project + 1 mark point for every 100,000 yuan	
Expert Activities	A	Attending international or national conferences	A1	Hosting/speaking/making keynote speech	4
				Common representative	1
		Attending conferences on other levels		Hosting/speaking/making keynote speech	2
				Common representative	0.5
		National Training Program	A2	Lecture	3
		Training on other levels		Lecture	1
		Participation in reception of survey and study visits from leaders at or above the sub-state level		Each Time	4
		Participation in reception of survey and study visits from leaders/experts at or above the provincial/ministerial level	A3	Each Time	1
		Participation in reception of survey and study visits from leaders/experts at other level		Each Time	0.5
Honors and Awards	H	Honors/awards at or above the provincial/ministerial level	H1	Each Time	2

The points and ranking of expert performance are not only openly available due to our privacy policy. Experts who need such information can obtain it by sending an email to ctti@nju. edu. cn.

5.4 University Think Tank Index Ranking Rules

As professional organizations for strategic and policy research and consultation, think tanks are a product of composite demands in politics, administration and social governance in contemporary society. It is also a product of further divisions of labor for both knowledge and society. Institutions of higher learning and think tanks are totally different social organizations. Generally speaking, universities are much older and larger than think tanks, and much more complex in structure and function. Most university think tanks form part of universities, with the think tank function being one of their multiple functions. The think tank capability of a university is generally in proportion to the number of its schools, departments and institutions engaged in strategic studies and policy studies. It is easy to find out that universities with powerful schools or departments with their characteristics for example, economy, government and administration, international relations and law, tend to have highly capable and influential think tanks. For instance, though away from the political center, Harvard ranks high among the top American universities in think tank capacity thanks to the influence of the John F. Kennedy School of Government. The university think tank index represents a description and assessment of a university's think tank capacity and the influence of its tanks.

The CTTI university think tank index is the sum of the integrated assessment scores of those among its source think tanks that belong to the same university. That sum is this university's total think tank value, which is defined as U^{ts}. Consequently, there must be a university with the highest value, which is marked as max U^{ts}. Then the U^{ts} of another university is divided by max U^{ts}. The ratio thus obtained, which must be equal to or smaller than 1, is multiplied by 100 to become the university's think tank index—index^{UT}. The specific formula is as follows:

$$\text{index}^{UT} = U^{ts}/\max U^{ts} \times 100$$

Detailed evaluation and analysis of this year's university think tank can be consulted in the *Report of the Top 100 CTTI University Think Tanks in 2018*.

5.5 MRPAI Assessment System

The MRPAI assessment system, which is in the background of CTTI, consists of three sub-systems—think tank ranking, expert ranking, and university think tank index ranking. Think tank ranking can be overall or by different types. The same is true of expert ranking and university think tank index ranking.

The MRPAI assessment system involves a deep understanding of the MRPAI indicator system, value assignment, and ranking rules. An advanced ranking algorithm has been employed and some basic machine-learning features have been included for real-time assessment of source think tanks.

In addition, the MRPAI assessment system is capable of searching and statistical analysis of data. It can not only pinpoint each think tank and expert, but also calculate the number of think tanks which have got 74 points as well as the number of experts who have got 48 points in the MRPAI indicutors. This makes it possible to compare such scores and reveal a think tank's strength and weaknesses in management, resources, products and activities, which is of enormous help for improving the management of think tanks.

Moreover, the points in the MRPAI indicators are in the form of adjustable parameters so that evaluators (which can be think tank supervising authorities, researchers, or users with special needs) can modify the values assigned to indicators according to their purposes and obtain customized ranking results. This reflects the flexibility of the MRPAI system.

It should be noted that the MRPAI assessment system is currently in the background and cannot be accessed from the foreground. This can help to protect the security of organization or expert assessment data as well as the privacy of experts. The CTTI project team will never disclose detailed results of assessment to any third party without consent from organzations or experts themselves. The data released this time are only primary indicator values and include no specific scores on secondary indicators. If any think tank needs information on specific scores, it can send an official email to ctti@nju.edu.cn. The CTTREC of Nanjing University will export the relevant outcomes to that particular think tank.

6 The Analysis of MRPAI Assessment Result Data

Following the principles of previous years, this year's assessment is not only based on a scientific and reasonable evaluation system, but also combined with a complete data filling situation of think tanks. According to the analysis of 706 CTTI think tanks' data filling situation, 520 of them have filled in relatively sufficient and accurate data. Therefore, these 520 think tanks are assessed and ranked as the main objects. This year's assessment, based on data accumulated over the years, principally falls into three categories: 1) assessment on private think tanks; 2) assessment on university think tanks (see *2018 Annual Report on CTTI University Think Tanks & Top 100 University Think Tanks*); 3) assessment on think tanks in various research areas. To protect the privacy of think tanks, we have only released the results for the most outstanding think tanks in each category. If a source think tank wants to know the specific ranking result, it can write an email to the CTTREC of Nanjing University (ctti@edu.nju.cn), which will provide relevant information one by one.

6.1 Examples of Evaluation Data on Private Think Tanks

After a review of data on private think tanks, 26 of them filled in more complete data. We rank them according to their output impact, i.e. *PAI* (the arithmetic sum of the value assigned to the three categories of indicators—product, activity and impact of media), and eventually select and publish the top 15 private think tanks, as shown in Table 5.

Table 5 Top 15 Private Think Tanks According to Performance in *PAI* assessment

(in alphabetical order according to the first letters of their names in pinyin spelling)

Names of Think Tanks	PAI	P	A	I
The Charhar Institute	132	108	24	0
Changjiang Education Research Institute	1 182.5	1 086.5	96	0
Chongqing Think-Tank Institution	486	366	120	0
China Region Development & Reform Institute (CRDRI)	127	52	75	0
South China Business Think Tank of Guangdong University of Finance and Economics	179	128	49	2
China Strategy Institute for Intellectual Property (Guangdong Zhongce Intellectual Property Research Institute)	322	237	76	9
Grandview Institution, Beijing	503	193	253	57
Intellisia Institute	583.5	321.5	257	5
The Pangoal Institution	698.5	412.5	286	0
Shanghai Finance Institute	103	58	45	0
Shenzhen Innovation and Development Institute	332	272	60	0
China Center for International Economic Exchanges	121.5	1.5	120	0
China Silk Road iValley Research Institute	783.5	783.5	0	0
Center for China & Globalization	4 217.5	3 354.5	836	27
China Institute of Science and Technology Evaluation	241	208	33	0

Compared with previous years, the assessment results of private think tanks have been relatively stable. It should be noted that most private think tanks don't record media reports, so I value is relatively low. But actually, they have exported a large number of intellectual achievements, which have had an important impact on the domestic society and even the international community. For example, Center for China & Globalization publishes 10 research works every year, including *Report on Globalization of Chinese Enterprises*, *Annual Report on the Development of Chinese Students Studying Abroad*, *Report on China's Regional International Competitiveness*, which are cooperatively published by Social Science Academic Press (China). It also undertakes the research project of many national ministries and commissions, holds multiple forums and think tank seminars, submits more than one hundred proposal reports to relevant ministries and commissions of the Chinese government, and possesses a large number of brand achievements and high media exposure. It is a leading global research institution of private think tanks in China. The sessions between China and Japan, China and America, China and Korea, and China and Europe, which are carried out by China Center for International Economic Exchanges, are of great significance to promote communication between China and other countries. The Global Think Tank Summit held by the Center is a feast of ideas and an important platform for exchanges and cooperation of global think tanks. The Pangoal Institution initiated the establishment of a global governance think tank linking nearly 20 first-rate think tanks from China, the United States, Germany, Italy, India, Singapore, Canada and other countries, which greatly enhanced the voice of Chinese think tanks in global governance. China Silk Road iValley Research Institute is committed to realizing China Dream and promoting the construction of the Belt and Road Initiative, which is a new think tank promoting the country to participate in governance and top-level design of international economic organization and international financial organization. It has been listed as one of the best think tanks by the Belt and Road Initiative Data Report, which is issued by the leading group office of the Belt and Road Initiative construction promoted by the central government and the the Belt and Road Initiative data center of State Information Center. The Charhar Institute has been one of the core institutions in the field of Chinese public diplomacy research since its establishment in 2009, effectively promoting the development of China's public diplomacy theory and practice and the improvement of private think tanks on international relations.

Some private think tanks excel in some specific areas. For example, Changjiang Education Research Institute has gathered a number of well-known education experts at home and abroad, and it has held Beijing-Changjiang Education Forum in Beijing before the National People's Conference (NPC) and the Chinese People's Political Consultative Conference (CPPCC) sessions every year since 2009, inviting NPC deputies, CPPCC members, well-known education experts and leaders of relevant departments and bureaus of the ministry of education to jointly discuss education reform and development; it has also released the annual education index——*China Education Index*, and *Top 10 Key Words of China Education* since 2015, which has widely influenced the society. Intellisia Institute provides scientific, fair and objective policy analysis, research reports and academic guidance for Chinese public and policy makers in a long term, steadily promotes researches in the fields of Sino-US relations, risk prediction, Southeast Asian political economy and the Belt and Road Initiative, and provides first-class intelligence support and decision-making consultation services for the government, enterprises and individual customers. China Strategy Institute for Intellectual Property (Guangdong ZHONGCE Intellectual Property Research

Institute) is the first state-level and high-end professional service institution of intellectual property in Guangdong, which focuses on intellectual property policy research, strategy formulation, industrial operation and other aspects. It has contributed an important force in the field of intellectual property. In recent years, China Institute of Science and Technology Evaluation has formed a series of national blue books, such as *Report on World Innovation Competitiveness*, *Report on Global Environmental Competitiveness*, *Report on the Development of Chinese Tea Industry*, which have authoritative influence on the construction of evaluation index system and the evaluation of competitiveness.

In addition, China Region Development & Reform Institute, Chongqing Think-Tank Institution and Grandview Institution have their own characteristics, providing strong decision-making support for the government. South China Business Think Tank of Guangdong University of Finance and Economics, as a new think tank this year, also boasts certain potential.

6.2　Examples of Evaluation Data on Think Tanks in Various Research Areas

We divide source think tanks into 12 policy research fields: macro-economy and international trade, industry and finance, regional research and international relations, Party building and national governance, social governance and public utilities, law and public security, culture and education, environment, energy and infrastructure, information and technology, three rural issues (agriculture rural areas, and rural residents), the Belt and Road Initiative and comprehensive think tank. In each research area, we measure and analyze the output impact (PAI) of source think tanks, and select and publish the results of top think tanks in each field. It should be noted that the results of each category are ranked in alphabetical order according to the names of think tanks in pinyin spelling.

6.2.1 Macro-Economy and International Trade

There are 62 think tanks engaged in the research of macroeconomic and international trade policy. Most of them focus on national economy, regional economic development, international or regional trade and other issues. Table 6 selects and publishes the assessment results of the top 15 think tanks. University think tanks have contributed a lot to this field by relying on the resource advantages of economics-related disciplines. For example, the Research Institute of Chinese Economy of Fudan University is positioned to provide forward-looking policy advice and suggestions for China's future medium-and-long-term economic growth and development, focusing on major strategic issues in China's economic growth and development in the next 20 years and writing a large number of internal references and think tank reports accordingly. Center for Quantitative Economics of Jilin University is good at using the method of quantitative analysis to study the frontier issues in China's economic field. It has developed the think tank information platform Economic and Social Index Research Database, and its website has been well constructed with nearly 60,000 visits. The College of Economic and Social Development of Nankai University, with its unique disciplinary advantages, aims to improve the ability of social transformation of scientific research achievements and give out Nankai's voice around the hot issues of economic and social development. In addition, some think tanks of Party and government organizations have performed well, such as the Development Research Center of Inner Mongolia Autonomous Region and Macroeconomic Research Institute in Hebei Province Development and Reform Committee, both of which have carried out a large number of surveys on hot and difficult issues in local economic and social operations, so as to ensure the local governments' policy decision in the economic field.

Table 6 Top 15 Think Tanks in Macro-Economy and International Trade According to Performance in *PAI* Assessment

(in alphabetical order according to the first letters of their names in pinyin spelling)

Names of Think Tanks	PAI	P	A	I
Institute of Anhui Economic Development Research, Anhui University of Finance and Economics	2 635.5	2 057.5	575	3
Institute of International Economics, University of Internatinal Business and Economics	1 376.5	1 376.5	0	0
Research Institute of Chinese Economy, Fudan University	1 212	1 020	192	0
Macroeconomic Research Institute in Hebei Province Development and Reform Committee	792	747	45	0
North Jiangsu Development Research Institute, Huaiyin Institute of Technology	755.5	753.5	2	0
Center for Quantitive Economics of Jilin University	1 351.5	1 141.5	179	31
Institute of Guangzhou Nansha Free Trade Test Area Research, Jinan University	734	650	84	0
Nankai University's College of Economic and Social Development	1 500.5	1 083.5	380	37
Jiangsu Yangtze Economic Belt Research Institute, Nanjing University	760.5	485.5	58	217
Development Research Center of Inner Mongolia Autonomous Region, Shanghai University of International Bussiness and Economics	2 333	2 292	41	0
Shanghai Center for Global Trade and Economic Governance	1 164	1 120	44	0
Beijing Economics and Social Development Policy Research Base, Capital University of Economics and Business	889.5	868.5	21	0
Tianjin Academy of Free Trade Area, Tianjin University of Finance and Economics	776.5	649.5	127	0

Continued

Names of Think Tanks	PAI	P	A	I
China Academy of Fiscal Sciences	802	792	10	0
China's Income Distribution Research Center, Zhongnan University of Economics and Law	753.5	548.5	205	0

6.2.2　Industry and Finance

There are also 62 think tanks engaged in industrial and financial research. Most of them focus on financial policies, various industrial policies, enterprise management, market consumption, innovation and development, etc. Table 7 selects and publishes the assessment results of the top 15 think tanks. In the field of finance, Chongyang Institute for Financial Studies of Renmin University of China has been officially recognized as the Secretariat of the Green Finance Committee of the Chinese Monetary Society by the Chinese government, and the Institute has hired 96 former politicians, bankers and well-known scholars from more than 10 countries as senior researchers. It enjoys a high reputation in the world, and it has also been reported by a large number of media and has played an important role in many fields. As a representative of first-class enterprise think tank, Suning Institute of Finance has also been an important intellectual source in this field. The think tank has set up columns in more than 30 mainstream financial and economic media and self-media platforms, published more than 400 columns monthly, received more than 100 media interviews, and actively voiced in the mainstream financial and economic forums, shaping its wide influence. Moreover, Suning Institute of Finance specially has established the daily work post of data management, arranging special personnel to update and maintain the data in the CTTI system, thus realizing the modern management of think tanks. In terms of enterprise operation, China Business Working Capital Management

Research Center is a leader in the industry. It has established a number of think tanks information platforms, thematic databases and comprehensive databases, and developed the Global Enterprise Capital Management Case Base. Both its results and media reports show its unique advantages.

Table 7 Top 15 Think Tanks in Industry and Finance According to Performance in *PAI* Assessment

(in alphabetical order according to the first letters of their names in pinyin spelling)

Names of Think Tanks	PAI	P	A	I
Innovative Development Institute, Anhui University	2 370.5	2 279.5	91	0
Research Base of Beijing Modern Manufacturing Development, Beijing University of Technology	659	614	45	0
National Research Center for Economic Comprehensive Competitiveness, Fujian Normal University Branch	576.5	517.5	59	0
Grandview Institution	503	193	253	57
Center for Beijing-Tianjin-Hebei Development Research, Hebei University of Technology	5 093	4 177	916	0
Institute of De Rong, Hebei Finance University	636	280	356	0
China (Henan) Innovation and Development Institute, Huanhe Science and Technology University	1 117	309	477	331
Research Institute of Machinery Industry Economic & Management	1 696	1 598	98	0
Yangtze Industrial Economics Institution, Nanjing University	3 284.5	817.5	2 344	123
Suning Institute of Finance	1 926.5	1 561.5	365	0
Modern Commerce Service Industry Development Research Center, Tianjin University	515.5	515.5	0	0
Survey and Research Center for China Household Finance, Southwestern University of Finance and Economics	678.5	367.5	188	123

Continued

Names of Think Tanks	PAI	P	A	I
China Business Working Capital Management Research Center, Ocean Univerisity of China	9 297	9 235	62	0
Chongyang Institute for Financial Studies, Renmin University of China	1 280	801	479	0
Collaborative Innovation Center of Industrial Upgrading and Regional Finance (Hubei), Zhongnan University of Economics and Law	2 171	1 108	1 060	3

6.2.3 Regional Research and International Relations

In order to further promote and strengthen the regional and national research in colleges and universities, the Ministry of Education of China held the First Working Conference on Regional and National Research in March 2012. In the following years, more than 100 universities and nearly 400 research institutes in China have become the national regional research record center of the Ministry of Education. Universities have shown a good momentum for rapid development of national and regional research, and think tanks of universities have become the main force of regional research. Among them, the Research Center for Co-Development with Neighboring Countries of East China Normal University establishes regional country studies on the basis of interdisciplinary collaborative studies of international political economics, geopolitics and history, launches a series of influential and important academic and consultative achievements, and establishes overseas studios to create a new model for think tanks to promote overseas research. The Africa-Wide Information of Zhejiang Normal University is the first comprehensive and substantive African research institute of Chinese universities established in 2007 with the support of the Ministry of Education and the Ministry of Foreign Affairs. After more than 10 years of development, it has become a widely influential African research institute in China and a national think tank of African affairs. The think tank has submitted more than 40 advisory reports to various ministries and commissions, many of which have been approved by national leaders or recruited by the *Special Journal of University Think Tanks of the Ministry of Education*. At the same time, it has also hosted a series of important academic conferences such as the Forum of China-Africa Think Tanks and the Seminar of China-Africa Media Think Tanks, which have a wide range of influence and receive a lot of reports from domestic and foreign media.

Besides the efforts of university think tanks, a small number of private think tanks and think tanks of the Academy of Social Sciences have also made important contributions to this field. In August 2018, the United Nations Economic and Social Council (ECOSOC) officially approved the granting of Special Consultative Status of non-governmental organizations to the Center for China & Globalization (CCG). CCG has become one of the few Chinese institutions with this qualification and the first Chinese think tank formally acquiring this status. CCG's accession to the consultative status indicates that China's think tanks are actively going global, giving full play to the international influence of non-governmental organizations and deeply participating in global governance. The Paris Peace Forum was held in Paris to achieve world peace and promote multilateral cooperation through innovative global governance from November 11 to 13. Two initiatives proposed by CCG, the establishments of the International Federation of Talents Organizations and the International E-commerce Union (D50), successfully broke through from nearly 900 projects and were highly recognized by the sponsors. At the same time, CCG President Wang Huiyao was elected to the Executive Committee of the Paris Peace Forum to guide and participate in the work of the forum as a member of the Executive Committee. This indicates that

Chinese think tanks have more opportunities to become deeply involved in global governance.

Pangoal Institution focuses on global governance, the Belt and Road Initiative, innovation driven projects, macroeconomic research and other fields, and it has especially won the recognized influence in the research of Sino-South Korean relations and Sino-Indian Relations. The Institute of European Studies of Chinese Academy of Social Sciences is a national scientific research institution specializing in European comprehensive research and national research. It has produced fruitful research results. At the same time, it has set up a network of exchange and cooperation among think tanks of Central and Eastern European countries. It plays an important role in promoting and strengthening China's second track diplomacy with Central and Eastern European countries.

Table 8 Top 15 Think Tanks in Regional Research and International Relations According to Performance in *PAI* Assessment

(in alphabetical order according to the first letters of their names in pinyin spelling)

Names of Think Tanks	PAI	P	A	I
Center for American Studies, Fudan University	885	207	609	69
Guangdong Institute for International Strategies, Guangdong University of Foreign Studies	1 941.5	1 622.5	290	29
China-ASEAN Research Institute, Guangxi University	646.5	401.5	245	0
the Research Center for Co-Development with Neighboring Countries, East China Normal University	5 965	4 546	1 419	0
Academy of Overseas Chinese Studies in Jinan University	800	604	187	9
Pangoal Institution	698.5	412.5	286	0
Middle East Studies Institute, Shanghai International Studies University	1 932.5	773.5	622	537

Continued

Names of Think Tanks	PAI	P	A	I
Center for Global Public Opinions of China, Shanghai International Studies University	1 155.5	1 155.5	0	0
Institute of South Asian Studies, Sichuan University	732.5	360.5	372	0
German Studies Center, Tongji University	767.5	367.5	400	0
Institute of Korean Peninsula Studies, Yanbian University	918	637	281	0
Center for China's Neighbor Diplomacy Studies, Yunnan Universty	2 004.5	1 801.5	184	19
Africa-Wide Information, Zhejiang Normal University	3 316.5	2 029.5	1 187	100
Institute of European Studies of Chinese Academy of Social Sciences	1 168	1 142	26	0
Center for China & Globalization	4 228.5	3 365.5	836	27

6.2.4 Party Building and National Governance

There are 26 source think tanks engaged in the research of Party building and national governance. These think tanks mainly focus on Party building, government, social system and other issues. Table 9 selects and publishes the assessment results of the top 10 think tanks.

In the aspect of Party building, the Institute for the Development of Socialism with Chinese Characteristics of Southeast University has performed well. Focusing on following up and explaining the Party's innovative theory and carrying out practice and countermeasure research on the development of socialism with Chinese characteristics, it has achieved fruitful theoretical results. It has published nearly 10 important theoretical articles in central media such as *People's Daily*, *Guang Ming Daily* and *Red Flag Manuscript*, held a number of relevant meetings and training programs, and actively built up its international influence. In terms of national governance, Beijing Institute of Letters to Government, based on a large number of detailed complaint reporting data and materials, has submitted more than 200 internal references and obtained a large number of instructions, which provides important support and reference for the government's relevant decision-making in the field of petition policy. At the same time, the Institute of State Governance Studies of Peking University has also made a certain contribution to this field, which is a comprehensive new think tank integrating scientific research, discipline construction, personnel training and social services. The institute has a relatively perfect management system and holds many important conference activities every year. Moreover, many internal references have been approved and instructed by the leaders at the national level, providing support for the decision-making of national governance modernization.

Table 9 Top 10 Think Tanks in Party Building and National Governance According to Performance in *PAI* Assessment

(in alphabetical order according to the first letters of their names in pinyin spelling)

Names of Think Tanks	PAI	P	A	I
Institute of State Governance Studies, Peking University	1 557.5	751.5	806	0
Beijing Institute of Letters to Government	3 049.5	2 503.5	546	0
Institute for the Development of Socialism with Chinese Characteristics, Southeast University	2 135	2 014	121	0
Institute of State Governance of Huazhong University of Science and Technology	503.5	233.5	270	0
Research Institute of Party Building Theory and Practice Innovation	444	444	0	0
Research Center of the Management-Decision Evaluation of Jiangxi Normal University	705	550	116	39
Chinese Government and Politics Unite Research Centre, Nankai University	296.5	135.5	82	79

Continued

Names of Think Tanks	PAI	P	A	I
Research Center of China Economic Reform Innovation and Assessment, Xi'an Jiaotong University	345.5	265.5	80	0
Shanghai Academy	1 900.5	739.5	971	190
China Society of Administrative Reform	523.5	145.5	42	336

6.2.5 Social Governance and Public Utilities

Among the 12 major think tanks classified in this report, 72 think tanks in the field of social governance and public utilities are the maximum number of source think tanks. Table 10 selects and publishes the results of the top 20 think tanks. Source think tanks in this field mainly focus on local governance, health, social security, regional planning and other aspects of public policy, each with its own characteristics. For example, based on the great needs of national construction and the leap-forward development of Hubei Province, Hubei Collaborative Innovation Center of Industrial Upgrading and Regional Finance carries out the coordinated tackling of key problems by government, learning, research, enterprise and using working as one entity, and constructs the Think Tank, Talent Tank, Theory Tank and Information Tank of the innovation of urban and rural community social management. The center has built a professional think tank information platform for urban and rural community social management, as well as a variety of thematic databases and comprehensive databases. The number of achievements is quite abundant. Its internal references have also received leadership instructions at different levels for many times, and its overall strength is strong. Soviet Area Revitalization Institute of Jiangxi Normal University is a key new think tank pilot construction unit in Jiangxi Province. Based on the integration of resources advantages of the university, it carries out the research on basic theories and application countermeasures of the revitalization of the Soviet area, providing intellectual support and social services for the revitalization and development of the former central Soviet area. More than 40 consulting reports and policy suggestions have been provided to the central committee, national ministries and commissions (offices), provincial commissions and provincial governments, and more than 30 of them have been approved and instructed by Party and state leaders, ministries and commissions, provincial commissions and provincial governments. The Center for Modern Chinese City Studies of East China Normal University, relying on the national key disciplines of human geography, sociology and economics, carries out researches on urban geography and urban society, undertakes a number of national key projects, holds a large number of relevant meetings every year, and conducts various reception and inspection activities, which has produced a certain range of influence.

Table 10　Top 20 Think Tanks in Social Governance and Public Utilities According to Performance in *PAI* Assessment

(in alphabetical order according to the first letters of their names in pinyin spelling)

Names of Think Tanks	PAI	P	A	I
Institute for Innovative City	476.5	425.5	51	0
Guangzhou Development Research Institute, Guangzhou University	581.5	405.5	133	43
Center for Modern Chinese City Studies of East China Normal University	2 449	1 364	870	215
Center of Social Governance Research, South China University of Technology	872	571	301	0
Institute of Modernization, Jiangsu Provincial Academy of Social Sciences	742.5	674.5	60	8
Jiangxi Academy of Social Sciences	1 258.5	1 218.5	40	0

Continued

Names of Think Tanks	PAI	P	A	I
Soviet Area Revitalization Institute of Jiangxi Normal University	1 963	1 760	167	36
Collaborative Innovation Center of Chinese Society Transformation Research, Jiangxi Normal University	1 220.5	1 162.5	28	30
MCA-ECNU Center for China Administrative Division Research	542.5	276.5	112	154
Academy of Healthy Jiangsu, Nanjing Medical University	420.5	358.5	50	12
Center for Health Management and Policy, Shandong University	486	231	255	0
Research Center for Local Governance, Shanghai University	686	472	214	0
China Institute for Urban Governance, Shanghai Jiaotong University	646	214	416	16
Collaborative Innovation Center or Security and Development Studies, Sichuan University	998	992	6	0
Center for Social Security Studies, Wuhan University	708.5	627.5	76	5
Hebei Provincial Public Policy Evaluation and Research Center, Yanshan University	1 699.5	1 658.5	41	0
Think Tank of Coastal Development, Yancheng Teachers University	636	602	33	1
Frontier Ethnic Problems Think-Tank of Yunnan University	929.5	910.5	19	0
China Academy of West Region Development, Zhejiang University	1 654.5	1 022.5	632	0
Collaborative Innovation Center of Industrial Upgrading and Regional Finance (Hubei), Zhongnan University of Economics and Law	26 574.5	20 974.5	5 034	566

6.2.6 Law and Public Security

There are 42 source think tanks engaged in the research of law and public security. Most of these think tanks are university think tanks. They carry out different professional research relying on relevant professional disciplines. Table 11 selects and publishes the results of the top 15 think tanks. The Institute of International Law of Wuhan University is an important academic center in the field of international law research in China. It is also one of the first batch of high-end national think tanks with fruitful achievements. In the past year, it has published a total of 15 books, which have generated great repercussions in the academic and practical circles at home and abroad. In addition, it has published more than 60 academic papers and submitted more than 50 consulting reports in *Chinese Journal of International Law*, *Hong Kong Law Journal*, *People's Daily*, *China Law* and other well-known domestic and foreign journals and newspapers, and undertaken nearly 30 horizontal and vertical research projects. The Institute for Food Safety Management of Jiangnan University, relying on its disciplinary advantages and the support of the competent authorities, has continuously expanded its research field on the basis of focusing on food safety risk management, established a series of brand achievements such as *China Development Report on Food Safety* and *China Development Report on Online Public Opinion of Food Safety*, served the government's decision-making, and developed the data mining platform of food safety incidents to provide data support for China's food safety governance. It has established a certain influence at home and abroad.

In the field of public safety, Jiangsu Public Security Institute has given full play to the functional advantages of the competent government departments and the research advantages of colleges and universities, constructed a cooperative and innovative mechanism for the deep integration of government organs, universities and scientific research institutes, took the lead in undertaking the research tasks of major public safety needs in the whole province, and written several articles with the approval of provincial and ministerial leaders, in order to promote public safety in Jiangsu Province. The modernization of governance system and capacity provides theoretical and intellectual support.

Table 11   Top 15 Think Tanks in Law and Public Security According to Performance in *PAI* Assessment

(in alphabetical order according to the first letters of their names in pinyin spelling)

Names of Think Tanks	PAI	P	A	I
Institute of Modern Policing Reform Ministry of Public Security	1 438.5	978.5	433	27
Guangxi Development Research Institute of Intellectual Property, Guangxi University	436	168	268	0
Institute for Food Safety Management, Jiangnan University	2 460	2 009	273	178
Jiangsu Public Security Institute, Jiangsu Police Institute	2 010.5	1 434.5	481	95
The Research Center of Intellectual Property Development in Jiangsu, Nanjing University of Science and Technology	385.5	182.5	192	11
Institute for Chinese Legal Modernization Studies, Nanjing Normal University	2 312.5	2 136.5	176	0
Center for Basic Laws of Hong Kong and Macao Special Administrative Regions, Shenzhen University	1 498.5	345.5	703	450
Research Base for the Implementation of National Intellectual Property Strategy, Tianjin University	552.5	188.5	360	4
Wuhan University Institute of International Law	4 738	4 624	114	0
Research Institute of Environmental Law, Wuhan Unversity	808.5	635.5	173	0
Center for Capital Social Safety, People's Public Security University of China	478	356	119	3

Continued

Names of Think Tanks	PAI	P	A	I
Center for the Development of Rule of Law and Judical Reform Research of Zhongnan University of Economics and Law	2 676.5	1 169.5	672	835
Center for Studies of Intellectual Property Rights, Zhongnan University of Economics and Law	2 700	1 677	888	135
Intellectual Property Research Institute of Central South University	811.5	406.5	404	1
Cultural Law Research Center of China Central South University	579	323	229	27

6.2.7 Culture and Education

A total of 70 think tanks are engaged in the research in the field of culture and education, involving language culture, ethnic culture, media, education and history, etc. Table 12 selects the list of think tanks with *PAI* ranking top 20. In this field, nearly 80% of think tanks are university think tanks. Universities have rich humanities and social science research resources, so they have natural academic advantages compared with other think tanks in carrying out decision-making consultation services in the field of culture and education. Think tanks of normal universities are outstanding especially in the field of education. The Institute of Curriculum & Instruction of East China Normal University focuses on the research fields and directions of internationalization of curriculum theory, curriculum evaluation and policy, subject curriculum, teachers' professional development and learning science. It has sponsored several publications, such as *Global Education*, *Frontiers of Curriculum Studies*, and led the research and development of policy texts, such as *National Basic Education Curriculum Reform Outline* and *Curriculum Standards of Teacher Education*. It also developed a think tank platform for monitoring the quality of curriculum implementation process in primary and secondary schools, which has made outstanding contributions to the new round of basic education curriculum reform and teachers' education curriculum reform in China. It is known as the national team in the field of curriculum and teaching research. The Center for Studies in Moral Culture of Hunan Normal University has established the China's Moral Status Assessment Data Center to dynamically grasp China's moral status and provide intellectual support for the government's decision-making. The Center for Studies of Media Development of Wuhan University is an important platform for the study of communication innovation in China. It regularly publishes the *Annual Report on China's Communication Innovation* and the *Research Report of China's Media Development*. It also won the Outstanding Contribution Award of China's Media Discipline in 2015 and 2016. It provides theoretical support and advisory services for the development of media and society in China.

Besides university think tanks, there are a few private think tanks, think tanks of Party/government organizations, such as Changjiang Education Research Institute, The Research Institute of Nanjing Massacre History & International Peace, China Youth and Children Research Center, and etc.

Table 12   Top 20 Think Tanks in Culture and Education According to Performance in *PAI* Assessment

(in alphabetical order according to the first letters of their names in pinyin spelling)

Names of Think Tanks	PAI	P	A	I
Institute of Beijing Study, Beijing Union University	663	553	102	8
Institute of International and Comparative Education, Beijing Normal University	966.5	719.5	247	0

Continued

Names of Think Tanks	PAI	P	A	I
China Academy of Education and Social Management, Beijing Normal University	4 030.5	3 741.5	289	0
International Institute of Chinese Studies, Beijing Foreign Studies University	3 157.5	2 439.5	718	0
National Research Centre for Language Capacity, Beijing Foreign Studies University	616.5	478.5	138	0
Changjiang Education Research Institute	1 182.5	1 086.5	96	0
Moral Development Think-Tank, Southeast University	1 672.5	1 386.5	286	0
Center for Studies in Moral Culture of Hunan Normal University	1 551	1 333	180	38
National Institute of Educational Policy Research, East China Normal University	1 061.5	887.5	0	174
The Institute of Curriculum & Instruction of East China Normal University	1 923	1 222	701	0
The Institute for Modern Chinese Thought and Culture, East China Normal University	1 255	1 150	105	0
The Research Institute of Nanjing Massacre History & International Peace	862.5	538.5	298	26
Zijin Media Think Tank, Nanjing University	1 702	1 245	427	30
Jiangsu Academy of Talent Development, Nanjing University of Science and Technology	732	678	54	0
Purple Academy of Culture & Creativity, Nanjing University of the Arts	850.5	248.5	602	0
Soochow University Think Tank, Soochow University	1 401.5	1 295.5	106	0
Center for Studies of Media Development, Wuhan University	2 001	914	1 012	75
Center for Collaborative Innovation in the Heritage and Development of Xizang Culture, Xizang Minzu University	611	553	42	16
Center for Higher Education Development of Xiamen University	2 766.5	2 575.5	161	30
Institute of China's Science, Technology and Education Policy, Zhejiang University	649	491	135	23

6.2.8 Environment, Energy and Infrastructure

The field of environment, energy and infrastructure mainly includes the development and protection of ecological environment, climate and meteorological issues, energy development, sustainable development, and infrastructure construction consisting of transportation, shipping, and other aspects, etc. It is mainly concentrated on university think tanks. A total of 30 think tanks from different sources are engaged in this field. Table 13 selects the top 10 think tanks according to *PAI* scores. The Research Center for Beijing Transportation Development of Beijing Jiaotong University conducts theoretical and empirical research on the construction of urban transportation system. It has published more than 900 academic papers and 80 books, and completed more than 300 scientific research projects, providing strong academic and intellectual support for the construction and development of Beijing transportation. Sichuan Oil & Gas Development Research Center of Southwest Petroleum University has successfully built famous academic brands such as Western Oil and Gas Forum and China Natural Gas Industry Prosperity Index. Many think tanks submit scientific advice and policy suggestions for local governments and energy enterprises to formulate medium-and-long-term development strategies, and provide the public and researchers with important references of correct assessment of the development situation of the oil and gas industry. Think Tank on Natural Disaster Prevention and Geological Environment Protection of Chengdu University of Technology has carried out research in the fields of geological disaster assessment and environmental protection. The research results have won nearly 70 awards with economic benefits of billions of yuan. It has published more than 50 monographs and textbooks, nearly 3,000 papers at home and abroad, and nearly 50 authorized invention patents. Shanghai International Shipping

Institute established by Shanghai Maritime University mainly provides decision-making consultation and information services for the government, domestic and foreign enterprises and shipping institutions. The China Shipping Database built by the institute is a public service platform integrating statistics and information resources in the field of port and shipping in China, aiming at providing one-stop data service with convenient query and data analysis functions to government organs, shipping enterprises, scientific research institutes and other types of users.

Table 13　Top 10 Think Tanks in Environment, Energy and Infrastructure According to Performance in *PAI* Assessment

(in alphabetical order according to the first letters of their names in pinyin spelling)

Names of Think Tanks	PAI	P	A	I
Research Center for Beijing Transportation Development, Beijing Jiaotong University	7 897	6 172	1 725	0
Beijing Logistics Informatics Research Base, Beijing Jiaotong University	771.5	391.5	380	0
Think Tank on Natural Disaster Prevention and Geological Environment Protection, Chengdu University of Technology	1 964	1 668	296	0
Electric Power Planning & Engineering Institute	1 785.5	1 365.5	420	0
State Grid Energy Research Institute	1 558	1 184	374	0
Beijing Energy Development Research Center, North China Electric Power University	514	481	33	0
Research Institute of Climatic and Environmental Governance, Nanjing University of Information Science and Technology	762	637	125	0
Shanghai International Shipping Institute, Shanghai Maritime University	1 700	1 312	327	61
APEC Sustainable Energy Center, Tianjin University	603	186	415	2
Sichuan Oil & Gas Development Research Center, Southwest Petroleum University	430	310	85	35

6.2.9　Information and Technology

The field of information and technology covers policy issues such as Internet, information technology, science and technology. 19 source think tanks are mainly engaged in this field. Table 14 selects the top three think tanks according to *PAI* scores. Most of these think tanks come from research institutes.

For example, Jiangxi Academy of Sciences Institute of Science & Technology Strategy is a high-end technology think-tank in Jiangxi Province, which carries out overall and forward-looking research around the major issues of Jiangxi's scientific, technological, economic and social development. It has built the Platform for Scientific Application and Information Sharing of the World's Lakes and written dozens of internal reference reports, which provide decision-making assistance for the development of science and technology in Jiangxi Province.

The Public Opinion Big Data Research Center of Guangzhou in Jinan University has established a big data dissemination laboratory, with a sound domestic and foreign public opinion data mining system and case base platform, which promotes the interdisciplinary communication and cross-boundary sharing of big data. In addition to think tanks of research institutes and universities, there are also some private think tanks, such as Shenzhen Innovation and Development Institute, China Institute of Science and Technology Evaluation, and Ali Research. Shenzhen Innovation and Development Institute has held a series of brand projects, such as Dameisha Chinese Innovation Forum, 30 People of Shenzhen Reform Forum, and Jinpeng Reform and Innovation Award. Since 2014, its *Annual Report on China's Reform and Innovation* has been published annually, which promotes the exchange of think tanks at home and abroad, and helps to improve the internationalization level of Chinese private think tanks.

Table 14 Top 3 Think Tanks in Information and Technology According to Performance in *PAI* Assessment

(in alphabetical order according to the first letters of their names in pinyin spelling)

Names of Think Tanks	*PAI*	*P*	*A*	*I*
The Public Opinion Big Data Research Center of Guangzhou, Jinan University	557.5	220.5	242	95
Jiangxi Academy of Sciences Institute of Science & Technology Strategy	1 165.5	1 072.5	93	0
Shenzhen Innovation and Development Institute	332	272	60	0

6.2.10 Three Rural Issues

Three Rural Issues refer to the studies of agriculture, rural areas and farmers. A total of 10 think tanks are engaged in the research of three rural issues, involving rural education, new rural construction, agricultural modernization, rural economy and other research directions. Table 15 selects the top 5 think tanks according to *PAI* scores. Institute of China Rural Studies in Central China Normal University dates back to the 1980s. For a long time, it has produced a large number of high-quality research results on the basis of field investigation and empirical research. It has established a development platform for rural think tanks in China. With the goal of One Tank Knows Farmers, it collects rural survey and multi-dimensional data to realize the three-dimensional display of rural morphology, change and reality. Zhejiang University's China Academy for Rural Development has formed a number of outstanding research results with certain international recognition and policy influence, for example, *Land Issues in the Process of Urbanization* won the first China Rural Development Research Work Award. It hosted a variety of high-level international and domestic academic seminars, such as jointly organizing International Academic Seminar on Frontiers and Development Strategies of Agricultural Economic

Management Discipline with the National Natural Science Foundation Committee. The International Symposium on China's Three Rural Issues jointly held with the Economic Association of China in the United States has had an important impact at home and abroad.

In addition to paying attention to the three rural issues in China, Jin Shanbao Agricultural Modernization Research Institute of Nanjing Agricultural University focuses on agricultural development in South America and African countries, summarizes the experience of agricultural modernization in East Asia such as Japan and Korea, and publishes a set of Jin Shanbao Blue Book every year, which includes its achievements in the field of agricultural economy and rural development in the past year. Jin Shanbao Agricultural Summit and Jiangsu Rural Development Forum are held annually to discuss the important events and problems in the agricultural economy and rural development of our country in that year, providing policy references for the agricultural modernization construction of Jiangsu Province and even our country as well as the implementation of agricultural going-out strategy.

Table 15 Top 5 Think Tanks in Three Rural Issues According to Performance in *PAI* Assessment

(in alphabetical order according to the first letters of their names in pinyin spelling)

Names of Think Tanks	PAI	P	A	I
Modern Agricultural Development Research Center, Northeast Agricultural University	607.5	486.5	81	40
China Institute of Rural Education Development, Northeast Normal University	786.5	741.5	45	0
Institute of China Rural Studies, Central China Normal University	8 870.5	8 125.5	737	8
Jin Shanbao Agricultural Modernization Research Institute, Nanjing Agricultural University	701	691	10	0

Continued

Names of Think Tanks	PAI	P	A	I
China Academy for Rural Development, Zhejiang University	1 552.5	656.5	534	362

6.2.11 The Belt and Road Initiative

Since China put forward the strategy of the Belt and Road Initiative, the research on related fields has always been a hot topic. According to the data from CTTI source think tank, a total of 17 think tanks are engaged in the Belt and Road Initiative research, involving many research directions such as international tourism resources development, high-end talent training, Sino-foreign trade and cultural exchanges international business cooperation, and regional and national social development research. Table 16 selects the top 5 according to PAI scores. 15 think tanks are university think tanks among these 17 think tanks, relying on the abundant research resources or geographical advantages of their universities. For example, Inner Mongolia University of Finance and Economics makes full use of geographical advantages, sets up the Research and Cooperative Innovation Center of China-Mongolia-Russia Economic and Trade Cooperation and the Construction of the Grassland Silk Road Economic Belt, carries out research around China-Mongolia-Russia Economic Corridor and Silk Road Economic Belt, and establishes multiple international cooperation platforms and research centers, such as the China-Mongolia Cooperation Research Institute, China-Mongolia Business School.

The establishment of the Institute of "The Belt and Road" Pilot Free Trade Zone by Xi'an Jiaotong University marks the new stage of internationalization, marketization and openness for the research work of the free trade pilot zone in the western region. It has become a new engine for the rapid development of Shaanxi Free

Trade Zone, and provides a strong think-tank support for Shaanxi to catch up with and surpass the development goals.

In addition to 15 university think tanks, there are two private think tanks, China Silk Road iValley Research Institute and the Hundred Talents Forum of the Belt and Road. The two private think tanks have brought together renowned experts, scholars, government officials, entrepreneurs and media practitioners from all over the world to provide intellectual support for the construction of the Belt and Road Initiative.

Table 16   Top 5 Think Tanks in the Belt and Road Initiative According to Performance in *PAI* Assessment

(in alphabetical order according to the first letters of their names in pinyin spelling)

Names of Think Tanks	PAI	P	A	I
China Academy of "One Belt and One Road" Strategy Institute, Beijing International Studies University	482.5	298.5	120	64
Institute of the Belt and Road, Jiangsu Normal University	504	400	104	0
Collaborative Innovation Center for the Study on China, Mongolia and Russia Economic and Trade Cooperation & Construction of Economic Belt on the Prairie Silk Road, Inner Mongolia University of Finance and Economics	1 503	1 043	460	0
XJTU Institute of "The Belt and The Road" Pilot Free Trade Zone	841.5	597.5	142	102
China Silk Road iValley Research Institute	783.5	783.5	0	0

6.2.12   Comprehensive Think Tank

In addition to the 11 main research areas mentioned above, there is also a type of comprehensive think tanks, mainly composed of local Party schools/administrative college and academies of social sciences, etc. Different from think tanks in other fields, comprehensive think tanks usually carry out interdisciplinary, multidisciplinary and comprehensive research. There are 46 comprehensive think tanks in total in CTTI source think tanks, and provincial social science academies account for nearly 60% of the 46 comprehensive think tanks. Comprehensive think tanks have carried out a lot of research on think tanks by virtue of their own institutional and resource advantages.

For example, the Academy of Social Sciences in Shandong, as one of the first pilot units for the construction of key new think tanks in Shandong Province, advocated the establishment of the Shandong Think Tank Alliance, set up online websites and WeChat official account, held the Taishan Think Tank Forum, and established *Shandong Social Sciences Report* to focus on introducing top-quality results of think tanks around the provincial central work of provincial Party committees and the construction of a powerful province of economy and culture. Party School of the Human Provincial Committee of C. P. C (Human Academy of Governance) carried out a large number of training and meetings. Moreover, *Decision Consulting Essentials*, *Think Tank Newsletter* and *Selected Results Anthology of Decision Consulting* founded by it had great impact on the province.

Party school of Zhejiang Provincial Committee of C. P. C (Zhejiang Institute of Administration) strives to enhance academic influence and the level of scientific research and consulting work. It has made positive and effective progress in building a model Party School of universities at a high level. The Party and government think tanks with high citations rank top in the number of papers.

Besides, some academies of social sciences also actively participate in the research and evaluation of think tanks. For example, some academies of social sciences have successively issued special evaluation reports on think tanks, such as Chinese

Academy of Social Sciences, Shanghai Academy of Social Sciences, Sichuan Academy of Social Sciences and Shandong Academy of Social Sciences.

7 Suggestions on Strengthening the Construction of New Think Tanks with Chinese Characteristics

According to the general goal of building new think tanks with Chinese characteristics by 2020 mentioned in "The Opinions", more than half of the time has passed since General Secretary Xi Jinping put forward the proposal of building a new type of think tanks with Chinese characteristics in April 2013. In the first half of the construction of new think tanks with Chinese characteristics for more than five years, remarkable achievements have been made. However, in the process of first half construction, some problems have gradually emerged. As General Secretary Xi Jinping pointed out, "Some think tanks pay more attention to quantity than quality, some pay more attention to form dissemination than content innovation, and some are formalistic practices such as setting up a platform, inviting celebrities and holding forums." Therefore, in the second half of the construction of new think tanks with Chinese characteristics, we should not only learn from the construction experience of the first half, but also focus on solving the problems left over from the first half.

7.1 Innovating the System and Mechanism of Think Tanks and Improving the Governance of Think Tanks

Since the 18th National Congress of the Communist Party of China proposed to "improve the decision-making mechanism and give play to the role of think tanks", China has issued a series of policy documents from the central and local governments to promote the development of think tanks. However, in the concrete practice of building new types of think tanks with Chinese characteristics, the development of think tanks is still limited due to the existing mechanisms and systems. The main reason is that most of the think tanks in China are institutional think tanks, including the Party schools, the schools of administration, the academies of social sciences and the think tanks of universities, etc. Most of them have competent units and do not have completely independent legal personality. Therefore, think tanks' operating is easily limited by a director unit, leading to think tank's construction into a "sandwich" trap, namely the upper of the sandwich as the administrative department of state/province ministries' think tanks, the middle one as the parent unit (e. g. college, Chinese academies of social sciences), and the lower as the think tank. State/province ministries need to work on the think tank through the parent unit, which to some extent causes difficulties in policy implementation and restricts the development of think tanks. In addition, there are still some problems such as the imperfect operation mechanism of the think tank itself, the unreasonable recognition and incentive system of the think tank's achievements.

The building of new types of think tanks with Chinese characteristics is not a decisive battle but a protracted one. Only by breaking the shackles of mechanism and system and improving the governance system of think tanks can we optimize the external environment for the development of think tanks and enhance the internal driving force for their development. On the one hand, the management system of think tanks should be improved, and the development policies of think tanks in central provinces and cities should be promoted, so that think tanks can fully enjoy the policy dividends. In the development of more than five years, part of the think tank development experience is worth using for reference. For example, Nanjing University established Yangtze Industrial Economics Institution and Zijin Media

Think Tank. At the same time, these two think tanks registered the "non-citizen" legal entity think tank in the provincial civil affairs department, which solved the "sandwich trap" of think tank development by means of "one entity, two brands", allowing two think tanks to enjoy the dividend of national policies and at the same time make convenient use of school resources. On the other hand, the operation mechanism of think tanks should be improved, the internal ecology of think tanks should be optimized, and the benign development of think tanks should be promoted. We will formulate a scientific and reasonable system for recognizing and encouraging the achievements of think tanks. First, attach importance to the establishment of the basic law of think tanks—the constitution of think tanks, so as to institutionalize and standardize the operation of think tanks. Second, change the previous academic evaluation model of discussing heroes in core journals, flexibly identify the achievements of think tanks, improve the enthusiasm of think tank researchers, and provide guarantee for think tank research.

7.2 Improving Think Tank Service Model and Providing Embedded Service

In addition to the government internal research office that is close to the decision-making department, there is a supply and demand information asymmetry between most think tanks and the decision-making departments. On the one hand, due to insufficient or limited disclosure of government information, think tanks have a single channel to obtain government information, so they cannot obtain detailed and reliable information data for research support. On the other hand, there's not enough interaction between the decision department and the think tank, and it's hard to get a chance to participate in a government policy seminar, and it's going to be a problem of "the file data is not available, the policy information is not available, and the feedback can't be seen". Secondly, at present, the research and consulting business of think tanks is too concentrated on the front end of the policy process, and the business model is top-heavy. That is to say, the policy consulting service provided by think tanks focuses on the drafting of policies, and pays less attention to the evaluation, feedback and education of policies. The business focus is superficial.

Building new types of think tanks with Chinese characteristics is an important way to improve the decision-making mechanism. First, focus on demand-side reform. The decision department has to value, trust, rely on, and support the think tank to provide decision counseling services, to provide the development of the think tank with policy support, financial support, information support, platform support, and to promote the cooperation of the policy lab in the government with the think tank. Second, think tanks need to change the previous consulting service mode and provide "embedded decision-making consulting services" for decision-making departments by embedding policy process, decision-making consulting process, decision-making consulting scenario and policy community. Specifically, through the embedding of policy process, think tanks provide full-chain services for decision-making departments from policy discussion and formulation to policy implementation, evaluation and feedback. Through the embedding of decision-making consultation process, from data collection to final report writing, it gives full play to the technical support of think tanks. Through the embedding of decision scenario, the cause and effect of a policy can be understood. Through the circle embedding of the policy community, it generates strong mutual trust with decision-making departments and policy research departments.

7.3 Optimizing the Distribution of Human Resources in Think Tanks and Enriching the Talent Team

Talent is the foundation of think tank development. In recent years, the number of Chinese intelligent library entities has rapidly increased, and CTTI alone has 700 think tanks distributed in more than 50 strategic and policy fields. However, it is worth noting that the talent team construction of think tanks has not kept pace with the growth of the number of think tanks. At present, the talent team of think tanks in China has many part-time staff but few full-time staff, many researchers but few support staff, and many research teams but few leading experts. Therefore, it is necessary to optimize the human resource layout of think tanks and enrich the talent team of think tanks, so as to provide continuous power for the development of think tanks and guarantee the high quality and high level of the research results of think tanks. Think tank talent team construction must pay attention to the following points:

First, pay attention to the proportion of auxiliary staff and researchers. Reasonable proportion of auxiliary staff and researchers is an important guarantee to improve research efficiency. Auxiliary personnel include administrators, research secretaries, and research assistants. For example, the experience of the Rand Corporation is that "two fellows are less efficient than one fellow and half a secretary". In addition to a large number of administrative affairs, the think tank studies are equally trifling, long-term and constancy. The auxiliary personnel can carry out the logistics support of the research for the researchers. Second, increase the proportion of full-time researchers. External researchers or part-time researchers can promote the exchange of ideas of think tanks, expand the research field of think tanks, and establish the brand effect of think tanks. However, if the number of part-time researchers is too large, it is not easy to form a stable and efficient think tank research team. Currently, however, the number of part-time researchers in some tanks is far beyond that of full-time research personnel, who need to incorporate more full-time researchers to build their own core research team. Third, think tank leaders are needed. On the one hand, think tank development needs academic leaders. In the initial stage of think tanks and the stage of think tank brand establishment, influential experts are needed to enhance the popularity of think tanks. On the other hand, the operation and management of think tanks need talents "who understand think tanks, are proficient in academics and have a general knowledge of management". Academic star type think tank managers tend to be a tiger with wings added to the development of think tanks. Fourth, absorb and cultivate "T" talents and optimize the talent structure. Think tank research is characterized by multi disciplines, broad fields, complexity and comprehensiveness. There are knowledgeable and specialized "T" type talents who have natural professional advantages in carrying out think tank research. In short, only by cultivating leading think tank talents, gathering top think tank experts, and rationally allocating human resources, can a certain scale of think tank research team layout be formed with leading talents as the guidance, senior experts as the core, researchers as the backbone, and research assistants as the assistance, so as to provide talent guarantee for the construction of new types of think tanks with Chinese characteristics.

7.4 Enhancing International Exchange and Cooperation to Make the World Understand China

As an important way to realize the modernization of China's governance capacity and system, the construction of new types of think tanks in China cannot be achieved behind closed doors. On the one hand, it is the demand for the construction of new think tanks with Chinese characteristics. Western think tanks developed earlier and their operating mechanisms are more mature. The construction of new think tanks in China is still in its infancy, and a large number of institutional problems need to be solved. Therefore, the construction of new types of think tanks with Chinese characteristics should be in line with the international standards, strengthen the international exchanges of think tanks, understand the dynamics of the western think tank industry, and learn from the development experience of western think tanks to know each other. Of course, learning from others is not the same as copying from others. To build new types of think tanks with Chinese characteristics, we need to keep in mind the words "special" and "new".

On the other hand, enhancing the international exchange of think tanks is the need of our diplomatic strategy. "Think tank diplomacy" has gradually become a "second track" beyond official diplomacy and people-to-people exchanges, and its core is the exchange of information and ideas. Think tanks play an important role in foreign exchanges because of their special relationship with official decision making and special status as professional policy researchers. They are more flexible and professional than official diplomacy and non-governmental exchanges. At present, China's comprehensive national strength is on the rise, and its interactions with the international community have become ever closer. China is actively participating in global governance and promoting the building of a global community of shared future. However, with the continuous changes in the world pattern and the strengthening of political and economic globalization, China's participation in global affairs is faced with more complex challenges and requires stronger, more professional and deeper theoretical and decision-making support. It also provides theoretical basis, policy advice and exchange platform for the development of China's major foreign country's diplomacy. Therefore, our nation's think tank has to focus on our country's strategic needs, to hit global hotspot issues, to make a "Chinese voice" in global governance, to increase the international influence of our nation's think tank, and to make the world understand China. For example, China has built a number of think tanks and international forums around the Belt and Road Initiative. These think tanks and forums have played an important role in promoting the Belt and Road Initiative and establishing China's international voice.

7.5 Establishing Brand Awareness of Think Tanks and Building Flagship Products

Professionalism is the basic attribute of think tanks. Without professionalism, think tank research will become "a tree without roots". However, at present there are thousands of domestic think tanks, involving a wide range of professional fields. How to stand out among the numerous think tanks is a question that must be considered in the process of think tank construction and development. Different from pure academic research institutions, think tanks are also media, shouldering the role of policy education and public opinion guidance, and the credibility of think tanks is the guarantee for think tanks to play the above functions. Therefore, think tanks must establish brand awareness, build flagship products, and improve the identification and credibility. First of all, think tank research should reflect "specialized, refined, special and excellent", which is the foundation of think tank. For example, the Institute of African Studies of Zhejiang Normal University has long focused on African studies, carried out systematic and comprehensive research, and accumulated a large number of research results. It is now the leader of African studies in China.

Second, focus on building think tanks flagship products. Think tanks and think tanks' flagship products complement each other, which means that, think tanks promote and disseminate the research results of think tanks through flagship products, while excellent think tank products in return help establish the brand image of think tanks. First, create well-known forums and conference. For example, Shanghai Forum hosted by the Development Research Institute of Fudan University is a large international academic forum, aiming to build a platform for the communication between Chinese and foreign political and business scholars, and make suggestions for regional development and national plans. Since its inception in 2005, the forum has attracted nearly 4,000 speakers at home and abroad. It has always been a pioneer in innovation to better serve the human advance, the development of the country, and the improvement of the people's life, and has gradually been a well-known brand of forum at home and abroad. Second, create a flagship publication. For example, the *Rand Review*, a flagship magazine published by the RAND corporation, an internationally renowned think tank, and *Globalization*, a publication founded by China Center for International Economic Exchanges, focusing on the major strategic issues of international and domestic economic and social development. Third, publish star products, for example, *Nanjing University Think Tank Collection* published by the Research and Evaluation Center of China Think Tank in Nanjing University, and the large-scale documentary *I Come from Africa* shot by the Institute of African Studies of Zhejiang Normal University mentioned above.

7.6 Promoting the Coordinated Development and Improving the System of Think Tank

"The Opinions" proposed to "promote the coordinated development of Party and government departments, academies of social sciences, Party school administration, universities, military, research institutes, enterprises and private think tanks. But the problems of incoordination also exist in the present state of development. According to CTTI source data, university think tanks account for half of the total number of think tanks in China, while enterprise think tanks and private think tanks account for less than one tenth. Other think tanks such as those of the Party, government and military, and the Chinese academies of social sciences, rank second in terms of number, but they have natural advantages in providing decision-making consultation services because of their close relationship with decision-making departments. In addition, think tanks are geographically unevenly distributed. For example, the number of think tanks in east and north China accounts for nearly 75% of the total number of think tanks, which are mainly concentrated in Beijing and Shanghai. Of course, the centralization and clustering of think tank industry are related to the political, economic and cultural status of Beijing and Shanghai. It is undeniable that although China's central and western regions are relatively backward in economic development, they also need professional think tanks to provide policy consulting services for local economic and social development. With the grand goal of building a moderately prosperous society in all respects, this demand is even more urgent. However, the development of think tanks in China's central and western regions is lagging behind.

Therefore, we should promote the coordinated development of think tanks. On the one hand, we should promote the coordinated development of all types of think tanks, especially private think tanks and enterprise think tanks. Other types of think tanks are more or less susceptible to institutional influence, while private think tanks have unique advantages, more objective, independent and flexible. Therefore, we must strongly support the development of social think tanks, give full play to the advantages of private think tanks, form "catfish effect", and prosper the policy market. On the other hand, we should support the development of local think tanks in the central and western regions. Based on the local conditions, we can provide strong intellectual support for local social and economic development.

Appendix: CTTI Source Think Tanks (2018 - 2019)

(in alphabetical order according to the pinyin spelling of names)

(Ⅰ) Think Tanks of Party/Government Organizations (69)

Beijing Institute of Letters to Government

Tariff Policy Research Center of Ministry of Finance of the People's Republic of China

International Economics and Finance Institute

Economic Information Center of Chongqing (Comprehensive Economic Institute of Chongqing)

China Center for Contemporary World Studies

Development Research Center of Fujian Provincial People's Government

Public Security Development Strategy Research Institute of the Ministry of Public Security

Institute of Modern Policing Reform Ministry of the Ministry Public Security

International Cooperation Center for National Development and Reform Commission

Academy of Macroeconomic Research of National Development and Reform Commission

China Institute for Marine Affairs

National Center for Education Development Research

Taxation Institute of State Administration of Taxation

China Institute of Sport Science

China National Health Development Research Center

National Institute of Hospital Administration

China Communication Research Center, State Administration of Press, Publication, Radio, Film and Television

National Center for Climate Change Strategy and International Cooperation

Intellectual Property Development Research Center of the State Intellectual Property Office

Strategic Research Center of Oil and Gas Resources, MLR

State Grid Energy Research Institute

Development Research Center of the State Council

The Institute of Fiscal Science and Policy of Hebei Province

Macroeconomic Research Institute in Hebei Province Development and Reform Committee

Policy Research Center for Environment and Economy, Ministry of Environmental Protection, People's Republic of China.

Research Institute of Machinery Industry Economics & Management

Development Research Center, the People's Government of Jilin Province

Research Institute of People's Government of Jiangsu Province

Jiangxi Provincial Research Center

Research Center for Social Science Development of Higher Education Institutions, the Ministry of Education

Development Research Center of Liaoning Provincial Government

The Research Institute of Nanjing Massacre History & International Peace

Development Research Center of Inner Mongolia Autonomous Region

Research Center for Rural Economy

National Society for the CPC Building Studies

Shandong Academy of Innovation Strategy

Shandong Macro-Economy Research Institute

Chinese Academy of International Trade and Economic Cooperation

Shanghai Academy of Development and Reform

Shanghai Academy of Educational Sciences

Shanghai Pudong Academy of Reform and Development [Institute of China (Shanghai) Free Trade Zone]

The Development Research Center of Shanghai Municipal People's Government

Ministry of Justice Crime Prevention Research Institute

Binhai Research Institute in Tianjin

Tianjin Innovation and Development Institute

Center for Studies of United Front

Zhejiang Development & Planning Institute (ZDPI)

Central Compilation & Translation Bureau

The Research of Marxism of Central Compilation & Translation Bureau

World Development Strategy Research of Central Compilation & Translation Bureau

Chinese Academy of Fiscal Sciences

China Center for Urban Development

China Institute of International Studies

Chinese Institute of Land and Resources Economy

National Institute of Education Sciences

Chinese Academy of Labour and Society Security

China Research Center on Aging

China Tourism Academy

Research Institute of Yangtze River Delta, China Executive Leadership Academy in Pudong

Research Institute of Leadership, China Executive Leadership Academy in Pudong

Research Institute of Socialism with Chinese Characteristics, China Executive Leadership Academy in Pudong

China Youth & Children Research Center

Financial Institute of the People's Bank of China

Chinese Academy of Personnel Science

National Statistical Society of China

Chinese Academy of Cultural Heritage

China Institutes of Contemporary International Relations

Chinese Academy of Press and Publication

Ministry of Civil Affairs of the People's Republic of China

(Ⅱ) Think Tanks of Academies of Social Sciences (51)

Anhui Academy of Social Sciences

Beijing Academy of Social Sciences

Chongqing Academy of Social Sciences

Chongqing Center for Productivity Development

Institute for Innovative City

Fujian Academy of Social Sciences

Gansu Academy of Social Sciences

Guangdong Academy of Social Sciences

Guangxi Academy of Social Sciences

Guizhou Academy of Social Sciences

Hainan Academy of Social Sciences

Hebei Academy of Social Sciences

Henan Academy of Social Sciences

Heilongjiang Provincial Academy of Social Sciences

Strategic Research Institute for Northeast Asia, Heilongjiang Provincial Academy of Social Sciences

Institute for Social Development and Local Governance of Heilongjiang, Heilongjiang Provincial Academy of Social Sciences

Hubei Provincial Academy of Social Sciences

Hunan Academy of Social Sciences

Jilin Academy of Social Sciences

Jiangsu Provincial Academy of Social Sciences

Institute of Modernization, Jiangsu Provincial Academy of Social Sciences

Jiangxi Provincial Academy of Social Sciences

Liaoning Academy of Social Sciences

Nanjing Academy of Social Sciences

Inner Mongolia Academy of Social Sciences

Ningxia Academy of Social Sciences

Qinghai Academy of Social Sciences

Institute of Modernization

Shandong Academy of Social Sciences

Shannxi Academy of Social Sciences

Shanghai Academy of Social Sciences

Sichuan Academy of Social Sciences

Tianjin Academy of Social Sciences

Tibetan Academy of Social Sciences, TAR

Xinjiang Academy of Social Sciences

Yunnan Academy of Social Sciences

Zhejiang Academy of Social Sciences

Chinese Academy of Social Sciences

National Academy of Economic Strategy, CASS

Marxist Political Economy Innovation Think Tank in Contemporary China, CASS

The Institute of Contemporary China Studies, CASS

National Institution for Finance & Development

National Institute of Global Strategy, CASS

Institute of European Studies of Chinese Academy of Social Sciences

Shanghai Academy

National Institute of Social Development

Institute of World Economics and Politics

Taiwan Institute of Chinese Academy of Social Sciences

Ideological Research Institute of Chinese Academy of Social Sciences

China National Center for Cultural Studies

China-CEEC Think Tanks Network

(Ⅲ) Think Tanks of Party Schools/Administrative College (48)

Research & Assessment Center for Anhui Public Policy of Anhui School of

Administration

    Gansu Institute of Public Administration

    China National School of Administration

    E-Governance Research Center of China National School of Administration

    Research Center for Development Strategy and Public Policy of China National School of Administration

    Advisory Committee for Party Decision of China National School of Administration

    Hebei Academy of Governance

    Research Institute of Party Building Theory and Practice Innovation in Jiangsu

    Shandong Academy of Governance

    Shannxi Academy of Governance

    Shanghai Party Institute of CPC (SPI), Shanghai Administration Institute (SAI)

    Institute for Great-Leap-Forward Development of Yunnan

    Anhui Provincial Committee Party School of CPC

    Party School of Beijing Municipal Committee of CPC, Beijing Administration College

    Party School of Chongqing Provincial Committee of CPC, Chongqing Institute of Administration

    Fujian Provincial Committee Party School of CPC, Fujian Administration College

    Gansu Provincial Party School of CPC

    Party School of the Guangdong Provincial Committee of CPC, Guangdong Institute of Public Administration

    Party School of Guangxi Autonomous Region Committee of CPC, Guangxi Institute of Public Administration

    Guizhou Provincial Party School of CPC, Guizhou Administration College

Hainan Provincial Party School of CPC, Hainan Academy of Governance

Hebei Provincial Party School of CPC

Henan Provincial Party School of CPC, Henan Academy of Governance

Heilongjiang Provincial Party School of CPC, Heilongjiang Academy of Governance

Hubei Provincial Party School of CPC, Hubei Academy of Governance

Party School of the Hunan Provincial Committee of CPC, Hunan Academy of Governance

Party School of the Jilin Provincial Committee of CPC, Jilin Academy of Governance

Party School of the Jiangsu Provincial Committee of CPC

Party School of the Jiangxi Provincial Committee of CPC, Jiangxi Academy of Governance

Party School of the Liaoning Provincial Committee of CPC

Party School of Inner Mongolia Autonomous Region Committee of CPC, Inner Mongolia Academy of Governance

Party School of Ningxia Autonomous Region Committee of CPC, Ningxia Academy of Governance

Party School of the Qinghai Provincial Committee of CPC, Qinghai Academy of Governance

Party School of the Shandong Provincial Committee

Party School of the Shannxi Provincial Committee

Party School of the Sichuan Provincial Committee of CPC

Party School of the Tianjin Municipal Committee of CPC, Tianjin Academy of Governance

Party School of the Tianjin Municipal Committee of CPC, Research Center of New-Era Innovative and Service-Oriented Government

Party School of the Tianjin Municipal Committee of CPC, Research Center of Tianjin New-Era Decision-Making of CPC

Party School of the Tianjin Municipal Committee of CPC, Research Center of New-Era Modern Economic System

Party School of Tibet Autonomous Region Committee of CPC, Tibet Autonomous Region Academy of Governance

Party School of Xinjiang Uygur Autonomous Region Committee of CPC, Xinjiang Uygur Autonomous Region Academy of Governance

Party School of Zhejiang Provincial Committee of CPC, Zhejiang Institute of Administration

Party School of Central Committee of CPC

Department of Party Building, Party School of Central Committee of CPC

Institute for International Strategic Studies

China Society of Administration Reform (CSOAR)

Research Institute for the China's Political Party System of the Central Institute of Socialism

(Ⅳ) University Think Tanks (441)

Institute of Anhui Economic Development Research, Anhui University Finance & Economics

Innovative Development Institute, Anhui University

Institute of Information and Strategy Studies, Peking University

National School of Development, Peking University

Institute of State Governance Studies, Peking University

Institute for Cultural Industries, Peking University

The Constitution and Administrative Law Research Center of Peking University

Research Center for China Urban Economy, Peking University

Beijing Research Institute of International Cultural Communication, Beijing International Studies University

Beijing Tourism Development Research Center, Beijing International Studies University

Beijing Research Institute of Cultural Trade of Beijing International Studies University

China Academy of One Belt and One Road Initiative Institute, Beijing International Studies University

Research Center of Capital Garment Culture and Industry of Beijing Institute of Fashion Technology

Beijing Social Building Research Base, Beijing University of Technology

Research Base of Beijing Modern Manufacturing Development, Beijing University of Technology

China Aeronautical Engineering Science and Technology Development Strategy Research Institute, Beihang University

Research Center for Beijing Transportation Development, Beijing Jiaotong University

Beijing Logistics Informatics Research Base, Beijing Jiaotong University

National Academy of Economic Security, Beijing Jiaotong University

Institute of Chinese Marxism and Cultural Development, Beijing Jiaotong University

Sustainable Development Research Institute for Economy and Society of Beijing, Beijing Institute of Technology

Institute of Beijing Studies, Beijing Union University

Beijing Research Center for New Countryside Construction, Beijing University of Agriculture

Institute of International and Comparative Education, Beijing Normal University

Capital Economics of Education Research Base, Beijing Normal University

Beijing Institute of Culture Innovation and Communication of Beijing Normal University

Smart Learning Institute of Beijing Normal University

Collaborative Innovation Center of Assessment for Basic Education Quality, Beijing Normal University

China Institute of Education and Social Development, Beijing Normal University

China Institute for Income Distribution, Beijing Normal University

Winter Olympics Culture Research Center of Beijing Sport University

International Institute of Chinese Studies, Beijing Foreign Studies University

National Research Center for State Language Capability, Beijing Foreign Studies University

Gulf Arab States Research Center, Beijing Foreign Studies University

National Research Center for Canadian Studies, Beijing Foreign Studies University

Center for Japanese Studies, Beijing Foreign Studies University

British Studies Centre, Beijing Foreign Studies University

Center for China-Germany People-to-People Exchange Studies, Beijing Foreign Studies University

Center for Central and Eastern European Studies, Beijing Foreign Studies University

Research Center for Knowledge Management, Beijing Information Science & Technology University

Beijing Literature Language and Cultural Heritage Center, Beijing Language and Culture University

Sichuan Mineral Resources Research Center, Chengdu University of Technology

Think Tank on Natural Disaster Prevention and Geological Environment Protection, Chengdu University of Technology

Institute of Urban-Rural Construction and Development, Chongqing University

Center for Public Economy & Public Policy Research, Chongqing University

Legal Strategy Research Institute of National Cyberspace Security and Big Data, Chongqing University

Consilium Research Institute, Chongqing University

Institute for Sustainable Development Research of CQU

Institute for China Public Service Evaluation and Research, Chongqing University

Research Center for Economy of Upper Reaches of the Yangtze River, Chongqing Technology and Business University

Think Tank for Yunnan Religious Governance and Ethnic Unity and Progress, Dali University

Belt and Road Initiative Research Institute, Dalian Maritime University

Northeast Asia Research Center, Dalian University of Foreign Language

Institute of Economic and Social Development, Dongbei University of Finance and Economics

China Academy of Northeast Revitalization, Northeastern University

Modern Agricultural Development Research Center, Northeastern Agricultural University

Institute of East-Asian Studies, Northeast Normal University

Research Institute of Rural Education, Northeast Normal University

Moral Development Think-Tank, Southeast University

Research Center for Anti-Corruption with Rule of Law, Southeast University

Research Center for Traffic Rule of Law and Development, Southeast University

Judicial Big Data Platform of People's Court, Southeast University

Research Center for Modern Management Accounting Innovation, Southeast University

China High Quality Development Evaluation Research Institute, Southeast University

Institute for the Development of Socialism with Chinese Characteristics, Southeast University

Institute of International Economics, University of International Business and Economics

Research Institute for Global Value Chains, University of International Business and Economics

China Institute for WTO Studies, University of International Business and Economics

National Research Center for Economic Comprehensive Competitiveness, Fujian Normal University

Fudan Development Institute, Fudan University

Center for American Studies, Fudan University

Fudan University Center for Population and Development Policy Studies

Center for Think Tanks Research and Management in Shanghai, Fudan University

Center for Asia-Pacific Cooperation and Governance, Fudan University

Center for Party Building and State Development Studies, Fudan University

Research Institute of Chinese Economy, Fudan University

China Institute, Fudan University

The Research Center for Investigative Theory and Application in Northwestern Ethnic Regions, Gansu Institute of Political Science and Law

National Economics Research Center, Guangdong University of Finance and Economics

Guangdong Institute for International Strategies, Guangdong University of Foreign Studies

Guangxi Research Institute for Innovation and Development of Guangxi University

China-ASEAN Research Institute, Guangxi University

Guangxi Development Research Institute of Intellectual Property, Guangxi University of Nationalities

Guangzhou Development Research Institute, Guangzhou University

Guizhou Research Institute of Big Data Industry Development and Application, Guizhou University

China-ASEAN Research Institute of Guizhou University

Institution of Public Market and Government Procurement, University of International Relations

Center for International Strategy and Security Studies, University of

International Relations

Heilongjiang Regional Innovation Driven Development Research Center, Harbin Engineering University

Heilongjiang Innovation and Entrepreneurship Research Center, Harbin Institute of Technology

"Belt and Road" Initiative Think Tank for Talent Strategy, Harbin Institute of Technology

Think Tank of Public Health Security and Medical Reform Strategy of Heilongjiang, Harbin Medical University

Hainan Policy and Industrial Reform Institute of Low-Carbon Economy, Hainan University

Hainan Institute of Development on International Tourist Destination, Hainan University

Research Center for Policy and Law of the South China Sea of Hainan Province, Hainan University

Hebei Research Center for Eco-Environment Sciences, Hebei University

Hebei University Research Center for Social Development of Islamic Countries

Center for Beijing-Tianjin-Hebei Development Research, Hebei University of Technology

Institute of De Rong, Hebei Finance University

Hebei Research Center for Moral Culture and Social Development, Hebei University of Economics and Business

Collaborative Innovation Center for Beijing-Tianjin-Hebei Integrated Development, Hebei University of Economics and Business

Collaborative Innovation Center of Social Governance by Law and Virtue, Hebei

University of Economics and Business

  Research Center for Changcheng Cultural Security, Hebei Normal University

  Research Base for Modern Service and Public Policy, Hebei Normal University

  Academy of Hinterland Development, Henan University

  Institute for Cultural Development and Strategy, Heilongjiang University

  Institute for Longjiang Revitalization and Development, Heilongjiang University

  Co-Innovation Center of Cultural Development and Strategy, Heilongjiang University

  Co-Innovation Center of Sino-Russia Strategy, Heilongjiang University

  Centre of Hubei Cooperative Innovation for Emission Trading System, Hubei Co-Innovation Innovation Center

  International Trade Research Center, Hunan University

  Financial Development and Credit Management Research Center, Hunan University

  Research Center of Honest Administration, Hunan University

  Research and Spread of National Studies in Yuelu Academy, Hunan University

  China Industrial Finance Collaborative Innovation Center, Hunan University

  China Center for Cultural Soft Power Research, Hunan University

  Center for Studies in Moral Culture, Hunan Normal University

  Human Research Institute of Chinese International Promotion, Hunan Normal University

  Institute of Core Socialist Values, Hunan Normal University

  Institute of Ecological Civilization, Hunan Normal University

  Beijing Energy Development Research Center, North China Electric Power University

Research Center for High Speed Railway and Regional Development, East China Jiaotong University

Center for Energy Economics and Environmental Management, East China University of Science and Technology

Research Center for Social Work and Management, East China University of Science and Technology

Research Center of Yangtze River Delta Regional Integration, East China Normal University

Center for Russian Studies of East China Normal University (CRS)

Institute for National Educational Policy Research, East China Normal University

Institute of Schooling Reform and Development, East China Normal University

Institute of Curriculum and Instruction, East China Normal University

Shanghai Innovation Research Base of Population Structure and Development Trend, East China Normal University

Center for the Study and Application of Chinese Characters, East China Normal University

The Center for Modern Chinese City Studies, East China Normal University

The Institute for Modern Chinese Thought and Culture, East China Normal University

Research Center for Co-development with Neighboring Countries, East China Normal University

East China Institute of Prosecution, East China University of Political Science and Law

Center for Rule of Law Strategy Studies, East China University of Political

Science and Law

Institute of Public Policy, South China University of Technology

Guangzhou Financial Services Innovation and Risk Management Research Base, South China University of Technology

Center of Social Governance Research, South China University of Technology

Center for Government Performance Appraisal, South China University of Technology

Non-traditional Security Centre of Huazhong University of Science and Technology

The Institute of State Governance, Huazhong University of Science and Technology

Academy of Health Policy and Management, Huazhong University of Science and Technology

Peikang Chang Institute for Development Studies, Huazhong University of Science and Technology

Institute of China Rural Studies, Central China Normal University

North Jiangsu Development Research Institute, Huaiyin Institute of Technology

China (Henan) Innovation and Development Institute, Huanghe Science and Technology College

Entrepreneurship and Innovation Graduate School, Jilin University

Center for Northeast Asian Studies, Jilin University

Research Center for Social Justice and Governance of Jilin University

Center for Quantitative Economics of Jilin University

China Center for Public Sector Economy Research at Jilin University

China Center for Aging Studies and Social-Economic Development, Jilin

University

    Chinese Culture Research Center, Jilin University

    Institute of Industrial Economics, Jinan University

    Institute of Guangzhou Nansha Free Trade Test Area Research, Jinan University

    The Public Opinion Big Date Research Center, Jinan University

    Academy of Overseas Chinese Studies, Jinan University

    Institute for Food Safety Risk Management, Jiangnan University

    Jiangsu Institute of Educational Modernization, Jiangsu Second Normal University

    Academy of Applied Maritime Talents of the "Belt and Road" Initiative, Jiangsu Maritime Institute

    Jiangsu Public Security Institute, Jiangsu Police Institute

    Institute of the "Belt and Road", Jiangsu Normal University

    Coordinated Innovation Center for Establishing an All-Around Affluent Society in Jiangxi, Jiangxi University of Finance and Economics

    The Collaborative Innovation Center of Strategic Emerging Industry Development of Jiangxi Province for Monitoring, Forecasting and Decision Supporting, Jiangxi University of Finance and Economics

    Research Center of Nonferrous Metal Industry Development, Jiangxi University of Science and Technology

    Research Center of the Management-Decision Evaluation of Jiangxi Normal University

    Jiangxi Industrial Transformation and Development Research Center, Jiangxi Normal University

    Soviet Area Revitalization Institute of Jiangxi Normal University

Collaborative Innovation Center of Chinese Society Transformation Research, Jiangxi Normal University

Yunnan Integrated Transport Development and Regional Logistics Management Think Tank, Kunming University of Science and Technology

Research Institute of Kunming Scientific Development, Kunming University

Silk Road Economic Research Institute of Lanzhou University of Finance and Economics

The Center for Afghanistan Studies of Lanzhou University

Research Center for Silk Road Belt Construction of Lanzhou University

Center of Studies of Ethnic Minorities in Northwest China of Lanzhou University

Evidence-Based Social Science Research Center of Lanzhou University

China Research Center for Government Performance Management, Lanzhou University

Institute for Central Asian Studies, Lanzhou University

Collaborative Innovation Center of the Opening of Northeast China for Northeast Asia, Liaoning University

China Academy of Northeast Revitalization, Liaoning University

Research Center for the Economics and Politics of Transitional Countries, Liaoning University

MCA-ECNU Institute for Administrative Division

Jiangxi Development Research Institute of Nanchang University

Tourism Planning and Research Center of Nanchang University

Research Center for Central China Economic and Social Development of Nanchang University

Modern Service Industry Think Tank of Nanjing University of Finance and

Economics

 Yangtze Industrial Economics Institution, Nanjing University

 Center for the Social and Economic Development of Yangtze River Delta of Nanjing University

 Institute of African Studies, Nanjing University

 Interdisciplinary Center for Risk, Disaster & Crisis Management, Nanjing University

 Collaborative Innovation Center of South China Sea Studies, Nanjing University

 Zijin Media Think Tank, Nanjing University

 Jiangsu Academy of Talent Development, Nanjing University of Science and Technology

 The Research Center of Intellectual Property Development in Jiangsu, Nanjing University of Science and Technology

 Jin Shanbao Agricultural Modernization Research Institute, Nanjing Agricultural University

 Institute for Chinese Legal Modernization Studies, Nanjing Normal University

 Research Institute of Climate and Environmental Governance, Nanjing University of Information Science & Technology

 Institute of Healthy Jiangsu Development, Nanjing Medical University

 Purple Academy of Culture & Creativity, Nanjing University of Arts

 Binhai Development Institute, Nankai University

 Institute of Issues in Contemporary China, Nankai University

 College of Economic and Social Development, Nankai University

 Japan Research Center of Nankai University

 APEC Study Center of Nankai University

Center for Studies of Political Economy of Nankai University

China Academy of Corporate Governance, Nankai University

Collaborative Innovation Center for China Economy, Nankai University

Chinese Government and Politics Unite Research Center, Nankai University

Jiangsu Yangtze Economic Belt Research Institute, Nantong University

Collaborative Innovation Center for the Study on China, Mongolia and Russia Economic and Trade Cooperation & Construction of Economic Belt on the Prairie Silk Road, Inner Mongolia University of Finance and Economics

Center for Studies of Mongolia, Inner Mongolia University

Center for Mongolian Studies, Inner Mongolia University

Donghai Institute of Ningbo University

Hui Institute of Ningxia University

China Institute for Arab Studies at Ningxia University

Qinghai Provincial Research Center, Qinghai University

Brookings-Tsinghua Center for Public Policy

Institute of International Relation, Tsinghua University

Institute for Contemporary China Studies, Tsinghua University

Research Center for Technological Innovation, Tsinghua University

Carnegie-Tsinghua Center for Global Policy

Research Center for Contemporary Management, Tsinghua University

Center for Crisis Management Research, Tsinghua University

Center for China in the World Economy, Tsinghua University

Institute of Contemporary World Socialism, Shandong University

Center for Confucius Institute Studies, Shandong University

Shandong School of Development at Shandong University

Shandong Regional Financial Reform and Development Research Center, Shandong University

Center for Health Management and Policy, Shandong University

The Institute for Studies in County Development, Shandong University

Center for Judaic and Inter-Religious Studies of Shandong University

Research Institute of Political Parties, Shandong University

Cooperative Innovation Center for Transition of Resource-Based Economics, Shanxi University of Finance and Economics

Institute of Management and Decision of Shanxi University

Institute for the Study of Jin-Merchants of Shanxi University

Center for Experimental Economics in Education at Shaanxi Normal University

Northwest Land and Resource Research Center, Shaanxi Normal University

Northwest Institute of Historical Environment and Sicio-Economic Development, Shaanxi Normal University

Central Asia Institute of Shaanxi Normal University

Language Resources Development Research Center, Shaanxi Normal University

Institute for Western Frontier Region of China, Shaanxi Normal University

Institute for Public Policy and Governance, Shanghai University of Finance and Economics

Shanghai Institute of International Finance Center, Shanghai University of Finance and Economics

China Industrial Development Institute, Shanghai University of Finance and Economics

China Public Finance Institute, Shanghai University of Finance and Economics

Collaborative Innovation Center of China Pilot Free Trade Zone, Shanghai

University of Finance and Economics

  Center for Drug and National Security in Shanghai University

  Research Center for Local Governance, Shanghai University

  Center for Latin American Studies, Shanghai University

  Center for Turkish Studies, Shanghai University

  Think Tank Industry Research Center of Shanghai University

  Shanghai Center for Global Trade and Economic Governance, Shanghai University of International Business and Economics

  Shanghai WTO Affairs Consultation Center, Shanghai University of International Business and Economics

  Shanghai International Shipping Institute, Shanghai Maritime University

  China Institute of FTZ Supply Chain, Shanghai Maritime University

  Institute of Urban Science in Shanghai Jiao Tong University

  The Center for Third Sector, Shanghai Jiao Tong University

  Center for Reform, Innovation and Governance at Shanghai Jiao Tong University

  Research Base on National Marine Rights and Strategy, Shanghai Jiao Tong University

  Cultural Industry Innovation & Development Academy, Shanghai Jiao Tong University

  Institute of Arts and Humanities, Shanghai Jiao Tong University

  Center for World-Class Universities, Shanghai Jiao Tong University

  Institute for Public Opinion Research, Shanghai Jiao Tong University

  China Institute for Urban Governance, Shanghai Jiao Tong University

  China Strategy Institute of Ocean Engineering, Shanghai Jiao Tong University

  Institute of Silk Road Strategy Studies of Shanghai International Studies

University (SISU)

    Centre for British Studies, SISU

    Middle East Studies Institute, SISU

    Center for Global Public Opinions, SISU

    Research of Foreign Language Strategies, SISU

    Shanghai Cooperation Organization Research Institute, Shanghai University of Political Science and Law

    Institute for the Security Studies of the "Belt and Road" Initiative, Shanghai University of Political Science and Law

    Institute of Urban Governance, Shenzhen University

    Center for Basic Laws of Hong Kong and Macao Special Administrative Regions, Shenzhen University,

    Institute of China Overseas Interests, Shenzhen University

    Institute of Human Resources Development and Management, Shenyang Normal University

    Beijing Economics and Social Development Policy Research Base, Capital University of Economics and Business

    Beijing Basic Education Research Base, Capital Normal University

    Institute of South Asian Studies, Sichuan University

    The Faculty of Social Development and Western China Development Studies, Sichuan University

    Collaborative Innovation Center for Security and Development of Western Frontier China, Sichuan University

    Center for Tibetan Studies of Sichuan University

    Soochow University Think Tank

Think Tank for Urban Development, Suzhou University of Science and Technology

Center for Economic Analysis of Law and Policy Evaluation, Tianjin University of Finance and Economics (TUFE)

Business Management Research Center of TUFE

Research Center for Finance and Insurance, TUFE

Tianjin Academy of Free Trade Area, TUFE

Coordinated Innovation Center for Binhai Finance in China, TUFE

China Center for Economic Statistics Research, TUFE

Research Center for Tianjin Urbanization and New Rural Construction, Tianjin Chengjian University

Research Base for the Implementation of National Intellectual Property Strategy, Tianjin University

Educational Science Research Center of Tianjin University

Center for Biosafety Research and Strategy, Tianjin University

APEC Sustainable Energy Center, Tianjin University

Collaborative Innovation Center for Cultural Inheritance of China's Traditional Villages & Architecture Heritages, Tianjin University

Research Institute of China Green Development of Tianjin University

International Research Centre for the Chinese Cultural Heritage Conservation, Tianjin University

Research Center of Tianjin Letters of the Rule of Law, Tianjin Polytechnic University

Research Center of Energy Environment and Green Development, Tianjin University of Science and Technology

Food Safety Strategy and Management Research Center of Tianjin University of Science and Technology

Research Center of Circular Economy d Green Development, Tianjin University of Technology

Think Tank for China's Major Engineering Technology "Going Out" Investment Model and Control, Tianjin University of Technology

Tianjin University of Commerce Modern Service Industry Development Research Center

Research Institute of Governance, Tianjin Normal University

Research Center of Regional Development Strategy and Reform, Tianjin Normal University

Center for Crisis Management Research, Tianjin Normal University

Institute of Free Economic Zone, Tianjin Normal University

Fitness Research Think Tank, Tianjin University of Sport

Northeast Asia Research Center, Tianjin Foreign Studies University

Tianjin Institute for the "Belt and Road" Initiative Studies, Tianjin Foreign Studies University

Institute of Finance and Economics of Tongji University

German Studies Center, Tongji University

Tongji University Sustainable Development and New Urbanization Think-Tank

Institute for China & World Studies, Tongji University

Wuhan University Institute of International Law

Institute of National Culture Development, Wuhan University

Research Institute of Environmental Law, Wuhan University

The Center for Economic Development Research of Wuhan University

Wuhan University Center of Economic Diplomacy

Center for Studies of Media Development, Wuhan University

Center for Social Security Studies of Wuhan University

Center for the Studies of Information Resources, Wuhan University

The Institute of Quality Development Strategy of Wuhan University

Wuhan University China Institute of Boundary and Ocean Studies

National Institute of Chinese Language Matters and Social Development, Wuhan University

Institute for the Development of Central China, Wuhan University

Research Institute of Eurasian Economy and Global Development, Xi'an Jiaotong University

Research Center for Social Governance and Social Policy Collaborative Innovation, Xi'an Jiaotong University

Silk Road Institute for International and Comparative Law of Xi'an Jiaotong University

Collaborative Innovation Centre for Silk Road Economic Belt Studies, Xi'an Jiaotong University

Research Center of China Economic Reform Innovation and Assessment, Xi'an Jiaotong University

Research Centre of Chinese Management, Xi'an Jiaotong University

China (Xi'an) Digital Economy Development Research Center, Xi'an Jiaotong University

Institute of the "Belt and Road" Pilot Free Trade Zone, Xi'an Jiaotong University

Research Institute of Silk Road Cultural Heritage Protection and Archeology,

Northwest University

   Institute of Middle Eastern Studies, Northwest University

   Economic Development Research Center of West China, Northwest University

   Research Center for Science, Technology and Industry Development for National Defense of Western China, Northwestern Polytechnical University

   The Gansu Province's Construction and Research Center of Cultural Resource and Chinese Civilization, Northwest Normal University

   Center for Targeted Poverty Alleviation & Regional Development Research, Northwest Normal University

   The Research Center for the "Belt and Road" Initiative and Education Development, Northwest Normal University

   Institute of Anti-Terrorism Studies, Northwest University of Political Science and Law

   Institute of National Religion of Northwest University of Political Science and Law

   Collaborative Innovation Center of Financial Security, Southwest University of Finance and Economics

   Survey and Research Center for China Household Finance, Southwest University of Finance and Economics

   Institute of Chinese Financial Studies of Southwest University of Finance and Economics

   Western Center for Economic Research in China, Southwest University of Finance and Economics

   The Research Center for Public Culture, Southwest University

   Research Center for Urban and Rural Education Development, Southwest

University

Center for Hellenic Studies, Southwest University

Center for Studies of Education and Psychology of Minorities in Southwest China of Southwest University

Center for Iranian Studies, Southwest University

Research Center of Western Transportation Strategy and Regional Development, Southwest Jiaotong University

Sichuan Province Cyclic Economy Research Center, Southwest University of Science and Technology

Development Research Center of Oil and Gas of Sichuan, Southwest Petroleum University

Human Rights Institute, Southwest University of Political Science and Law

Institute for Tibetan Sustainable Development, Tibet University

Center for Collaborative Innovation in the Heritage and Development of Xizang Culture, Xizang Minzu University

Center for Southeast Asian Studies, Xiamen University

Center for Higher Education Development of Xiamen University

Center for Macroeconomic Research, Xiamen University

Taiwan Research Institute of Xiamen University

China Institute for Studies in Energy Policy, Xiamen University

Local Legislation and Social Governance Research Center, Xiangtan University

Public Administration and Regional Economic Development Research Center of Xiangtan University

The Studying Center of Mao Zedong Thought, Xiangtan University

Government Performance Evaluation and Management Innovation Research

Center of Xiangtan University

Research Center of Revolutionary Spirit and Cultural Resources of the Communist Party of China, Xiangtan University

Hebei Provincial Public Policy Evaluation and Research Center, Yanshan University

Hebei Design Innovation & Industrial Development Research Center, Yanshan University

Institute of Korean Peninsula Studies, Yanbian University

Think Tank of Coastal Development, Yancheng Teachers University

Center for Advanced Study of Public Policy, Yunnan University of Finance and Economics

Research Institute for Indian Ocean Economics, Yunnan University of Finance and Economics

Yunnan Think Tank on Disaster Prevention and Mitigation, Yunnan University of Finance and Economics

Frontier Ethnic Problems Think-Tank of Yunnan University

Institute of Myanmar Studies, Yunnan University

Culture Development Institute of Yunnan University

Center for China's Neighbor Diplomacy Studies, Yunnan University

National Institute for Innovation Management, Zhejiang University

Center for Non-Traditional Security and Peaceful Development Studies, Zhejiang University

Public Policy Research Institute of Zhejiang University

Center for Research of Private Economy, Zhejiang University

Institute of China's Science, Technology and Education Policy, Zhejiang

University

China Academy for Rural Development of Zhejiang University

China Academy of West Region Development, Zhejiang University

The Collaborative Innovation Center for the "Belt and Road" Initiative, Zhejiang University

Center for China Farmers' Development, Zhejiang A & F University

Institute of African Studies, Zhejiang Normal University

Ningbo Maritime Silk Road Institute, Zhejiang Wanli University

National Center for Radio and Television Studies, CUC

The Capital's Research Base of Media Economy (BJ Media), CUC

Institute of Marine Development, Ocean University of China

Center for Japanese Studies, Ocean University of China

China Business Working Capital Management Research Center, Ocean University of China

Anhui Province Key Laboratory of Big Data Analysis and Application, University of Science and Technology of China

Research Center of Anhui Science and Technology Innovation and Regional Development, University of Science and Technology of China

China Urban Public Security Management Think Tank, China University of Mining and Technology

Institute of Airport Economics, Civil Aviation University of China

Research Center for Environment and Sustainable Development of the China Civil Aviation, Civil Aviation University of China

Research Center for International Development, China Agricultural University

Institute of China Agricultural Economics and Rural Development, China

Agricultural University

    Center for Land Policy and Law, China Agricultural University

    Chongyang Institute for Financial Studies, Renmin University of China

    National Academy of Development and Strategy, Renmin University of China

    The Research Center of Civil and Commercial Jurisprudence of Renmin University of China

    Population and Development Studies Center, Renmin University of China

    Collaborative Innovation Center for Social Transformation and Social Governance, Renmin University of China

    The Research Center of Criminal Justice at Renmin University of China

    China Financial Policy Research Center, Renmin University of China

    Center for Capital Social Safety, People's Public Security University of China

    School of Law-Based Government, China University of Political Science and Law

    Institution for Human Rights at China University of Political Science and Law

    Collaborative Innovation Center of Judicial Civilization of China, China University of Political Science and Law

    China Society of Administrative Reform, China University of Political Science and Law

    Collaborative Innovation Center of Industrial Upgrading and Regional Finance (Hubei), Zhongnan University of Economics and Law

    The Co-Innovation Center for Social Management of Urban and Rural Communities in Hubei Province, Zhongnan University of Economics and Law

    Center for the Development of Rule of Law and Judicial Reform Research of Zhongnan University of Economics and Law

    Center for Studies of Intellectual Property Rights, Zhongnan University of

Economics and Law

China's Income Distribution Research Center, Zhongnan University of Economics and Law

Institute for Local Governance of Central South University

Legislative Research Base for Education of Central South University

Institute of Metal Resources Strategy, Central South University

Collaborative Innovation Center for Resource Conserving & Environment-friendly Society and Ecological Civilization

Center for Social Stability Risk Assessment of Central South University

Political Consultation Office of United Front Department, CSU

Institute of Medical and Health Law, CSU

Applied Ethics Research Center of CSU

Intellectual Property Research Institute of Central South University

Research Center of Chinese Village Culture, Central South University

China Center for Cultural Law Research of Central South University

Institute of State Governance, Sun Yat-sen University

Institute of South China Sea Strategic Studies, Sun Yat-sen University

Institute of Guangdong, Hong Kong and Macao Development Studies, Sun Yat-sen University

Institute of Public Procurement, Central University of Finance and Economics

International Institute of Green Finance, Central University of Finance and Economics

China Center for Internet Economy Research Central University of Finance and Economics

Center for China Fiscal Development, Central University of Finance and

Economics

Research Center for China's Banking Industry, Central University of Finance and Economics

(V) Military Think Tanks (6)

Beijing System Engineering Research Institute

Research Center for Defense Technology and Civil Military Integration of National University of Defense Technology

National Defense Science and Technology Strategy Research Center of National University of Defense Technology

International Studies Center of National University of Defense Technology

National Defense University of People's Liberation Army, NDU, PLA

Academy of Military Sciences, PLA, China

(VI) Think Tanks of Research Institutes (34)

Beijing Research Center for Science of Science

Surveying and Mapping Development Research Center, NASG

Rural Development Research Institute of Hunan

Jiangsu Information Institute of Science and Technology (Jiangsu Science and Technology Development Strategy Research Institute)

Jiangsu Suke Academy of Innovation Strategy

Jiangxi Academy of Sciences Institute of Science & Technology Strategy

International Engineering Education Center, United Nations Educational, Scientific and Cultural Organization

Research Center of Science and Technology for Development of Liaoning

Qingdao Institute of Science and Technology Development Strategy

Institute of Science and Technology for Development of Shandong

Shanghai Institutes for International Studies

Shanghai Institute of Science & Technology Policy (Shanghai Institute of Science & Technology Management)

Shanghai Institute for Science of Science

Capital Institute of Science and Technology Development Strategy

Development Research Center of the Ministry of Water Resources of P. R. China

Tianjin Research Institute of Economic Development

Western China Think Tank on Resources, Environment and Development

China Steel Development & Research Institute

Zhejiang Institute of Science and Technology Information (Zhejiang Institute of Science and Technology Development Strategy)

China Center for Information Industry Development

Chinese Academy of Engineering

China Aerospace Engineering Science and Technology Development Strategy Research Institute

Chinese Research Academy of Environmental Sciences

National Academy of Innovation Strategy

Chinese Academy of Science and Technology for Development

Institute of Scientific and Technical Information of China

Chinese Academy of Sciences

Institutes of Science and Development, Chinese Academy of Sciences

Center for Forecasting Science, Chinese Academy of Sciences

CNPC Economics & Technology Research Institute

China Academy of Information and Communication Technology

China Institute of Science and Technology Development Strategies on Information and Electronic Engineering

Center of Cutural Development and Strategy, Chinese National Academy of Arts

Think Tank for Traditional Chinese Medicine, China Information Association for Traditional Chinese Medicine and Pharmacy

(Ⅶ) Corporate Think Tanks (8)

Ali Research

Beijing Greatwall Enterprise Institute

Electric Power Planning & Engineering Institute

Institute of China Development Bank

Suning Institute of Finance

Tengyun Think Tank

Advising Committee for China Academy of Management Science

CITIC Foundation for Reform and Development Studies

(Ⅷ) Private Think Tanks (36)

International Institute for Urban Development, Beijing

The Charhar Institute

Changjiang Education Research Institute

Institute of Industry Development Research, Changsha

Chongqing Think Tank

China Region Development & Reform Institute (CRDRI)

South China Business Think Tank of Guangdong University of Finance and

Economics

    Asia-Pacific Innovation Economic Research Institute of Guangdong

    China Strategy Institute for Intellectual Property (Guangdong ZHONGCE Intellect Property Research Institute)

    Grandview Institution

    Intellisia Institute

    Hainan Institute for World Watch

    Research and Development International, Chinese Academy of Social Sciences

    The Association of Soft Science Research of Liaoning

    The Pangoal Institution

    Chunqiu Institute for Development and Strategic Studies

    Shanghai FC Institute of Economics Forecast CO., Ltd.

    Shanghai Academy of Huaxia Social Development Research

    Shanghai Institute of Finance and Law

    Shanghai Finance Institute

    Shenzhen Innovation and Development Institute

    Wanb Institute

    New Silk Road Economic Institute

    Knowfar Institute for Struggles and Defense Studies

    China Center for International Economic Exchanges

    China Finance 40 Forum

    China Society of Economic Reform

    China Institute for Leadership Science

    National Institute for South Sea Studies

    China Enterprise Reform and Development Society

China Silk Road iValley Research

Center for China & Globalization

China Institute for Reform and Development

China Institute of Science and Technology

China Development Institute

the "Belt and Road"

(IX) Media Think Tanks (13)

YICAI Research Institute

Cover Institute

Phoenix International Think Tank

Research Center of Cultural and Creative Industry at *Guangming Daily*

Guangming Think Tank

Guangzhou Daily Data & Digit Institute

China Economic Trends Research Institute

Liaowang Institute

Nanfang Media Think Tank

South Reviews Media Institute

Shengjinghui Think Tank

People's Daily Online New Media Institute

Xinhua News Agency

2018 CTTI 高校智库暨百强榜报告

高等学校是人才密集、学科齐备、国际交往活跃的机构,在我国人才培养、科学研究和社会服务中有着重要地位。经过党的十八大以来对中国特色新型智库建设的宣传引导、大力推进,我国高等学校里大部分承担对策研究功能的研究中心、研究基地和研究所都逐渐形成了"智库行业自觉",更加认同智库概念,积极向新型智库转型,在咨政启民、公共外交、推动学科发展、繁荣哲学社会科学等方面取得了长足进步。

1 高校系统高度重视新型智库建设

教育部高度重视新型智库建设。2014年2月10日,教育部印发了《中国特色新型高校智库建设推进计划》,其中凝练了8个主攻方向,提出了4条高校智库建设路径,强调了高校智库队伍建设的重要性,指出要拓展成果应用渠道,打造高端发布平台,改革管理方式,创新组织形式等重要意见。2015年1月20日,中共中央办公厅、国务院办公厅印发《关于加强中国特色新型智库建设的意见》,指出要推动高校智库发展完善,发挥高校学科齐全、人才密集和对外交流广泛的优势,深入实施中国特色新型高校智库建设推进计划,推动高校智力服务能力整体提升。为贯彻中央新型智库建设部署,2015年1月底,教育部印发了《教育部2015年工作要点》,指出要全面落实《中国特色新型高校智库建设推进计划》,深化人文社会科学重点研究基地管理方式和组织形式改革,启动高端智库建设。随后,在2015—2018年教育部的多份文件中,均提到推进中国特色新型高校智库建设。

各省市及自治区教育主管部门也根据自身实际制定了相应的文件。早在2011年,上海市教育委员会就发文指出,要树立上海高校智库品牌。2013年11月,湖北省教育厅和财政厅印发了《湖北省普通高等学校哲学社会科学繁荣计划(2013—2020年)》,努力打造一批"湖北急需、国内一流、制度先进、贡献重大"的特色新型高校智库,以前瞻性眼光为湖北省高校智库建设提供了政策指引。2015年后,上海市、甘肃省、浙江省、广西壮族自治区、湖南省、天津市、山东省、重庆市、辽宁省、吉林省等先后印发相关文件,加强高校智库建设,发挥高校智库功能。各地区的政策响应为高校智库建设蓬勃发展奠定了良好基础。

2 高校在新型智库建设中的独特作用

2.1 学科齐全,便于开展跨学科的问题导向研究

大学是专家学者的聚集地,也是知识生产与积累的重要场所,集中了各领域的精英。许多高校建立起了门类齐全的学科体系,尤其是综合性大学,它们办学历史悠久、学术积累深厚、基础研究力量强大,在前瞻性、储备性的政策研究中占有学科综合的资源优势。当前,全面建成小康社会进入决定性阶段,破解改革发展问题和应对全球性问题的复杂性前所未有,单一学科在解决国家应对的难题时常常力不从心,需要横跨自然科学、人文社会科学,凝聚多个学科的力量共同探索解决方案。另外,高校的学科优势还体现在高校智库可以依托本校的紧密型专家网络,成为智库人才网络的整合中心。比如,南京大学紫金传媒智库的主力部队就是由该校社会学院、法学院、政府管理学院、新闻学院和信息管理学院五大学院相关团队相互联合、交叉渗透所形成的。也因为这样的研究队伍架构,高校智库得以避免变成学校中的"孤岛",而是成为推进大学学科交叉的"催化剂"。

2.2 人才富集,有利于开展大规模数据工程

智库从事的是基于证据的政策研究。各种类型的特色数据库是政策分析的基础。数据库建设中,有大量数据收集和整理工作,高校的研究生是从事数据收集、整理和分析的最佳人选。研究生还是智库高级研究员(教授)的得力行政助手。不少著名高校智库都广泛利用了研究生这支生力军。

2.3 高校智库有开展公共外交的便捷通道

世界知名大学都存在着广泛而频繁的学术交流与合作,具有自由度高、学科领域广泛、起点高等特点。相比党政部门智库,高校智库的研究人员在出国交流上的限制更少,有利于开展学术交流和人文交流,全面了解国外有关信息,减少信息不对称,降低信息壁垒,避免误读误判。

2.4 高校智库舆论公信力较高

学术机构的任务是"求真""求知",使知识得以生产和传播。学者的学术观点通常具有一定的权威性,尤其是知名专家经常具有强大的社会公信力。高校智库可以把握好自身的专业性、科学性,积极发挥引导社会舆论的功能优势。

2.5 高校智库专业特征明显

与平台型的社科院、党校行政学院智库相比,高校智库一般体量不大,与决策端的距离较远,但是高校智库专业特色和领域划分明显,有利于为党政系统提供技术密集、知识密集、数据密集的专业服务。从智库知识服务来讲,政府需要的不仅是政策设计思路,也需要真实数据和明确的规划方案。比如,天津大学生物安全战略研究中心作为专业性高校智库,在生物技术发展、生物军控履约、国际法等多领域开展决策咨询,先后参与起草科技部《生物技术研究开发安全管理办法》、参与修订《人类遗传资源管理条例》,负责起草的"生物科学家行为准则范本"在联合国《禁止生物武器公约》第八次审议大会上作为中国政府的两项提案之一,受到国际社会的广泛关注和好评。2017年11月,该中心获批成为联合国《禁止生物武器公约》中国首家非政府组织(NGO),并多次在联合国日内瓦总部代表中国作大会发言。

3 高校智库在新型智库体系中占据了重要地位

截至2018年11月20日,中国智库索引(CTTI)共收录706家来源智库,其中高校智库441家,占比达62%。在2018年新增补的105家来源智库中,有94家是高校智库,占比高达90%。目前,CTTI系统共收录了来自高校智库的7 110篇内参、

17 646 份报告、4 978 篇报纸文章、6 220 本图书和 45 130 篇论文,分别占 CTTI 系统内各成果总量的 74%、81%、52%、80%、85%。高校智库已经成为智库内容生产的主力军,这也是中国智库建设的一大特色。公认拥有众多高水平智库的美国,高校智库数量占比远低于中国。可见,高校智库在中国特色新型智库体系中的地位十分重要,应当予以高度重视。

3.1 高校智库的地域分布

CTTI 系统数据显示,高校智库地域分布不均衡,各省市和自治区之间差异较大,少数省份高度集中。从表 1 来看,在遴选进入 CTTI 的高校智库中,北京市拥有 78 家,占比 17.7%。数量排名前六位的省市分别为北京、上海、天津、江苏、湖南和湖北,共有 233 家高校智库入选,占据了高校智库的半壁江山。东部地区入选高校智库数量多,有 263 家;中部和西部入选高校智库较少,只有 178 家。

这些省市的来源高校智库能在总量中占据如此高的比例,很大原因是这六个省市"985 高校""211 高校"集中,拥有丰富且优质的智力资源。可见,要办好高校智库,学术研究基础和学科发展水平是重中之重。

表 1　CTTI 来源智库中高校智库地域分布情况

地域	数量	地域	数量	地域	数量
北京市	78	浙江省	12	安徽省	4
上海市	58	甘肃省	11	山西省	3
天津市	39	山东省	11	内蒙古自治区	3
江苏省	32	江西省	11	广西壮族自治区	3
湖南省	26	云南省	10	河南省	2
湖北省	23	河北省	10	宁夏回族自治区	2
陕西省	21	吉林省	10	海南省	2
广东省	17	黑龙江省	9	贵州省	2
四川省	13	辽宁省	8	青海省	1
重庆市	13	福建省	6	西藏自治区	1

3.2 中国高校智库类型及研究领域分布

我国高校智库可以分为综合型智库和专业型智库两大类。在CTTI系统填报专业范围的286家高校智库中，仅有33%（94家）属于综合型，这类智库横跨多个研究领域；其余的67%皆为专业型智库。

CTTI系统数据显示，高校智库的十大政策研究领域分别为产业政策（87家）、金融政策（81家）、文化政策（66家）、外交政策（60家）、市场政策（53家）、安全政策（42家）、对外贸易政策（40家）、资源政策（38家）、社会建设与社会政策（36家）和司法政策（35家）。而高校智库研究较少的领域为水利政策、公安政策、检察政策、审计政策、药品政策和林业政策等，仅有1至3家智库有所涉及。

3.3 高校智库的规模

CTTI系统中有325家高校智库填报了人员数据，其中有10家智库的总人数超过100人，如南开大学中国特色社会主义经济建设协同创新中心、南京大学长江产业经济研究院、华中师范大学中国农村研究院等，这些智库规模较大，人员构成较为复杂。其余智库的人员规模基本都处于10至100人之间，尤其集中于10至50人，有一半以上的高校智库人数都在这一区间，属于中型规模智库。单就智库全职研究员人数来看，近80%的高校智库拥有10名以上全职研究员。可见，我国高校智库目前普遍处于第二发展阶段，面对的是向智库成熟发展转型的关键时期。

3.4 中国大学智库指数

CTTI大学智库指数是把来源智库中直属于同一所大学的各个智库的综合测评分值进行求和，得出该大学的智库总值，定义该值为U^n，旨在衡量一个大学的智库功能。其具体原理阐述和计算办法见总报告有关部分。大体而言，一所大学入选CTTI来源智库数量越多，成果越丰富，大学的智库指数越高。为了公平比较不同类型和体量的高校，本报告依然把我国高校分为三档进行排序，每档按照高校名称音序排列（表2，表3，表4）。位居前列的高校有北京大学、清华大学、复旦大学、南开大学、武汉大学、浙江大学、北京师范大学、南京大学等，由于这些高校拥有实力较强的经济管理学院、政府管理学院、国际关系学院、法学院等特色院系,能够为智库的运作提供必要的智力支持与运营技巧,能够发挥智库更大的影响力。

表2 原"985高校"大学智库指数前20名(按音序排列)

北京大学
北京师范大学
东南大学
复旦大学
华东师范大学
华中科技大学
吉林大学
南京大学
南开大学
清华大学
上海交通大学
四川大学
天津大学
武汉大学
西安交通大学
厦门大学
浙江大学
中国海洋大学
中国人民大学
中南大学

表 3 原"211 高校"大学智库指数前 20 名(按音序排列)

安徽大学
北京交通大学
北京外国语大学
东北师范大学
广西大学
河北工业大学
湖南师范大学
华中师范大学
暨南大学
江南大学
南京理工大学
南京师范大学
陕西师范大学
上海大学
上海外国语大学
苏州大学
延边大学
云南大学
中国政法大学
中南财经政法大学

表 4 普通高校智库指数前 30 名(按音序排列)

安徽财经大学
北京第二外国语学院
北京联合大学
成都理工大学
福建师范大学
广东外语外贸大学

(续表)

广州大学
河北大学
河北金融学院
河北经贸大学
淮阴工学院
江苏警官学院
江苏师范大学
江西师范大学
南京信息工程大学
南京艺术学院
南通大学
内蒙古财经大学
上海对外经贸大学
上海海事大学
深圳大学
首都经济贸易大学
首都师范大学
天津财经大学
西北师范大学
西藏民族大学
燕山大学
盐城师范学院
云南财经大学
浙江师范大学

4 CTTI 高校智库百强评价愿景与原则

4.1 CTTI 高校智库百强评价的界定

CTTI 高校智库百强评价,是将收录于中国智库索引的441家高校智库,从智库产品（product）、智库活动（activity）、智库媒体影响（impact）和智库专家主观评价（expert）四个维度进行的综合评价，按照分数高低选出 100 家优秀智库，将它们评定为"A 区高校智库"，并形成"CTTI 高校智库百强榜"。因此这又称为"PAI-E 100 评价"，这个榜单也可以谐音称为"湃 100 高校智库"，寓意是肯定我国高校智库澎湃的发展潜能。根据排名将所有 A 区高校智库细分为 A+、A、A-三个等级，三个等级分别有 25 家、35 家和 40 家智库，而其他未入围的智库则为 B 区、C 区高校智库。2018 年报告只公布 A 区高校智库的名单。

PAI-E 100 评价与 MRPAI 综合评价有所区别。首先，PAI-E 100 评价是产出导向型评价，倾向于对智库的成果产出和影响进行评价，不将智库的管理（management）与资源（resource）投入纳入评价体系；其次，PAI-E 100 评价是智库填报的客观数据和专家主观意见评价相结合的新型评价体系，将专家主观评价纳入评价体系中，结合了两种评价方法的优点，从而更加全面客观地衡量智库建设的水平；最后，PAI-E 100 评价只针对高校智库进行评价，各智库产生智库成果、发挥智库功能、产生智库影响的方式有较高的相似性，与把不同类型智库放在一起评价相比，使用相同的评价尺度能够更加合理地度量和评价智库建设的水平。

4.2 CTTI 高校智库百强评价的目的

南京大学中国智库研究与评价中心和光明日报智库研究与发布中心（以下简称"两个中心"）始终恪守本心，坚持开放、共建、共享原则，为智库提升管理质量提供专业服务。CTTI 高校百强智库评价的目的，是通过对来源高校智库进行评价的方式，促进中国特色新型高校智库建设健康发展。

中国特色新型高校智库建设正如火如荼开展。许多高校尤其是知名高校非常重视新型智库建设，以前许多高校文科建设工作汇报的内容大多以学科建设为主，而现在却会分配一定的篇幅汇报一年来高校新型智库建设的情况，智库建设已成为高校文科工作的重要方面和学科建设的重要指标。然而，这不意味着所有的高校智库都充分发挥了智库功能、符合国家智库建设的预期目标。一部分高校智库存在着治理和营运方面的问题，它们对自身的定位不准、认识不清，智库产品质量有待提高，智库建设水平还有相当大的提升空间。从宏观上看，全国高校智库发展质量也是参差不齐的，地域之间、高校之间、不同研究领域之间的智库发展水平存在一定差距，这既需要国家政策的支持，也需要智库界专业意见的引导。

本次评价的愿景是通过 CTTI 高校智库百强评价的方式，遴选一批优秀的高校智库，邀请它们分享智库建设经验和成果，发挥它们在智库领域的标杆和示范作用，将其先进的智库建设理念提供给广大高校智库，作为参考和学习的范例。"世界上没有两片完全相同的树叶"，纳入榜单的高校智库有各自的独到之处，其建设经验也并非放之四海而皆准。其他高校智库可以与同类优秀智库进行比较、分析、判断，结合自身实际，调整出最合适自己的发展路径，将百强高校智库的建设经验"以我为主、为我所用"，不断赶超优秀智库的建设步伐，使中国特色高校智库建设不断刷新成绩。

中国智库索引自发布以来，得到了广大智库的充分认可，许多来源智库将入选中国智库索引视为一种专业性肯定。"两个中心"希望"CTTI 高校智库百强榜"能成为一种服务来源智库、宣传来源智库的全新方式，鼓励各来源智库继续推进数据的共建共享、质量的切实提升，最终达到"以评促建"的目的。

4.3 CTTI 高校智库百强评价的原则

(1) 客观性与独立性

"两个中心"的评价工作始终秉持客观和独立的原则，并将此原则贯彻到 CTTI 高校智库百强评价工作的每一环节。"两个中心"坚持客观性原则，尽可能全面、准确地收集各高校智库建设的数据，以获取到的数据为依据，忠于事实、实事求是，力求使评价结果真实地展现出各家高校智库的建设水平。评价所依据的数据来源于 CTTI 系统各来源高校智库的填报、智库专家评价意见以及各类公开信息。"两个中心"以第三方智库研究机构的身份开展评价工作，坚持独立性原则，确保不受其他机构和个人的影响，无偏见地公平对待每家来源高校智库填报的数据，尊重专家打分和评价意见，使评价工作达到应有的专业水准。

(2) 保护用户隐私

保护各来源智库的数据是"两个中心"从始至终恪守的原则。CTTI 高校智库百强评价使用的数据均在后台生成,为了保护各来源智库的隐私,本次榜单不公开机构的各项得分。但来源智库可以以机构名义向南京大学中国智库研究与评价中心发函查询,届时可获得自己的各项得分。

(3) 以结果为导向

CTTI 高校智库百强评价采用 PAI - E 100 评价体系,侧重于对智库的生产力和影响力进行评价,看智库多大程度上发挥了政策影响力、学术影响力和社会影响力。

CTTI 高校智库百强评价创新性地分离出 PAI 值指标,是符合高校智库发展实际的。首先,中国高校管理体制具有一致性,高校在进行智库管理时的方式也有很高相似度,M 值对 CTTI 高校智库评价结果影响有限,于是在本次评价中不使用 M 值。其次,高等院校是专家学者的主要科研场所,高校智库天然具有聚集顶尖智力资源的能力和优势。然而,一部分高校智库虽然聘用了许多知名智库研究专家,但由于大部分专家为兼职聘用、资源整合能力有限等因素,智库未能充分激发和利用专家的科研力量,名义上占有众多资源,却不具备与之匹配的产出能力。将 R 值纳入评价体系会产生潜在的不公平因素,会导致某些资源充足但成果偏少的智库分数较高,而某些资源不占优势但成果和影响力喜人的优秀智库无法入选,使用 PAI 值则很好地解决了这一问题。除此之外,PAI 值作为对生产力和影响力的评价指标,符合 CTTI 高校智库百强评价的预期目标,让充分发挥智库功能的智库脱颖而出,而非选出资源上最占优势的智库。

(4) 客观数据与专家主观意见相结合

CTTI 高校智库百强评价的数据来源分为两种:一是中国智库索引内各家来源智库主动填报的数据,二是智库专家打分与评选意见。评价以客观数据为主、专家主观意见为辅,两类数据相辅相成,以更加客观地反映来源高校智库的建设成果。

CTTI 系统建立了共建共享的数据采集机制,目前系统采集数据的方式有三种:

(1) 依靠来源智库和专家自主填报的方式;(2) 南京大学中国智库研究与评价中心手工收集;(3) 网上数据自动抓取。其中第一种方式是主流,数据由智库机构管理员或者专家本人录入,提交给 CTTI 系统后台进行严格的质量审核,每一条数据只有在审核准确无误后才提交到数据库。这种数据采集机制表面上人工投入巨大,实际上由于采用了共建"众包"(众筹)模式,实现了数据共建共享,数据采集成本分摊到每一个参与者,反而比较低廉。通过人工模式搜集数据,数据的精准性、客观性和有效性能够得到充分的保障,使数据能够准确反映出各高校智库建设取得的各项成果。为减少人为干扰影响力数据的情况,除后台管理员填报的少数字段外,CTTI 系统内每个智库、每位专家的影响力数值,都是根据填报的数据自动计算出来的。这与以网络大数据分析为主的评价有很大的不同。虽然大数据具有数据量大、数据种类多样等优点,但是也具有数据质量不高、数据价值密度低、可能存在误导性等缺点。此外,由于内参专报、领导批示等信息具有严格的保密性,网络大数据很大程度上缺少了对政策产生直接影响力的内参信息。某些智库产品和活动不具备公开性,在网络上没有被披露,网络大数据无法完全反映智库咨政建言的能力和成绩。

本系统数据的准确性和客观性,保证了 CTTI 高校智库百强评价结果的可靠性。然而,仅靠系统采集数据也存在一定问题。首先,有些来源智库不能在截止时间前填报完成果信息,也有极少数智库存在夸大成果的情况。其次,PAI 值虽然具备诸多优点,但在实际的数据采集中更侧重于体现智库的生产力,尚不能精确反映出智库的影响力。党政机关对智库的政策建言是否真正满意、学界对智库的研究成果是否真正认可、智库声誉是否能得到业界同行的肯定、智库发声是否在社会上产生积极反响,这些都是客观数据——PAI 值难以计算出来的。目标受众的主观反馈无疑是非常重要的评价指标,于是,系统引入了"E 值",即专家对智库进行打分评价,来弥补客观数据的不足之处,将 PAI 值难以衡量的定性指标进行量化。因此,$PAI-E$ 100 评价是客观数据与专家主观评价相结合的评价体系。

(5) 邀请高校智库进行自我评价

结合CTTI高校智库百强评价工作的初衷,"两个中心"采用第三方评价与机构自我评价相结合的原则开展此项工作。第三方评价,即与评价对象、管理部门等当事人无直接关系的第三方对评价主体做出的独立、公正、客观的评估或建议。"两个中心"作为超脱于高校智库与其管理部门的第三方,进行CTTI高校智库百强榜排名和发布,属第三方评价。除此之外,本次评价将机构自我评价也纳入评价体系当中,这是同一项评估工作的另一个环节,是对第三方评价的有益补充。最了解各个高校智库建设成就的,不是评价机构,恰恰是高校智库自身,它们最清楚自己的竞争力,最能准确地总结自己的建设经验。因此,在百强榜出炉之后,我们将邀请上榜智库撰写各自的"智库小传",以高校智库自我评价的方式,为中国特色新型高校智库建设提供经验与借鉴。

5 CTTI高校智库百强评价体系及算法

5.1 CTTI高校智库百强评价体系构建

(1) CTTI系统客观数据及其赋值

CTTI高校智库百强评价使用"PAI-E评价体系",其中PAI值为CTTI系统后台根据智库填报的数据自动计算得出,属客观评价数据;E值为使用调查问卷法,通过CTTI系统向权威智库专家发放问卷所得,属主观评价数据。

PAI值由三部分构成,是P值、A值、I值三者之和(表5)。P值是将智库各种类型的产品,通过分别赋值的方式,转化成的数值型数据。纳入P值计算的智库产品包括单篇内参、被批示内参、智库主办或承办的期刊、正式出版的图书、研究报告、发表在《人民日报》《求是》《光明日报》等媒体的文章、论文、纵向项目、横向项目等9类成果,是智库产生学术影响力、政策影响力、权威媒体影响力的直接反映。智库与传统的科研机构有所区别,传统科研机构重视学术研究,而智库更加重视对策研究、政策研究,发挥舆论引导功能,产生政策影响力和社会影响力。因此,在CTTI系统的赋值体系中,期刊论文、图书等学术性成果分值较低,而内参尤其是党政机关领导予以批示的内参、研究报告以及发表在国家权威媒体上的文章等政策咨询类、舆论引导类成果,则被赋予了相当高的分值。我们希望通过这样的方式鼓励高校智库转变传统的学术思维,避免学术路径依赖,加强战略研究、咨政建言,加强舆论引导,充分发挥智库功能。

A 值是将高校智库举办的活动,如会议、培训、机构考察等,通过赋值的方式计算转化成的数值型数据,用以测量智库的活跃度,直观反映智库属性和智库影响力。我们认为,活动多的智库未必就是优秀智库,但活动很少、活跃度过低的智库一定智库特征不明显,更像是传统的大学研究中心。参照国际经验来看,智库要发挥影响力,举办高层次高水平的论坛和会议是其重要途径之一,世界著名智库几乎都是会议中心,几乎都是重大政策路演的主要平台,因此,CTTI 系统对于智库举办的全国性会议和国际性会议给予较高的赋值。调研考察是具有中国特色的智库研究方法,没有调查研究就没有发言权,因此 CTTI 系统也给予此类活动较高的赋分。

I 值是度量高校智库媒体影响力的指标,是把电视新闻、报纸新闻、网络新闻三大类新闻报道,通过赋值的方式转化成的数值型数据,是反映智库媒体影响力和知名度的有效指标。世界知名智库大都非常重视智库成果传播,并且在智库成果传播方面非常专业,善于并乐于与大型媒体开展深度合作。CTTI 系统按照报道的媒体级别的不同,分别予以赋分,旨在唤醒高校智库的传播意识。

表 5　高校智库 PAI 测评指标及其赋值

一级指标	代码	二级指标	计分规则	分值
智库成果	P	单篇内参(无论是否被批示)	按篇赋值	2
		被批示内参	正国级/每条	30
			副国级/每条	20
			省部级/每条	10
			副省部级/每条	5

（续表）

一级指标	代码	二级指标	计分规则	分值
		智库主办/承办期刊	每种 CSSCI 来源刊	20
			每种普通期刊	10
			每种通讯/内参集	8
		图书（正式出版）	每种赋值	2
		研究报告	每份赋值	4
		《人民日报》理论版、《求是》、《光明日报》	每篇赋值	5
		论文	CSSCI 来源刊论文/每篇	1
			SSCI/A&HCI 收录/每篇	2
			CSCI/EI 收录/每篇	1
			其他普通论文/每篇	0.5
		纵向项目	纵向-国家社科重大/教育部社科重大	10
			纵向-国家社科重点/国家自科重点	6
			纵向-国家社科一般项目/青年项目	4
			纵向-省部级项目	2
			纵向-其他	0.5
		横向项目	每项基本分 2＋每 10 万赋值 1 分	
智库活动	A	会议	主办承办全国性会议/每次	10
			省市自治区一级会议/每次	5
			国际性会议/每次	10
			其他会议/每次	3
		培训	全国性培训活动/每次	8
			其他层次培训	2
		调研考察	接受副国级领导以上调研活动/每次	15
			接受省部级领导/专家调研/每次	5
			接受其他层次领导/专家调研/每次	2
			外出调研考察	1

（续表）

一级指标	代码	二级指标	计分规则	分值
		参与政策和法规文件起草	负责中央级别政策和法规的主要起草工作/每次	10
			参与中央级别政策和法规文件起草/每次	3
			负责省部级政策和法规文件主要起草工作/每次	5
			参与省部级政策和法规文件起草/每次	2
			负责其他级别文件主要起草工作/每次	2
			参与其他级别文件起草/每次	1
		参与咨政会议	参加中央级咨政会议	5
			参加省部级咨政会议	2
			参加其他级别咨政会议	1
		获得各类奖项或荣誉	国际组织授予奖项或荣誉（如联合国等）/每项	8
			国家级奖项或荣誉/每项	10
			省部级奖项或荣誉/每项	5
			其他级别奖项或荣誉/每项	3
智库媒体影响力	I	报纸新闻报道	中央级	5
			省部级	4
			地方级	3
			境外媒体	2
			其他媒体	1
		电视新闻报道	中央级	5
			省部级	4
			地方级	3
			境外媒体	2
			其他媒体	1

(续表)

一级指标	代码	二级指标	计分规则	分值
		网络新闻报道	中央级	5
			省部级	4
			地方级	3
			境外媒体	2
			其他媒体	1

(2) 智库专家主观评价数据

CTTI高校智库百强评价引入专家评价意见,咨询智库领域的权威专家,从五大方面为高校智库进行打分,形成主观评价数据——"E 值"。为了全面考察高校智库在战略研究、政策建言、人才培养、舆论引导和公共外交方面的功能,"两个中心"在选择智库专家时充分考虑到了他们的专业性、代表性和多元性,最终选择向三类专家咨询评价意见:一是专门从事智库研究的专家学者,他们的研究方向长期聚焦于智库研究与评价,具有广博的国际视野和丰富的研究经验,通晓国内外智库建设的专业知识,同时对国内高校智库建设情况也有较为全面准确的把握,他们的专业判断力能够相对科学地评价高校智库建设的水平。二是党政机关下设智库机构的专家学者。智库作为党政机关"外脑",是智库产品的提供者,而党政机关作为智库对策和政策研究成果的用户,其对智库的认可度和满意度能够在一定程度上反映出智库整体水平的高下。三是供职于高校智库的业内专家,由他们采用同一标准,对高校智库进行同行评议。此类专家具有丰厚的智库建设经验,对其他高校智库的信息也有较为充分的把握,有资格也有能力对其他智库进行评价。三类专家共同评价所赋予的分值,经过平均值计算,构成了最终的 E 值。

智库专家主要从五大方面进行智库评价(表6)。

一是智库是否具有灵活的体制机制,包括人员考核指标是否多样化、学术交流平台与成果转化渠道层次是否多元、整合高校优质资源的能力是否强大,等等。高校的人员考核标准通常以论文和纵向项目为主，而智库成果如内参、报告、报纸文章鲜被纳入专家职称评定和晋升的认定体系中。高校智库需要转变传统学术观念，在人员考核上有所创新，丰富和完善智库人员的考核指标。相比党政部门的智库，高校智库在成果转化渠道上有一定的劣势，智库声音要传达到党政机关，需要建立有效的意见通道。智库也需要增强自身影响力，不断丰富成果转化渠道。大学积聚了大批优质科研力量，但高校智库能否充分发挥好资源优势、将智力资源充分调动起来，则有赖于创新、高效的体制机制。综合以上考虑，CTTI系统对高校智库是否具有灵活的体制机制一项所赋分值为20。

二是智库是否具有较强的发展潜力，包括资金来源保障情况、可持续吸引领军人物和精英人才的能力等，所赋分值为20。

三是智库是否具有较高的声誉，包括智库决策咨询成果能否获得各级决策者重视、被各级部门采纳，智库是否具备社会知名度和公众影响力，智库在公共外交和国际交流上是否能够发挥较大作用，所赋分值为20。

四是智库是否具有特色鲜明的研究领域，该研究领域是否具有专业性、现实性、针对性、前瞻性，具体研究方向是否为国际前沿或国家急需，所赋分值为20。

五是智库是否在学科建设与人才培养上具有较强影响力，是否对于高校整体发展而言发挥了重要作用，所赋分值为20。

表6 高校智库 E 值测评指标及其赋值

一级指标	代码	二级指标	积分规则	满分分值
专家评价	E	智库是否具有灵活的治理体制机制	优秀18~20分；良好15~17分；较好12~14分；合格9~11分；较差0~8分	20
		智库是否具有较强的发展潜力		20
		智库是否具有较高的声誉		20
		智库是否具有特色鲜明的研究领域		20
		智库是否在学科建设与人才培养上具有较强影响力		20

(3) CTTI 高校智库百强评价指标计算方法

CTTI 系统针对所有来源高校智库进行 PAI 值计算，根据数值从大到小的顺序进行排序，PAI 值计算方式为

$$PAI_i = P_i + A_i + I_i$$

其中 PAI_i、P_i、A_i、I_i 值分别为每家高校智库的 PAI 值、P 值、A 值和 I 值。

为了使数据更加直观化，我们首先将 PAI 值进行归一化处理，把有量纲表达式变成无量纲表达式，具体公式为

$$\text{Adjusted } PAI_i = \frac{PAI_i - PAI_{\min}}{PAI_{\max} - PAI_{\min}},$$

其中 PAI_i 为每家机构的 PAI 值，$PAI_{\max}$ 为所有机构 PAI 值的最大值，$PAI_{\min}$ 为所有机构 PAI 值中的最小值。Adjusted PAI_i 为归一化处理后的 PAI 值，记为 $APAI_i$。

E 值的计算方法为

$$E_i = \frac{1}{n}\sum_{j=1}^{n} E_j, 1 \leqslant j \leqslant n$$

$$E_{\max} = \max\{E_i\}$$

$$E_{\min} = \min\{E_i\}$$

其中 E_j 为每位专家对智库的评分，E_i 为每家机构的最终得分，$E_{\max}$ 为所有机构最终得分的最高分，$E_{\min}$ 为所有机构最终得分的最低分。

同理，E 值也进行归一化处理，公式为

$$\text{Adjusted } E_i = \frac{E_i - E_{\min}}{E_{\max} - E_{\min}}$$

Adjusted E_i 是归一化处理后的 E 值，记 Adjusted E_i 为 AE_i。

令 $PAIE_i = \alpha APAI_i + (1-\alpha) AE_i, 0 \leqslant \alpha < 1$

其中 α 为客观数据 PAI 值占 PAI - E 评价的比重，该数值通过德尔菲法获得。$PAIE_i$ 值即 CTTI 高校智库评价的最终综合得分。

5.2 CTTI高校智库百强榜遴选过程

CTTI高校智库百强榜的遴选过程分为五个步骤：

第一步，在统一的时间节点11月20日24:00，导出CTTI系统内所有高校智库的PAI值，按照PAI值的大小进行排序。"两个中心"选取了PAI值排序为前130名的高校智库入围"CTTI高校智库百强榜"评选，同时根据普遍性与特殊性相结合的原则，将5家数据填写不够完整的国家高端智库也纳入入围榜单，进入专家意见评审阶段。

第二步，使用德尔菲法确定PAI值和E值在本次评价中所占比例。根据专家意见，"两个中心"最终将排名前130的来源智库的α值定为0.6，即客观数据PAI值和专家主观意见E值在本次评价中的比例分别为60%和40%。

第三步，遴选出专家评价组，确保专家的代表性、专业性和多元性，并向所有专家发放调查问卷，问题涉及E值覆盖的所有方面，并在统一的时间节点前回收问卷。

第四步，计算最终的$PAIE$值，根据各机构$PAIE$值的大小进行排序，确定"CTTI来源高校智库百强榜"榜单。

第五步，将最终入选的高校智库确认等级，按照等级高低分为A+、A、A-三个等级，各级别分别有25家、35家和40家来源高校智库。CTTI高校智库百强榜榜单按照智库名称音序排列（表7、表8、表9）。

5.3 CTTI高校智库百强榜名单

表7 CTTI高校智库A+级榜单（按音序排列）

序号	等级	智库名称
1	A+	北京大学国家发展研究院
2	A+	北京大学国家治理研究院
3	A+	北京师范大学中国教育与社会发展研究院
4	A+	北京外国语大学国际中国文化研究院
5	A+	复旦大学美国研究中心

(续表)

序号	等级	智库名称
6	A+	复旦大学中国经济研究中心
7	A+	复旦大学中国研究院
8	A+	河北工业大学京津冀发展研究中心
9	A+	湖南师范大学道德文化研究院
10	A+	华东师范大学周边合作与发展协同创新中心
11	A+	华中师范大学中国农村研究院
12	A+	江南大学食品安全风险治理研究院
13	A+	南京大学长江产业经济研究院
14	A+	南京师范大学中国法治现代化研究院
15	A+	清华大学国情研究院
16	A+	四川大学南亚研究所
17	A+	武汉大学国际法研究所
18	A+	厦门大学高等教育发展研究中心
19	A+	浙江大学中国西部发展研究院
20	A+	浙江师范大学非洲研究院
21	A+	中国人民大学重阳金融研究院
22	A+	中国人民大学国家发展与战略研究院
23	A+	中南财经政法大学城乡社区社会管理湖北省协同创新中心
24	A+	中南财经政法大学知识产权研究中心
25	A+	中山大学粤港澳发展研究院

表8 CTTI高校智库A级榜单(按音序排列)

序号	等级	智库名称
26	A	北京交通大学北京交通发展研究基地
27	A	北京师范大学国际与比较教育研究院
28	A	北京外国语大学国家语言能力发展研究中心
29	A	东南大学道德发展智库

(续表)

序号	等级	智库名称
30	A	东南大学中国特色社会主义发展研究院
31	A	对外经济贸易大学国际经济研究院
32	A	对外经济贸易大学中国世界贸易组织研究院
33	A	复旦发展研究院
34	A	广东外语外贸大学广东国际战略研究院
35	A	广西大学中国—东盟研究院
36	A	华东师范大学中国现代城市研究中心
37	A	华中科技大学国家治理研究院
38	A	暨南大学华侨华人研究院
39	A	江苏警官学院江苏省公共安全研究院
40	A	江西师范大学苏区振兴研究院
41	A	南京大学中国南海研究协同创新中心
42	A	南京大学紫金传媒智库
43	A	南京艺术学院紫金文创研究院
44	A	南开大学经济与社会发展研究院
45	A	上海海事大学上海国际航运研究中心
46	A	上海交通大学中国城市治理研究院
47	A	上海外国语大学中东研究所
48	A	上海外国语大学中国国际舆情研究中心
49	A	深圳大学港澳基本法研究中心
50	A	四川大学中国西部边疆安全与发展协同创新中心
51	A	苏州大学苏州东吴智库文化与社会发展研究院
52	A	武汉大学环境法研究所
53	A	武汉大学媒体发展研究中心
54	A	延边大学朝鲜半岛研究院
55	A	云南大学周边外交研究中心
56	A	浙江大学中国农村发展研究院

（续表）

序号	等级	智库名称
57	A	中国海洋大学中国企业营运资金管理研究中心
58	A	中南财经政法大学法治发展与司法改革研究中心
59	A	中南大学知识产权研究院
60	A	中南大学中国村落文化研究中心

表9 CTTI高校智库A一级榜单（按音序排列）

序号	等级	智库名称
61	A−	安徽财经大学安徽经济发展研究院
62	A−	安徽大学创新发展研究院
63	A−	北京工业大学北京现代制造业发展研究基地
64	A−	北京师范大学中国基础教育质量监测协同创新中心
65	A−	成都理工大学自然灾害防治与地质环境保护研究智库
66	A−	东北师范大学中国农村教育发展研究院
67	A−	福建师范大学竞争力研究中心
68	A−	广州大学广州发展研究院
69	A−	华东师范大学国家教育宏观政策研究院
70	A−	华东师范大学课程与教学研究所
71	A−	华东师范大学中国现代思想文化研究所
72	A−	华南理工大学社会治理研究中心
73	A−	吉林大学数量经济研究中心
74	A−	吉林大学中国国有经济研究中心
75	A−	暨南大学广州市舆情大数据研究中心
76	A−	南京理工大学江苏人才发展战略研究院
77	A−	南京医科大学健康江苏研究院
78	A−	南开大学中国特色社会主义经济建设协同创新中心
79	A−	南通大学江苏长江经济带研究院

序号	等级	智库名称
80	A−	内蒙古财经大学中蒙俄经贸合作与草原丝绸之路经济带构建研究协同创新中心
81	A−	山东大学卫生管理与政策研究中心
82	A−	上海大学基层治理创新研究中心
83	A−	上海对外经贸大学国际经贸治理与中国改革开放联合研究中心
84	A−	上海海事大学中国（上海）自贸区供应链研究院
85	A−	天津财经大学天津市自由贸易区研究院
86	A−	天津大学国家知识产权战略实施研究基地
87	A−	天津大学亚太经合组织可持续能源中心
88	A−	同济大学德国研究中心
89	A−	武汉大学国家文化发展研究院
90	A−	武汉大学经济发展研究中心
91	A−	武汉大学社会保障研究中心
92	A−	西安交通大学"一带一路"自由贸易试验区研究院
93	A−	西南财经大学中国家庭金融调查与研究中心
94	A−	西藏民族大学西藏文化传承发展协同创新中心
95	A−	盐城师范学院沿海发展智库
96	A−	云南大学边疆民族问题智库
97	A−	浙江大学中国科教战略研究院
98	A−	中国人民公安大学首都社会安全研究基地
99	A−	中南财经政法大学产业升级与区域金融湖北省协同创新中心
100	A−	中南财经政法大学中国收入分配研究中心

6 CTTI高校智库百强榜数据分析

6.1 CTTI百强高校智库地域分布

2018年CTTI高校智库百强榜中，上海市入选的高校智库最多，共17家；北京市入选15家，紧跟其后；江苏省有14家智库入选，排名第三；其次是湖北省、广东省、天津市和浙江省,分别有12家、7家、6家、5家智库入选。上海市和北京市拥有一大批"985高校"和"211高校",高校综合实力强,学科基础雄厚,为高校智库发展奠定了学术基础。江苏、湖北、广东等省份也集聚了大批"双一流"高校,在国家政策的扶持下,高校智库建设迅猛发展,成绩斐然(图1)。

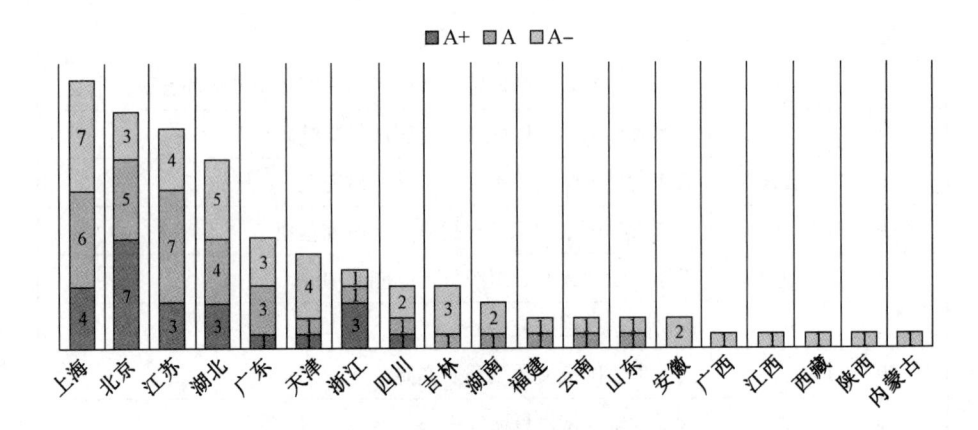

图1 CTTI百强高校智库地域分布

在25家A+级高校智库中,北京占7家,数量居于首位,其次是上海、江苏、湖北、浙江。顶级的高校智库,都拥有着实力不凡的学术基础。如北京大学国家发展研究院,是以经济学为基础的多学科综合性学院,北京大学应用经济学一级学科在第四轮学科评估中获得A+;再如江南大学食品安全风险治理研究院依托江南大学食品科学与工程一级学科,该学科同样在第四轮学科评估中获得A+。因此高校智库建设"打铁还需自身硬",首先要打牢学术研究基础。

6.2 CTTI百强高校智库大学分布

本次CTTI高校智库百强榜共有64所高等院校入围,其中武汉大学有6家来源高校智库入围评选,位居榜首;华东师范大学和中南财经政法大学均有5家智库入选百强榜;其次是复旦大学、北京师范大学、南京大学和浙江大学,分别有4家、3家、3家、3家来源智库入选,这些高校充分发挥了智库功能。复旦大学在本次评选中的表现可圈可点,共有3家智库被定为A+,是入选A+级别智库中最多的院校(表10)。

表 10　CTTI 百强高校智库大学分布表

大学名称	A+	A	A−	总计	大学名称	A+	A	A−	总计
武汉大学	1	2	3	6	南京师范大学	1			1
中南财经政法大学	2	1	2	5	清华大学	1			1
华东师范大学	1	1	3	5	厦门大学	1			1
复旦大学	3	1		4	浙江师范大学	1			1
南京大学	1	2		3	中山大学	1			1
北京师范大学	1	1	1	3	北京交通大学		1		1
浙江大学	1	1	1	3	广东外语外贸大学		1		1
北京大学	2			2	广西大学		1		1
中国人民大学	2			2	华中科技大学		1		1
北京外国语大学	1	1		2	江苏警官学院		1		1
四川大学	1	1		2	江西师范大学		1		1
东南大学		2		2	南京艺术学院		1		1
对外经济贸易大学		2		2	上海交通大学		1		1
上海外国语大学		2		2	深圳大学		1		1
中南大学		2		2	苏州大学		1		1
暨南大学		1	1	2	延边大学		1		1
南开大学		1	1	2	中国海洋大学		1		1
上海海事大学		1	1	2	安徽财经大学			1	1
云南大学		1	1	2	安徽大学			1	1
吉林大学			2	2	北京工业大学			1	1
天津大学			2	2	成都理工大学			1	1
河北工业大学	1			1	东北师范大学			1	1
湖南师范大学	1			1	福建师范大学			1	1
华中师范大学	1			1	广州大学			1	1
江南大学	1			1	华南理工大学			1	1

(续表)

大学名称	A+	A	A−	总计	大学名称	A+	A	A−	总计
南京理工大学			1	1	天津财经大学			1	1
南京医科大学			1	1	同济大学			1	1
南通大学			1	1	西安交通大学			1	1
内蒙古财经大学			1	1	西藏民族大学			1	1
山东大学			1	1	西南财经大学			1	1
上海大学			1	1	盐城师范学院			1	1
上海对外经贸大学		1	1	中国人民公安大学			1	1

7 高校新型智库建设中的主要问题

7.1 缺乏明确的政策咨询信息，供求信息不对称

高校智库作为党政机关的"外脑"，往往遇到政策咨询供求信息不对称的困局。大部分高校智库无法在第一时间获取各级党政决策部门对于政策咨询、对策研究的需求信息。因此，高校智库的一些政策建议不精准、不适用、不解渴。另外，学术语言体系和政策语言体系的差异，使高校智库与党政部门的沟通质量和效率受到影响，制约了双方的长久合作。

7.2 传播意识淡薄，忽视宣传工作

CTTI系统收录的八成左右内参、论文、报告、图书，都出自高校智库，而来源于高校智库的报纸文章仅占总量的52%。由此可见，很多高校智库对于舆论引导、公开宣传不够重视，没有充分利用报纸渠道传播智库思想。而在新媒体渠道日新月异的今天，仍有相当多高校智库没有自己的独立门户网站，有些即使有网站，网站的运维也无专人负责，信息长期不更新，有英文网站的高校智库更是鲜见。

7.3 智库治理机制需要优化

一是高校智库主体性缺位。由于高校智库在财政、人事及行政运作多方面受到诸多限制，因此缺乏主体性和自主性。在资金来源上，高校智库属于高校的内部机

构,当前活动经费主要依靠高校分拨及政府部分支持,接受企业、社会基金和个人捐赠等社会资金很少。现行的经费制度致使高校智库对高校和政府具有高度依附性,资金来源渠道单一化,尚未形成"自我造血"的经费募集机制。另一方面,在人员管理上,缺乏自主的人事管理权造成人员流动困难,导致智库实体化运作程度较低。据CTTI高校智库数据显示,54%的高校智库中全职人员数量少于兼职人员,未能建立科学合理的人才配置结构。其中也不乏研究员职称分布不合理、缺少研究辅助人员和行政人员、缺乏资历深厚的智库专业人士等问题。并且,高校智库目前尚未形成一套灵活的考核激励机制,重考核、轻激励的现象也会进一步削弱对于智库人才的吸引力。

二是缺乏开拓创新的智库组织文化。智库研究不同于学术研究,智库研究需要脚踏实地、广接地气。高校智库长期"生活"在象牙塔里,容易产生"闭门造车"的情况,弱化了智库的服务意识。学术型组织文化也限制了高校智库的开拓能力和创新能力。高校智库目前存在的研究质量不高、内容创新不足等问题,与其尚处在实体化建设和制度化建设的初级阶段,未能形成自己的创新文化有很大关系。

三是粗放管理影响高校智库的营运能力提升。一方面,一部分高校智库已经进入精细化管理的时代,比如,南京大学长江产业经济研究院已经明确提出"营运为政策研究赋能"的理念,大力提升智库营运能力,提高政策研究的保障水平;中国人民大学重阳金融研究院形成了二十多万字的完整的研究员和职员激励考核体系。另一方面,一部分高校智库对自身的年度成果数据尚不能做到有效管理,无法及时更新CTTI系统数据。与此相对的是,企业智库和社会智库数据管理能力普遍优于高校智库。例如,苏宁金融研究院作为一家企业智库,把CTTI数据填报纳入智库行政岗日常工作,并纳入KPI考核,数据更新日常化、常规化,使自身对智库的产品与活动心中有数。

四是成果认定体系不适应智库发展需要。传统高校成果认定体系将论文尤其是SCI、SSCI、CSSCI和CSCD论文,纵向项目等作为硬性考察指标,一些高校智库专家撰写的内参、报纸文章不被纳入成果认定范围,这一定程度上打击了高校学者,尤其是中青年学者参与智库建设的积极性。高校智库要完善政策配套支持,鼓励专家学者产出智库产品。以湖南师范大学为例,2018年3月8日该校印发了《湖南师范大学关于进一步加强新型智库建设的实施意见(试行)》,《意见》明确了新的成果认定与推广规定,将智库成果纳入考评体系中,按照采纳应用部门的不同分四级认定,分别享有同《中国社会科学》、权威刊物论文、重要刊物论文和CSSCI来源刊物论文一样的成果待遇。配套的政策支持是湖南师范大学智库在本次评价中取得良好成绩的原因之一。

8 加强高校新型智库建设的几点建议

第一,高校要明确认识到新型智库建设对"双一流"建设的重要意义。智库是专门从事基于证据的政策分析机构,和高校学术研究机构有联系,但是也有明确的分工,有自己独特的组织文化、研究方式、运营模式。现代高校智库最大的特色是知行统一,是教学研做合一的机构。对于高校智库而言,在高校内部承担的更多的是成果转化、政策孵化、政策教育和政策评估等服务党和国家、服务社会的功能。智库是大学的名片,是大学联系党委政府和社会的纽带,是通向国际政策研究界的桥梁。

一个好的智库对大学而言不可或缺。事实证明,高校智库建设和学科建设完全可以相得益彰。据上海交通大学资料显示,第四轮学科评估中,该校智库提供的学科社会服务案例就达近200个。可见,高校学科建设与智库建设并不矛盾,良好的智库建设会促进学科建设和应用型社会科学建设。南京大学长江产业经济研究院是一所主要从事应用经济学研究的国家高端培育智库,它直接帮助南京大学应用经济学学科在第四轮学科评估中得到A等次。华南理工大学是一所以理工、工程学科见长的高校,但在2017年却能成功申请4项教育部重大攻关项目,这与该校智库建设水平密不可分。华南理工大学下设的IPP(公共政策研究院)智库,在智库研究、对策研究方面的成功经验以及一整套的理念与方法,对华南理工大学应用型社会科学具有很大启发,因此促进了学校文科学科建设的整体水平。

纵观近年来的国家社科基金项目,国家急需的对策性、应用性研究比重可观,而这正是智库最擅长的战略性、方案性研究。如果一所高校的智库较强,那么它承担国家重大项目的能力就强。习近平总书记在哲学社会科学工作座谈会上的重要讲话以及后来一系列文件,其宗旨就是加快构建中国特色哲学社会科学。我国现在的哲学社会科学评价指标体系正在发生重大变化,党中央和国务院文件多次就此提出意见,要求改变论文挂帅的评价体系。今天,部分省市、高校制定的新政策已经明确了不同层次的智库成果对应怎样的奖励机制。如南京大学规定,智库成果获得副省级以上领导批示就相当于发表一篇 C 刊文章。可见,哲学社会科学本身评价机制的变化,对智库发展是有利的。

第二,高校智库建设的突破口是体制机制和选对智库运营的"关键少数"。高校智库数量的增长并不意味着智库新型体制机制的落地生根,我国高校智库的治理体制仍未突破固有瓶颈。

国家高端智库是体制机制创新的"领头羊"。高端智库建设试点工作开展以来,中央和有关部门在经费管理、人员出国、奖励激励、会议管理等方面出台了一系列含金量很高的政策,赋予试点单位很大的自主权和政策空间,但就高校智库的情况来看,对这些政策承接、落实不到位的现象还较为普遍,人员管理、薪酬待遇、职称评定、财务管理等方面的掣肘比较突出。产生这种现象的根本原因是我国大部分高校智库都是附属型智库,国家、省市部委智库管理部门无法直接对其进行管理,而要通过高校才能作用到智库。这在无形中削弱了国家、省市部委智库管理部门和非独立智库之间的直接联系。

如何破解这一问题?一些高校正在试水,把非独立智库变成独立法人实体机构。比如南京大学支持其下属的两家省级重点智库——长江产业经济研究院、紫金传媒智库在省民政厅注册为"民非"法人实体智库。独立的法人实体智库可以直接执行中央、省市部委智库管理部门有关智库治理的政策文件。浙江大学公共政策研究院也采取同样机制解决了法人化和实体化办智库的问题。

有了好的体制机制并不意味着就可以办好智库,制度和人事是一个问题的两个方面。再好的体制机制,没有关键少数发挥作用,也无法释放制度"红利"。因此,高校如何为下设智库配备年富力强、开拓进取、作风正派的掌门人和首席专家也是办好高校智库的关键所在。一个优秀的智库离不开学术领军人物的引领,也需要真正的智库掌门人和操盘手。西方智库界有个概念叫"政策企业家",即具备企业家的创业精神、真正把智库作为事业来做的负责人。我国高校智库能否成为业界翘楚,在某种意义上取决于能否形成这样的一支关键少数队伍。

第三,采用嵌入式决策咨询服务模式,消除信息不对称,提供精准的政策研究成果。习近平总书记指出,"要加强决策部门同智库的信息共享和互动交流,把党政部门政策研究同智库对策研究紧密结合起来,引导和推动智库建设健康发展、更好发挥作用",强调的其实就是"政府内脑"和"智库外脑"的协同。内脑要指导、引导和推动外脑的对策研究,努力消除需求和供给之间的信息不对称;智库要主动采用嵌入式决策咨询服务模式,解决政策研究和对策研究两张皮的问题。嵌入首先说明了智库和政府政策研究部门之间存在一定的区别,同时也意味着智库的对策研究有独立的价值,有自己独特的属性。嵌入式决策咨询服务包括政策过程嵌入、决策咨询流程嵌入、决策咨询场景嵌入和政策共同体圈层嵌入。政策过程嵌入是指智库应该嵌入一个政策的完整过程,和内脑开展紧密合作,从议程设置、政策辩论、决策与推广、政策执行、政策教育、政策评估和政策反馈全过程参与和发挥作用,不仅要关心政策文本的产生,还要促进政策文本的落地,并检验评估政策文本落地后的效果。决策咨询流程嵌入是指要在调查研究、数据采集、数据分析、分析研判和撰写报告等过程中和内脑紧密合作,充分发挥智库技术支援的优势,服务内脑的政策研究。决策咨询场景嵌入是指积极参加决策部门的调研活动、决策咨询会议和政策路演活动,获得决策咨询活动的现场感与语境,更加了解政策产生的前因后果。政策共同体圈层嵌入是指智库要和政府决策者、政策研究部门形成密切的联系,产生强烈的互信关系。当然,政策共同体中并非只有决策者和政策研究者(内脑),还包含其他的要素,智库应和这些要素之间都形成密切的圈层嵌入。如果智库能实现上述四种形式的嵌入,就有望解决对策研究脱离实际、不接地气、没有市场的困境,成为党委政府想得起、用得上、离不开的智库。

第四,高校智库要积极探索并实施推广科学客观的成果认定与激励制度。成果认定和激励制度是引导智库发展的指挥棒,但目前这个指挥棒设计不够合理,是制约智库健康发展的主要问题之一。我国高校智库成果认定标准相对单一,各类智库都看重领导批示、追求批示的行政级别。其实,政策评估、政策教育、政策规划等技术支援性决策咨询服务,也应纳入高校智库成果的认定范围。

南京大学中国智库研究与评价中心研究助理　于亮(执笔)

附录：CTTI 高校智库百强机构小传

安徽大学创新发展研究院

安徽大学创新发展研究院成立于 2016 年 5 月，同年被确定为"安徽省重点智库"，并参与发起成立长江经济带智库合作联盟。研究院秉持国家创新驱动战略，着眼安徽乃至全国经济社会现代化发展重点、热点、难点问题，聚焦科技创新、产业创新、社会建设创新和治理制度创新等战略性问题，观测新现象、研讨新问题、提出新思路、谋划新对策。两年来研究院编发报送了 46 期决策咨询专报《安大智库》，受到中央和安徽省领导 10 多次批示。

安徽财经大学安徽经济发展研究院

安徽经济发展研究院是安徽省重点智库，正努力打造成为立足安徽、面向全国的财经智库。年度经费 300 余万元。

研究院连续 13 年公开出版、发布 12 部研究安徽经济社会发展的系列研究报告，在此基础之上形成的政策建议获得国家级和省部级领导批示 20 余篇，多篇研究成果被中共中央政策研究室《群言》、省经济发展研究中心的《决策》等内参选用。研究院还承担省扶贫开发工作领导小组安排的脱贫攻坚第三方评估工作。从 2016 年 9 月至 2018 年 12 月，5 次共组织 2 700 余名师生完成涵盖 25 个县的脱贫攻坚第三方监测评估和摘帽评估任务。

网址：http://ahjj.aufe.edu.cn
邮箱：2816260994@qq.com
电话：0552 - 3111482/0552 - 3126631

北京大学国家发展研究院

北京大学国家发展研究院(NSD)是北京大学的一个以经济学为基础的多学科综合性学院。在智库建设方面,国发院秉承"小机构、大网络"的理念,聚合北大乃至全球的研究资源,在政府与市场的关系、新农村建设、土地问题、国企改革、电信改革、股市治理、人口政策以及经济结构调整等诸多重大问题上,提出了一批有影响力的政策建议,并被政府所采纳。经过多年的耕耘,国发院于 2016 年入选国家首批高端智库。国发院拥有"中国经济观察报告会"、"格政"和"国家发展论坛"三个智库品牌活动,并牵头组织"中美经济对话"和"中美卫生对话",在中美民间外交方面做出了突出的贡献。

邮编:100871

传真:86 - 10 - 62751474/86 - 10 - 62750030

北京大学国家治理研究院

北京大学国家治理研究院是教育部人文社会科学百所重点研究基地——政治学研究基地。研究院现有国内外专兼职研究人员 55 名,年度经费 140 万。

自成立以来,研究院以国家治理现代化为研究主题积极开展学术和对策研究,同时以"国家治理论坛"为平台,协同国内外知名高校举办学术会议和学术讲座。研究院正式出版《国家治理现代化研究》辑刊、《国家治理研究丛书》等,致力于中国特色社会主义国家治理现代化和政治学、公共管理等一流学科建设,提供咨政支持,开展人才培养。

网址:http://www.isgs.pku.edu.cn/

邮箱:gjzlxtcx@pku.edu.cn

电话:010 - 62754337/62756937

北京工业大学北京现代制造业发展研究基地

北京现代制造业发展研究基地是由北京市哲学社会科学规划办公室和北京市教育委员会于 2004 年批准建立的市属哲学社会科学研究基地之一。基地以北京现代制造业发展为中心，围绕北京现代制造业发展战略、问题及对策，展开一系列研究。基地积极承担各项重大课题，发表学术论文 200 余篇，出版研究报告和专著 10 余部，提交的各类报告 50 多份，获得中央部门表彰和批示，相关成果在政府委办局和企业得到诸多应用。基地将以面向全球治理、面向治国理政、面向国计民生为导向，为构建我国现代决策咨询体系而贡献力量。

北京交通大学北京交通发展研究基地

北京交通发展研究基地成立于 2005 年，是北京交通大学最早建设的以应用经济学一级学科及相关管理学科为基础、以运输经济与物流管理为优势特色的重点研究基地，是经北京市哲学社会科学办公室和北京市教育委员会批准建立的北京市哲学社会科学研究基地之一。基地自成立以来，三次验收均被评为优秀，一次获得免检。基地在咨政建议、科研项目、学术论文、媒体影响力方面成果丰硕。连续举办六届北京交通大学运输与时空经济论坛，国内外影响力日益增强。

北京师范大学国际与比较教育研究院

北京师范大学国际与比较教育研究院创立于 1961 年，是中国成立最早和影响最大的比较教育研究机构，是全国唯一的比较教育学国家重点学科点，教育部人文社会科学重点研究基地、教育部国别和区域研究培育基地、APEC 高等教育研究中心秘书处依托单位。研究院秉持"立足中国，放眼世界"的原则，积极发挥咨政建言、舆论引导、社会服务、公共外交作用，服务党和政府的科学民主决策。2012 年以来向各级教育行政部门提交并被采纳的政策咨询报告有 90 余份，多份咨询报告得到中央领导、教育部领导及其他领导的批示和肯定。

北京师范大学中国基础教育质量监测协同创新中心

基础教育质量监测协同创新中心成立于 2012 年 7 月,是我国教育学和心理学领域唯一的国家级协同创新中心。中心由北京师范大学牵头,下设华东师范大学等 8 个分中心。中心秉持科学、准确、及时"把脉"全国基础教育质量状况,促进亿万儿童青少年全面、个性发展的宗旨,开展基础教育政策等方面的研究。设立了教育评价云平台和专题数据库。2016 年,中心两项成果获得第五届全国教育科学研究优秀成果一等奖,两项成果获得二等奖,四项成果获得三等奖。

电话:010 - 58800158

传真:010 - 58800158

邮箱:xtxxbs@bnu.edu.cn

北京师范大学中国教育与社会发展研究院

北京师范大学中国教育与社会发展研究院成立于 2010 年 10 月,是北京师范大学整合校内外资源,培养社会领域高层次人才、开展社会治理政策咨询和科学研究的实体性机构。研究院以推进中国特色教育现代化和社会建设为使命,以教育改革发展和社会治理创新为研究特色,重点打造"七大工程",即一策、一库、一典、一论坛、一刊、一书、一调查。研究院积极推进与美国、英国、俄罗斯、新加坡、日本等国家和地区的著名智库,以及一流高校、科研机构的广泛交流和深入合作,不断增强和扩大中院的国内外影响力。

电话:010 - 58802885

传真:010 - 58804062

E-mail:casm@bnu.edu.cn

北京外国语大学国际中国文化研究院

北京外国语大学国际中国文化研究院(IICS)成立于 1996 年。研究院以沟通中外文化为己任，承担起"将中国介绍给世界"新的历史使命，旨在探索中国文化在全球发展的战略问题，探究中国文化在世界各民族中间的传播和影响。在中外文化交流史的背景下追踪中国文化典籍外传的历史与轨迹，梳理中国文化典籍外译的历史、人物和各种译本，并通过对各国重要的汉学家、汉学名著的翻译和研究，勾勒出世界主要国家汉学（中国学）的发展史。从跨文化的角度，研究中国文化在海外的影响，揭示世界各国的中国形象及其形成的机制，探索中国文化走向世界的轨迹和路径。

北京外国语大学国家语言能力发展研究中心

北京外国语大学国家语言能力发展研究中心成立于 2014 年 7 月，系国家语委科研机构，由教育部语言文字信息管理司与北京外国语大学共建共管。中心以"服务国家、服务社会、服务学科"为理念，聚焦于"国家语言能力、国别语言政策、世界语言生活"三大研究方向。2014 年中心成功申请并获批"语言政策与规划学"二级学科硕士和博士学位授予权，先后创办了《世界语言战略资讯》（内刊）、《语言政策与规划研究》（集刊），承接了十多项国家级和省部级项目，是中国语言学会语言政策与规划研究会主要成员，国家级学术智库之一。

网址：https://gynf.bfsu.edu.cn/

成都理工大学自然灾害防治与地质环境保护研究智库

智库是依托于地质灾害防治与地质环境保护国家重点实验室（成都理工大学）建设的，主要为公益性自然灾害和人类工程建设中地质灾害防治提供科技支撑，其研究成果曾两次独立获得国家科技进步一等奖。实验室的固定研究人员共 75 人，年度科研经费约 5 000 万元。

2017 年，该智库在国际上首次提出构建空-天-地一体化的"三查"体系（即基于高精度遥感＋InSAR 的"普查"；基于机载 LiDAR＋无人机航拍的"详查"；基于地面调查复核的"核查"），得到相关部门的广泛认可。

网址：http://www.sklgp.cdut.edu.cn

邮箱：sklgp@cdut.edu.cn

电话：028-84073193

传真：028-84073193

东北师范大学中国农村教育发展研究院

东北师范大学中国农村教育发展研究院成立于1999年，现有专职研究员14人，兼职研究员11人。研究所以"研究农村教育，服务农村教育，发展农村教育"为宗旨，开展基础教育政策、文化政策、财政政策研究，为国家农村教育改革与发展提供政策咨询。近年来，基于大型课题项目的强力推进和农村教育经验的理论反思，农村教育研究所持续提交高质量的教育政策咨询报告，多篇被国务院、教育部以及民进中央等部门采纳，受到上级部门领导的高度赞扬。

电话：0431-85099422

邮箱：qihp644@nenu.edu.cn

东南大学道德发展智库

东南大学道德发展智库成立于2015年，是江苏省首批重点高端智库。目前智库拥有一支高层次科研创新团队，包括长江学者特聘教授、讲座教授4名，以及国家"万人计划"首批哲学社会科学领军人才、中宣部"四个一批"人才、教育部新世纪人才等。2018年智库共募集科研经费280万元。智库始终定位于全面、系统、科学、专业地呈现改革开放40年来中国伦理道德发展状况，揭示当代中国伦理道德发展的基本规律与发展趋势，为新时代中国伦理道德发展的国家战略规划提供科学依据与理论资源。

联系电话：025-52090923

网址：http://mdi.seu.edu.cn

微信公众号：seu-moral

东南大学中国特色社会主义发展研究院

东南大学中国特色社会主义发展研究院成立于 2015 年 11 月 16 日,是江苏省首批重点高端智库。目前研究院建立起了一支由近 30 名专家学者组成的专兼职结合的研究队伍,年度经费达 300 余万元。成立以来,研究院围绕中国特色社会主义的理论和实践开展深入研究,先后在《求是》《人民日报》《光明日报》等中央媒体发表理论文章 20 余篇,提交决策咨询报告 40 余篇,获省部级领导批示 8 篇,为党的创新理论研究阐释以及党和政府科学决策做出了重要贡献。研究院获得 2017CTTI-BPA 智库最佳管理一等奖,成功入选"2018 年 CTTI 来源高校智库百强榜单"并获评 A 类智库。

网址:http://idscc.seu.edu.cn/

邮箱:ddztzk@sina.com

电话:025-83795265

对外经济贸易大学国际经济研究院

对外经济贸易大学国际经济研究院前身是成立于 1982 年 10 月的国际贸易问题研究所,2003 年 11 月更为现名。研究院在基础理论研究、国家政策研究、商业咨询服务三个层面开展研究工作,涉及世界经济和中国对外经济贸易等诸多领域,完成多项国家社会科学基金和自然科学基金课题,商务部、农业部、科技部等部委课题,省、市地方政府课题,以及国际组织、行业协会、企业等委托课题。每年组织出版的《中国外商投资报告》《中国出口产业国际竞争力报告》受到学界、政府、社会的普遍认同和广泛好评。

电话:86-10-64492251

传真:86-10-64493899

对外经济贸易大学中国世界贸易组织研究院

研究院是以科学研究、学科发展、智库建设和人才培养为主要职能的学校直属实体性研究机构。2000年8月被教育部评选为"普通高等学校人文社会科学重点研究基地"。

研究院致力于中国对外开放经济规律等问题研究并提供高质量的咨询服务。研究院承担了众多国家级、省部级重大课题和政府、企事业单位咨询项目，形成了一系列高水准的研究成果和学术品牌。中国世界贸易组织研究院已经成为中国WTO研究领域最重要的学术创新基地和交流平台。

研究院网址：ciwto.uibe.edu.cn

研究院邮箱：ciwto@uibe.edu.cn

研究院电话：010-64495778

福建师范大学竞争力中心

福建师范大学竞争力中心成立于2006年，现拥有研究人员33人，年度经费300多万元。中心的《中国省域经济综合竞争力》蓝皮书、《中国省域环境竞争力》绿皮书、《二十国集团（G20）国家创新竞争力》黄皮书、《世界创新竞争力》黄皮书、《金砖国家创新竞争力》黄皮书、《全球环境竞争力》绿皮书和《中国城市创新竞争力》蓝皮书等"七大产品"被纳入国家权威品牌"皮书"系列。出版50多部研究著作，英文著作5部；近百篇专项研究报告获各级部门领导批示、采纳，多位成员成为G20和金砖会议科技专家组成员。

联系方式：0591-83465205

网址：jjxy.fjnu.edu.cn

复旦大学美国研究中心

复旦大学美国研究中心成立于1985年，是我国最早建立的专门从事美国研究的主要机构之一,是教育部普通高等学校人文社会科学重点研究基地,美国研究国家哲学社会科学创新基地。中心现有专职科研人员 14 人,中心定期出版《美国问题研究》、《宗教与美国社会》以及《21 世纪的美国与世界》丛书。

中心以美国研究和中美关系研究为特色,涵盖美国政治、经济、外交、社会和文化、中国对美政策及中美关系等领域。在 2016 年最新一轮教育部人文社科重点研究基地评比中,中心在多方面排名国内前列。

网址:www.cas.fudan.edu.cn

单位邮箱:cas@fudan.edu.cn

联系电话:021 - 65642269

复旦大学中国经济研究中心

复旦大学中国经济研究中心于 2013 年获上海高校智库正式立项,中心以复旦大学中国社会主义市场经济研究中心的专职研究人员为主体。

中心兼具科学研究基础和中国问题导向的特点,定期向党和国家决策机构提供有关中国经济发展和改革的政策报告。

成立以来,中心报送各类政策专题报告 280 余篇,获得国家领导人批示 4 篇次,省部级领导人 1 篇;被中央和各级政府部门采纳 70 余篇,另有多篇专报被各级别内刊录用。已举办"中国大问题"讲堂 13 期、RICE-CCES 沙龙系列讲座 26 期、公共政策讲座 20 期,吸引了政商学界近万人次参与。

复旦大学中国研究院

中国研究院属复旦大学二级学院,是国家高端智库首批试点单位,团队人员 140 多人。院长是张维为教授。经费来源于国家智库办拨款和自筹经费。

研究院在研究、资政、传播和培训四个方向均做到国内领先。研究院组织年度国际思想者论坛、中国话语高端论坛等多项活动。出版编辑《东方学刊》《中国研究院简报》《中国研究院专报》等公开和内部刊物,为中国道路、中国模式和中国话语提供研究、交流和学习的平台,为国家决策提供政策建言。

网址:http://www.cifu.fudan.edu.cn/

邮箱:ci_fa@fudan.edu.cn

微信:ChinaInstituteFDU

电话:021-65641825

复旦大学发展研究院

复旦大学发展研究院成立于1993年,是改革开放以来国内最早设立的智库之一,是光明日报"十大影响力智库"。研究院拥有一支30人规模的"智库运营团队",聚集一支数百人的专家团队,设立了"政策规划学社"。

研究院每年举办上海论坛、中国大学智库论坛。研究院围绕区域经济、科技创新、产业发展、全球城市、网络治理等五大研究领域,已建和在建数据库近20个。国际化是研究院的鲜明特色,首创"海外中国研究中心"、"国际智库中心"、拉美大学联盟,与多个国家和地区建立了合作关系。

网址:http://fddi.fudan.edu.cn

邮箱:fdifudan@fudan.edu.cn

电话:86-21-55670203

传真:86-21-55670203

广东外语外贸大学广东国际战略研究院

广东国际战略研究院成立于2009年,是广东省人民政府设置成立的独立法人智库。现有正式员工25人,年度预算经费800万元。

研究院聚焦21世纪海上丝绸之路、全球经济治理等研究。完成各类政府决策咨询研究报告190余份,非洲工业化进程的调研报告获习近平总书记等中央领导肯定。

创办海上丝绸之路国际智库论坛等国际学术平台,发挥了二轨外交作用。

研究院是教育部战略研究基地、外交部政策研究重点合作单位、中联部"一带一路"智库合作联盟理事单位、广东省首批重点智库,连续三年在一带一路地方性智库中排名第3位。2018年获广东五一劳动奖章。

网站:http://giis.gdufs.edu.cn

邮箱:giis2015@qq.com

电话:020-36205613

广西大学中国-东盟研究院

广西大学中国-东盟研究院成立于2005年1月,本着跨学科、跨区域、跨国家的开放式研究平台建设思维,整合国内外该领域研究力量,依托中国-东盟区域发展协同创新中心这一重要平台,建设教育部战略研究基地和国别与区域研究中心。研究院的研究成果或入选教育部社会科学委员会专家建议,中共中央对外联络部、教育部内参和成果摘报,或获得党中央、国务院和自治区主要领导批示,在学术界和社会上有较大的影响。

电话:0771-3274451

广州大学广州发展研究院

广州大学广州发展研究院成立于2003年,是广州大学校属综合性重点科研机构、广东省高校人文社科重点研究基地、广东省高校协同创新发展中心、广东省社会科学研究基地、广州市第一批新型智库试点建设单位。该院以"高校新型智库"与"重点科研基地"为目标,实施基础研究与应用研究"双轮驱动"战略。目前全院共有在编及兼职研究人员30余人,已形成《决策内参》《广州蓝皮书系列》、"广州学"等多个智库品牌,其中《决策内参》批示率达96%,采纳率达40%;《广州蓝皮书系列》连续七年共获得17个全国皮书奖项。

网址:http://gda.gzhu.edu.cn/

电话:020-86236001

河北工业大学京津冀发展研究中心

河北工业大学京津冀发展研究中心成立于2012年,先后被列为河北省软科学基地、河北省高等学校人文社科重点研究基地、河北省新型智库重点培育基地。中心坚持"以服务京津冀及环渤海区域经济建设为主,积极辐射全国,为京津冀协同发展提供人才支持和智力支撑"的发展方针在科学研究、咨询服务、学术交流、人才培养四个方面为各级政府各类重大决策提供咨询服务,形成以《河北经济发展报告》《京津冀经济社会发展报告》为主的标志性成果,积极为服务区域经济社会发展做出应有贡献。

网址:http://jjj.hebut.edu.cn/

湖南师范大学道德文化研究院

湖南师范大学道德文化研究院成立于1983年10月,是在以湖南师范大学伦理学学科为主体、整合校内外优势资源的基础上组建的教育部人文社会科学重点研究基地。研究院重视伦理学学科的现实服务功能,研究人类道德文化发展的普遍规律和大趋势,积极应对我国社会发展和世界形势变化所提出的各种突出道德问题,大力推进中华道德文化的历史、理论和实践研究,建构中国特色社会主义道德文化的理论体系、话语体系、传承传播体系和实践体系,为提升中国道德文化的综合实力、核心竞争力、理论感召力和实践影响力做贡献。

邮编:410081

电话:0731-88872593

华东师范大学国家教育宏观政策研究院

国家教育宏观政策研究院成立于2014年,由教育部和上海市人民政府共建,依托华东师范大学和上海市教育科学研究院联合建立。研究院实体化运行,致力于建成国家宏观决策服务的教育智库。研究方向包括国家教育现代化发展监测与评价、国家教育决策支持服务系统开发、国家教育战略与教育规划发展、国际教育发展与政策趋向、教育与社会经济协调发展、教育政策分析与评论、教育实践调查与分析。研究院以学术研究、政策研究为导向,在做出一流学术研究成果的同时为教育决策科学化和治理现代化提供专业支撑服务。

邮箱:office2014@admin.ecnu.edu.cn

电话:021-62231103

华东师范大学课程与教学研究所

华东师范大学课程与教学研究所成立于1999年,是教育部首批人文社会科学重点研究基地,课程所现有科研岗位人员17人。课程所主办基地学术CSSCI刊物《全球教育展望》以及网络在线刊物《课程研究前沿》。课程所专家相继领衔研制起草了《国家基础教育课程改革纲要》和《教师教育课程标准》等重要政策性文本,为我国新一轮基础教育课程改革和教师教育课程改革做出杰出贡献,被誉为课程与教学研究领域的"国家队"。多项成果获得中央级和省部级表彰。

电话:010-62233405

邮箱:ici@ecnu.edu.cn

华东师范大学中国现代城市研究中心

华东师范大学中国现代城市研究中心成立于2003年3月,2014年正式成为我国普通高等学校人文社会科学重点研究基地。中心现有专职研究员15名,兼职研究员40余名,行政管理人员3名,办公面积500平方米,年度经费320万。

中心依托学校人文地理学国家重点学科以及社会学、经济学等主要学科,开展城市地理、城市社会等方面的研究。中心研究人员承担多项重要研究项目,取得了一批具有重要影响力的标志性成果，其中获国家级和省部级奖项共计86项。

网址：http://ccmc.ecnu.edu.cn/

邮箱：cmccs@mail.ecnu.edu.cn

电话：021-62232980

华东师范大学中国现代思想文化研究所

华东师范大学中国现代思想文化研究所成立于1999年，属教育部人文社会科学重点研究基地。中国哲学学科点被评为上海市重点学科。近年来研究所承担多项研究课题，出版多本著作。基地研究人员在《中国社会科学》等权威刊物发表学术论文数十篇，被《新华文摘》等多家刊物转载，有的还被翻译为德语、日语、英语、韩文等。多项成果获得了国家级与省部级等各种奖项，在学术界产生了较大的影响。目前主办刊物《思想与文化》。

华东师范大学周边合作与发展协同创新中心

华东师范大学周边合作与发展协同创新中心成立于2012年，是由华东师大牵头，北京大学和复旦大学共同参与建设的协同创新平台。2013年经华东师大重组，入选首批上海高校智库。

中心以丰厚的历史档案与扎实的田野调查为基础，以我国周边发展、合作、安全为研究重点，推出了一系列有影响力的咨政与学术成果，承接并完成了一批国家和省部级重大课题，并发布多项启民新媒体作品。每年定期举办"瓦尔代"中俄论坛、学术精英讲习班等活动。在华盛顿、莫斯科设有海外工作室，专门培养复合型智库精英人才。

网址：https://zhoubian.ecnu.edu.cn/

邮箱：zhoubiancenter@126.com

电话：021-62235320

华南理工大学社会治理研究中心

华南理工大学社会治理研究中心,成立于 2015 年 3 月,是广东省目前唯一以社会治理为主题的省级智库。中心目前形成了"10 位教授+12 位副教授+8 位讲师"的科研团队,主要开展社会保障政策、民政政策、社会建设与社会政策、安全政策等方面研究。中心的多项成果获得国家和省市级领导的批示。承担项目 10 余项,可支配经费 400 多万元。中心成员发表了学术论文 10 多篇,多篇被高水平期刊转载和收录。中心具有稳定的政府合作渠道和国际学术交流平台。一项成果获得中央级奖项,多项成果获得省部级奖项。

电话:020-87114133

邮箱:hghszl@scut.edu.cn

华中科技大学国家治理研究院

华中科技大学国家治理研究院系国内首家以"国家治理研究院"命名的高校智库,现为国家治理湖北省协同创新中心入选智库。

欧阳康教授担任研究院院长,研究院现有专兼职研究员 35 人,外籍客座研究员 18 人。

国家治理研究院成立以来,已成功举办 4 届"全球治理·东湖论坛"国际学术研讨会,5 届"国家治理现代化高峰论坛",主持并完成近 20 项国家治理方面的课题,成功发布、出版国内首个由高校智库公开发布、出版的地方性、全国性绿色 GDP 绩效评估报告,该系列成果获得多个奖项。

网站网址:http://isg.hust.edu.cn/

微信公众号:hustgjzl

华中师范大学中国农村研究院

中国农村发展智库依托华中师范大学中国农村研究院成立,是从事农村与农民问题研究的专门性学术机构,是教育部签约智库,是被刘延东副总理认可的国内初具雏形的四大高校智库之一。

中农智库以建设"四个全球顶级"为目标,坚持"大调查、大数据、大服务、大平台"的要求,积极发挥智库的作用。截至目前,中农智库已向决策部门提交政策咨询报告580份,得到诸多单位的批示与采纳400次。撰写的有关农村集体经济、农村基层组织、乡村振兴的调查研究成果均为中共中央一号文件所采纳。

吉林大学数量经济研究中心

吉林大学数量经济研究中心为教育部普通高等学校人文社会科学重点研究基地,直属于吉林大学。现有专、兼职研究人员41人,各类项目年度总经费近千万元。

中心长期为各级政府部门提供咨询报告,连续出版《吉林大学数量经济研究中心政策咨询报告》,CSSCI来源集刊《数量经济研究》,多年连续主办"数量经济学国际学术会议"和"数量经济学国际讲习班",在中国经济学界具有重要影响力。

中心2017年成功入选中国智库索引(CTTI)来源智库高校智库100强,其中,经济与贸易领域智库综合排名进入前30名。

网址:http://jlucqe.jlu.edu.cn

邮箱:qe_journal@jlu.edu.cn

电话:0431-85166059

吉林大学中国国有经济研究中心

吉林大学中国国有经济研究中心是普通高等学校人文社会科学重点研究基地、吉林大学"985工程"中国国有经济改革与发展研究哲学社会科学创新基地。中心成功举办了18届"中国国有经济发展论坛"国内或国际学术研讨会,连续出版学术集刊《国有经济评论》及《中国国有经济发展报告》《中央企业自主创新报告》《国有经济论丛》等系列学术著作,年到账经费200余万元,发表大量高水平学术论文,每年都有研究报告受到省级以上有关领导肯定性批示。

网站:ccpser.jlu.edu.cn

邮箱:ccpser@jlu.edu.cn

电话:0431-85168829

暨南大学广州市舆情大数据研究中心

暨南大学广州市舆情大数据研究中心成立于2012年,是广州市人文社会科学重点研究基地建设优秀基地,主要开展互联网管理政策、网络安全政策、港澳台政策、意识形态政策、新闻政策等方面的研究工作。拥有完善的境内外舆情数据挖掘系统与案例库平台,可监测国内主要新闻媒体、微博与超过500万的微信公众号,拥有的境外舆情监测平台覆盖国际200多个国家和地区、超过90种语言的媒体,同时可监测国际社交主流平台,设有专题数据库5个。多项成果获得省部级奖项。

电话:020-38374980

邮箱:bdclab@jnu.edu.cn

暨南大学华侨华人研究院

暨南大学华侨华人研究院成立于2006年11月,是教育部人文社科重点研究基地。研究院以中国和平发展的战略需求为导向,立足于为国家的改革开放和现代化建设服务、为社会服务,致力于多学科和国际视野下的前沿研究,优化重组各相关机构的基础条件和研究力量,引进高水平人才。研究院学术刊物有《东南亚研究》(双月刊)以及《世界侨情报告》,还与学校图书馆共建华侨华人研究文献中心。

邮箱:ohqhr@jnu.edu.cn

电话:020-85226108

江南大学食品安全风险治理研究院

食品安全风险治理研究院由江南大学与江苏省市场监管局共建,是江苏省委宣传部批准的全省 15 个重点培育智库之一,是全省唯一的以食品安全风险治理为主业的专业性智库。

智库成立以来,在省部级内参上发表咨询报告 30 余篇,10 多个咨询报告获得党和国家领导人、省部级领导人的肯定性批示。发表 100 余篇新闻报道、言论、评论与科普类文章。智库完成了一批国家级重要研究项目。《中国食品安全风险治理体系与治理能力现代化考察报告》、系列《中国食品安全发展报告》、食品安全风险监督抽检大数据服务平台等项目获奖。

江苏警官学院江苏省公共安全研究院

江苏警官学院江苏省公共安全研究院是公安部首批建设的两个部级智库之一,是江苏省重点培育智库。智库现有专职研究人员 18 名,兼职研究人员 30 多名,研究团队 4 个,年度经费 450 万。

部省智库重要研究成果以《智库专报》《公安智库研究》的形式报送公安部和省委省政府领导参阅。每年编撰出版《国外警务智库研究年度报告》《江苏省公共安全年度报告》,出版了《现代警务研究》学术丛书 12 卷。智库先后举办 10 次全国性和国际性研讨会。有两个项目获得表彰。

网址:http://jwzx.jspi.cn/

微信公众号:公安部现代警务改革研究所

邮箱:wangchi@jspi.cn

电话:025 - 52881589

江西师范大学苏区振兴研究院

江西省重点智库,全国百强智库,江西省哲学社会科学重点研究基地。致力于为苏区、革命老区振兴发展提供智力支持和社会服务。承办《苏区振兴论坛》《苏区振兴论坛策论专报》的编辑任务。拥有专兼职研究人员30多名以及二级学科硕士点"马克思主义与当代中国经济社会发展"。承担多项基金项目。多份资政报告获得国家和省级领导人批示。形成了"丛书""专报""高峰论坛""蓝皮书"等四大产品系列。

电话:0791-88121059

邮编:330022

Email:sqzxyjy@163.com

南京大学长江产业经济研究院

南京大学长江产业经济研究院是江苏省首批重点高端智库,国家高端智库建设培育单位。研究院以南京大学经济学、管理学及其他相关学科平台为核心,以中国沿海地区高度开放、发达的实体经济为背景,深入研究探索中国实体经济的走势、趋向与政策,为国家实现"两个一百年"奋斗目标总结经验,探索中国特色社会主义经济发展道路。研究院形成了《长江产经决策咨询报告》《中国产经热点研讨》《中国经济动能指数报告》等代表性研究成果,多项成果获中央领导及江苏省主要领导肯定性批示,在社会各领域产生广泛影响力。

邮箱:idei@nju.edu.cn

电话:025-83576316

南京大学中国南海研究协同创新中心

南京大学中国南海研究协同创新中心成立于2012年7月,是国家认定的首批14家"2011协同创新中心"之一。

中心以国家重大战略需求为导向,以实现南海权益最大化为目标,以多学科协同创新为主体,以"文理-军地-校所-校校协同"为路径,以体制机制改革为保障,全面推动南海问题综合研究,服务国家南海战略决策。中心围绕基础研究、动态监测、战略决策等三大方向,构建"南海史地与文化""南海资源环境与海疆权益""南海法律研究""南海航行自由与安全稳定"等九大研究平台,全力打造集学术创新体、高端智库、人才培养基地、国际交流对话四大功能与目标于一身的中国特色新型智库。

电话:025 - 83597212

邮箱:nanhai@nju.edu.cn

南京大学紫金传媒智库

南京大学紫金传媒智库于2015年10月挂牌。智库下设六个中心,拥有近40位专家及4名运营人员。每年江苏省委宣传部拨款200万元,另有与外界企事业单位合作项目的经费支持。

智库以大数据及大样本数据研究见长,成立三年来发布了《2016中国股市风潮中期报告》、《2016及2018中国A股上市公司创新指数报告》、《互联网公益大数据报告》及《江苏省职业年金认知度调查报告》等十余份研究报告,拥有丰富的基础性研究成果,为建言献策提供扎实论据。

网站:www.zijimtt.com

邮箱:zijin@nju.edu.cn

电话:025 - 89681258

南京理工大学江苏人才发展战略研究院

江苏人才发展战略研究院成立于2015年5月12日,是江苏省依托南京理工大学成立的人才发展研究平台。研究院旨在汇聚一流研究力量,对人才发展战略问题进行综合性、长期性、前瞻性研究,为党委和政府提供政策建议、咨询意见和人才服务。依托省内外知名高校院所,设立八个研究中心,通过组织开展重点课题研究、举办高层次学术论坛、发布研究成果等方式为党委政府及有关部门提供决策咨询,为园区、企业、高校院所等用人单位提供智力服务,为省委省政府"迈上新台阶、建设新江苏"的目标建言献策。

电话：025-84303966

邮箱：jatd2015@163.com

南京师范大学中国法治现代化研究院

中国法治现代化研究院是依托南京师范大学成立的江苏省首批重点高端智库，是组织开展当代中国法治现代化领域决策咨询的非营利性公共研究机构。下设7个中心。

研究院现已形成"年度十大法治影响力事件"（荣获"最佳智库活动一等奖"）、"方德法治研究奖"两个具有全国影响力的智库品牌活动。研究院组织的"民法总则立法建议"项目荣获中国智库咨政建言"国策奖"，"大运河文化带建设法律与立法研究"项目获得"江苏省智库实践十佳案例"称号。

网址：http://iclms.njnu.edu.cn/

邮箱：yuhaimei_galya@163.com

电话：025-85891703

南京医科大学健康江苏研究院

健康江苏研究院，成立于2016年，是江苏省重点培育智库。南京医科大学校党委书记王长青教授担任研究院院长、首席专家。目前在研专家20人，年度拨款经费40万元人民币。

研究院以咨询决策为先导、以问题研究为核心、以健康维护为目的的组织发展体系，主要致力于三方面工作：（一）为政府决策提供咨询，将健康中国战略融万策。（二）积极承担政府卫生政策的相关评估和研究工作。（三）加强合作交流，助力"一带一路"健康发展。研究院有多篇政策建议获省委市委录用及重要批示。

网址：http://jkjs.njmu.edu.cn

邮箱地址：jkjs@nkjs.edu.cn

联系电话：025-86868591

南京艺术学院紫金文创研究院

南京艺术学院紫金文创研究院成立于2016年3月，由江苏省委宣传部、省文投集团和南京艺术学院共建。研究院下设"文创发展研究中心""文创策划与产业服务中心""文创信息与数据中心"，政策研究领域包括文化政策、消费政策、广播电视政策、市场政策等，与海内外众多政府部门、文化机构、高等院校建立良好合作关系。研究院整合了海内外专家多元化的学术背景与学术专长，围绕文化创意产业重大理论问题与前沿问题，结合国家重大关切和省内发展实际，开展相关研究。

南开大学经济与社会发展研究院

南开大学经济与社会发展研究院成立于1998年，以建设国内领先的应用经济研究平台为目标，创建国内首屈一指的效率与生产率研究机构，依托国际高水平学术交流平台的中国区域政策研究中心，注重服务国家战略，举办一系列高水平论坛，多篇决策咨询报告获得中央及省部级领导批示。每年代表中国政府发布《中国现代物流发展报告》（中英文），让世界把握中国的现代物流发展脉搏。

2016年入选教育部中国教育智库联盟执行委员，同年入选天津市首批高校智库。

网站：http://esd.nankai.edu.cn/

电话：022-23508549

南开大学中国特色社会主义经济建设协同创新中心

南开大学中国特色社会主义经济建设协同创新中心成立于2014年，汇聚了300余名专家学者。中心编辑报送《成果要报》近200篇，并自建研究数据库，为中央和地方决策提供智力支持；建设多个海外研究基地并搭建联合培养平台，成功举办国内外学术论坛 300 余场；创立"政治经济学大讲堂"，培训专业人才近 2 000 人；创办经济学拔尖创新人才试点班，其成果《经济学基础创新人才培养模式的理论与实践探索》获得第六届国家级教学成果一等奖。

联系方式：

网址：http://chinaeconomy.nankai.edu.cn/

联系电话：022-23500235

邮箱：cicce@nankai.edu.cn

南通大学江苏长江经济带研究院

江苏长江经济带研究院成立于 2014 年，2016 年被江苏省委宣传部确定为省重点培育智库。目前，研究院拥有经济学等学科背景的专兼职研究人员 45 人，年度经费约 100 万元。

研究团队创新性提出了协调性均衡发展理论。研究成果在人民出版社出版以及权威期刊发表，多篇决策咨询报告得到党和国家领导人、省部级主要领导肯定性批示并被政府部门采纳应用。研究院 2015 年创办了首届长江经济带发展论坛，随后主办了三届论坛。2018 年获评江苏省智库实践十佳案例。

联系方式：

网站：http://yhyjy.ntu.edu.cn/

邮箱：chenweizhong@ntu.edu.cn

电话：0513-85012972

中蒙俄经贸合作与草原丝绸之路经济带构建研究协同创新中心

中蒙俄经贸合作与草原丝绸之路经济带构建研究协同创新中心成立于 2015 年 1 月。中心设有六大研究平台和两个研究中心，拥有专家学者 120 余人，经费充足。

智库主要在中蒙俄经济合作与草原丝绸之路经济带建设相关领域开展学术研究，并在战略规划、制度设计、政策扶持等方面进行开创性探索。同时，为经济带建设培养人才。智库于2017年入选内蒙古自治区首批"高端智库试点单位"。

联系方式：0471-5300158

电子邮件：nmstar@vip.sina.com

通信地址：内蒙古呼和浩特市北二环路185号

网址：http://www.imufe.edu.cn/kyc/xtcxzx

微信公众号：gh_8f29d9a5ee3d

清华大学国情研究院

清华大学国情研究院成立于2011年12月，并在2015年入选全国首批国家高端智库建设试点单位。国情研究院坚持"维护国家最高利益，认清国家长期发展目标，积极影响国家宏观决策"的发展宗旨，遵循"获取决策知识，创新决策知识，传播决策知识，通过国情研究报告影响决策与政策"的发展路径，按照原创性、前沿性和权威性并重的知识品牌建设原则，已建设成为国内外具有重要影响的公共政策研究机构。

国情研究院长期为国家重大决策提供咨询服务，很多研究成果被采纳，出版的《国情报告》已成为中央和地方政府决策的重要参考；积极与世界对话，通过国际学术交流、研究成果出版和主流媒体宣介，在国际舞台上发出响亮的中国声音。

电话：010-62772199

邮箱：ccsoffice@tsinghua.edu.cn

山东大学卫生管理与政策研究中心

山东大学卫生管理与政策研究中心于2002年成立，是山东大学独立建制的二级单位，拥有专职人员23人，兼职人员20人，2018年度到位经费500余万元。中心拥有国家卫生健康委员会"卫生经济与政策研究重点实验室""山东大学-瑞典卡罗琳斯卡医学院全球健康研究联合实验室",2016年成功入选山东省重点新型智库试点建设单位。

中心以卫生经济与政策研究为特色研究领域,围绕国内卫生改革与发展的需要,紧跟国际卫生研究发展前沿,利用已有的国际合作优势,通过承担各级政府部门课题和国际合作项目、开展政策咨询、卫生人才培训等多种形式发挥智库功能。

网址:http://www.chmp.sdu.edu.cn

邮箱:shcm@sdu.edu.cn

电话:0531-88380061

上海大学基层治理创新研究中心

上海大学基层治理创新研究中心系上海市教委资助的首批上海高校智库之一。研究中心围绕国家加强和创新社会治理、建设和谐社会的战略目标,研究中国基层社会治理模式转型的基本走势,以及在此背景下社会管理体制、基本公共服务体系和现代社会组织体制在制度建设上的互适性,从而为加快推进上海基层治理转型提供经验和理论层面的决策依据。自成立以来,中心入选首批"十三五"上海民政科研基地,获2017年社会类智库专业影响力第6名。

网址:http://www.rclgshu.org/

邮箱:rclgshu@126.com

微信公众号:RCLGSHU

电话:021-66135205

上海对外经贸大学国际经贸治理与中国改革开放联合研究中心(SC-GTEG)

上海对外经贸大学国际经贸治理与中国改革开放联合研究中心成立于2013年,是上海市首批高校智库之一。中心以我国唯一世界贸易组织讲席计划为学术支撑,以国内外团队联合研究为主要工作方式。智库每年出版《国际经贸治理重大议题年报》和《国际经贸治理评论》，每月发布《国际经贸治理动态》，在《国际商报》开设"国际经贸治理"专栏。智库被中国服务贸易协会授予"全国服务贸易创新研究基地"。

邮箱：maoyitanpan@126.com

电话：021-52067321

上海海事大学上海国际航运研究中心

上海国际航运研究中心是国际航运业发展的研究和咨询机构，成立于2008年。中心先后入选上海市第一批高校知识服务平台——高级战略研究中心、上海高校人文社会科学重点研究基地和上海市高校协同创新中心。

中心产生大量对政府和国内外航运界有影响的重要成果，每年对外发布指数和行业报告近百本，已建立多元化、立体化信息发布渠道。建设了国际上第一个数据完整、功能全面的"中国航运数据库"，建设的"港航大数据实验室"被列为上海国际航运中心建设重点任务，在航运大数据研究方面居于国内领先地位。

上海海事大学中国（上海）自贸区供应链研究院

中国（上海）自贸区供应链研究院于2013年10月成立，是上海市社会科学创新研究基地，年均科研经费达到1000余万元。

研究院主办、联办或承办首届中国国际进口博览会物流业重要配套论坛——2018全球贸易与国际物流高峰论坛、博鳌国际物流论坛、首届中国自贸试验区检验检疫创新发展论坛等国内外会议，为国内外相关机构提供合作交流平台。

研究院承担众多决策咨询课题研究，委托单位包括各地政府、大型企业、国内高校、国际机构等，涉及战略规划、制度创新、政策评估、企业转型、社会化采信等领域，形成多份专报，得到领导批示和关注。

研究院网址：http://cifsc.shmtu.edu.cn

上海交通大学中国城市治理研究院

中国城市治理研究院由上海交通大学和上海市人民政府发展研究中心合作建设，其目标是建成国际知名、具有中国特色的新型智库，优秀人才汇聚培养基地和高端国际交流合作平台。研究院通过跨学科交叉集成，凝练了城市应急管理、城市环境治理、城市社会治理、创新驱动和可持续发展、宜居和公共服务、城市文化与城市形象等研究领域，为党和政府科学决策提供智力支持。研究院多渠道报送咨政建言70余篇，公开发表学术论文和媒体文章各70余篇；成功举办2016、2017全球城市论坛；与联合国人居署、世界银行等国际组织和咨询机构积极合作。

电话：021-62934788

邮箱：ciug@sjtu.edu.cn

网址：ciug.sjtu.edu.cn

上海外国语大学中东研究所

上海外国语大学中东研究所为教育部人文社会科学重点研究基地、上海市教委首批"上海高校智库"，现有编制22名，年度经费投入400万元。

研究所积极发挥资政、育人、启民、咨商的智库作用。现承担课题21项，主办《阿拉伯世界研究》和 *Asian Journal of Middle Eastern and Islamic Studies*，出版《中东地区发展年度报告》6卷，主办"亚洲与中东"高层国际论坛6届；编印中东问题研究《专报》《简报》近200期，咨询报告已获党和国家主要领导人批示多次。研究所入选中联部"一带一路"智库合作联盟。

网址：http://mideast.shisu.edu.cn

邮箱：zdssisu@163.com

微信公众号：MESI_SISU

电话：021-35373278

上海外国语大学中国国际舆情研究中心

上海外国语大学中国国际舆情研究中心成立于 2008 年 6 月,是上海外国语大学校级学术研究机构,致力于国际舆情和国际传播领域的研究。中心现有研究人员和行政团队 14 人,兼职研究人员 20 人。

主持多项国家社科基金。2015 年入选中宣部舆情信息直报点。截至 2018 年,中心提交的决策咨询报告有近百篇获中央领导同志批示,有 300 余篇被中宣部、中共中央办公厅、上海市委对外宣传办公室等政府机构采纳。荣获 2017 年、2018 年中宣部舆情信息"优秀单位"称号。

网址:http://www.rcgpoc.shisu.edu.cn

电话:021-35372559

邮箱:globalopinion@shisu.edu.cn

深圳大学港澳基本法研究中心

深圳大学港澳基本法研究中心是全国最早独立设置的专门从事港澳基本法研究的科研实体机构,2011 年 5 月被遴选为部级人文社会科学重点研究基地。中心现有 13 人,年度经费(含人员工资)预算 550 万元。中心围绕服务国家发展战略和港澳工作大局,开展科学研究和咨询服务,发挥对外学术交流平台作用。中心取得的工作成绩得到中央、省、市港澳工作机构的重视和肯定,得到同行专家的好评,具有良好的学术影响力和社会影响力。

中心 http://cbl.szu.edu.cn

邮箱 cbl@szu.edu.cn

电话 0755-26733093

四川大学南亚研究所

四川大学南亚研究所坚持"以研究政治经济现状为主,兼及历史文化"的方针,加强对南亚国家政治经济现状的研究,并结合我国社会经济发展的实际为我国社会经济发展服务。研究所先后承担并完成国家社科基金和政府有关部门的科研课题20多项,出版学术专著20多部,发表学术论文800多篇,并向中央政府有关部门和有关单位提供研究报告50多份。研究所对南亚经济发展和南亚军事安全等的研究具有优势,在全国南亚研究领域走在前列,对南亚社会政治发展的研究也有相当实力。

邮箱:nanyasuo@163.com

电话:028-85412638

四川大学中国西部边疆安全与发展协同创新中心

中国西部边疆安全与发展协同创新中心成立于2012年,由四川大学与云南大学、西藏大学、新疆大学、国家民委民族理论政策研究室、国务院发展研究中心民族发展研究所等单位联合组建。

中心建立了涉藏问题研究、新疆研究、西部周边研究、"一带一路"重大问题研究、西部边疆史地研究、边疆理论与治理战略研究等平台。中心以新时期国家安全与发展的重大战略需求为导向,研究西部边疆治理战略,探索西部边疆安全与发展新路,为兴边富民、强国睦邻和国家长治久安提供智力支持。

电话:028-85416270

邮箱:cwf-scu@163.com

网址:http://cwf.scu.edu.cn/index.htm

苏州大学东吴智库文化与社会发展研究院

苏州大学东吴智库文化与社会发展研究院于2011年经苏州市民政局注册成立,是"江苏高校哲学社会科学重点研究基地""创建新型智库先进单位""江苏省重点培育智库"。2017年,智库年度经费802万元。

智库以"城镇化与城市发展"为关键词,以"城市经济与管理""城市与社会治理"

"城市文化与传播""城市规划与建设"为主要研究领域,以"名城名校 融合发展"战略工作为主要抓手。"对话苏州"系列活动是东吴智库的品牌活动,现已持续举办五年。

网址:http://sutt.suda.edu.cn/

邮箱:sutt@suda.edu.cn

电话:0512-65228625

天津财经大学天津市自由贸易区研究院

天津市自由贸易区研究院成立于2014年,秉承服务政府、服务社会的理念,是"中国自由贸易试验区协同创新中心"核心协同单位,"中国高校自贸区研究联盟"发起单位。自成立以来,研究院进行了多项课题研究,获批国家"十三五"重点出版项目(自贸区研究),组织召开了各种国际性和全国性的自贸区学术与政策研讨会,并开展了一系列自贸区相关的专题讲座和培训活动,受到市委、市政府和自贸区管委会等部门的高度重视,产生了广泛的社会影响。

网址:http://tafta.tjufe.edu.cn

微信公众号:TAFTA-TJUFE(天津自贸区研究院)

邮箱:tafta_tjufe@126.com

电话:022-88186335

天津大学国家知识产权战略实施研究基地

国家知识产权战略实施(天津大学)研究基地于2013年4月设立,张维教授担任主任。研究基地秉承管、法、经、工交叉融合,助力知识产权强国建设的使命,努力打造成为面向国家知识产权政策制定、面向企业知识产权战略管理、面向高校知识产权人才培养的智库平台。2016年入选"天津市首批高校智库"、2017年加入天津智库联盟。研究团队30余人,刊发51期《信息速递》,22期获得国知局领导批示,7期得到进一步转化应用。

邮箱:liulinshanipr@tju.edu.cn

电话:022-27401360

天津大学亚太经合组织可持续能源中心(APSEC)

亚太经合组织可持续能源中心,成立于2014年第11届APEC能源部长会议,是外交部备案的17家APEC中心之一。中心隶属于国家能源局,是中国政府牵头成立的第一家能源国际合作机构,由天津大学负责日常运营管理。

APSEC办公面积300平方米,专职人员14名,有稳定财政经费支持。现国际智力网络含9个APEC经济体60名专家,设立2个项目联合运营中心,在APEC区域固定出版核心研究成果2部,服务国家APEC能源国际合作报送资讯70期、简报21期,统筹协调国内36家单位参与APEC能源工作,形成特色品牌旗舰论坛2个,与全球10座城市和15家机构签订合作协议。

网址:http://apsec.tju.edu.cn/

邮箱:apsec2014@126.com

电话:022-27400847

同济大学德国研究中心

同济大学德国研究中心成立于2012年,是同济大学直属的实体性研究机构、同济大学首个新型智库建设项目,也是教育部国别和区域研究培育基地。中心目前已汇聚校内外、国内外专兼职研究员近60名,研究范围涵盖德国及欧洲政治、外交、经济、社会、文化、教育及中德、中欧关系等领域。

中心从2012年起每年编写《德国发展报告》暨德国蓝皮书;出版《德国研究》季刊(CSSCI来源期刊);每年在各类媒体发表署名文章百余篇;迄今已有多篇内参获中央主要领导批示。此外,中心与全球德国与欧洲研究领域的有关智库建立有实质性合作,每年联合举办中德论坛等国际会议。

网址:http://german-studies-online.tongji.edu.cn/

微信公众号:tongji_dgyj

办公地点:上海市四平路1239号同济大学中德大楼9楼

邮箱:gso@tongji.edu.cn

电话:021 - 65980328

武汉大学国际法研究所

武汉大学国际法研究所成立于1980年,是我国高校系统第一个国际法专门研究机构。获批法学领域首批硕士点、博士点,获评国家级重点学科,是教育部人文社会科学重点研究基地。2015年被中宣部批准为国家高端智库首批试点建设单位。汇聚了一批理论素养深厚,在决策咨询、国际交流和公共外交方面能力突出的专家。坚持国际公法、国际私法、国际经济法与比较法的全面综合研究,在智库建设方面秉持"有机融合中国立场、独立意识与理论论证"的理念,向中央和决策部门提供咨询、直接参与案件处理、深度参与国际谈判,多篇报告被党和国家领导人批示,不少建议被有关部门采纳。编辑出版的《武大国际法评论》《中国国际私法与比较法年刊》《中国促进国际法治报告》和SSCI期刊 *Chinese Journal of International Law*,在国内外学术界和实务界具有重要影响。

武汉大学国家文化发展研究院

武汉大学国家文化发展研究院成立于2009年,由文化部与武汉大学统一领导,湖北省文化厅参与共建,现有专职学者12人,兼职学者13人。研究院主要组织文化创新基础理论和相关课题研究,为我国文化创新发展提供理论支撑,培养各类文化创新专门人才,为我国文化创新体系建设提供人才保障;提供政策咨询与信息服务,为国家和各级政府部门决策提供智库支持;关注国际文化创新发展与研究的进程。跟踪关注我国文化创新理论前沿,承担并完成国家和地方政府部门交给的文化创新课题研究任务。

电话:027-68766957/027-68761537

邮箱:nccirwhu@126.com

武汉大学环境法研究所

武汉大学环境法研究所始建于1981年,1999年首批入选中国普通高等学校人文社会科学重点研究基地,是中国法学会环境资源法学研究会的秘书处所在地,亦是最高人民法院环境资源司法理论研究基地。现有教授6人,副教授4人,讲师1人,所长为秦天宝教授。

研究所先后承担或参与了《环境保护法》等几乎所有国家环境法律以及百余部国家环境法规和地方环境法规的起草和修改工作,并向全国人大、环境保护部外交部等各级政府机关提交了200余份咨询报告。

研究所在教育部社科司组织的2015年基地测评中,在基地服务社会能力的单项排名中进入全国前50强。

网址:www.riel.whu.edu.cn

邮箱:riel2@whu.edu.cn

电话/传真:027-68752091

微信公众号:whu_riel

武汉大学经济发展研究中心

武汉大学经济发展研究中心创立于1990年,是依托武汉大学经济学领域四个国家级重点学科,集聚校内外发展经济学领域优秀学者而构建的集理论研究、政策分析和教学于一体的智库。2000年被批准为教育部人文社会科学重点基地。中心的宗旨是,集聚和培养一批创新人才,全面提升教学、科研和咨政三位一体的创新能力,致力于推进发展经济学的中国化与时代化、中国经济发展实践的理论化与国际化,努力办成国内顶尖国际知名的学术平台和具有社会影响力的智库,为中国经济发展贡献智慧。

武汉大学媒体发展研究中心

武汉大学媒体发展研究中心是教育部人文社会科学重点研究基地,2015 年、2016 年连续荣获中国传媒经济学科杰出贡献奖(机构类),被誉为有创新活力的研究中心。中心现有专兼职研究员 50 余位,聚焦互联网传播形态与中国传播创新,深入开展中国传播创新实践调研,多篇报告被中央和省部级单位采用。中心搭建了如"跨文化传播国际学术会议(ICIC)""比较传播研究国际研讨会""中国传播创新论坛""瑞中跨文化传播夏令营"等交流平台,定期出版《中国传播创新研究报告》(蓝皮书)、《中国媒体发展研究报告》,以及《跨文化传播研究丛书》《新闻传播学:问题与方法丛书》等丛书,不懈探索中国传播创新与社会发展的核心问题。

武汉大学社会保障研究中心

武汉大学社会保障研究中心是教育部直属的人文社会科学重点研究基地,拥有全国唯一的社会保障国家级重点学科和国家级社会保障研究创新基地。目前,中心有专兼职研究人员 71 人,年度经费 400 余万元。近年来,中心向各级政府部门报送并被采纳的咨询报告达 100 多份,部分咨询报告受到国家领导人的批示;每年都与实务部门合作撰写《中国社会保障改革与发展报告》,并联合召开成果发布会。2015 年在全部参与评估的 151 个教育部人文社科重点研究基地中,中心决策支持能力排名第 5。2017 年中心成为高校高端智库联盟成员单位。

网址:http://csss.whu.edu.cn

邮箱:csss6@sina.com

电话:027 - 68752238/027 - 68755887

西安交通大学"一带一路"自由贸易试验区研究院

西安交通大学"一带一路"自由贸易试验区研究院成立于2017年3月,实行理事会下的院长负责制,下设服务贸易、政府治理与创新、法律治理三个研究中心,建立了博士后进站制度。

研究院累计争取到经费1 100余万元,承担各类课题共计50余项,形成研究报告超过100万字,提交《决策建言》批复率达60%以上,编撰《自贸院之声》8期,参与改革研讨、专家咨询上百次,举办"陕西省自贸区创新发展高端论坛"等系列活动,被人民网、新华网等主流媒体报道转载。研究院在探索"文章"变"文件",将知识优势转化为战略优势、策略优势、政策优势,实现高校社会服务职能中发挥了积极作用。

网址:http://skc-zm.xjtu.edu.cn/

邮箱:xjtu_zmy@163.com

电话:029-82663967

西藏民族大学西藏文化传承发展协同创新中心

西藏民族大学西藏文化传承发展协同创新中心于2013年4月被西藏自治区认定为自治区级"2011协同创新计划"重点培育和建设项目,2018年12月,被教育部认定为首批省部共建协同创新中心。

中心以"立足西藏、协同合作、创新机制、服务社会"为工作思路,紧紧围绕西藏区域创新发展的重大需求,以西藏重大创新任务为牵引,抓住西藏经济社会发展急需解决的重大现实问题,积极组织开展科学研究,大力推动成果转化,充分发挥了高校智库和咨政服务作用。中心产出各类研究成果百余篇,其中6项研究成果被国家领导人批示,50余项成果被国家民委、西藏自治区以及有关部门采纳。

中心网址:http://www.xzmy.edu.cn/xtcx/

联系电话:029-33755894

邮　　箱:xzmyxietong@sina.com

西南财经大学中国家庭金融调查与研究中心

中国家庭金融调查与研究中心成立于 2010 年，是集数据采集、数据研究及政策研究于一体的公益性高校智库机构，包含中国家庭金融、小微企业和城乡社区治理三大数据库，为相关问题的学术研究及政策制定提供参考，在国内外享有较高声誉。中心积极开展收入分配、家庭金融、农村发展、房产与城镇化、城乡治理等方面的问题研究，在智库建设、政策建议、社会服务等方面取得了重要进展。同时，中心是"高等学校学科创新引智计划"（简称"111 计划"）的文社科类创新引智基地之一。

中心：http://chfs.swufe.edu.cn/

联系电话：028 - 87352163

联系邮箱：pr@chfs.cn

厦门大学高等教育发展研究中心

厦门大学高等教育发展研究中心组建于 2000 年 1 月，是全国唯一一家以高等教育为研究对象的教育部人文社会科学重点研究基地。中心始终以高等教育为研究特色，以服务国家重大需求为宗旨，长期参与国家教育政策的研究和咨询工作，在高等教育基本理论研究、高等教育考试研究、高等教育体制与管理研究等领域取得了奠基性、领先性的科研成果，为国家高等教育战略规划设计、高考改革方案研制、高等教育质量建设等提供政策咨询意见，已成为国家高等教育决策的重要智库。

网址：https://che.xmu.edu.cn/

邮箱：xmdxgjzx@xmu.edu.cn

电话：0592 - 2187552

延边大学朝鲜半岛研究院

延边大学朝鲜半岛研究院成立于 2014 年 11 月，与朝鲜韩国研究中心（教育部人文社会科学重点研究基地）和亚洲研究中心（与韩国高等教育财团合办）两个研究中心合署办公。

延边大学是国内唯一从政治、经济、法律、历史、语言文学、教育、艺术等各学科、各领域全面综合研究朝鲜半岛的高校。研究院充分发挥其综合研究特点和地域优势,同中国社会科学院、吉林大学、朝鲜金日成综合大学、韩国首尔大学、日本早稻田大学等国内外知名高校和学术机构建立广泛的学术交流合作机制,实现合作研究、人员互访、资料信息共享。

盐城师范学院沿海发展智库

盐城师范学院沿海发展智库成立于2007年,是江苏省重点培育智库,拥有一支35人组成的研究团队,其中正高职称22人。智库主要致力于江苏乃至全国沿海发展的重大理论与实践问题,以服务江苏省委省政府和沿海各市党委政府科学决策为导向。自成立以来,共推出了100多项决策咨询研究成果,其中有4项成果先后获得党和国家领导人的批示,15项成果获得省领导批示。6篇成果刊登省智库办《智库专报》,5篇成果刊登省社科联《决策参阅》,江苏沿海发展的决策咨询研究处于全省领先水平。

电话:0515-88233887

传真:0515-88213020

邮箱:jsyhkf@163.com

云南大学边疆民族问题智库

云南大学边疆民族问题智库由云南大学西南边疆少数民族研究中心牵头成立、中国陆地边疆地区7所高校共同合作组建,年度经费240万元。智库按照"自愿参与、平等合作、优势互补、互利共赢、共同发展"原则,合力建设中国民族问题智库,致力于促进民族团结进步和中华民族共同体建构。智库每年开展田野调查并编写《中国边疆民族发展报告》,建设"中国边疆地区民族工作案例库",编印《中国边疆民族问题咨询报告》，迄今已提交20余份高质量咨询报告，在昆明、呼和浩特和南宁举办了"中国边疆民族智库论坛"共3届。

邮箱：cber_7@163.com

电话：(0871)65031748

云南大学周边外交研究中心

云南大学周边外交研究中心是云南省第一批高校智库，在2016年度省内考核中名列第一名。中心现有专职研究人员20余人，其中教授（研究员）12人，副教授（副研究员）7人。中心先后获得4项国家社科基金重大项目、2项教育部重大项目，有2篇咨询报告得到中央领导批示、1篇报告入选教育部《智库专刊》。中心主办《云大地区研究》（集刊）和《周边要报》（内刊），出版《研究丛书》和《智库报告》两个系列丛书，每年出版《澜湄合作发展报告》《缅甸国情报告》等蓝皮书。

电话/传真：+86-871-65033130/65034082

邮箱：ccnds@ynu.edu.cn

微信公众号：周边外交研究

网址：http://www.ccnds.ynu.edu.cn

浙江大学中国科教战略研究院

浙江大学中国科教战略研究院聚焦工程教育、科教创新、院校研究三大优势特色领域，为国家和区域创新发展提供战略咨询服务。目前共有正高级职称15名，副高级职称及讲师10名，同时邀请了一批国内外知名的智库咨询专家。

战略院近五年承担国家自然科学基金8项、社会科学基金2项，教育部、工程院、科技部等国家部委课题30项，提供高质量咨询报告100余篇。战略院已建立广泛的国际合作网络，每年举办科教发展战略国际研讨会，与国内外学者深入交流探讨科教战略与工程教育前沿热点问题，目前已成功举办了13届。

网址：http://www.icstep.zju.edu.cn/

邮箱：icstep@zju.edu.cn

电话：0571-88981232

浙江大学中国农村发展研究院

浙江大学中国农村发展研究院（CARD，中文"卡特"）是教育部首批国家人文社会科学重点研究基地，也是国家"985"工程人文社会科学创新基地。"卡特"核心学科"农林经济管理"在第四轮全国学科评估中荣列A+，被列入国家"双一流"建设学科。

"卡特"立足浙江、服务全国、走向世界，将理论研究与中国"三农"发展与改革实践相结合，积极咨政建言，提出了一系列具有创新性、前瞻性、可操作性的农村改革与发展的决策报告，其中有100多项受到中央和省部领导的肯定与批示，充分发挥了"卡特"在服务"三农"中的高端智库作用。

浙江大学中国西部发展研究院

浙江大学中国西部发展研究院成立于2006年10月，是国家高端智库建设培育单位和浙江省新型重点专业智库。

西部院聚焦西部大开发、"一带一路"建设和区域协调发展相关重大问题，已凝练形成"区域经济合作与区域协调发展""民心相通与区域协调发展""生态文明建设与区域协调发展"三大研究领域和"国际规则与风险防控""数据资源库与政策评估"两大决策支撑，承担的一批重要咨询报告多次获国家领导人重要批示，参与了一系列党中央、国务院重要文件的起草，先后完成10多项国务院印发或批复的战略规划。

地址：浙江省杭州市浙江大学紫金港校区中国西部发展研究院大楼

主页：http://www.cawd.zju.edu.cn/

联系方式：0571-88981422

浙江师范大学非洲研究院

浙江师范大学非洲研究院(IASZNU)成立于 2007 年 9 月,系中国高校首个综合性、实体性非洲研究院,是一所集学术研究、人才培养、政策咨询、国际交流为一体的智库。研究院迄今承担国家社科基金项目 19 项,教育部、外交部等部委和国际合作课题 80 余项;建有国内高校首个非洲博物馆、非洲翻译馆、非洲文献中心与特色数据库,建成了五种文字服务的智库网站。2011 年创办的"中非智库论坛"已成为影响广泛的中非人文交流和公共外交的高端平台。研究院立足国家战略需求,在深入非洲调研基础上提交大量咨询报告,多项政策建议被中央领导批示或采纳。研究院现已成为服务国家非洲事务的舆论引导与公共外交中心。

网站:http://ias.zjnu.cn
邮箱:ias@zjnu.cn
电话:0579-82287076

中国海洋大学中国企业营运资金管理研究中心

中国企业营运资金管理研究中心由中国海洋大学与中国会计学会于 2009 年 8 月合作设立。研究中心以独创的"资本效率与财务风险分析体系"为支撑,持续开展中国上市公司营运资金管理调查,编撰发布《营运资金管理发展报告》系列丛书,举办中国资金管理智库高峰论坛,扩充"中国资金管理智库数据平台"(http://cmttc.ouc.edu.cn/data),是我国资金管理领域的"思想库""文献库""信息库""案例库"。研究成果被中国石油天然气集团公司等著名企业采纳应用,获得省部级以上教学、科研成果奖励 20 多项。

中国人民大学国家发展与战略研究院

国家发展与战略研究院于 2013 年正式成立,2015 年成为全国首批"国家高端智库"建设试点单位。人大国发院是以习近平总书记治国理政思想为指导,以"四个全面"战略为研究框架,以"国家治理现代化"为特色研究领域,通过机制和体制创新,整合中国人民大学优质智库研究资源而打造的、独立的非营利实体研究机构,坚守"国家战略、全球视野、决策咨询、舆论引导"的目标,着眼于思想创新和全球未来,致力于发展成为具有国际影响力的中国特色新型智库,服务于国家发展战略与社会进步。

电话:010-62515049/0329

网站:http://nads.ruc.edu.cn

Email:nads_ruc@126.com(行政)

nads04@ruc.edu.cn(媒体)

中国人民大学重阳金融研究院

中国人民大学重阳金融研究院成立于2013年1月19日,是重阳投资董事长裘国根先生向其母校捐赠并设立教育基金运营的主要资助项目。作为中国特色新型智库,人大重阳聘请了全球数十位前政要、银行家、知名学者为高级研究员,旨在关注现实、建言国家、服务人民。目前,人大重阳下设7个部门、运营管理3个中心(生态金融研究中心、全球治理研究中心、中美人文交流研究中心)。近年来,人大重阳在金融发展、全球治理、大国关系、宏观政策等研究领域在国内外均具有较高认可度。

电话:8610-62516805

邮箱:rdcy-info@ruc.edu.cn

网站:www.rdcy.org

新浪微博:@人大重阳

微信:@rdcy2013

中国人民公安大学首都社会安全研究基地

首都社会安全研究基地是首批北京市哲学社会科学研究基地,由中国人民公安大学治安学院建设管理,现有专兼职研究人员40余人,年度研究经费150万余元。

近年来,研究基地承担了国家重点研发计划、国家社科基金重大项目、教育部哲学社会科学重大攻关项目等一系列社会安全领域重大国家课题,"无人机管控""扫黑除恶""地铁反恐"等多项研究成果得到中央或省部级领导批示;出版《平安北京》蓝皮书,召开首都社会安全论坛,参与社会安全立法,制定北京-张家口2022年冬奥会安保规划,为海南省、武汉市、东莞市、克拉玛依市等多地制定社会治安防控体系规划,充分发挥了智库作用。

网站:http://ccss.ppsuc.edu.cn/

邮箱:CCSS2004@126.com

联系电话:010-83903413

中南财经政法大学产业升级与区域金融湖北省协同创新中心

中南财经政法大学产业升级与区域金融湖北省协同创新中心成立于2014年,是湖北省实施"高等学校创新能力提升计划"(即"2011"计划)第二批认定的15个湖北省协同创新中心之一,也是中南财经政法大学首个获批的面向区域发展的省级协同创新中心,是"产业升级与区域金融"的智库、思想库、信息库和人才库。主要在金融政策、产业政策、市场政策等领域开展研究,下设分支机构7个,直属机构14个。2015年以来,1项成果获中央级奖项,多项成果获省部级奖项。

电话:027-88386955

邮箱:chtl@zuel.edu.cn

中南财经政法大学城乡社区社会管理湖北省协同创新中心

城乡社区社会管理湖北省协同创新中心成立于2012年,是中共湖北省委改革智库及民政部全国民政政策理论研究基地。湖北省级财政每年支持300万元,固定办公场地400余平方米,研究平台5个:社会建设和社会治理、生态治理和绿色发展、就业创业和社会保障、乡村振兴和精准扶贫、健康湖北和医疗改革。

生态公民建设受到习近平总书记的肯定,咨政报告获中央领导和湖北省领导的批示,研究成果获省部级咨政成果特等奖和一、二等奖。

中心网址:www.smjic.org

电话:027-88387563

中南财经政法大学法治发展与司法改革研究中心

中南财经政法大学法治发展与司法改革研究中心成立于2011年11月,现与湖北法治发展战略研究院合署,是专门从事法治发展战略研究的智库。2015年入选中国法学会首家法治研究基地,系最高人民检察院检察应用理论研究基地、湖北省人文社科重点研究基地。智库按照"高起点、跨越式、重协同、建机制"的思路,着力为国家提供社会治理法治卓越人才,为中央和地方立法与决策提供高质量的咨询服务。通过协同创新搭建和运用"法治社会·长江论坛""法治中国大讲堂""1 000名决策者服务行动计划"等平台,在打造社会治理法治学术体系、话语体系、传播体系和人才培养等方面取得了显著绩效。

中南财经政法大学知识产权研究中心

十余年来,中心秉持"问题导向、理论创新、打造智库、服务社会"之理念,以"世界知名、中国一流"为目标,构建多个高端研究平台,开展全方位协同创新,全力打造知识产权国家智库。

中心拥有学术结构、学缘结构、年龄结构优化的各类高端人才组建的学术团队;承担了包括国家"双重大"研究项目、国家自科基金、社科基金项目在内260余项;在《中国社会科学》《法学研究》《中国法学》等国内外期刊上发表高水平论文600余篇;创办了知识产权南湖论坛等重要学术平台,为国家知识产权制度建设贡献了卓越智慧。

中南财经政法大学中国收入分配研究中心

中南财经政法大学中国收入分配研究中心于 2010 年 11 月成立。中心旨在建设成为具有国际水准的收入分配研究中心和创新人才培养基地,推进我国收入分配的理论与实践研究的深入开展。中心举办多场国际学术会议并与国外多所高校建立合作关系。自成立以来,发表了一批高质量的研究成果,其中多项成果发表后被《中国社会科学文摘》等刊物转载,多项研究成果获得了国家级和省部级的各类奖励。所撰写的多份研究报告多次获得省部级主要领导的重要批示并在实际中被采纳,取得了良好的社会影响。

电话:027-88986475

邮箱:sunqunli@sina.com

中南大学知识产权研究院

中南大学知识产权研究院成立于 2011 年,由中南大学和湖南省知识产权局联合共建,具有"战略、协同、共享"的特性,构建了"高校+政府+企业+中介"的智库运行模式,形成了"特色鲜明、制度创新、引领发展、服务社会"的建设思路。研究院是湖南省委宣传部认定的湖南省省级重点智库·专业特色智库,也是湖南省普通高等学校哲学社会科学重点研究基地和湖南省科协省级海智基地。

2013 年,研究院成为全国专利保护重点联系机制单位;2012 年和 2015 年先后两次获评全国知识产权系统知识产权人才工作先进集体;2018 年,研究院被国务院知识产权战略实施工作部际联席会议办公室评选为"国家知识产权战略实施先进集体"。

邮箱:hnipyiy@126.com

电话:0731-88660480

网址:http://law.csu.edu.cn/zscq/

中南大学中国村落文化研究中心

中国村落文化研究中心是我国创建年代最早、规模最大的以研究和保护中国传统村落为主的创新平台,把中国传统村落文化的保护成功推向了国家文化保护战略,把中国村落文化的研究引入了国家人文学科研究的领域,并首次界定了"中国传统村落"的定义。中心获得国家、省部级项目30多项,多次主办中国传统村落文化保护研究论坛等重要学术活动,持续开展全国性大规模田野调查,相关调研报告多次得到党和国家领导人的重要批示,发布了我国首部《中国传统村落蓝皮书》,相关成果先后入选CTTI八大智库精品成果、CTTI-BPA智库最佳研究报告一等奖、湖湘智库研究十大金策奖等。

联系方式:http://village.csu.edu.cn/

邮箱:village@csu.edu.cn

电话:0731-88877027

中山大学粤港澳发展研究院

中山大学粤港澳发展研究院成立于2015年,是首批国家高端智库试点单位。研究院下设"一国两制"与港澳基本法研究中心、港澳政治与公共治理研究中心、港澳经济研究中心、港澳社会研究中心、港澳历史文化与价值观研究中心、港澳与内地合作研究中心、海上丝绸之路与粤港澳国际合作研究中心等7个研究中心,主要围绕港澳发展动态、港澳治理、粤港澳合作发展等重大问题,服务于党和政府的重大决策需求。研究院建有粤港澳档案文献中心、粤港澳研究数据平台,拥有港澳经济、社会等多个专题追踪数据库。

网址:http://ygafz.sysu.edu.cn

2018 Annual Report on CTTI University Think Tanks & Top 100 University Think Tanks

As institutions with intensive talents, comprehensive disciplines and active international exchanges, colleges and universities play a significant role in talent training, scientific research and social service in China. Since the 18th National Congress of the Communist Party of China (CPC), the construction of new types of think tanks with Chinese characteristics has been publicized, guided and greatly promoted. Most of the research centers, research bases and research institutes which conduct countermeasure research in China's colleges and universities have gradually formed the "industry consciousness of think tanks", who identify with the concept of think tanks more than ever before, actively transform themselves into new types of think tanks, and make solid progress in providing political consultation, enlightening the general public, promoting public diplomacy, pushing forward the development of disciplines, and flourishing philosophy and social sciences.

1 Great Importance Attached to the Construction of New Types of University Think Tanks

The Ministry of Education attaches great importance to the construction of new types of think tanks. On February 10, 2014, the Ministry of Education distributed "Plan for the Construction of New Types of University Think Tanks with Chinese

Characteristics" ("The Plan"), in which eight main targets were concluded, four ways of constructing university think tanks were put forward, the importance of building university think tank teams was emphasized, and such significant opinions as expanding channels for outcomes application, creating high-end publishing platforms, carrying out reforms in management modes, and making innovations in organizational forms were stated. On January 20, 2015, the General Office of the CPC Central Committee (GOCPCCC) and the General Office of the State Council distributed "Opinions on Improving the Construction of New Types of Think Tanks with Chinese Characteristics" ("The Opinions"). "The Opinions" stated that we shall move forward with the development and improvement of university think tanks, give full play to the advantages of comprehensive disciplines, intensive talents and active international exchanges of universities, thoroughly implement the plan for the construction of new types of think tanks with Chinese characteristics and promote the overall improvement of universities' capability to provide intelligence service. To act upon the arrangement made by the CPC Central Committee for the building of new types of think tanks, the Ministry of Education issued "Key Points for the Work of the Ministry of Education in 2015" in late January in 2015, which stated that "The Plan" should be carried out in an all-round way, reforms in the ways to manage and organize key research bases for humanities and social sciences should be deepened and the building of top think tanks should be started. "The Plan" was mentioned in many documents issued by the Ministry of Education from 2015 to 2018.

Education authorities of all provinces, municipalities and autonomous regions have formulated relevant documents according to their own situation. Early in 2011, Shanghai Municipal Education Commission had once issued a document that stated the need to build Shanghai university think tanks brand. In November 2013, Hubei

Provincial Department of Education and Hubei Provincial Department of Finance distributed "Plan for the Flourishment of Philosophy and Social Sciences of Regular Colleges and Universities in Hubei (2013 - 2020)" which required that great efforts should be spared to build a number of new think tanks with the characteristics of being "urgently needed by Hubei, first-class in China, advanced in institutions, significant in contributions". It has provided forward-looking policy guidance for the building of university think tanks in Hubei. After the year of 2015, Shanghai City, Gansu Province, Zhejiang Province, Guangxi Zhuang Autonomous Region, Hunan Province, Tianjin City, Shandong Province, Chongqing City, Liaoning Province and Jilin Province successively distributed relevant documents to strengthen the construction of university think tanks and perform the functions of university think tanks. The active responses to the policy from various regions have laid a good foundation for the vigorous development of the construction of university think tanks.

2 The Unique Role Played by Universities in the Construction of New Types of Think Tanks

2.1 Comprehensive Disciplines Make It Easier to Conduct Interdisciplinary Problem-Oriented Researches

University is not only a gathering place for experts, scholars and elites from various fields, but also an important place for the production and accumulation of knowledge. Many universities have established a complete discipline system, especially those comprehensive ones which boast a long history, profound academic accumulation and strong capacity on fundamental researches. With integrated disciplines, these universities have resource superiority in forward-looking policy research that is reserved for the future. Currently, as China has embarked on a decisive stage in building a moderately prosperous society in all respects, it is more complicated to solve the problems of reform and development and to deal with global issues than ever before. Single discipline is far from enough to cope with the difficulties faced by China, thus strength of multi-disciplines including natural science, humanities and social sciences should be pooled to seek a solution. In addition, another discipline advantage of universities is that university think tanks can serve as an integration center for think tank personnel networks by drawing on their intensive networks of experts. For example, Zijin Media Think Tank of Nanjing University mainly consists of teams of five schools of the university which are interconnected and interwoven, including School of Social and Behavioral Sciences, Law School, School of Government, School of Journalism & Communication and School of Information Management. Thanks to such a framework of research teams, university think tanks are able to become a "catalyst" for the intersection of different disciplines rather than an "island" among universities.

2.2 Abundant Talents Are Conducive to the Implementation of Large-Scale Data Projects

Think tanks are engaged in evidence-based policy research grounded in various types of characteristic databases. During the process of database construction, masses of data need to be collected and classified. Graduate students in universities are optimal candidates for data collection, classification and analysis, and they are also the competent administrative assistants for senior researchers (professors) of think tanks. Therefore, a lot of prestigious university think tanks have made use of such a new force of graduate students.

2.3 University Think Tanks Provide an Easy Approach to Developing Public Diplomacy

World-renowned universities are all characterized by extensive and frequent academic exchanges and cooperation, a high degree of freedom, a wide range of disciplines and a high starting point. Compared with think tanks of Party/government organizations, researchers in university think tanks have fewer restrictions on outbound visits, which makes it easier for them to carry out academic and cultural exchanges, get a comprehensive understanding of relevant information in other countries, reduce information asymmetry, lower information barriers and get rid of misinterpretations and misjudgments.

2.4 University Think Tanks Have a High Level of Public Credibility

The mission of academic institutions is to "seek truth" and "seek knowledge", so that knowledge can be produced and disseminated. Academic views of scholars are usually authoritative, especially those of leading experts who have great social credibility. University think tanks can make use of their advantages of being specialized and scientific, and play an active role in guiding social opinions.

2.5 University Think Tanks Have Distinct Specialized Characteristics

Compared with such platform-oriented think tanks as think tanks of academies of social sciences and think tanks of Party schools or administrative colleges, university think tanks are usually small in size and less influential in decision-making. However, they have distinct specialized characteristics and clear division of research fields, which helps provide Party and government organizations with technology-intensive, knowledge-intensive and data-intensive service. In terms of the knowledge service of think tanks, what government needs are not only ideas of policy design, but also clear planning schemes. For example, as a specialized university think tank, Center for

Biosafety Research and Strategy of Tianjin University has carried out decision-making consultation in fields of biotechnology development, implementation of biological arms control and international laws. It took part in the drafting of "Measures for Safety Management of Biotechnology Research and Development" of the Ministry of Science and Technology and revision of "Regulations on Human Genetic Resources Management". Besides, it took charge of the drafting of "Model Code of Conduct for Biological Scientists", which received widespread attention and praises from the international community as one of the two proposals submitted by Chinese government on the 8th Review Conference for "Biological Weapons Convention" of the United Nations. In November 2017, the Center was approved by the United Nations as the first non-governmental organization (NGO) in China under the "Biological Weapons Convention", and made many speeches on behalf of China at the United Nations Headquarters in Geneva.

3 The Important Role Played by University Think Tanks in the System of New Types of Think Tanks

By the end of November 20, 2018, the Chinese Think Tank Index (CTTI) has included 706 source think tanks, among which there are 441 university think tanks, accounting for 62% of the total. Of the 105 source think tanks added in 2018, 94 are university think tanks, accounting for 90% of the total. Currently, CTTI system includes 7,110 internal references, 17,646 reports, 4,978 newspaper articles, 6,220 books and 45,130 academic papers from university think tanks, respectively making up 74%, 81%, 52%, 80% and 85% of the total outcomes in the CTTI system. University think tanks have played a dominant role in content production, which is one of the major features of think tank construction in China. Despite the fact that the

United States is widely recognized as having a large number of top think tanks, the proportion of university think tanks in the United States is far less than China. Therefore, university think tanks play a crucial part in the system of new think tanks with Chinese characteristics and great importance should be attached to them.

3.1 Regional Distribution of University Think Tanks

According to the data in the CTTI system, the regional distribution of university think tanks is uneven, which is embodied in the relatively great difference among provinces, cities and autonomous regions as well as highly-centralized distribution in a few provinces. As is shown in Fig. 1, of all think tanks selected in the CTTI, 78 are in Beijing, making up 17.7% of the total; Beijing, Shanghai, Tianjin, Jiangsu, Hunan and Hubei take the first six places in the regional ranking of selected think tanks, with a total of 233 selected university think tanks, accounting for half of the total number. East China has a large number of selected university think tanks (263), while Central China and West China have a relatively small number (178).

The high proportion of source university think tanks in these six provinces and cities is largely ascribed to the fact that they boast a large number of "Universities of 985 Project" and "Universities of 211 Project" with abundant and high-quality intellectual resources. Therefore, foundation of academic research and development of disciplines are the top priority to run university think tanks.

Table 1 Regional Distribution of University Think Tanks in the CTTI Source Think Tanks

Region	Number	Region	Number	Region	Number
Beijing City	78	Zhejiang Province	12	Anhui Province	4
Shanghai City	58	Gansu Province	11	Shanxi Province	3
Tianjin City	39	Shandong Province	11	Inner Mongolia Autonomous Region	3

Continued

Region	Number	Region	Number	Region	Number
Jiangsu Province	32	Jiangxi Province	11	Guangxi Zhuang Autonomous Region	3
Hunan Province	26	Yunnan Province	10	Henan Province	2
Hubei Province	23	Hebei Province	10	Ningxia Hui Autonomous Region	2
Shaanxi Province	21	Jilin Province	10	Hainan Province	2
Guangdong Province	17	Heilongjiang Province	9	Guizhou Province	2
Sichuan Province	13	Liaoning Province	8	Qinghai Province	1
Chongqing City	13	Fujian Province	6	Tibet Autonomous Region	1

3.2 Distribution of University Think Tanks in China by Type and by Area of Research

University think tanks in China can be classified into two types: comprehensive think tanks and specialized think tanks. Of the 286 university think tanks which have submitted the data of their research fields to the CTTI system, only 33% (94) are comprehensive ones involving multiple research fields, and the rest 67% are all specialized ones.

According to the data in the CTTI system, the top ten fields of policy research studied by university think tanks are industrial policy (87), financial policy (81), cultural policy (66), diplomatic policy (60), marketing policy (53), security policy (42), foreign trade policy (40), resource policy (38), social construction and social policy (36) and judicial policy (35). However, few university think tanks (only 1 - 3) conduct research into water conservancy policy, public security policy, supervision and monitoring policy, auditing policy, drug policy and forestry policy.

3.3 Scale of University Think Tanks

Among the 325 university think tanks that have submitted personnel data in the CTTI system, ten have more than 100 members of staff, including Collaborative Innovation Center for China Economy of Nankai University, Yangtze Industrial Economic Institute of Nanjing University and Institute of China Rural Studies in East China Normal University. These think tanks have a relatively large scale and complex staff composition. The remaining think tanks usually have the staff number between 10 to 100, especially between 10 to 50, which are called medium-sized think tanks. More than half of the university think tanks are medium-sized. In terms of the number of full-time researchers, nearly 80% of university think tanks have over 10 full-time researchers. That means China's university think tanks are generally in the second stage of development, a critical period of transformation to mature development.

3.4 University Think Tank Index in China

The CTTI university think tank index is the sum of the integrated assessment scores of all think tanks that belong to the same university in source think tanks, which is defined as U^{ts}. This index is intended to measure the think tank function of a university, and as for its detailed principles and calculation methods, please refer to the general report. Generally speaking, the think tank index of a university will be higher if the university has more think tanks being selected as the CTTI source think tanks and is more fruitful in think tank products. To compare universities of different types and scales in a fair way, universities in China are divided into three grades in this report, and universities of the same grade are sorted in alphabetical order according to pinyin spelling of names. The leading universities include Peking University, Tsinghua University, Fudan University, Nankai University, Wuhan

University, Zhejiang University, Beijing Normal University and Nanjing University. Since these universities possess such strong and distinctive schools as School of Economics and Management, School of Government, School of International Studies and School of Law, they can provide necessary intellectual support and skills for the operation of think tanks and enable think tanks to have a greater influence.

Table 2 Top 20 Universities of the Original "University of 985 Project" According to the University Think Tank Index

(in alphabetical order according to pinyin spelling of names)

Peking University
Beijing Normal University
Southeast University
Fudan University
East China Normal University
Huazhong University of Science and Technology
Jilin University
Nanjing University
Nankai University
Tsinghua University
Shanghai Jiao Tong University
Sichuan University
Tianjin University
Wuhan University
Xi'an Jiaotong University
Xiamen University
Zhejiang University
Ocean University of China
Renmin University of China
Central South University

Table 3 Top 20 Universities of the Original "University of 211 Project" According to the University Think Tank Index

(in alphabetical order according to pinyin spelling of names)

Anhui University
Beijing Jiaotong University
Beijing Foreign Studies University
Northeast Normal University
Guangxi University
Hebei University of Technology
Hunan Normal University
Central China Normal University
Jinan University
Jiangnan University
Nanjing University of Science and Technology
Nanjing Normal University
Shaanxi Normal University
Shanghai University
Shanghai International Studies University
Soochow University
Yanbian University
Yunnan University
China University of Political Science and Law
Zhongnan University of Economics and Law

Table 4 Top 30 Universities According to the University Think Tank Index

(in alphabetical order according to pinyin spelling of names)

Anhui University of Finance and Economics
Beijing International Studies University
Beijing Union University
Chengdu University of Technology
Fujian Normal University
Guangdong University of Foreign Studies
Guangzhou University
Hebei University
Hebei Finance University
Hebei University of Economics and Business
Huaiyin Institute of Technology
Jiangsu Police Institute
Jiangsu Normal University
Jiangxi Normal University
Nanjing University of Information Science & Technology
Nanjing University of the Arts
Nantong University
Inner Mongolia University of Finance and Economics
Shanghai University of International Business and Economics
Shanghai Maritime University
Shenzhen University
Capital University of Economics and Business
Capital Normal University
Tianjin University of Finance and Economics
Northwest Normal University
Xizang Minzu University
Yanshan University
Yancheng Teachers University
Yunnan University of Finance and Economics
Zhejiang Normal University

4 Visions and Principles of the CTTI Top 100 University Think Tanks Evaluation

4.1 Definition of the CTTI Top 100 University Think Tanks Evaluation

The CTTI Top 100 University Think Tanks Evaluation is a comprehensive evaluation of 441 university think tanks included in the Chinese Think Tank Index from four dimensions of Product (P), Activity (A), Impact (I) and Expert (E), among which 100 outstanding think tanks with the highest scores are assessed as "A-Level University Think Tanks" and "The CTTI Top 100 University Think Tanks". It is also called "PAI-E 100 Evaluation", or "PAI 100 University Think Tanks" (pai, a homophone for "upsurge" in Chinese) which means China's university think tanks have a huge potential for development. All A-Level university think tanks can be subdivided into three levels: A+ (25), A (35) and A-(40). The rest fall into B-Level and C-Level university think tanks. The 2018 annual report only publishes a list of "A-Level University Think Tanks".

"PAI-E 100 Evaluation" is different from "MRPAI Comprehensive Evaluation". First of all, the former is an output-oriented evaluation which focuses on evaluating Products (P) and Impact (I) of think tanks and excludes Management (M) and Resource (R) input in the system. Secondly, "PAI-E 100 Evaluation" is a new type of evaluation system that combines objective data in think tanks and opinions and evaluations of experts. By combining the advantages of these two evaluation methods, it can measure the level of think tank construction in a more comprehensive and objective way. Finally, "PAI-E 100 Evaluation" is only directed at university think tanks. Considering that each think tank produces products, functions and exerts influences in a quite similar way, it's more reasonable to evaluate the construction level of different types of think tanks with the same measurement.

4.2　Purpose of the CTTI Top 100 University Think Tanks Evaluation

China Think Tank Research and Evaluation Center of Nanjing University and Think Tank Research and Release Center of *Guangming Daily* ("The Two Centers") have always been committed to their missions, adhered to the principle of achieving shared growth through openness and collaboration, and provided professional services for high-quality management of think tanks. The purpose of the CTTI Top 100 University Think Tanks Evaluation is to promote healthy development of the construction of new types of university think tanks with Chinese characteristics by evaluating source university think tanks.

The construction of new types of university think tanks with Chinese characteristics is in full swing. Many universities, especially those prestigious universities, lay much emphasis on this work. In the past, lots of universities focused on presenting discipline construction in their reports on the construction of liberal arts, but now they report on the construction work of new types of think tanks of the past year. The building of think tanks has already been an important part of universities' liberal arts work and a critical indicator for discipline construction. However, not all universities think tanks have given full play to the role of think tanks or reached the expected goal of national think tank construction. Some university think tanks are facing problems in management and operation, positioning and self-cognition and the quality of their products. They still have a long way to go in improving their construction. In the macroscopic view, the development quality of national university think tanks varies greatly, which embodies in the development disparity among different regions, universities and research fields. The solution to such problems entails the support of national policies as well as the guidance and professional advice from other think tanks.

The vision of the CTTI Top 100 University Think Tanks Evaluation is to select a group of excellent university think tanks, invite them to share their experience and achievements in think tank construction, allow them to play an exemplary and demonstration role in the field of think tanks, and promote their advanced ideas of think tank construction which can be learnt by other university think tanks. There is an old saying that goes, "There are no two identical leaves in the world". The university think tanks on the list all have their own unique advantages, but their experience in think tank construction can not be applied to all. Other university think tanks should compare themselves with these excellent think tanks, make rational analysis and judgement and take their own situation into consideration, and only in this way can they find out the development path that is most suitable for them, can they internalize and make full use of the experience of the top 100 university think tanks, can they catch up with and finally surpass those excellent think tanks and can they make more brilliant achievements in the construction of new types of university think tanks with Chinese characteristics.

Since its publication, the Chinese Think Tank Index has been widely recognized by a large number of think tanks. Many source think tanks regard the selection for the CTTI as a kind of professional affirmation. "The Two Centers" hope that the CTTI Top 100 University Think Tanks list can act as a new way to serve and publicize source think tanks and encourage them to push forward with the sharing of data through collaboration and the improvement of their quality, so as to achieve the goal of "promoting construction by evaluation".

4.3 Principles of the CTTI Top 100 University Think Tanks Evaluation

(1) Objectivity and Independence

"The Two Centers" always stick to the principle of being objective and independent, and thoroughly implement the principle in every step of the CTTI Top 100 University Think Tanks Evaluation. Adhering to the principle of objectivity, "The Two Centers" collect the construction data of all university think tanks as comprehensively and correctly as possible, and strive to present the actual construction level of all university think tanks on the basis of data, fact and truth. The evaluation is based on the data of all source university think tanks in the CTTI system, the opinions from think tank experts and a variety of public information. "The Two Centers" carry out the assessment work as third-party think tank research institutions. Adhering to the principle of independence, they try best to ensure that the evaluation work will not be affected by other institutions or individuals, treat the data submitted by each source university think tank impartially and fairly, and respect the decisions, opinions and evaluations from experts, so as to make the evaluation work reach the required professional level.

(2) Protection of Users' Privacy

"The Two Centers" have always stuck to the principle of protecting the data of all source think tanks. The data used by the CTTI Top 100 University Think Tanks Evaluation is generated in the backend, and the scores of each institution will not be accessible to the public in order to protect the privacy of all source think tanks. However, the source think tank can send an official letter to the China Think Tank Research and Evaluation Center of Nanjing University in the name of the institution to get its specific scores.

(3) Being Result-Oriented

The CTTI Top 100 University Think Tanks Evaluation adopts the "PAI-E 100" evaluation system which focuses on the evaluation of productivity and impact of think tanks on policy, academy and society.

The CTTI Top 100 University Think Tanks Evaluation innovatively extracts the indicator PAI, which conforms to the actual development of university think tanks. First of all, universities in China have the same school management system, and they also have a quite similar way to manage their think tanks. Considering that M has a limited impact on the results of CTTI university think tank evaluation, it is excluded in this evaluation. Secondly, institutions of higher education are the main places for experts and scholars to carry out research, so university think tanks naturally have the ability and advantages of gathering top intellectual resources. Some university think tanks hire many well-known experts in think tank research. However, due to the fact that most of the experts are part-time members with limited resource integration ability, these think tanks fail to fully inspire or take advantage of the research capabilities of these experts. Although they occupy numerous resources, they are void of matching productive competence. Integrating R into the evaluation system will bring about potential unfairness that think tanks with abundant resources but few products can get high scores while those excellent thinks tanks that gain satisfactory achievements and great influence in spite of limited resources fail to be selected as the top 100 university think tanks, but the use of PAI can solve these problems well. Besides, as an evaluation index of Products and Impact, PAI conforms to the expected goal of the CTTI Top 100 University Think Tanks Evaluation which allows the think tanks that give full play to their roles, rather than those dominant in resources, to stand out from the competition.

(4) Combination of Objective Data and Opinions from Experts

The CTTI Top 100 University Think Tanks Evaluation is based on the data submitted by all source university think tanks in the CTTI system and the scores and opinions given by think tank experts. The former plays a main role while the latter serves as a supplement in the evaluation. The two complement each other and reflect the construction outcomes of all source university think tanks in a more objective way.

The CTTI system has established a sharing data collection mechanism through the collaboration of all members. Currently, there are three major sources of the system data: (1) data submitted by source think tanks and experts (2) data collected by members of the China Think Tank Research and Evaluation Center of Nanjing University (3) data automatically extracted online. The first one is the most widely-used approach. The data is input by think tank administrators or experts and then submitted to the CTTI background system for strict quality audit. All data must be confirmed before being entered in the database. Apparently, such a data collection mechanism involves a large number of human resources, however, it turns out to be a cost-effective way. By employing the mode of data sharing through "crowdsourcing" and co-construction, it makes the cost apportioned among each participant. Manual collection of the data ensures the accuracy, objectivity and validity of the data and allows them to accurately reflect the construction achievements of all university think tanks. In order to reduce man-made interference in the scores of Impact, except for a small amount of data entered by the administrators, the Impact scores of all think tanks and experts in the CTTI system are calculated automatically according to the reported data. This is quite different from the evaluation based on network big data analysis. Although big data contains a mass of various types of data, its quality and value density are not high and may be misleading. In addition, given that such information as internal reference reports, special reports and comments made by leaders is highly confidential, network big data, to a large degree, is short of internal reference information which can have a direct impact on policies. Moreover, products and activities of some think tanks are not accessible to the public or disclosed on the Internet, so network big data fails to fully reflect the capability and performance of think tanks in providing consultation and suggestions for policymaking.

The accuracy and objectivity of the system data ensure the reliability of the results of the CTTI Top 100 University Think Tanks Evaluation. However, taking the data collected by the system as the only measurement may bring about some problems. First, some think tanks may fail to enter their construction outcomes in the system before the deadline and few think tanks may exaggerate their achievements. Second, despite the fact that the *PAI* boasts numerous advantages, it focuses on the productivity of think tanks during its data collection and cannot accurately reflect the impact of think tanks. It is difficult to get the following objective data through *PAI*: Are the Party and government organizations truly satisfied with the suggestions on policymaking given by think tanks? Are their research results truly recognized by academia? Is their reputation accepted by their peers? Do their calls receive positive responses from the society? Subjective feedback from targeted audience is undoubtedly a critical evaluation index. To make up the deficiency of objective data and to quantify the qualitative index that *PAI* fails to measure, the system introduces the "*E*" which allows experts to score and evaluate think tanks.

(5) Inviting University Think Tanks for Self-Evaluation

Considering the original intention of the CTTI Top 100 University Think Tanks Evaluation, "The Two Centers" adopt the method of third-party evaluation and self-evaluation from institutions in the evaluation work. Third-party evaluation refers to an independent, impartial and objective evaluation or suggestion made by a third party that has no direct relationship with the evaluation object and administrative departments. As a third party independent of university think tanks and their administrative departments, "The Two Centers" rank and publish the CTTI Top 100 University Think Tanks, which is a third-party evaluation. Besides, the evaluation involves the self-evaluation from institutions in the evaluation system. Serving as another link in the evaluation work, the self-evaluation is a good complement to the third-party evaluation. It is not evaluation agencies, but university think tanks that know their construction results and competitiveness best and can accurately sum up their experience in construction. Therefore, after the release of the CTTI Top 100 University Think Tanks, we will invite the listed think tanks to write their own "Brief Biographies of Think Tanks" (self-evaluation) in the hope that they may provide experience for the construction of new types of university think tanks with Chinese characteristics.

5 The CTTI Top 100 University Think Tanks Evaluation System and Algorithm

5.1 Establishment of the CTTI Top 100 University Think Tanks Evaluation System

(1) Objective Data in the CTTI System and Their Assigned Values

The CTTI Top 100 University Think Tanks Evaluation employs the "PAI-E Evaluation System". *PAI* is a kind of objective evaluation data automatically calculated by the CTTI background system on the basis of the data submitted by all think tanks; E is a kind of subjective evaluation data acquired by sending questionnaires to think tank experts through the CTTI system.

PAI is the arithmetic sum of P, A and I. P is the metric data calculated by assigning values to nine categories of products of think tanks, including single internal reference reports, internal reference reports commented by leaders, journals sponsored/undertaken by think tanks, officially published books, research reports, articles published in the theoretical edition of *People's Daily*, *Seeking Truth*, or *Guangming Daily*, academic papers, vertical projects and horizontal projects. It can directly reflect the academic influence, policy influence and authoritative media influence of think tanks. Think tanks are different from traditional scientific research institutions. The former focus on countermeasure research, policy research, public opinion guidance and exertion of policy and social influence while the latter lay more emphasis on academic research. Therefore, in the assignment system of the CTTI, low values are assigned to such academic products as journals, academic papers and books, while high values are assigned to products that can provide policy consultation and public opinion guidance, such as internal reference reports, especially those commented by leaders of Party/government organizations, research reports and articles published in national authoritative media. In this way, we hope to encourage university think tanks to transform their traditional academic thinking, avoid academic path dependence, strengthen strategic research, improve their ability to provide consultation and suggestions for policymaking and public opinion guidance, and give full play to their functions of think tanks.

A is the metric data calculated by assigning values to such activities organized by university think tanks as conferences and meetings, trainings and observations. It is intended to measure the liveness of think tanks and directly reflect their attributes and influence. In our opinion, think tanks with rich activities are not necessarily excellent thinks tanks, but those with few activities are bound to lack the characteristics of think tanks and are more likely to be traditional university research centers. According to the experience of the international community, one of the important ways for think tanks to exert their influence is to hold high-level forums and conferences. Almost all world-renowned think tanks serve as conference centers as well as major platforms for the promotion of significant policies. Therefore, the CTTI system assigns high values to national and international conferences held by think tanks. Surveys and observations are research methods of think tanks with Chinese characteristics, as an old saying in China that goes, "He who makes no investigation and study has no right to speak". The CTTI system assigns relatively high values to such activities.

I is the metric data calculated by assigning values to such items as television coverage, newspaper coverage and Internet coverage. It is an effective indicator intended to measure the media impact and popularity of university think tanks. Almost all world-famous think tanks attach great importance to and are quite proficient in the dissemination of think tank outcomes. They are good at and take delight in carrying out in-depth cooperation with large media. The CTTI system assigns different values to the coverage given by media at different levels in the hope of raising university think tanks' awareness of spreading their achievements.

Table 5 Assessment Indicators for *PAI* of University Think Tanks and Their Assigned Values

Primary Indicator	Code	Secondary Indicator	Scoring Rule	Points
Products Activities	P	Single internal reference reports with or without leaders' comments	Value assigned to each title	2
		Internal reference reports commented by leaders	State level/per comment	30
			Sub-state level/per comment	20
			Provincial or ministerial level/per comment	10
			Sub-provincial or ministerial level/per comment	5
		Journals sponsored/run by think tanks	Each CSSCI source journal	20
			Each common journal	10
			Each bulletin/collection of internal reference reports	8
		Books (officially published)	Value assigned to each book	2
		Research reports	Value assigned to each report	4
		Articles published in the theoretical edition of *People's Daily*, *Seeking Truth*, or *Guangming Daily*	Value assigned to each article	5
		Academic papers	Each paper in CSSCI source journal	1
			Each paper included in SSCI/A&HCI	2
			Each paper included in CSCI/EI	1
			Each of other papers	0.5
		Vertical projects	Vertical: major project supported by National Social Science Fund or Social Science Fund of Ministry of Education	10

Continued

Primary Indicator	Code	Secondary Indicator	Scoring Rule	Points
			Vertical: key project supported by National Social Science Fund or Social Science Fund of Ministry of Education	6
			Vertical: common/young scholar project supported by National Social Science Fund	4
			Vertical: provincial/ministerial-level project	2
			Vertical: Other	0.5
		Horizontal projects	2 basic points for each project+1 mark point for every 100,000 yuan	
Activities	A	Conferences and Meetings	Each national conference sponsored or organized	10
			Each conference at the level of province, municipality or Autonomous Region	5
			Each international conference	10
			Other meetings	3
		Trainings	Each national training program	8
			Training on other levels	2
		Surveys and Observations	Each survey by leaders/experts at or above the sub-state level	15
			Each survey by leaders/experts at or above the provincial/ministerial level	5
			Each survey by leaders/experts at other levels	2
			Outbound visits for survey or observation	1
		Participation in the drafting of policies, laws and regulations	Taking charge of the drafting of national policies, laws and regulations/each time	10

Continued

Primary Indicator	Code	Secondary Indicator	Scoring Rule	Points
			Participation in the drafting of national policies, laws and regulations/each time	3
			Taking charge of the drafting of policies, laws and regulations at the provincial or ministerial level/each time	5
			Participation in the drafting of policies, laws and regulations at the provincial or ministerial level/each time	2
			Taking charge of the drafting of documents at other levels/each time	2
			Participation in the drafting of documents at other levels/each time	1
		Participation in political consultative conferences	Participation in national political consultative conferences	5
			Participation in political consultative conferences at the provincial or ministerial level	2
			Participation in political consultative conferences at other levels	1
		Honors and Awards	Each honor and award granted by international organizations (such as the United Nations)	8
			Each national honor and award	10
			Each honor and award at the provincial or ministerial level	5
			Each honor and award at other levels	3
Impact	I	Newspaper coverage	Central level	5
			Provincial or ministerial level	4
			Local level	3

Continued

Primary Indicator	Code	Secondary Indicator	Scoring Rule	Points
			Overseas media	2
			Other media	1
		TV coverage	Central level	5
			Provincial or ministerial level	4
			Local level	3
			Overseas media	2
			Other media	1
		Web coverage	Central level	5
			Provincial or ministerial level	4
			Local level	3
			Overseas media	2
			Other media	1

(2) Subjective Evaluation Data from Think Tank Experts

The CTTI Top 100 University Think Tanks Evaluation introduces opinions from authoritative experts in the field of think tanks, scores university think tanks in five aspects, and finally generates the subjective evaluation data—E. In order to comprehensively examine the functions of university think tanks in strategic research, political consultation, personnel training, public opinion guidance and public diplomacy, "The Two Centers" fully consider the expertise, representativeness and diversity of the selected think tank experts, and ultimately decide on three types of experts for consultation. The first are scholars and experts who specialize in think tank research and evaluation. With a broad international vision, rich research experience and a comprehensive understanding of both professional knowledge of think tank construction at home and abroad and the construction of university think tanks in China, they are fully qualified to evaluate the construction level of university think tanks in a relatively scientific way. The second are experts and scholars from think tanks of Party and government organizations. On the one hand, as the "external brain" of Party and government organizations, think tanks provide products for these organizations; on the other hand, as the users of countermeasure and policy research outcomes of think tanks, the organizations' recognition and satisfaction of the think tanks can reflect the overall level of the think tanks to a certain extent. The third are experts who work in university think tanks. They make peer reviews on think tanks according to a unified standard. Given that they have rich experience in think tank construction and are well-informed about other university think tanks, they are qualified and able to evaluate other think tanks. The average value of the values assigned to the evaluations of these three types of experts constitutes E.

Think tank experts carry out the evaluation in five aspects.

The first is the flexibility of management systems of think tanks, including the diversity of personnel assessment indicators, academic exchange platforms and channels for achievement transformation and the capability of integrating high-quality resources in universities. The personnel assessment in universities is usually based on academic papers and vertical projects, while such think tank products as internal reference reports, reports and newspaper articles are seldom included in the identification system for the professional-title evaluation and promotion. University think tanks should change their traditional academic concepts, make innovations in personnel assessment and enrich and improve the assessment indicators for think tank personnel. Compared with think tanks of Party/government organizations, university think tanks have certain disadvantages in the channels for achievement transformation, so effective channels must be established to convey the ideas of think tanks to Party/

government organizations. At the same time, think tanks should enhance their own influence and constantly open up new channels for achievement transformation. Universities boast a large number of high-quality scientific research forces, but whether university think tanks can give full play to the advantages of resources and fully mobilize intellectual resources depends on the innovative and efficient mechanisms. Based on the considerations above, the CTTI system assigns 20 points to the flexibility of management systems of university think tanks.

The second is the development potential of think tanks, including the guarantee of capital sources and the capability to constantly attract leading figures and elites. 20 points are assigned to this item.

The third is the reputation of think tanks, including whether the outcomes of their decision-making consultation can receive attention from policymakers at all levels or be adopted by departments at all levels, whether they have popularity and public influence and whether they can play an important role in public diplomacy and international exchanges. 20 points are assigned to this item.

The fourth is whether think tanks have distinctive research fields which are professional, realistic, targeted and prospective and whether their specific researches are urgently needed by the international community or our country. 20 points are assigned to this item.

The fifth is whether think tanks have a great influence on discipline construction and personnel training and whether they play an important role in the overall development of universities. 20 points are assigned to this item.

Table 6 Assessment Indicators for E of University Think Tanks and Their Assigned Values

Primary Indicator	Code	Secondary Indicator	Scoring Rule	Full Marks
Expert Evaluation	E	Flexibility of management systems of think tanks	Excellent: 18 - 20 points; Good: 15 - 17 points; Fair: 12 - 14 points; Qualified: 9 - 11 points; Poor: 0 - 8 points	20
		Development potential of think tanks		20
		Reputation of think tanks		20
		Distinctive research fields of think tanks		20
		Influence of think tanks on discipline construction and talent training		20

(3) Calculation Method for the CTTI Top 100 University Think Tanks Evaluation Indicators

The CTTI system calculates the PAI of each source university think tank and sorts them by numerical value in descending order. The PAI is calculated as follows:

$$PAI_i = P_i + A_i + I_i$$

Where PAI_i, P_i, A_i and I_i are respectively the PAI, P, A and I of each university think tank.

To make the data more intuitive, we first normalize the PAI and turn the dimensional expression into a dimensionless expression. The specific formula is:

$$\text{Adjusted } PAI_i = \frac{PAI_i - PAI_{\min}}{PAI_{\max} - PAI_{\min}},$$

Where PAI_i is the PAI of each think tank, $PAI_{\max}$ is the maximum PAI among that of all think tanks and $PAI_{\min}$ is the minimum PAI among that of all think tanks. Adjusted PAI_i is the normalized PAI, and is denoted by $APAI_i$.

The E is calculated as follows:

$$E_i = \frac{1}{n} \sum_{j=1}^{n} E_j, 1 \leqslant j \leqslant n$$

$$E_{max} = \max\{E_i\}$$

$$E_{min} = \min\{E_i\}$$

Where E_j is the score of each think tank given by expert, E_i is the final score of each think tank, E_{max} is the highest final score among that of all think tanks, and E_{min} is the lowest final score among that of all think tanks.

Similarly, we normalize the E, and the specific formula is:

$$\text{Adjusted } E_i = \frac{E_i - E_{min}}{E_{max} - E_{min}}$$

Adjusted E_i is the normalized E, and is denoted by AE_i.

Let $PAIE_i = \alpha APAI_i + (1-\alpha)AE_i$, where $0 \leqslant \alpha < 1$.

Where α is the proportion of objective data PAI in the PAI-E evaluation and it is obtained by Delphi Method. $PAIE_i$ is the final comprehensive score of the CTTI University Think Tanks Evaluation.

5.2 Selection Process of the CTTI Top 100 University Think Tanks

The selection process of the CTTI Top 100 University Think Tanks consists of four steps:

In the first step, at 24:00 on November 20, the PAI of all university think tanks in the CTTI system were derived and sorted in ascending order. "The Two Centers" selected the top 130 university think tanks for the next round of the CTTI Top 100 University Think Tanks Evaluation. Adhering to the principle of universality and particularity, five top national think tanks with incomplete data were also on the list for the next stage of expert review.

In the second step, the Delphi Method was used to determine the proportion of the PAI and E in this evaluation. According to expert opinions, "The Two Centers" finally set the α value of the top 130 source think tanks to 0.6, which means objective data PAI and expert opinions (E) respectively account for 60% and 40% in this evaluation.

In the third step, we selected a group of experts who are professional, representative and diversified. Questionnaires covering all aspects of E were distributed to all experts and collected before a unified time node.

In the fourth step, the final $PAIE$ of all think tanks were calculated and sorted in ascending order so as to make the list of the CTTI Top 100 Source University Think Tanks.

In the fifth step, all university think tanks on the list are subdivided into three levels: A+, A and A−. 25 think tanks fall into A+ level, 35 into A level and 40 into A− level. The CTTI top 100 university think tanks are arranged in alphabetical order according to their names in pinyin spelling.

5.3 The CTTI Top 100 University Think Tanks

Table 7　The CTTI "A+" University Think Tanks

(in alphabetical order according to pinyin spelling of names)

No.	Grade	Name of Think Tanks
1	A+	National School of Development, Peking University
2	A+	Institute of State Governance Studies, Peking University
3	A+	China Institute of Education and Social Development, Beijing Normal University
4	A+	International Institute of Chinese Studies, Beijing Foreign Studies University
5	A+	Center for American Studies, Fudan University
6	A+	Research Institute of Chinese Economy, Fudan University
7	A+	China Institute, Fudan University
8	A+	Center for Beijing-Tianjin-Hebei Development Research, Hebei University of Technology
9	A+	Center for Studies in Moral Culture of Hunan Normal University

Continued

No.	Grade	Name of Think Tanks
10	A+	Research Center for Co-Development with Neighboring Countries, East China Normal University
11	A+	Institute for China Rural Studies, Central China Normal University
12	A+	Food Safety Risk Management Institute, Jiangnan University
13	A+	Yangtze Industrial Economic Institute, Nanjing University
14	A+	Institute for Chinese Legal Modernization Studies, Nanjing Normal University
15	A+	Institute for Contemporary China Studies, Tsinghua University
16	A+	Institute of South Asian Studies, Sichuan University
17	A+	Wuhan University Institute of International Law
18	A+	Center for Higher Education Development of Xiamen University
19	A+	China Academy of West Region Development, Zhejiang University
20	A+	Institute of African Studies, Zhejiang Normal University
21	A+	Chongyang Institute for Financial Studies, Renmin University of China
22	A+	National Academy of Development and Strategy, Renmin University of China
23	A+	The Co-Innovation Center for Social Governance of Urban and Rural Communities in Hubei Province, Zhongnan University of Economics and Law
24	A+	Center for Studies of Intellectual Property Rights, Zhongnan University of Economics and Law
25	A+	Institute of Guangdong, Hong Kong and Macao Development Studies, Sun Yat-sen University

Table 8　The CTTI "A" University Think Tanks

(in alphabetical order according to pinyin spelling of names)

No.	Grade	Name of Think Tanks
26	A	Research Center for Beijing Transportation Development, Beijing Jiaotong University
27	A	Institute of International and Comparative Education, Beijing Normal University

Continued

No.	Grade	Name of Think Tanks
28	A	National Research Center for State Language Capacity, Beijing Foreign Studies University
29	A	Moral Development Think-Tank, Southeast University
30	A	Institute for the Development of Socialism with Chinese Characteristic, Southeast University
31	A	Institute of International Economy, University of International Business and Economics
32	A	China Institute for WTO Studies, University of International Business and Economics
33	A	Fudan Development Institute
34	A	Guangdong Institute for International Strategies, Guangdong University of Foreign Studies
35	A	China-ASEAN Research Institute of Guangxi University
36	A	The Center for Modern Chinese City Studies, East China Normal University
37	A	The Institute of State Governance, Huazhong University of Science and Technology
38	A	Academy of Overseas Chinese Studies, Jinan University
39	A	Jiangsu Public Security Institute, Jiangsu Police Institute
40	A	Soviet Area Revitalization Institute of Jiangxi Normal University
41	A	Collaborative Innovation Center of South China Sea Studies, Nanjing University
42	A	Zijin Media Think Tank, Nanjing University
43	A	Purple Academy of Culture & Creativity, Nanjing University of the Arts
44	A	College of Economic and Social Development, Nankai University
45	A	Shanghai International Shipping Institute, Shanghai Maritime University
46	A	China Institute for Urban Governance, Shanghai Jiao Tong University
47	A	The Middle East Studies Institute, Shanghai International Studies University
48	A	Center for Global Public Opinions of China, Shanghai International Studies University
49	A	Center for Basic Laws of Hong Kong and Macao Special Administrative Regions, Shenzhen University

No.	Grade	Name of Think Tanks
50	A	Collaborative Innovation Center for Security and Development of Western Frontier China, Sichuan University
51	A	Soochow University Think Tank
52	A	Research Institute of Environment Law, Wuhan University
53	A	Center for Studies of Media Development, Wuhan University
54	A	Center for Korean Peninsula Studies, Yanbian University
55	A	Center for China's Neighbor Diplomacy, Yunnan University
56	A	China Academy for Rural Development, Zhejiang University
57	A	China Business Working Capital Management Research Center, Ocean University of China
58	A	Center for the Development of Rule of Law and Judicial Reform Research, Zhongnan University of Economics and Law
59	A	Intellectual Property Institute of Central South University
60	A	Research Center of Chinese Village Culture, Central South University

Table 9　The CTTI "A—" University Think Tanks

(in alphabetical order according to pinyin spelling of names)

No.	Grade	Name of Think Tanks
61	A—	Institute of Anhui Economic Development Research, Anhui University of Finance and Economics
62	A—	Innovative Development Institute, Anhui University
63	A—	Research Base of Beijing Modern Manufacturing Development, Beijing University of Technology
64	A—	Collaborative Innovation Center of Assessment for Basic Education Quality, Beijing Normal University
65	A—	Think Tank on Natural Disaster Prevention and Geological Environment Protection, Chengdu University of Technology
66	A—	China Academy of Rural Education Development, Northeast Normal University

Continued

No.	Grade	Name of Think Tanks
67	A—	National Research Center for Economic Comprehensive Competitiveness, Fujian Normal University
68	A—	Guangzhou Development Research Institute, Guangzhou University
69	A—	National Institute of Education Policy Research, East China Normal University
70	A—	Institute of Curriculum and Instruction of East China Normal University
71	A—	The Institute for Modern Chinese Thought and Culture, East China Normal University
72	A—	Center of Social Governance Research, South China University of Technology
73	A—	Center for Quantitative Economics of Jilin University
74	A—	China Center for Public Sector Economy Research, Jilin University
75	A—	The Public Opinion Big Data Research Center of Guangzhou, Jinan University
76	A—	Jiangsu Academy of Talent Development, Nanjing University of Science and Technology
77	A—	Institute of Healthy Jiangsu Development, Nanjing Medical University
78	A—	Collaborative Innovation Center for China Economy, Nankai University
79	A—	Jiangsu Yangtze Economic Belt Research Institute, Nantong University
80	A—	Collaborative Innovation Center for the Study on China, Mongolia and Russia Economic and Trade Cooperation & Construction of Economic Belt on the Prairie Silk Road, Inner Mongolia University of Finance and Economics
81	A—	Center for Health Management and Policy, Shandong University
82	A—	Research Center for Local Governance, Shanghai University
83	A—	Shanghai Center for Global Trade and Economic Governance, Shanghai University of International Business and Economics
84	A—	China Institute of FTZ Supply Chain, Shanghai Maritime University
85	A—	Tianjin Academy of Free Trade Area, Tianjin University of Finance and Economics
86	A—	Research Base for the Implementation of National Intellectual Property Strategy, Tianjin University

Continued

No.	Grade	Name of Think Tanks
87	A—	APEC Sustainable Energy Center, Tianjin University
88	A—	German Studies Center, Tongji University
89	A—	National Institute of Culture Development, Wuhan University
90	A—	The Center for Economic Development Research of Wuhan University
91	A—	Center for Social Security Studies of Wuhan University
92	A—	Institute of the "Belt and Road" Pilot Free Trade Zone, Xi'an Jiaotong University
93	A—	Survey and Research Center for China Household Finance, Southwestern University of Finance and Economics
94	A—	Center for Collaborative Innovation in the Heritage and Development of Xizang Culture, Xizang Minzu University
95	A—	Think Tank of Coastal Development, Yancheng Teachers University
96	A—	Frontier Ethnic Problems Think-Tank of Yunnan University
97	A—	Institute of China's Science, Technology and Education Policy, Zhejiang University
98	A—	Center for Capital Social Safety, People's Public Security University of China
99	A—	Collaborative Innovation Center of Industrial Upgrading and Regional Finance (Hubei), Zhongnan University of Economics and Law
100	A—	China's Income Distribution Research Center, Zhongnan University of Economics and Law

6　Data Analysis of the CTTI Top 100 University Think Tanks

6.1　Regional Distribution of the CTTI Top 100 University Think Tanks

On the list of the 2018 CTTI Top 100 University Think Tanks, Shanghai takes the first place with 17 university think tanks, closely followed by Beijing, which has 15. Jiangsu ranks third with 14 think tanks, followed by Hubei, Guangdong, Tianjin and Zhejiang with 12, 7, 6 and 5 think tanks respectively. Shanghai and Beijing boast a large number of "Universities of 985 Project" and "Universities of 211 Project" with strong comprehensive strength and solid discipline foundation, laying a sound academic foundation for the development of university think tanks. Such provinces as Jiangsu, Hubei and Guangdong possess plenty of "Double First-Class" universities. With the support of the national policies, they have made solid progress and remarkable achievements in the construction of university think tanks.

REGIONAL DISTRIBUTION OF UNIVERSITY THINK TANKS TOP 100

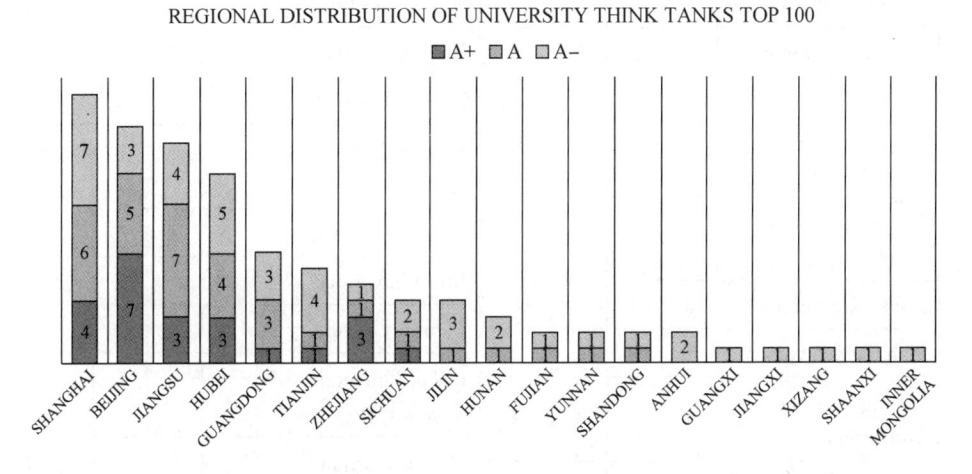

■A+ ■A ■A-

Fig. 1 Regional Distribution of the CTTI Top 100 University Think Tanks

Among the 25 "A+" university think tanks, Beijing ranks first with 7 think tanks, followed by Shanghai, Jiangsu, Hubei and Zhejiang. There is no doubt that top university think tanks all have outstanding academic foundation. For example, National School of Development at Peking University is a multi-disciplinary comprehensive school based on economics, and its first level discipline Applied Economics got A+ in the fourth round of national discipline evaluation; Institute for Food Safety Risk Management at Jiangnan University is based on its first level discipline Food Science and Engineering which also got A+ in the fourth round of national discipline evaluation. Therefore, a solid foundation on academic research is necessary to the construction of university think tanks.

6.2 Distribution of the CTTI Top 100 University Think Tanks in Colleges or Universities

Table 10   Distribution of the CTTI Top 100 University Think Tanks in Colleges or Universities

Names of Colleges or Universities	A+	A	A−	Total	Names of Colleges or Universities	A+	A	A−	Total
Wuhan University	1	2	3	6	Jinan University		1	1	2
Zhongnan University of Economics and Law	2	1	2	5	Nankai University		1	1	2
					Shanghai Maritime University		1	1	2
East China Normal University	1	1	3	5	Yunnan University		1	1	2
					Jilin University			2	2
Fudan University	3	1		4	Tianjin University			2	2
Nanjing University	1	2		3	Hebei University of Technology	1			1
Beijing Normal University	1	1	1	3					
					Hunan Normal University	1			1
Zhejiang University	1	1	1	3					
Peking University	2			2	Central China Normal University	1			1
Renmin University of China	2			2					
					Jiangnan University	1			1
Beijing Foreign Studies University	1	1		2	Nanjing Normal University	1			1
Sichuan University	1	1		2	Tsinghua University	1			1
Southeast University		2		2	Xiamen University	1			1
University of International Business and Economics		2		2	Zhejiang Normal University	1			1
Shanghai International Studies University		2		2	Sun Yat-sen University	1			1
Central South University		2		2	Beijing Jiaotong University		1		1

Continued

Names of Colleges or Universities	A+	A	A−	Total	Names of Colleges or Universities	A+	A	A−	Total
Guangdong University of Foreign Studies		1		1	Fujian Normal University			1	1
Guangxi University		1		1	Guangzhou University			1	1
Huazhong University of Science and Technology		1		1	South China University of Technology			1	1
Jiangsu Police Institute		1		1	Nanjing University of Science and Technology			1	1
Jiangxi Normal University		1		1	Nanjing Medical University			1	1
Nanjing University of the Arts		1		1	Nantong University			1	1
Shanghai Jiao Tong University		1		1	Inner Mongolia University of Finance and Economics			1	1
Shenzhen University		1		1					
Soochow University		1		1	Shandong University			1	1
Yanbian University		1		1	Shanghai University			1	1
Ocean University of China		1		1	Shanghai University of International Business and Economics			1	1
Anhui University of Finance and Economics			1	1	Tianjin University of Finance and Economics			1	1
Anhui University			1	1					
Beijing University of Technology			1	1	Tongji University			1	1
Chengdu University of Technology			1	1	Xi'an Jiaotong University			1	1
Northeast Normal University			1	1	Xizang Minzu University			1	1

Continued

Names of Colleges or Universities	A+	A	A−	Total	Names of Colleges or Universities	A+	A	A−	Total
Southwestern University of Finance and Economics			1	1	People's Public Security University of China			1	1
Yancheng Teachers University			1	1					

64 universities are included in the CTTI Top 100 University Think Tanks list, among which Wuhan University ranks first with 6 university think tanks. East China Normal University and Zhongnan University of Economics and Law rank second with 5 think tanks, followed by Fudan University, Beijing Normal University, Nanjing University and Zhejiang University which have 4, 3, 3, and 3 respectively. The universities mentioned above give full play to the roles of think tanks. Fudan University delivers a remarkable performance in this evaluation. With 3 think tanks being rated as A+, it is the most influential university in terms of the number of A+ think tanks.

7 Major Problems in the Construction of New Types of University Think Tanks

7.1 Lack of Clear Information on Policy Consultation and Imbalance between Information Supply and Demand

As the "external brain" of the Party and government organizations, university think tanks usually find themselves in a woeful predicament that there exists an imbalance between information supply and demand. Most university think tanks cannot be informed of the demands on policy consultation and countermeasure research from decision-making departments of the Party and government organizations at all levels timely. Therefore, some policy proposals of think tanks are not precise, applicable and effective. In addition, the differences between the system of academic language and that of policy language not only affect the quality and efficiency of communication between university think tanks and Party and government organizations, but also restrain the long-term cooperation between the two parties.

7.2 Weak Awareness of Communication and Publicity

About 80% of the internal references, academic papers, reports and books included in the CTTI system are from university think tanks, while only 52% of the newspaper articles are from university think tanks. Thus, many university think tanks do not pay enough attention to public opinion guidance and publicity and fail to take full advantage of such media as newspaper to express their opinions. Nowadays, new media channels have been changing with each passing day, while quite a large number of university think tanks are void of either independent portals or people responsible for the operation and maintenance of their portals so that the information may not be updated for a long time. Besides, just a few university think tanks have English websites.

7.3 Management Mechanisms of Think Tanks Required to Be Improved

Firstly, university think tanks are wanting in initiative. Given that university think tanks are subject to many restrictions in finance, personnel and administrative operation, they lack initiative and autonomy. On the one hand, in terms of source of funds, since university think tanks are internal organizations of universities, they mainly depend on universities and partly government to cover their activity fees, and seldom receive funds from society, corporations and individuals. The current funding system leads university think tanks to be highly dependent on universities and government. The source of funds is single, and the funding system which enables university think tanks to raise funds by themselves has not been established. On the other hand, university think tanks lack independent personnel management right, which leads them to have difficulties in employee turnover and in operating as entities. According to the CTTI university think tanks data, 54% of university think tanks have fewer full-time members than part-time ones, failing to establish a scientific and reasonable personnel allotment system. Besides, there are some other problems, such as unreasonable distribution of researchers of different professional titles and a lack of research assistants, administrative staff and senior think tank experts. Moreover, university think tanks have not yet established a set of flexible performance appraisal and incentive system. Too much emphasis on assessment and little emphasis on encouragement will further weaken their attraction to think tank talents.

Secondly, university think tanks lack pioneering and innovative culture. Different from academic research, think tank research should be down-to-earth. The long-term "life" in the ivory tower may lead university think tanks to carry out researches without reference to what the world requires and weaken their awareness of serving others. Besides, the culture of such academic organizations as universities also restricts the innovation and exploration ability of university think tanks. Poor quality of research and insufficient content innovation in university think tanks are largely due to the fact that they are still at the initial stage of the substantiation and institutionalization construction and fail to form their own innovative culture.

Thirdly, the extensive management hinders university think tanks from improving their operation capability. On the one hand, some university think tanks have entered the era of fine management. For example, Yangtze Industrial Economics Institution of Nanjing University has clearly put forward the concept of "operation energizing policy research" and advocates that university think tanks should spare no efforts to improve their operation capability and the policy research guarantee; Chongyang Institute for Financial Studies of Renmin University of China has formed a complete performance appraisal and incentive system for its researchers and employees with a total Chinese character count of more than 200,000. On the other hand, some university think tanks cannot effectively manage the data on their annual outcomes or update the data in the CTTI system timely. By contrast, enterprise think tanks and social think tanks are generally better than university think tanks at data management. For instance, as an enterprise think tank, Suning Institute of Finance takes the submission of CTTI data as one of the daily routines of its administrative staff as well as a key performance indicator. Through routine and regular data update, it can be well-informed of its think tank products and activities.

Fourthly, the result ratification system does not fit the development of think tanks. Traditional result ratification system of universities takes vertical projects and academic papers, especially SCI, SSCI, CSSICI and CSCD papers as a rigid index, while intenal reference reports and newspaper articles written by some think tank experts are not taken into consideration, which discourages university scholars, especially those young and middle-aged scholars from participating in the construction of think tanks to a certain degree. University think tanks should improve policy support and encourage experts and scholars to produce think tank products. Taking Hunan Normal University as an example, on March 8, 2018, the school distributed the "Opinions on How to Improve the Construction of New Types of Think Tanks of Hunan Normal University (Trial)" ("The Opinions"). "The Opinions" clarified new regulations on result ratification and promotion, and involved products of think tanks in the evaluation system. The products would be classified into four levels according to the departments which are responsible for products adoption and application, and would respectively share the same treatment as *Social Sciences in China*, papers published in authoritative academic journals, papers published in important academic journals and CSSCI papers. The matched policy support is one of the reasons why the think tanks of Hunan Normal University have achieved good results in this evaluation.

8 Suggestions on How to Improve the Construction of New Types of University Think Tanks

Firstly, universities should be fully aware that the construction of new types of think tanks has a great significance for the "Double-First Class" initiative. Think tanks are institutions specializing in evidence-based policy analysis. They are in connection with institutions of academic research in universities, and at the same time have their own clear division of labor, unique organizational culture, research methods and operation modes. The most prominent features of modern university think tanks are the unity of knowledge and practice and the combination of teaching and research. University think tanks mainly undertake the tasks of serving the Party, country and society, such as achievement transformation, policy incubation, policy education and policy evaluation. Think tanks are the business cards of universities, the links between universities and Party committees, government and society, and the bridges to international policy research community.

An excellent think tank is indispensable for a university. Think tank construction and discipline construction in universities have been proved to complement each other. According to the data from Shanghai Jiao Tong University, in the fourth round of discipline evaluation, there were nearly 200 cases in which think tanks of the school made use of their disciplines to provide social service. Therefore, there is no contradiction between think tank construction and discipline construction in universities. Instead, sound think tanks construction will promote discipline construction and the construction of applied social sciences. Yangtze Industrial Economics Institution of Nanjing University is a national top think tank which is mainly engaged in applied economics research. It helped the school's Applied Economics get A in the fourth round of discipline evaluation. South China University of Technology is an institution of higher education that specializes in science and engineering, however, its successful application for four key projects of the Ministry of Education in 2017 was closely related to its high-level think tanks. Institute of Public Policy (IPP) is a think tank of the school, whose success in ideas and methods of think tank research and countermeasure research have greatly inspired the applied social sciences of the school and improved the overall level of the liberal arts construction in the school.

In the projects supported by the National Social Science Fund of China for the past few years, the proportion of countermeasure research and applied research urgently needed by our country is quite considerable, and such strategic and programmatic research is exactly what think tanks do best in. If a university has strong think tanks, it will be more capable of undertaking national major projects. The important speech delivered by the General Secretary Xi Jinping at the Symposium on Philosophy and Social Sciences and subsequent documents are all aimed at accelerating the construction of philosophy and social sciences with Chinese characteristics. Our current evaluation system of philosophy and social sciences is witnessing major changes. The Central Party Committee and the State Council have repeatedly proposed in their documents that the evaluation system which gives top priority to academic papers should be changed. At present, some provinces, municipalities and universities have formulated new policies to clarify the incentive mechanism for different levels of think tank products. As stipulated by Nanjing University, a think tank product commented by assisting roles of provinces is equivalent to a CSSCI paper. It can be seen that the changes in the evaluation mechanism of philosophy and social sciences are beneficial to the development of think tanks.

Secondly, to make a breakthrough in the construction of university think tanks, sound systems and mechanisms and a team of pivotal think tank operators is quite important. The increasing number of university think tanks does not mean the establishment of new systems. No breakthrough has yet been made in the management system of China's university think tanks.

National top think tanks are the bellwether of institutional innovation. Since the pilot project of constructing top think tanks was carried out, the Central Party Committee and related departments have introduced a series of high-quality policies on funds and conference management, outbound visits and incentives and have given pilot units great autonomy and sufficient policy space. However, still many university think tanks fail to implement these policies, and constraints on personnel and financial management, compensation package and professional-title evaluation are still prominent. The root cause of this phenomenon is that most of our university think tanks are affiliated think tanks which are not under the direct leadership of think tank management departments of state, provincial and municipal ministries and commissions. Instead, they are only in the charge of universities. This has weakened the direct links between the think tank management departments of state, provincial and municipal ministries and commissions and those affiliated think tanks.

How to solve this problem? Some universities are trying to turn affiliated think tanks into independent corporate entities. For example, with the support of Nanjing University, its two affiliated provincial key think tanks—Yangtze Industrial Economics Institution and Zijin Media Think Tank are registered as "private non-enterprise" entities in the Department of Civil Affairs of Jiangsu Province. Such think tanks can directly implement the policies on think tank management made by related departments of state, provincial and municipal ministries and commissions. Public Policy Research Institute of Zhejiang University has adopted the same mechanism in the building of think tanks into corporate entities.

A top think tank needs more than sound systems and mechanisms. Institution and personnel are two critical factors in the construction of an excellent university think tank. Without pivotal operators, the system cannot bring benefits no matter how good it is. Therefore, to build good university think tanks, it is crucial that universities should equip the think tanks with leaders and chief experts who are daring, vigorous, enterprising, honest and upright. An outstanding think tank needs the leadership of both top academic experts and competent operators. Among western think tanks, there is a group of people called "policy entrepreneurs", referring to those enterprising directors who regard the construction of think tanks as a cause. Whether our university think tanks can come out among the best in the world depends, in a sense, on the formation of such a team of leaders.

Thirdly, embedded modes of advisory service for decision making should be adopted to remove information asymmetry and provide accurate policy research outcomes. The General Secretary Xi Jinping pointed out, "Information sharing and interaction should be promoted between the decision-making sector and think tanks; policy research by Party and government organizations should be more closely linked with countermeasure research by think tanks in an effort to guide the latter towards sound development and more effective service." What he emphasized is the synergy between the "internal brain" (government) and the "external brain" (think tanks). Government should guide, lead and promote the countermeasure research of think tanks, and strive to eliminate the imbalance between information supply and demand; think tanks should actively adopt the embedded modes of advisory service for decision making so as to solve the divorce between policy research and countermeasure research. The embedded mode not only illustrates that there are some differences between think tanks and policy research departments of government, but also indicates that countermeasure research of think tanks has its own independent value and unique attributes. Embedded advisory services for decision-making include imbedding of decision-making process, embedding of decision-making consultation process, embedding of decision-making consultation scenario and embedding of a community of shared policy. Policy-making process embedding requires think tanks to take part in the complete policy-making process, which includes working closely with government, participating in and playing a role in agenda setting, policy debating, decision making and promotion, policy implementation, policy education, policy evaluation and policy feedback, being concerned with the generation of policy documents, pushing forward with the implementation of policies, and evaluating the effects of policies. Decision-making consultation process embedding requires think tanks to develop close cooperation with government during investigation and research, data collection and analysis, study and determination and report writing, and take full advantage of their expertise to support the policy research of government. Decision-making consultation scenario embedding requests that think tanks take an active part in such activities as investigation and survey, decision-making consultation meetings and policy promotion that are organized by decision-making sections and gain first-hand experience in these activities so as to have a better understanding of why and how the policies are generated. The embedding of a community of shared policy requires think tanks to be tied up with policymakers and policy research departments and build strong mutual trust between each other. Apart from policymakers and policy research departments (government), the community also contains other elements, and tanks should build close relationship with all these elements. Once think tanks adopt the above four embedded modes, they are expected to extricate themselves from the current predicament that their countermeasure research is not realistic, down-to-earth or needed by market, and be indispensable to Party committees and government.

Fourthly, university think tanks should actively explore, implement and promote a scientific and objective result ratification and incentive system. Result ratification and incentive system serves as a baton guiding the development of think tanks, but its design is not reasonable enough, which is one of the major problems restricting the healthy development of think tanks. In China, the relatively single criterion for result ratification leads all kinds of think tanks to lay too much emphasis on the administrative levels of the comments made by leaders. In fact, policy evaluation, policy education, policy planning and other supportive advisory services for decision making should also be included in the scope of result ratification.

Appendix: Brief Biographies of the CTTI Top 100 University Think Tanks

Innovative Development Institute, Anhui University

Innovative Development Institute of Anhui University was established in May 2016. In the same year, it was assessed as the "Key Think Tank of Anhui Province" and participated in the initiation and establishment of the Changjiang Economic Belt Think Tank Cooperation Alliance. Adhering to the national strategy of innovation-driven development, the Institute focuses on key, hot and difficult issues in the development of economic and social modernization in Anhui and even the whole country and on strategic issues such as scientific and technological innovation, industrial innovation, social construction innovation and governance system innovation. It spares no effort to observe new phenomena, discuss new issues, put forward new ideas and work on new countermeasures. Over the past two years, the Institute has compiled and distributed 46 issues of *Think Tank of Anhui University*— special reports on decision-making consultation, which have received more than 10 instructions or comments from the leaders of the Central Committee and Anhui Province.

Institute of Anhui Economic Development Research, Anhui University of Finance and Economics

As a key think tank of Anhui Province, Institute of Anhui Economic Development

Research is striving to make itself a financial and economic think tank based on Anhui and open to the whole country. The Institute has an annual funding of more than 3 million yuan.

It has published 12 series of research reports on Anhui's economic and social development for 13 consecutive years. More than 20 pieces of policy recommendations based on the reports have received instructions or comments from the leaders at the national and provincial/ministerial levels, and many of the research results have been included in the internal reference magazines, such as *Popular Tribune* of the Policy Research Office of the CPC Central Committee and *Decision-Making* of the Anhui Research Center for Economic Development. The Institute also undertakes the third-party evaluation of poverty alleviation arranged by the provincial leading group on poverty alleviation and development. From September 2016 to December 2018, for five times, a total of more than 2,700 teachers and students were organized to complete the third-party monitoring and assessment and result assessment of poverty alleviation work covering 25 counties.

Website: http://ahjj.aufe.edu.cn

Email: 2816260994@qq.com

Tel: 0552-3111482; 0552-3126631

National School of Development, Peking University

National School of Development (NSD) of Peking University is a school that features multidisciplinary study on economics. NSD sticks to building itself into "small institute with large network" and brings together research resources of Peking University and those from all over the world. Over the years, it has produced influential decision-making support on important issues concerning the relationship between the government and the market, rural reconstruction, land issues, SOE reform, telecommunication reform, stock market administration, population policy and economic structure adjustment, etc. Some of them have been adopted by the government. Years of endeavor and accumulation won the school a place in the first batch of high-end think tanks in China in 2016. NSD not only hosts three highly recognized think-tank events: China Economic Observer, NSD Policy Talk and China Development Forum, but also serves as the organizer of US-China Economic Dialogue and US-China Health Dialogue, making great contributions to Sino-American non-governmental diplomacy.

Website: http://www.nsd.pku.edu.cn/

Zip Code: 100871

Fax: 86 - 10 - 62751474 / 86 - 10 - 62750030

Institute of State Governance Studies, Peking University

Institute of State Governance Studies of Peking University is the Key Politics Research Base, one of the 100 key humanities and social sciences research bases approved by the Ministry of Education of People's Republic of China. Currently, the Institute has 55 full-time and part-time researchers from home and abroad, with an annual funding of 1.4 million yuan.

Since its establishment, the Institute has actively carried out academic and countermeasure research on the modernization of State Governance. Besides, it has organized many academic conferences and lectures in collaboration with the well-known universities at home and abroad on the platform of "Forum on State Governance" and has officially published the *Research on Modernization of State Governance* and *Research on State Governance Series*. It is devoted to constructing such first-class disciplines as socialism with Chinese characteristics and modernization of state governance, politics and public management, providing political consultation and conducting personnel training.

Website: http://www.isgs.pku.edu.cn/

Email: gjzlxtcx@pku.edu.cn

Tel: 010 - 62754337 / 62756937

Research Base of Beijing Modern Manufacturing Development, Beijing University of Technology

Research Base of Beijing Modern Manufacturing Development was established in 2004 as one of the municipal philosophy and social sciences research bases granted by Beijing Planning Office of Philosophy and Social Sciences and Beijing Municipal Education Commission. The Base revolves around the development of Beijing's modern manufacturing industry and conducts a series of researches on the development strategy, problems and countermeasures of Beijing's modern manufacturing. Proactively undertaking major research projects, it has published more than 200 academic papers and a dozen of research reports and monographs, and has submitted more than 50 reports of various types. The reports have been commended and approved by the central government, and the research achievements have been put into practice by government agencies and enterprises. Oriented towards global governance, national governance, national economy and people's livelihood, the Base will keep contributing its part to the construction of China's modern consultation system for decision-making.

Research Center for Beijing Transportation Development, Beijing Jiaotong University

Founded in 2005, Research Center for Beijing Transportation Development (RCBTD) is the first key research base established by Beijing Jiaotong University. Developing on the basis of a Level I discipline of applied economics and relative management disciplines, specializing in transportation economy and logistics management, RCBTD is one of the research bases on philosophy and social sciences in Beijing granted by the Beijing Planning Office of Philosophy and Social Sciences and the Beijing Municipal Education Commission. Since its inception, the Center has been assessed as Outstanding Institute for three times and exempted from assessment for once. Its achievements in providing decision-making support and policy advice, fulfilling scientific research projects, publishing academic papers and casting influences on media are considerable. It has hosted International Conference on Transportation and Space-Time Economics in Beijing Jiaotong University for six consecutive years and gained influence at home and abroad.

Institute of International and Comparative Education, Beijing Normal University

Established in 1961, Institute of International and Comparative Education (IICE) is the earliest and most influential comparative education research institute in China, a key research base on humanities and social sciences granted by the Ministry of Education, a research base on international and regional studies granted by the Ministry of Education and a supporting agency for the Secretariat of the APEC Higher Education Research Center. Committed to researches that cater to China's status quo and embrace international theories and practices, IICE has been providing decision-making support, policy advice, public opinion guidance, social service and public diplomacy, so as to facilitate scientific and democratic decision-making of CPC and the central government. As of 2012, IICE has had 90 policy advisory reports submitted to and adopted by educational administrations of all levels. A number of advisory reports have been commended and approved by the leaders of the central government, the Ministry of Education and other departments.

Collaborative Innovation Center of Assessment for Basic Education Quality (CICA-BEQ)

Collaborative Innovation Center of Assessment for Basic Education Quality (CICA-BEQ), founded in July 2012, is the only national collaborative innovation center in education and psychology in China. Led by Beijing Normal University, it has eight sub-centers including one in East China Normal University. The Center conducts researches on basic education policies by monitoring basic education quality in a scientific, accurate and timely manner, striving to promote an all-round and individualized development of hundreds of millions of children and adolescents. It has established an educational evaluation cloud and thematic databases. In 2016, two of the Center's research achievements were awarded with the first prize in the 5th National Education Science Education Sciences Research Achievement Assessment, two with the second prize, and four with the third prize.

Website: http://cicabeq.bnu.edu.cn/zzhx

Tel: 010 - 58800158

Fax: 010 - 58800158

Email: xtxxbs@bnu.edu.cn

China Institute of Education and Social Development, Beijing Normal University

China Institute of Education and Social Development of Beijing Normal University, founded in the October of 2010 by Beijing Normal University with resources in and out of the university, strives to cultivate high-level talents in social sciences as well as provide advice and consultation on social governance. Aspiring to promote the development of a modern education and society with Chinese characteristics, the Academy features researches on education reform and development and social governance innovation, and concentrates its efforts on seven aspects, namely, making suggestions to CPC committees and governments, constructing the Research Database of China Social Governance Innovation, compiling *Great Events in Modern China Society*, organizing China Social Governance Forum, hosting the journal of *Social Governance*, publishing social governance think tank book series, and conducting social governance investigation. The institute has been actively promoting extensive exchanges and in-depth cooperation with worldly recognized think tanks, leading universities and research institutes in the United States, Britain, Russia, Singapore, Japan as well as other countries and regions in an effort to continuously enhance and expand its influence at home and abroad.

Tel: 010-58802885

Fax: 010-58804062

Email: casm@bnu.edu.cn

International Institute of Chinese Studies, Beijing Foreign Studies University

International Institute of Chinese Studies (IICS) of Beijing Foreign Studies University was established in 1996. It undertakes the mission of disseminating Chinese culture and other cultures in the world and introducing China to the rest of the world. Aspiring to fathom into the Chinese culture's development strategy in the world, IICS studies the transmission and influence of Chinese culture among other nations, tracks the history of disseminating Chinese cultural classics to the outside world in the context of the study on cultural exchange history between China and other countries, sorting out the history, figures and versions of Chinese cultural classics translations, and illustrates the development history of sinology, i. e. Chinese studies by studying important sinologists and translating famous works on sinology. From the perspective of cross-cultural studies, IICS studies the influence of Chinese culture overseas, unveils the China's images in other countries and how they are formed, and explores the ways in which Chinese culture could be known to the world.

National Research Centre for State Language Capacity, Beijing Foreign Studies University

Established in July 2014, National Research Centre for State Language Capacity of Beijing Foreign Studies University is a scientific research institution of the State Language Commission jointly founded and managed by the Department of Language and Information Management of the Ministry of Education and Beijing Foreign Studies University. Adhering to the idea of "serving the country, society and disciplines", the Center is committed to the research on state language capacity, language policies in individual countries and language life in foreign countries. In 2014, it applied for and was granted the right to confer master's and doctoral degrees in the second-level discipline of "Language Policy and Planning", successively established *Information on Strategies of foreign languages* (internal publication) and *Journal of Language Policy and Language Planning* (collection of papers), and took on over ten projects at the national and provincial/ministerial levels. It is a major member of the Language Policy and Planning Research Association of the Chinese Linguistics Society as well as a national academic think tank.

Website: https://gynf.bfsu.edu.cn/

Think Tank on Natural Disaster Prevention and Geological Environment Protection, Chengdu University of Technology

Based on State Key Laboratory of Geohazard Prevention and Geoenvironment Protection (Chengdu University of Technology), the think tank focuses on providing scientific and technological support for the public service prevention and treatment of natural disasters and geological disasters in engineering construction. Its research achievements have won the first prize of the National Prize for Progress in Science and Technology twice. The laboratory has a total of 75 permanent researchers, with an annual research funding of about 50 million yuan.

In 2017, the think tank proposed for the first in the world to build a survey system covering air, space and land (including the "general survey" based on high-precision remote sensing and InSAR technology, the "detailed survey" based on airborne LiDAR and UAV aerial photographs and the "verification" based on the review of ground survey), which was widely recognized by relevant departments.

Website: http://www.sklgp.cdut.edu.cn

Email: sklgp@cdut.edu.cn

Tel: 028 - 84073193

Fax: 028 - 84073193

Research Institute of Rural Education, Northeast Normal University

Founded in 1999, Research Institute of Rural Education of Northeast Normal University currently has 14 full-time researchers and 11 part-time researchers. The Institute endeavors to study, serve and develop rural education; it has been providing policy advice for the reform and development of national rural education by carrying out studies on basic education policy, cultural policy and fiscal policy research. Along with the considerable progress in large-scale research projects and theoretical reflection on rural education practices in recent years, the Institute has been producing high-quality advisory reports on education policy, many of which have been adopted by the State Council, the Ministry of Education and the Central Committee of Democratic Progressive Party and have received commendations from the leaders of higher authorities.

Website: http://ire.nenu.edu.cn/

Tel: 0431 - 85099422

Email: qihp644@nenu.edu.cn

Moral Development Think-Tank, Southeast University

Moral Development Think-Tank of Southeast University, founded in 2015, is one of the first key top think tanks in Jiangsu Province. Currently, the think tank boasts a high-level scientific research & innovation team, including four distinguished professors and chair professors from the Chang Jiang Scholars Program, talents from the first batch of leading personnel in philosophy and social sciences under the National Special Support Program for High-Level Personnel Recruitment, talents from the Four Batches of Talents Program of the Publicity Department of the Communist Party of China, and talents from the Support Program for New Century Excellent Talents of the Ministry of Education. In 2018, the think tank raised 2.8 million yuan for scientific research. It has been committed to presenting the moral and ethical development in China over the past 40 years of reform and opening up in a comprehensive, systematic, scientific and professional way, revealing the basic laws and trends of the moral and ethical development in contemporary China, and providing scientific basis and theoretical resources for the national strategic planning of the moral and ethical development in the new era.

Tel: 025 - 52090923

Website: http://mdi.seu.edu.cn

Official WeChat: seu-moral

Institute for the Development of Socialism with Chinese Characteristics, Southeast University

Institute for the Development of Socialism with Chinese Characteristics (IDSCC) was founded on November 16th, 2015, serving as one of the first batch of key think tanks of Jiangsu Province. IDSCC has a team of nearly 30 experts and scholars who work full-time or part-time for the institute and an annual funding of more than three million yuan. Fathoming into the theory and practice of socialism with Chinese characteristics, it has published more than 20 theoretical articles in organs of the Central Committee of the Communist Party of China, including *Qiushi*, *China Daily* and *Guangming Daily*. It has also submitted over 40 decision-making advisory reports to the government, among which eight of them were approved by provincial and ministerial leaders. The Institute has contributed greatly to interpreting and researching innovative theories of CPC and facilitating a scientific decision-making process. Accordingly, IDSCC was awarded with the first prize of 2017 CTTI-BPA Think Tank Management; it also ranked among Top 100 CTTI University Think Tanks in 2018 and was listed as a Class-A think tank.

Website: http://idscc.seu.edu.cn/

Email: ddztzk@sina.com

Tel: 025 - 83795265

Institute of International Economy, University of International Business and Economics

Institute of International Economy of University of International Business and Economics was the former International Trade Research Institute founded in the October of 1982 and was renamed in the November of 2003. The Institute conducts researches on fundamental theories, national policy and business consulting services, which covers a wide range of areas from world economy and China's foreign trade. It has undertaken and fulfilled a number of projects commissioned by the National Social Sciences Fund of China, the National Natural Science Foundation of China, the Ministry of Commerce, the Ministry of Agriculture and Rural Affairs, the Ministry of Science and Technology, provincial and municipal governments as well as international organizations, industry associations and enterprise. The annually published *China Foreign Investment Report* and *Report on the Competitiveness of China's Exporting Industry* have been universally recognized and recommended by the academia, the government and the society.

Website: http://iie.uibe.edu.cn/

Tel: 86-10-64492251

Fax: 86-10-64493899

China Institute for WTO Studies, University of International Business and Economics (CIWTO)

China Institute for WTO Studies (CIWTO) is a research institute bearing functions of scientific research, discipline development, think tank construction and personnel training. The Institute was granted by the Ministry of Education as a key research base on humanities and social sciences in universities in August 2000.

The Institute is committed to studying the laws of economy of China's opening up and providing high-quality consulting services. It has undertaken a number of national, provincial and ministerial research projects as well as consulting projects commissioned by the government, enterprises and institutional organizations, yielding a series of high-level research achievements and an academic fame. Currently, CIWTO has become the most important academic innovation base and exchange platform for China's WTO studies.

Website: http://ciwto.uibe.edu.cn

Email: ciwto@uibe.edu.cn

Tel: 010-64495778

National Research Center for Economic Comprehensive Competitiveness, Fujian Normal University

National Research Center for Economic Comprehensive Competitiveness of Fujian

Normal University, founded in 2006, currently has 33 research fellows and an annual budget of over three million yuan. Its flagship products, including *Blue Book of China's Provincial Competitiveness*, *Green Book of Environmental Competitiveness*, *Yellow Book of G20 National Innovation Competitiveness*, *Yellow Book of World Innovation Competitiveness*, *Yellow Book of BRICS*, *Green Book of Global Environmental Competitiveness* and *Blue Book of City Innovation Competitiveness*, have been listed among the national "Pishu series". The Center has published more than 50 academic monographs and five of them are in English; nearly 100 specialized research reports it submitted have been approved and adopted by leaders of all levels, among whom many are on the technical experts team of G20 Summit and BRICS Summit.

Tel: 0591 - 83465205

Website: http://jjxy.fjnu.edu.cn

Center for American Studies (CAS), Fudan University

Center for American Studies (CAS), established in 1985, is one of the earliest major research institutes for American studies in China. In December 2000, the CAS was designated by the Ministry of Education as one of the key research institutes on humanities and social sciences in China; it is also a philosophy and social sciences innovation base for American study. There are currently 14 full-time research fellows in the Center. Its periodical publications include *Fudan American Review*, *Religion and American Society* and *Series on the United States and the World in the 21st Century*.

Featuring American studies and Sino-US relations studies, CAS covers a wide range of research topics, including politics, economy, diplomacy, society and culture of the United States, as well as China's American policy and Sino-American relations. According to the latest round of assessment on key research bases on humanities and social sciences granted by the Ministry of Education in 2016, CAS ranked among the top in a number of aspects.

Website: http://www.cas.fudan.edu.cn

Email: cas@fudan.edu.cn

Tel: 021-65642269

Research Institute of Chinese Economy (RICE), Fudan University

Research Institute of Chinese Economy (RICE) of Fudan University was granted by Shanghai Universities Think Tanks in 2013, run mainly by full-time research fellows of China Center for Economic Studies of Fudan University.

Featuring social science research and problem-solving on Chinese issues, RICE has been providing CPC and national decision-making bodies with policy reports on China's economic development and reform.

Since its inception, the Institute has submitted over 280 policy reports on different issues, among which four have been approved by the state's leaders, one has been approved by provincial and ministerial leaders, over 70 have been adopted by the central government and government of all levels, while a number of others have been accepted by internal references. RICE has held 13 lectures themed on "Big Issues in China", 26 series lectures of RICE-CCES and 20 lectures on public policy, attracting nearly 10,000 participants from the political and business circles.

China Institute, Fudan University

China Institute, a secondary school of Fudan University, is among the first batch of national pilot high-end think tanks. The dean is Professor Zhang Weiwei who leads a team of 140 members. Its funding is granted by the National Think Tank Office grants and partly self-financed.

The Institute plays a leading role in research, consulting, communication and training. It not only organizes multiple activities, such as International Thinkers Forum of the Year and China Discourse High-End Forum, but also publishes public and internal journals like *Dongfang Journal*, *China Institute Newsletters* and *China Institute Special Report*, etc. China Institute has been serving as a platform for the researches and exchanges on Chinese way, Chinese models and Chinese discourse, while also providing policy advice for national decisions.

Website: http://www.cifu.fudan.edu.cn/

Email: ci_fa@fudan.edu.cn

WeChat Official Account: ChinaInstituteFDU

Tel: 021 - 65641825

Fudan Development Institute (FDDI), Fudan University

Founded in 1993, Fudan Development Institute (FDDI) is one of the first think tanks established in China since the reform and opening up and has been listed as a Top 10 Influential Think Tanks by *Guangming Daily*. With a 30-person think tank operating group and an expert team of hundreds of researchers, it has established a Policy Planning Society.

FDDI hosts Shanghai Forum and China University Think Tank Forum every year and has a total number of 20 databases that have been built or are being built on regional economy, technological innovation, industrial development, global cities and network governance. Featuring international cooperation and exchanges, FDDI has established cooperative relationships with many countries and regions and is the first domestic think tank to establish the Overseas Center for China Studies, International Think Tank Center and Fudan-Latin America University Consortium.

Website: http://fddi.fudan.edu.cn

Email: fddifudan@fudan.edu.cn

Tel: 86 - 21 - 55670203

Fax: 86 - 21 - 55670203

Guangdong Institute for International Strategies, Guangdong University of Foreign Studies

With the approval of the People's Government of Guangdong Province, Guangdong Institute for International Strategies was established in 2009 as an independent legal entity think tank. It currently has 25 full-time staff and an annual budget of eight million yuan.

The Institute has committed itself to researches on the 21st Century Maritime Silk Road and global economic governance, etc. It has completed 190 decision-making and advisory reports for governments of all levels; its research report on the industrialization progress in Africa has been commended by national leaders like General Secretary Xi Jinping. The international academic platforms it built, such as the Maritime Silk Road International Think Tank Forum, have functioned as Track II diplomacy.

GIIS is a strategy research base of the Ministry of Education, one of the key cooperation units for strategy research of the Ministry of Foreign Affairs, one of the presidencies of the "Belt and Road" Initiative Think Tank Association granted by the International Department of CPC and one of the first batch of key think tanks in

Guangdong Province. It has been ranked 3rd among local think tanks on the "Belt and Road" Initiative for three consecutive years; in 2018, it was awarded with May 1st Labor Medal of Guangdong Province.

Website: http://giis.gdufs.edu.cn。

Email: giis2015@qq.com。

Tel: 020 - 36205613

China-ASEAN Research Institute, Guangxi University

China-ASEAN Research Institute of Guangxi University was founded in January 2005. It is designed as an interdisciplinary, trans-regional and trans-national open research platform that integrates research powers at home and abroad, which has been constructing a strategic research base and a country and regional research center of the Ministry of Education on the key platform of China-ASEAN Collaborative Innovation Center for Regional Development. Research findings of CARI has been recommended by experts in the Social Sciences Commission of the Ministry of Education, selected as internal references and briefings for the International Department of the CPC Central Committee and the Ministry of Education, or approved by leaders in the CPC Central Committee, the State Council and Guangxi Autonomous Region, bringing considerable influence to the academia and the society.

Website: http://cari.gxu.edu.cn/

Tel: 0771 - 3274451

Guangzhou Development Research Institute, Guangzhou University

Guangzhou Development Research Institute of Guangzhou University, established in 2003, is a comprehensive key research institute affiliated to Guangzhou

University, a key research base on humanities and social sciences in Guangdong Province, a collaborative innovation and development center of Guangdong universities, a social science research base of Guangdong Province, and one of the first batch of new-type pilot think tanks in Guangzhou. With the goal of developing itself into a new-type university think tank and key research bases, the Institute attaches equal importance to basic researches and applied researches. With the joint effort of over 30 researchers working full-time or part-time in the Academy, it has created several flagship products, including *Internal Reference to Decision-Making*, *Blue Book of Guangzhou*, as well as the study of Cantonology, among which 96% of its *Internal Reference to Decision-Making* have been approved and 40% adopted, while *Blue Book of Guangzhou* has won 17 National Pishu Awards within seven years.

Website: http://gda.gzhu.edu.cn/

Tel: 020 - 86236001

Center for Beijing-Tianjin-Hebei Development Research, Hebei University of Technology

Center for Beijing-Tianjin-Hebei Development Research, founded in 2012, is listed as a soft science base in Hebei Province, a key research base on humanities and social sciences in Hebei Province, and a prioritized new-type think tank in Hebei Province. Striving to provide talent support and intellectual support for the collaborative development of Beijing, Tianjin and Hebei, facilitating economic development of Beijing-Tianjin-Hebei and Circum-Bohai-Sea Region, and casting positive influence on the rest of the country, the Center has been providing consulting services for major government decisions at all levels from four aspects, namely, scientific research, consulting services, academic exchanges, and personnel training. The outstanding achievements are *Annual Report on Economic Development in Hebei* and *Annual Report on Economic and Social Development in Beijing-Tianjin-Hebei*. In these ways, the Center has been paying great efforts to regional economic and social development.

Website: http://jjj.hebut.edu.cn/

Center for Studies in Moral Culture of Hunan Normal University

Center for Studies in Moral Culture of Hunan Normal University, established in October, 1983, is a key research base on humanities and social sciences granted by the Ministry of Education. Its main body is the ethics discipline of Hunan Normal University combining advantageous resources on and off the campus. Attaching great importance to the service function of ethics as a discipline, the Institute studies the universal laws and general trends of human beings' ethical culture development, strives to cope with a variety of crucial ethical issues emerging with China's social development and global changes. It has paid great efforts in promoting historical, theoretical and practical researches in Chinese ethical culture and constructing the theoretical system, discourse system, inheritance & dissemination system and practical system of ethical culture of socialism with Chinese characteristics, which contributes to improving the strength, competitiveness, appeal and influence of Chinese ethical culture.

Website: http://ethics.hunnu.edu.cn/

Zip Code: 410081

Tel: 0731 - 88872593

Institute for National Educational Policy Research, East China Normal University

Institute for National Educational Policy Research was co-built in 2014 by the Ministry of Education and Shanghai Municipal People's Government, and is affiliated to East China Normal University and Shanghai Institute of Education Sciences. The Institute endeavors to grow into an educational think tank serving for national decision-making whose research directions range from the monitoring and evaluation of China's development in educational modernization, the development of supporting systems to China's educational decision-making, national education strategy and education development planning, international education development and policy trends, the coordinated development of education and social economy, analysis of and comment on educational policy, to investigation and analysis of educational practices. Directing itself towards academic researches and policy study, NIEPR not only yields first-class academic achievements, but also professionally supports scientific educational decision-making and modern governance.

Email: office2014@admin.ecnu.edu.cn

Tel: 021 - 62231103

Institute of Curriculum and Instruction, East China Normal University

Established in 1999, the Institute of Curriculum and Instruction (ICI), at the East China Normal University, Shanghai, is a key research institute on humanities and social sciences designated by the Ministry of Education. There are currently 17 research fellows in the Institute. ICI issues the journal of *Global Education* (abstracted and indexed in CSSCI) and an online journal named *Journal of*

Curriculum Studies. ICI has initiated and drafted key policy documents like "Guideline of National K-12 Curriculum Reform" and "National Curriculum Standard of Teacher Education", which made great contributions to the new-round K-12 curriculum reform and teacher education reform of China. It thus earns the fame of the "national team" in curriculum and instruction research. Many academic achievements of ICI have won national and provincial awards.

Website: http://www.kcs.ecnu.edu.cn/

Tel: 010 - 62233405

Email: ici@ecnu.edu.cn

Center for Modern Chinese City Studies, East China Normal University

Center for Modern Chinese City Studies was established in March 2003 and was officially granted as a key research base on humanities and social sciences in universities in 2014. The Center currently has 15 full-time researchers, over 40 part-time researchers and three administrative staff with an office space of 500 square meters and an annual funding of 3.2 million yuan.

Supported by the national key discipline of human geography in East China Normal University and other major disciplines such as sociology and economics, the Center conducts researches on urban geography and urban society. Its research fellows have undertaken a number of major research projects and harvested a number of influential academic achievements, among which 86 were awarded with national, ministerial or provincial prizes.

Website: http://ccmc.ecnu.edu.cn/

Email: cmccs@mail.ecnu.edu.cn

Tel: 021 - 62232980

The Institute for Modern Chinese Thought and Culture, East China Normal University

The Institute for Modern Chinese Thought and Culture, founded in 1999, is a key research base on humanities and social sciences granted by the Ministry of Education. Its discipline, Chinese philosophy, has been rated as a key discipline in Shanghai. The Institute has undertaken a number of research projects and published multiple academic monographs. A dozen of academic papers of its research fellows have been published on *Social Sciences in China* and reprinted by media like *Xinhua Wenzhai*, some of which have been translated into German, Japanese, English, and Korean and other languages. It also hosts the publication of *Thoughts & Culture*. Multiple research achievements have won national, provincial or ministerial awards, bringing major influence in the academia.

Research Center for Co-Development with Neighboring Countries, East China Normal University

Research Center for Co-Development with Neighboring Countries, founded in 2012, is a collaborative innovation platform launched by East China Normal University and co-built by Peking University and Fudan University. After being restructured by East China Normal University in 2013, it was selected as one of the first-batch university think tanks of Shanghai.

On the basis of a profusion of historical archives and solid field investigations, the Center has released a series of influential policy advice and academic achievements, undertaken and completed a number of national and provincial research projects, and launched multiple enlightening new media publicity works, all of which done with constant focus on economic development, cooperation and security issues with China's neighboring countries. Other activities include the Valdai Sino-Russian Forum that is annually organized, academic elite workshops and so on. The Center has set up overseas studios in Washington and Moscow to cultivate interdisciplinary talents for think tanks.

Website: https://zhoubian.ecnu.edu.cn/

Email: zhoubiancenter@126.com

Tel: 021 - 62235320

Center of Social Governance Research (CSGR), South China University of Technology

Center of Social Governance Research (CSGR) of South China University of Technology, established in March 2015, is the only provincial think tank in Guangdong Province themed on social governance. The research team that consists of 10 professors, 12 associate professors and 8 lecturers are mainly engaged in researches on social security policy, civil administration policy, social construction and social policy, as well as security policy. Multiple academic achievements of the Center have been approved by national, provincial and municipal leaders. CSGR has undertaken over 10 projects with a disposable fund of more than four million yuan. The research fellows have published more than 10 academic papers, many of which have been reprinted and included in high-level journals. The Center is privileged with stable government cooperation channels and international academic exchange platforms. Among the research findings, one has won a national awards and multiple others have been awarded with provincial and ministerial prizes.

Tel: 020 - 87114133

Email: hghszl@scut.edu.cn

The Institute of State Governance (ISG), Huazhong University of Science and Technology

The Institute of State Governance (ISG) of Huazhong University of Science and Technology is the first university think tank in China named as "State Governance" and has been listed among think tanks as Collaborative Innovation Center for State Governance of Hubei Province.

Led by Professor Ouyang Kang as president of the Institute, it currently has 35 research fellows working full-time or part-time as well as 18 foreign visiting researchers.

Since its inception, ISG has successfully held the international academic conferences of East Lake Forum on Global Governance for four times and Summit on the Modernization of State Governance for five times, hosted and completed about 20 research projects on state governance, and has released and published the first local and national performance reviews that are fulfilled by a university think tank, which are all award-winning research achievements.

Website: http://isg.hust.edu.cn/

WeChat Official Account: hustgjzl

Institute of China Rural Studies, Central China Normal University

Institute of China Rural Studies, supported by the Institute of China Rural Studies of Central China Normal University, is a specialized academic institute for the study of problems facing rural areas and rural population, a think tank granted by the

Ministry of Education and one of the four major university think tanks in China that has been recognized by Deputy Prime Minister Liu Yandong.

With the goal of becoming a top-notch think tank worldwide, Think Tank for China Rural Policies strives to conduct large-scale investigations, gather big data, provide policy service, build national platforms and thus plays its role as a think tank. As of now, it has submitted 580 policy advisory reports to the decision-making departments, among which 400 have been approved and adopted. Its research achievements on rural collective economy, rural grassroots organizations, and revitalization of rural areas have all been adopted by the No. 1 Document issued by the Central Committee of CPC.

Center for Quantitative Economics of Jinlin University

Center for Quantitative Economics Research, directly affiliated to Jilin University, is a key research institute on humanities and social sciences granted by the Ministry of Education. The Center has 41 research fellows who work full-time or part-time with an annual funding of nearly ten million yuan.

The Center has been providing advisory reports to government agencies of all levels, periodically publishing *Policy Advisory Report of Center for Quantitative Economics of Jinlin University* and the CSSCI-sourced collection of *Quantitative Economics Research*. Coupled with the International Conference on Quantitative Economics and International Quantitative Economics Workshop that it has held for years, the Center has gained its influence in China's economics academia.

In 2017, the Center was selected among top 100 university think tanks in China Think Tank Index (CTTI) and top 30 in the areas of economy and trade.

Website: http://jlucqe.jlu.edu.cn

Email: qe_journal@jlu.edu.cn

Tel: 0431 - 85166059

China Center for Public Sector Economy Research of Jilin University

China Center for Public Sector Economy Research of Jilin University is a key research institute on humanities and social sciences and a philosophy and social sciences innovation base on the reform and development of China's public sector economy granted by "Project 985" in Jilin University. The Center has successfully held Chinese State-Owned Economy Development Forum nationally or internationally for 18 times consecutively; it has also been publishing collected papers of *Review of Public Sector Economies*, and a series of academic monographs including *Chinese State-Owned Economy Development Report*, *Report on Independent Innovation of Central State-Owned Enterprises*, *Journey of State-Owned Economy Study*, etc. With an annual funding of over two million yuan, it has published a profusion of quality academic papers and submitted a number of research reports that were approved by provincial or even national leaders.

Website: http://ccpser.jlu.edu.cn;

Email: ccpser@jlu.edu.cn;

Tel: 0431 - 85168829。

The Public Opinion Big Date Research Center, Jinan University

The Public Opinion Big Date Research Center, founded in 2012, is one of the outstanding cases of key research institutes on humanities and social sciences of Guangzhou. The researched areas include Internet management policies, network security policies, Hong Kong, Macao and Taiwan policies, ideological policies, and news policies. Boasting a comprehensive domestic and overseas public opinion data mining system and case library, the Center is capable of monitoring major domestic news media, Weibo and more than five million WeChat public accounts. with its overseas public opinion monitoring platform for specific, it covers media of more than 90 languages in more than 200 countries and regions, and is able to monitor international mainstream social media and has set up five thematic databases. A number of academic achievements of the Center have won provincial and ministerial awards.

Tel: 020 - 38374980

Email: bdclab@jnu.edu.cn

Academy of Overseas Chinese Studies in Jinan University

Academy of Overseas Chinese Studies in Jinan University, established in the November of 2006, is a key research base on humanities and social sciences granted by the Ministry of Education. Directing itself for China's strategy of peaceful development, the Academy strives to serve China's reform & opening up and modernization as well as Chinese society. Its endeavor in conducting multidisciplinary cutting-edge researches with an international vision involves restructuring affiliates, optimizing research power and introducing top-tier talents. It has been hosting journals like *Southeast Asian Studies* issued bimonthly and *Overseas Chinese Report*, while co-building the Documentation Center for Overseas Chinese Study with the university library.

Website: https://hqhryj.jnu.edu.cn/

Email: ohqhr@jnu.edu.cn

Tel: 020 - 85226108

Institute for Food Safety Risk Management, Jiangnan University

Institute for Food Safety Risk Management, co-founded by Jiangnan University and Jiangsu Provincial Administration for Market Regulation, is one of the prioritized think tanks of Jiangsu Province granted by the Publicity Department of the CPC Jiangsu Provincial Committee and the only professional think tank specializing in food safety risk governance in Jiangsu Province.

Since its inception, the Institute has published over 30 advisory reports on provincial and ministerial internal references, among which over 10 have been approved by the Party and state's leaders as well as provincial and ministerial leaders. It has also published more than 100 news reports, speeches, comments and popular science articles and fulfilled a number of major national research projects. Its publications like *Investigation Report on Modernization of China Food Safety Risk Management System and Governance Capability* and *Series Introduction to China Development Report on Food Safety* as well as projects like Big Data Service Platform for Monitoring and Inspection on Food Safety Risk have all been awarded.

Jiangsu Public Security Institute, Jiangsu Police Institute

Jiangsu Public Security Institute (JPSI) is one of the two first-batch ministerial think tanks built by the Ministry of Public Security and is also a prioritized think tank in Jiangsu Province. The Institute currently has four research teams consisting of 18 full-time researchers and over 30 part-time researchers with an annual funding of 4.5 million yuan.

Major research achievements are compiled as *Think Tank Special Report* and *Think Tank Research on Public Security* that are submitted to the Ministry of Public Security, CPC Jiangsu Provincial Committee and Jiangsu provincial government.

Apart from that, JPSI also compiles and publishes *Annual Report of Foreign Policing Think Tanks Research*, *Annual Report of Public Security in Jiangsu Province*, and the 12-volume academic book series of *Research on Modern Policing*. It has held 10 national or international symposiums and completed two award-winning research projects.

Website: http://jwzx.jspi.cn/

WeChat Official Account: gonganbuzhiku-impr

Email: wangchi@jspi.cn

Tel: 025 - 52881589

Soviet Area Revitalization Institute of Jiangxi Normal University

Soviet Area Revitalization Institute of Jiangxi Normal University is a key think tank of Jiangxi Province, one of the Top 100 Think tanks in China and also a key research base on philosophy and social sciences in Jiangxi Province. It is committed to providing intellectual support and social services for the revitalization and development for the original Soviet areas and bases for the National Revolutionary Army. It hosts two journals, namely *Jiangxi Soviet Areas Rejuvenation Forum* and *Editorials for Jiangxi Soviet Areas Rejuvenation Forum*. With a total of over 30 research fellows and a Level II master program called Marxism and the Economic and Social Development of Contemporary China, it has undertaken a number of funded research projects. Many of its advisory reports have been approved by national and provincial leaders and its research findings have been complied into different publishing series including Book Series, Special Reports, Summits and Blue Books.

Website: http://sqzxyjy.jxnu.edu.cn/

Tel: 0791 - 88121059

Zip Code: 330022

Email: sqzxyjy@163.com

Yangtze Industrial Economics Institution, Nanjing University

Yangtze Industrial Economics Institution (Yangtze IDEI) is one of the first-batch high-end think tanks in Jiangsu Province and a national high-end think tank. The Institute, undergirded by Nanjing University's economics and management study, delves into the trends and policies of China's real economy in the context of the highly open and developed real economy in China's coastal areas, which serves to gain experience for achieving the Two Centenaries and explore the economic development of socialism with Chinese characteristics. Its major achievements include *Advisory Report for Decision-Making on Yangtze River Industrial Economics*, *Hot Spot on China's Industrial Economics* and *China Economic Dynamic Index Report*. a number of which have been approved by the central and Jiangsu's provincial leaders, casting an extensive influence on all walks of life.

Website: http://www.yangtze-idei.cn/

Email: idei@nju.edu.cn

Tel: 025 - 83576316

Collaborative Innovation Center of South China Sea Studies, Nanjing University

Collaborative Innovation Center of South China Sea Studies (CICOSCSS), founded in the July of 2012, is one of the 14 first batch of "collaborative innovation centers in 2011" granted by the Ministry of Education.

Driven by the demands of major national policies and aiming to safeguard China's maritime rights in South China Sea, the Center seeks to adopt collaborative innovation among multiple disciplines and takes the route of arts and sciences studies, military and civilian studies, university-center cooperation, as well as the collaboration among universities. Coupled with the reform of systems and mechanisms, it has been conducting South China Sea issues as an integrated whole in an all-round manner at the service of the nation's strategic decision-making on these issues. Revolving around the monitoring of academic trending and strategic decision-making, the Center has set up nine research platforms on the history and culture of South China Sea, the resource environment and coastal & territorial rights and interests of South China Sea, South China Sea law study, navigation freedom, security and stability on South China Sea, etc. It endeavors to build a new-type think tank with Chinese characteristics integrating academic innovation, high-end think tank, personnel training and international exchanges and dialogues.

Website: http://nanhai.nju.edu.cn/

Tel: 025 - 83597212

Email: nanhai@nju.edu.cn

Zijin Media Think Tank, Nanjing University

Zijin Media Think Tank (ZMT) was activated in October 2015. There are almost 40 experts and four operating staff running six centers affiliated to ZMT. It receives an annual subsidy of two million yuan from the Publicity Department of Jiangsu Provincial Committee of CPC and is funded by enterprises and institutional organizations for cooperation projects.

ZMT, known for its research on big data and large data sets, has established a dozen of research reports during the three years since its inception, including *Interim Report 2016 of China Stock Market*, *Innovation Index Report on China's Listed Companies in 2016 and 2018*, *Report on Big Data of Internet Philanthropy* and *Investigation Report on the Knowledge about Occupation Pension in Jiangsu Province*. Such a profusion of fundamental researches has laid a solid foundation for its decision-making support and policy advice.

Website: http://www.zijimtt.com

Email: zijin@nju.edu.cn

Tel: 025-89681258

Jiangsu Academy of Talent Development, Nanjing University of Science and Technology

Jiangsu Academy of Talent Development (JATD), founded on May 12, 2015, is a research platform on talent development established by Nanjing University of Science & Technology in Jiangsu Province. The Institute aims to bring together top-notch research forces, conduct an integrated, long-term and forward-looking research on talent development strategy issues, so as to provide policy advice, decision-making support and talent services to the committees of CPC and the government. JATD has set up eight research centers in China's well-known colleges and research institutes. Decision-making support is provided to the committees of CPC and the government by undertaking key research projects, hosting high-level academic forums and publishing research findings; intellectual services are provided to employers such as parks, enterprises, as well as colleges and research institutes. It has been contributing its constructive advice to CPC Jiangsu Provincial Committee and Jiangsu provincial government for a new and upgraded Jiangsu.

Website: http://www.jatd.org/

Tel: 025-84303966

Email: jatd2015@163.com

Institute for China Legal Modernization Studies, Nanjing Normal University

Institute for China Legal Modernization Studies (ICLMS) is a first-batch high-end think tank of Jiangsu Province established on the basis of Nanjing Normal University. It is a non-profit public research institute with seven affiliated research centers that provides decision-making consultations in the studies of China legal modernization.

The Institute has developed two flagship activities with national influence, namely Ten Rule of Law Cases of the Year that won the First Prize for Best Think Tank Activities and Fangde Rule of Law Research Award. As for research projects, Legislation Advice on General Principles of Civil Law won "National Policy Award" of China's Think Tank Consultation, while the Law and Legislation Research on Construction of the Grand Canal's Cultural Belt was entitled to be Top Ten Best Cases of Think Tank Practice in Jiangsu Province.

Website: http://iclms.njnu.edu.cn/

Email: yuhaimei_galya@163.com

Tel: 025-85891703

Institute of Healthy Jiangsu Development, Nanjing Medical University

Institute of Healthy Jiangsu Development is a prioritized think tank of Jiangsu Province founded in 2016. It's presided over by Professor Wang Changqing, Secretary of the Party Committee of Nanjing Medical University, who also serves as a leading expert. Currently it has 20 experts and an annual subsidy of 400 thousand yuan.

The Institute develops itself on the basis of decision-making consultation, problem-oriented researches and an aim of health maintenance. Accordingly, its endeavor is three-fold: integrating a healthy China into its decision-making advice for the government; undertaking evaluation and researches related to the government's health policy; strengthening cooperation and exchanges as a facilitation to the Belt and Road Initiative. A number of policy recommendations of the Institute have been approved and adopted by the provincial and municipal party committee.

Website: http://jkjs.njmu.edu.cn

Email: jkjs@nkjs.edu.cn

Tel: 025 - 86868591

Purple Academy of Culture & Creativity, Nanjing Medical University

Purple Academy of Culture & Creativity (PACC) was co-built by the Publicity Department of the CPC Jiangsu Provincial Committee, Jiangsu Cultural Investment and Nanjing College of Art in March 2016. The Academy is composed of Culture & Creativity Development Research Center, Culture & Creativity Planning and Industrial Service Center as well as Culture & Creativity Information and Data Center. Cultural policy, consumption policy, radio and television policy and market policy all fall into PACC's research areas. Sound cooperative relations are built with many government departments, cultural institutions, and universities at home and abroad. Incorporating the diversified academic backgrounds and specialties of experts from home and abroad, PACC conducts researches on major theoretical issues and state-of-the-art topics on culture & creativity industry as well as issues of national concern or that upon Jiangsu's development in the industry.

College of Economic and Social Development (CESD), Nankai University

Nankai University's College of Economic and Social Development (CESD) was established in 1998. Heading towards the goal of building a leading applied economy research platform in China, the College has established an efficient productive research institute that is second to none in China. Its China Regional Policy Research Center is supported by high-level academic exchange platforms. CESD, striving to serve national strategies, has held a series of high-level forums and submitted a number of advisory reports that were approved by national and provincial leaders. On behalf of Chinese government, CESD annually publishes *Report of China Logistics Development* both in Chinese and English, allowing the world to get informed of the logistic development of contemporary China.

CESD was granted as one of the executives of China Education Think Tanks Union by the Ministry of Education and selected as one of the first batch of university think tanks in Tianjin in 2016.

Website: http://esd.nankai.edu.cn/

Tel: 022 - 23508549

Collaborative Innovative Center for China Economy (CICCE), Nankai University

Collaborative Innovative Center for China Economy (CICCE), founded in 2014, is home to over 300 experts and scholars. About 200 research briefings have been published by the Center, along with its own research database, have been providing intellectual support to the decision-making of the central and local government. It has built multiple overseas research bases and collaborative training platform, hosted over 300 academic forums at home and abroad, launched the Lecture on Political Economics that has trained almost 2,000 professional personnel; apart from that, it has founded a pilot class for outstanding innovation talents, whose project of Theory and Practice Exploration on Training Model of Talents for Economics Innovation won a First Prize in the 6th National Teaching Achievement.

Website: http://chinaeconomy.nankai.edu.cn/

Tel: 022-23500235

Email: cicce@nankai.edu.cn

Jiangsu Yangtze Economic Belt Research Institute (JYEBRI), Nantong University

Jiangsu Yangtze River Economic Belt Research Institute (JYEBRI), established in 2014, was granted as a highly-valued think tank by the Publicity Department of the Jiangsu Provincial Committee of CPC. The Institute currently has an annual funding of about one million yuan as well as 45 researchers with academic backgrounds in economics or other disciplines working full-time or part-time.

The research team has innovatively proposed a collaboratively balanced development theory and had other research achievements published by People's Publishing House and other authoritative journals. Many of its decision-making advisory reports were approved by leaders of the Central Committee of CPC and the provincial and central government and adopted by government agencies. Having launched the First Yangtze River Economic Belt Development Forum in 2015, the Institute has hosted the forum for three consecutive years since then. In 2018, it was awarded with Top Ten Cases of Think Tank in Jiangsu.

Website: http://yhyjy.ntu.edu.cn/

Email: chenweizhong@ntu.edu.cn

Tel: 0513-85012972

Collaborative Innovation Center for the Study on China, Mongolia and Russia Economic and Trade Cooperation & Construction of Economic Belt on the Prairie Silk Road, Inner Mongolia University of Finance and Economics

Collaborative Innovation Center for Sino-Mongolian-Russian Economic and Trade Cooperation and the Construction of the Economic Belt of the Prairie Silk Road (high-end think tank), founded in January 2015, is composed of six research platforms and two research centers with a research group of over 120 experts and scholars and ample funds.

Focusing on the researches on Sino-Mongolian-Russian economic and trade cooperation as well as the construction of the economic belt of the Prairie Silk Road, the Center explores into strategy planning, system designing and policy making of the researched topics; meanwhile, it endeavors to cultivate talents for the construction of the economic belt. In 2017, the Center was granted as one of the first batch of pilot high-end think tanks of the Inner Mongolia Autonomous Region.

Tel: 0471-5300158

Email: nmstar@vip.sina.com

Address: No. 185, North Second Ring Road, Hohhot, Inner Mongolia

Website: http://www.imufe.edu.cn/kyc/xtcxzx

WeChat Official Account: gh_8f29d9a5ee3d

Institute for Contemporary China Studies (ICCS), Tsinghua University

Institute for Contemporary China Studies (ICCS), founded in December 2011, was selected as one of the first batch of national high-end pilot think tanks in 2015. ICCS develops itself on the basis of safeguarding the highest state interests, recognizing the long-term development goals of the country and proactively facilitating national decision-making; it develops itself by acquiring, innovating and disseminating decision-making knowledge and facilitating decision-making and policy-making with contemporary China studies report. Attaching equal importance to originality, innovation and authority of this knowledge brand, ICCS has been built into a public policy research institute with important influence at home and abroad.

The Institute has long been providing consulting services for major national decisions, with many research findings adopted; for example, *China Study* published by ICCS has become an important reference for the decision-making of central and local governments. It also has constant dialogues with the world—airing resonant voice of China on the global stage through international academic exchanges, publication of research achievements and publicity of mainstream media.

Website: http://www.iccs.tsinghua.edu.cn/

Tel: 010 - 62772199

Email: ccsoffice@tsinghua.edu.cn

Center for Health Management and Policy, Shandong University

Founded in 2002, the Center for Health Management and Policy of Shandong University is a secondary unit independent from Shandong University. It has 23 full-time staff and 20 part-time staff with an annual budget of about five million yuan in 2018. It is in charge of the Key Laboratory on Health Economy and Policy and

Shandong University-Karolinska Institute Joint Laboratory for Global Health issued by National Health Commission of PRC. In 2016, it entered the list of key new-type pilot think tanks of Shandong Province.

The Center specializes in the research of health economy and policy, caters to the domestic need for health reform and development, keeps abreast of the state-of-the-art development of international health research, and exploits its advantages in international cooperation. By means of undertaking projects issued by governments of all levels as well as international cooperation programs, it fully plays its role of a think tank by providing policy consultation and personnel training.

Website: http://www.chmp.sdu.edu.cn

Email: shcm@sdu.edu.cn

Tel: 0531 - 88380061

Research Centre for Local Governance, Shanghai University

Research Centre for Local Governance (RCLG) of Shanghai University is one of the first batch university think tanks funded by the Shanghai Education Committee. In order to facilitate the transformation of Shanghai's local governance empirically and academically, RCLG centers on China's strategic goal of strengthening and innovating social governance as well as fostering a harmonious society, based on which it studies the basic trend of the transformation of China's local governance model and the compatibility among the social management system, the fundamental public service system and the modern social organization system under this background. Since its inception, the center has been selected as one of the first batch of Shanghai Civil Affairs Research Institutes during the 13th Five-Year Plan, and was ranked 6th for Academic Influence of Think Tanks of Social Sciences in 2017.

Website: http://www.rclgshu.org/

Email: rclgshu@126.com

WeChat Official Account: RCLGSHU

Tel: 021-66135205

Shanghai Center for Global Trade and Economic Governance, Shanghai University of International Business and Economics

Shanghai Center for Global Trade and Economic Governance (SC-GTEG), founded in 2013, is one of the first-batch university think tanks in Shanghai. SC-GTEG stands on the basis of China's World Trade Center Negotiation Plan and works collaboratively from domestic and abroad. The Center publishes annually *Global Trade and Economic Governance Annual Report* and *Review of Global Trade and Economic Governance* and monthly *Developments and Trends of Global Trade and Economic Governance*, while also hosts a column named "Global Trade and Economic Governance" on *International Business Daily*. It has been awarded as National Innovative Research Institute for Trade in Services by China Association of Trade in Services.

Email: maoyitanpan@126.com

Tel: 021-52067321

Shanghai International Shipping Institute (SISI), Shanghai Maritime University

Shanghai International Shipping Institute (SISI), founded in 2008, is a research and consulting institute for the development of the international shipping industry.

The Center has been granted as one of the first-batch university knowledge service platforms in Shanghai (Advanced Strategic Research Center) and key research institutes on humanities and social sciences in Shanghai; it has also been selected as the Collaborative Innovation Center of Shanghai's Universities.

The Institute has yielded a profusion of research achievements that influence the government and the shipping industry at home and abroad. Boasting a diversified and comprehensive information distribution channel, SISI publishes nearly 100 indexes and industry reports every year and has established the first China Shipping Database with complete data and comprehensive functions. The China Shipping Database and Shipping & Port Big Data Laboratory it launched has been granted as a major task for the construction of Shanghai International Shipping Center, performing a leading role in the research of shipping big data.

China Institute of FTZ Supply Chain, Shanghai Maritime University

Founded in October 2013, China Institute of FTZ Supply Chain (CIFSC) is a research base for social sciences innovation in Shanghai with an annual funding of 10 million yuan.

CIFSC has hosted, co-hosted or been commissioned with a series of cooperation and exchange platforms for organizations at home and abroad, including the 2018 Global Trade and International Logistics Summit Forum that serves as a supporting forum on logistics to the 1st China International Import Expo, Boao International Logistics Forum, and the 1st China Free Trade Zone Inspection and Quarantine Innovation and Development Forum.

CIFSC has been undertaking many decision-making consulting projects commissioned by local governments, large enterprises, domestic universities and international institutions, etc. on areas ranging from strategic planning, institutional innovation, policy evaluation, enterprise transformation, socialized information adoption and so on, based on which it has produced multiple thematic reports that were approved and highly valued by the clients.

Website: http://cifsc.shmtu.edu.cn

China Institute for Urban Governance, Shanghai Jiao Tong University

China Institute for Urban Governance (CIUG) is co-built by Shanghai Jiao Tong University and the Development Research Center of Shanghai Municipal Government, aspiring to build itself into a world-renowned new-style think tank with Chinese characteristics, a pool of talents and a high-end international exchange and cooperation platform. It has been providing intellectual support for the scientific decision-making of the Party and the government through interdisciplinary studies on urban emergency management, urban environmental governance, urban social governance, innovation-driven and sustainable development, livable and public services, as well as urban culture and urban image. CIUG has submitted more than 70 advisory reports for government's decision-making and has published more than 70 academic papers and editorials. It has also held Global Cities Forum (GCF) in 2016 and 2017 and maintained cooperation with international organizations and consultation agencies, such as United Nations Human Settlements Programme (UN-HABITAT) and World Bank.

Tel: 021-62934788

Email: ciug@sjtu.edu.cn

Website: ciug.sjtu.edu.cn

Middle East Studies Institute (MESI) of Shanghai International Studies University

Institute of Middle East Studies (MESI) of Shanghai International Studies University is designated as one of the key research bases on humanities and social sciences in universities designated by the Ministry of Education and one of the first-batch university think tanks in Shanghai by the Education Committee of Shanghai.

With an authorized size of 22 staff and an annual budget of four million yuan, MESI is playing an active role in providing suggestions for the government and enterprises as well as cultivating academic talents and informed citizens. It is currently presiding over 21 research projects and hosting *Arab World Studies* and *Asian Journal of Middle Eastern and Islamic Studies*; it has published six volumes of *Reports on Middle East Development*, hosted the International Forum on Asia and the Middle East for six years, complied about 200 features and briefings on Middle East issues, and had its advisory reports approved by leaders of CPC and central government. It is listed in the Think Tank Network for the Belt and Road Initiative launched by the International Liaison Department (ILD) of the Central Committee of CPC.

Website: http://mideast.shisu.edu.cn

Email: zdssisu@163.com

WeChat Official Account: MESI_SISU

Tel: 021-35373278

Center for Global Public Opinions of China, SISU

Center for Global Public Opinions of China, founded in the June of 2008, is a research institute affiliated to Shanghai International Studies University that strives for the study of international public opinion and international communication. It currently has 14 full-time researchers and administrative staff as well as 20 part-time researchers.

The Center is currently presiding over a number of projects of National Social Sciences Fund and was selected as one of the public opinion information sources of the Publicity Department of CPC. As of 2018, nearly 100 advisory reports of the Center have been approved by leaders of the Central Committee of CPC and more than 300 advisory reports were adopted by Publicity Department of CPC, Central Office of CPC and the Publicity Office of Shanghai Municipal Committee and other government agencies. It was awarded as Outstanding Organ of Public Opinion by the Publicity Department of CPC in 2017 and 2018 consecutively.

Website: http://www.rcgpoc.shisu.edu.cn

Email: globalopinion@shisu.edu.cn

Tel: 021 - 35372559

Center for Basic Laws of Hong Kong and Macao Special Administrative Regions, Shenzhen University

Center for Basic Laws of Hong Kong and Macao Special Administrative Regions of Shenzhen University is the first independent research institute on the basic laws of Hong Kong and Macao. It was selected as a ministerial key research base on humanities and social sciences in May 2011. With 13 staff and an annual budget (including salaries) of 5.5 million yuan, it has been centering its scientific researches and consulting services on national development strategy and the holistic development of Hong Kong and Macao and serving as an academic exchange platform. CBL's achievements have been valued by institutes on Hong Kong and Macao of all levels and have been recognized by peer experts, which demonstrates its academic and social influence.

Website: http://cbl.szu.edu.cn

Email: cbl@szu.edu.cn

Tel: 0755 - 26733093

Institute of South Asian Studies (ISAS), Sichuan University

Institute of South Asian Studies (ISAS) bases its research on the political and economic status quo and history and culture of South Asian countries and facilitates China's social and economic development in light of national conditions. The Institute has undertaken and completed more than 20 research projects granted by National Social Sciences Fund of China and relevant government departments, published over 20 academic monographs and 800 academic papers, and submitted over 50 research reports to relevant departments and organs of the central government. ISAS runs ahead its peers in South Asian Studies thanks to its advantages in the research on economic development and military security in South Asian countries; it is also competent in the researches on social political development in this region.

Website: http://www.isas.net.cn/

Email: nanyasuo@163.com

Tel: 028 - 85412638

Collaborative Innovation Center for Security and Development of Western Frontier China, Sichuan University

Collaborative Innovation Center for Security and Development of Western Frontier China was co-founded in 2012 by Sichuan University, Yunnan University, Tibet University, Xinjiang University, Ethnic Minority Groups Theory and Policy Research Room of the National Ethic Affairs Commission of PRC and Ethnic Minority Groups Development Research Institute of the Development Research Center of the State Council.

The Center has established research platforms on Tibet-related issues, Xinjiang studies, studies of neighboring countries of West China, major issues of the Belt and Road Initiative, studies of the history and geography of western frontiers, and the study of border theory and governance strategies. Aiming to serve the national strategy on security and development in the new era, it studies the governance strategy on western frontiers, explores new means for the security and development of this area, and provides intellectual support for the prosperity of people in western frontiers, for a harmonious relationship with neighboring countries, and for the long-term stability of China.

Tel: 028-85416270

Email: cwf-scu@163.com

Website: http://cwf.scu.edu.cn/index.htm

Soochow University Think Tank (SUTT)

Soochow University Think Tank (SUTT) was registered at Suzhou Civil Affairs Bureau in 2011 and was granted with 8.02 million yuan financially in 2017. It has been awarded as a key research base of philosophy and social sciences in Jiangsu Province, an exemplary think tank, a prioritized think tank of Jiangsu Province and one of the core think tanks of China.

Featuring urbanization and urban development, SUTT mainly studies urban economy and management, city and social governance, urban culture and communication as well as urban planning and construction, and adopts the strategy of integrated development of Suzhou as a well-known city and Soochow University as a prestigious university. Dialogue with Suzhou, its flagship series activity, has been held for five years.

Website: http://sutt.suda.edu.cn/

Email: sutt@suda.edu.cn

Tel: 0512 - 65228625

Tianjin Academy of Free Trade Area, Tianjin University of Finance and Economics

Tianjin Academy of Free Trade Area (TAFTA), established in 2014, has been adhering to the mission of serving the government as well as the society. It serves as a core coordination organ of Collaborative Innovation Center for China Pilot Free Trade Zone and co-launched Research Association on Free Trade Zone of China's Universities. Since its inception, the Academy has conducted a number of research projects and has been approved as a key publishing project (Free Trade Zone Research) of the National 13th Five-Year Plan. It has also organized various international and national academic and policy symposiums on free trade zone and carried out a series of lectures and training on this topic, which had extensive influence on the society and were highly valued by Tianjin Municipal Committee of

CPC, Tianjin Municipal Government and Administrative Committee of Free Trade Zone.

Website: http://tafta.tjufe.edu.cn/

We Chat Official Account: TAFTA-TJUFE

Email: tafta_tjufe@126.com

Tel: 022 - 88186335

Research Base for the Implementation of National Intellectual Property Strategy (Tianjin University)

Research Base for the Implementation of National Intellectual Property Strategy (Tianjin University) was founded in the April 2013 and was led by Professor Zhang Wei. Striving for the inter-and-trans-disciplinary study of management, law, economics and engineering and aiming to contribute to China's development in intellectual property, the Base is on the quest of becoming an intellectual-property-specialized think tank for the country to better policy-making, for the enterprises to better strategic management, and for universities to cultivate talents in this field of expertise. It was listed among the first batch of university think tanks in Tianjin in 2016 and joined Tianjin Think Tank Alliance in 2017. With a research group of over 30, it has published 51 briefings, among which 22 of them were approved by National Intellectual Property Administration (NIPA) and seven of them were put into practice.

Email: liulinshanipr@tju.edu.cn

Tel: 022 - 27401360

APEC Sustainable Energy Center, Tianjin University

APEC Sustainable Energy Center (APSEC), one of the seventeen APEC centers registered by the Ministry of Foreign Affairs of PRC, was founded at the 11th APEC Energy Ministerial Meeting in 2014. Affiliated to the National Energy Administration (NEA), the center is the first international energy cooperation agency led by the Chinese government; currently, it's under the management of Tianjin University.

APSEC is under stable financial support with an office area of 300 square meters and 14 full-time staff. Its international intelligence network consists of 60 experts from nine APEC economies and two joint project operating centers. It has completed two publications of core research achievements in the APEC members, and released 70 reports and 21 briefings in service of APEC international energy cooperation. Besides, the Center has coordinated 36 domestic organs in APEC energy affairs, incubated two flagship forums with their own features, and signed cooperation agreements with 10 cities and 15 institutes around the world.

Website: http://apsec.tju.edu.cn/

Email: apsec2014@126.com

Tel: 022-27400847

German Studies Center (DFZ) of Tongji University

The German Studies Center (German: Deutschlandforschungszentrum, DFZ) of Tongji University, founded in 2012, is the first new-type think tank directly affiliated to Tongji University and one of centers for "countries and areas studies" funded by the Chinese Ministry of Education. As an inter-and-transdisciplinary platform in the university with a focus on Germany and Europe, the DFZ has currently 60 full-time, part-time or guest researchers from China as well as Germany. The research field of the DFZ covers politics, diplomacy, economy, society, culture, education of Germany and Europe, as well as the Sino-German and Sino-European relations, etc.

The most important publications of the DFZ include the *Annual Development Report of Germany* (*Blue Book of Germany*) since 2012 and the Quarterly Journal *Deutschland-Studien* (CSSCI source journal). Researchers of the DFZ publish more than 100 articles in various media each year. So far, the DFZ has got written instructions or comments from the main leaders of the Central authority for several internal reports. In addition, the DFZ has established substantive cooperation with relevant think tanks in the field of German and European research worldwide and jointly organizes international conferences such as the Sino-German Forum every year.

Website: http://german-studies-online.tongji.edu.cn/

WeChat Official Account: tongji_dgyj

Address: Zhongde Dalou (Sino-German Building), 9th fl.

1239 Siping Road, Tongji University, Shanghai

Email: gso@tongji.edu.cn

Tel.: 021 - 65980328

Wuhan University Institute of International Law

Founded in 1980, Wuhan University Institute of International Law was the first college-based academic institute on international law research and one of the earliest to grant master, doctoral and postdoctoral degrees in the science of law. The Institute has its study approved as a national key discipline and is granted as a key research base on humanities and social sciences by the Ministry of Education. Having gathered a group of experts with profound theoretical literacy and outstanding ability in decision-making consultation, international exchange and public diplomacy, it was granted as one of the first batch of pilot institutes of national high-end think tank by the Publicity Department of the Central Committee of the Communist Party of China (CCPPD) in 2015. The Institute adheres to an integrated and comprehensive study of international public law, international private law, international economic law and comparative law. Upholding the principle of "organically integrating China's standpoint, maintaining independent thinking and putting forward theoretical argumentation", it has been providing consultation to the Central Committee of CPC and other decision-making departments and involved directly in cases handling and engaged thoroughly in international negotiations—a number of reports have been approved by the Party and the state's leaders, while many proposals have been adopted by relevant departments. In terms of publication, *Wuhan University International Law Review*, *Chinese Yearbook of Private International Law and Comparative Law*, *Annual Report on China's Practice in Promoting the International Rule of Law*, as well as *Chinese Journal of International Law* (covered by SSCI), edited and published by the Institute, have been casting great influence on academic and practical circles at home and abroad.

Institute of National Culture Development, Wuhan University

Founded in 2009, Institute of National Culture Development in Wuhan University is under the charge of the Ministry of Culture of PRC and Wuhan University, and is co-built by Hubei Provincial Department of Culture. It currently has 12 full-time research fellows and 13 part-time research fellows. Focusing on studying basic theories of cultural innovation, the Institute functions as a cradle and academic reservoir for talents of cultural innovation who will establish China's cultural development system; as a think tank, it provides reform consultation and information services for the decision-making of government of all levels and pays close attention to the trending of international cultural innovation development and study. Paying equal attention to the development of China's cultural innovation theory, it has undertaken and completed the cultural innovation research projects granted by the state and local government agencies.

Website: http://nccc.whu.edu.cn/

Tel: 027 - 68766957, 027 - 68761537

Email: nccirwhu@126.com

Research Institute of Environmental Law, Wuhan University

Research Institute of Environmental Law, Wuhan University (RIEL), founded in 1981, was one of the first institutes to be granted as a key research base on humanities and social sciences by the Ministry of Education in 1999. It is home to the Secretariat of China Environmental and Resources Law Society and also the research base on environmental and resources judicial theories for Supreme People's Court. Led by Professor Qin Tianbao, RIEL's staff is composed of six professors, four associate professors and one lecturer.

RIEL has undertaken or participated in the drafting and revision of almost all the national environmental laws, such as the Environmental Protection Law and over 100 national or local environmental regulations; it has submitted more than 200 advisory reports to the National People's Congress (NPC), the Ministry of Environmental Protection, the Ministry of Foreign Affairs and other government agencies.

According to the base assessment organized by the Department of Social Sciences of the Ministry of Education in 2015, the Institute was ranked top 50 in China in terms of social service ability.

Website: http://www.riel.whu.edu.cn

Email: riel2@whu.edu.cn

Tel/Fax: 027 - 68752091

WeChat Official Account: whu_riel

The Center for Economic Development Research (CEDR) of Wuhan University

Founded in 1990, the Center for Economic Development Research (CEDR) of Wuhan University is a think tank incorporating functions of theoretical research, policy analysis and teaching. It is supported by the four national key disciplines in economics of Wuhan University and a group of eminent economic scholars in and out of Wuhan University. It was granted as a key research base on humanities and social sciences by the Ministry of Education in 2000. Bearing the goal of gathering and fostering innovative talents and enhancing innovation capability in teaching, research and consulting, CEDR has been striving to develop economics that keeps up with the step of time and enjoys Chinese characteristics to transform China's economic development into theories and communicate them with the rest of the world. Efforts are being made to become a well-known top-notch academic platform at home and abroad as well as a think tank with social influence, so as to contribute its wisdom to the economic development of China.

Center for Studies of Media Development (CSMD), Wuhan University

Center for Studies of Media Development (CSMD) of Wuhan University is a research base on humanities and social sciences granted by the Ministry of Education with 50 research fellows working full-time or part-time. In 2015 and 2016, it won the Outstanding Contribution Award for China's Media Economics Study and earned the fame as a research center with innovation and vitality. CSMD has been fathoming into the communication pattern of Internet and China's communication innovation, conducting in-depth investigation and research on China's communication innovation practice. Many of its reports have been adopted by CPC as well as provincial and ministerial government agencies. On the relentless quest of exploring into China's communication innovation and social development, it has launched a number of exchange platforms, including International Conference on Intercultural Communication (ICIC), Comparative Communication Study International Symposium, Forum on Communication Innovation in China, Sino-Swedish Cross-Cultural Communication Summer Camp, etc; its has been publishing *Annual Report on China's Communication Innovation* (Blue Book) and *Research Report of China's Media Development*, as well as book series of Cross-Cultural Communication and the Problems and Methods in Journalism and Communication.

Center for Social Security Studies (CSSS) of Wuhan University

Center for Social Security Studies (CSSS) of Wuhan University is a key research institute on humanities and social sciences directly affiliated to the Ministry of Education. It is home to the only national key discipline for social security and is a national innovation base for social security research. The Center currently has 71 researchers working full-time or part-time with an annual funding of more than four million yuan. In recent years, more than 100 advisory reports it submitted have been adopted by government departments of all levels, some of which have been approved by national leaders. Collaborating with Social Security Bureaus, it annually compiles *Reform and Development of Social Security Report* and holds news conference for achievements of the year. In 2015, the Center was ranked fifth among the 151 evaluated key research bases on humanities and social sciences granted by the Ministry of Education in terms of decision-making support. In 2017, it joined the Alliance of High-End University Think Tank.

Website: http://csss.whu.edu.cn

Email: csss6@sina.com

Tel: 027 - 68752238; 027 - 68755887

Institute of the "Belt and Road" Pilot Free Trade Zone, Xi'an Jiaotong University

XJTU Institute of the "Belt and Road" Pilot Free Trade Zone, established in March 2017, is presided by the Dean who reports to the university commission. It is composed of three research centers for service trade, government governance and innovation, and legal governance respectively, where postdoctoral researchers are admitted.

With an annual budget of over 11 million yuan, the Institute has undertaken a total of 50 research projects and produced research reports of over one million words. More than 60% of the *Decision-Making Advice* it submitted have been approved and eight issues of the *Voice of Institute of Free Trade Zone* have been compiled and published. Apart from more than one hundred reform symposiums and expert consultations, the Institute has also held serial activities such as the Free Trade Zone

Innovation and Development (Xi'an) Summit Meeting that was reported and reprinted by people.cn, Xinhua Net and other mainstream media. In the process of turning academic papers to policy documents issued by the government, the Institute is transforming its advantage in knowledge into those in strategy, tactics and policy, so that it can contribute more in social service.

Website: http://skc-zm.xjtu.edu.cn/

Email: xjtu_zmy@163.com

Tel: 029 - 82663967

Center for Collaborative Innovation in the Heritage and Development of Xizang Culture, Xizang Minzu University

Center for Collaborative Innovation in the Heritage and Development of Xizang Culture was granted as an autonomous-region-level prioritized project of "2011 Collaborative Innovation Plan" by Tibet Autonomous Region in April 2013 and was granted as one of the first batch of province-ministry co-built collaboration centers by the Ministry of Education in December 2018.

Committed to Tibet issues, cooperation, innovation and social service, the Center delves into the innovation development and innovation projects of Tibet. It has been conducting researches on the most urgent and realistic problems confronting the social and economic development of Tibet; along with its endeavor in transforming research findings to real-life changes, the Center gives full play to its role of a university think tank and consultation agency. The Center has published over 100 research findings, among which six were approved by the national leaders and 50 were adopted by National Ethic Affairs Commission, Tibet Autonomous Region and other departments.

Website: http://www.xzmy.edu.cn/xtcx/

Tel: 029 - 33755894

Email: xzmyxietong@sina.com

Survey and Research Center for China Household Finance of Southwestern University of Finance and Economics

Established in 2010, Survey and Research Center for China Household Finance is a commonweal university think tank that integrates data collection, data research and policy research. It contains three databases of family finance, small and micro enterprises and urban and rural community governance in China and provides support for academic research and policy making in related issues, for which it enjoys a high reputation at home and abroad. The Center actively conducts research on income distribution, family finance, rural development, real estate and urbanization and urban and rural governance, and has made significant headway in the construction of think tanks, policy proposal and social services. Moreover, it is one of the bases for introducing overseas expertise for innovation in humanities and social sciences of the "Overseas Expertise Introduction Project for Discipline Innovation". ("111 Project")

Website: http://chfs.swufe.edu.cn/

Tel: 028 - 87352163

Email: pr@chfs.cn

Center for Higher Education Development of Xiamen University

Center for Higher Education Development of Xiamen University, founded in the January of 2000, is the only major research base on humanities and social sciences granted by the Ministry of Education that focuses on higher education study. Featuring higher education study, abiding by the principle to serve the country's major demand, CHE has long dedicated itself to the research and consultation of national education policy and has gained groundbreaking academic achievements in the studies on the basic theories of higher education, higher education examination, higher education system and management. With its policy advice for the planning and design of national higher education strategy, the formulation of college entrance examination reform, and the promotion of higher education quality, the Center has become a crucial think tank for the decision-making of China's higher education.

Website: https://che.xmu.edu.cn/

Email: xmdxgjzx@xmu.edu.cn

Tel: 0592-2187552

Institute of Korean Peninsula Studies, Yanbian University

Institute of Korean Peninsula Studies (IKPS), established in the November of 2014, consists of two research centers, namely Center for North and South Korea Studies of Yanbian University, which is one of the key research institutes on humanities and social sciences granted by the Ministry of Education, and Asia Research Center that is jointly established by Yanbian University and the Korea Foundation for Advanced Studies (KFAS).

Yanbian University is the only university in China that conducts an all-round Korean Peninsula studies in a wide variety of disciplines and fields including politics, economy, law, history, language and literature, education, and art. Taking full advantage of its comprehensive disciplines and geographical features, IKPS has maintained extensive academic exchanges with well-known universities and academic institutes at home and abroad, such as Chinese Academy of Social Sciences (CASS), Jinlin University, Kim Il-Sung University, Seoul National University and Waseda University, realizing cooperative researches, personnel exchange as well as documentation and information sharing.

Think Tank of Coastal Development, Yancheng Teachers University

Think Tank of Coastal Development (TTCD), founded in 2007, is listed among the prioritized think tanks of Jiangsu Province. It has 35 research fellows among whom 22 are professor-level researchers. The mission of TTCD is to study the major theoretical and practical issues of the development of Jiangsu Province and other costal areas and to serve for the scientific decision of CPC Jiangsu Provincial Committee, Jiangsu Provincial government, as well as the CPC municipal committees and municipal governments of other costal cities. Since its inception, it has released over 100 research findings for decision-making, among which four were approved by the Party and state's leaders and 15 were approved by provincial leaders. TTCD holds outshining consultation competency on coastal development in Jiangsu Province with six research findings published on *Think Tank Proceeding* issued by the Jiangsu Provincial Think Tank Office and five findings published on *Reference for Decision-Making* issued by Jiangsu Federation of Philosophy and Social Sciences.

Tel: 0515 - 88233887

Fax: 0515 - 88213020

Email: jsyhkf@163.com

Frontier Ethnic Problems Think-Tank of Yunnan University

Frontier Ethnic Problems Think-Tank of Yunnan University is led by the

Research Center for Ethnic Minority on Southeastern Frontier of Yunnan University and co-built by seven universities located on the China's terrestrial frontier. It has an annual funding of 2. 4 million yuan. Adhering to free will, equality, cooperation, complementary advantages, mutual benefit and common development, it is developing itself into a think tank for ethnic issues in China that strives for national solidarity and Chinese national community. The think tank conducts field investigations every year, produces the *Report on China's Frontier Ethnic Development*, builds China's Frontier Ethnic Work Case Library, and compiles *China Frontier Ethnic Issues Advisory Report*—20 high-quality advisory reports have been submitted. It has held China Frontier Ethnic Think Tank Forum in Kunming, Hohhot and Nanning respectively.

Email: cber_7@163.com;

Tel: (0871) 65031748

Center for China's Neighbor Diplomacy Studies (CCNDS), Yunnan University

Center for China's Neighbor Diplomacy Studies (CCNDS) of Yunnan University is one of the first batch of university think tanks of Yunnan Province and was ranked first in the provincial assessment of think tanks in 2016. There are currently about 20 research fellows in the Center, among whom 12 are professors (researchers) and seven are associate professors (associate researchers). CCNDS has undertaken four major projects granted by National Social Science Fund of China and two major projects granted by the Ministry of Education. Two of the consultation reports submitted by the Center have been approved by leaders of the central government and one was selected into the *Special Issue for Think Tanks* released by the Ministry of Education. It not only hosts collective papers named *Regional Research of Yunnan*

University and an internal journal called *Key Reports on Neighbors*, but also publishes *Research Book Series* and *Think Tank Report Series*, as well as the annually-released *Report on the Development of the Lancang-Mekong Cooperation* and *Report on Myanmar's National Situation*.

Fax: +86 - 871 - 65033130; 65034082

Email: ccnds@ynu.edu.cn

WeChat Official Account: CCNDS_YNU

Website: http://www.ccnds.ynu.edu.cn

Institute of China's Science, Technology and Education Policy of Zhejiang University

Institute of China's Science, Technology and Education Policy of Zhejiang University focuses on three distinctive research fields of strength, including engineering education, innovation in science, technology and education and research of colleges and universities, and it provides strategic advisory services for national and regional innovation and development. Currently, the Institute is equipped with 15 professors, 10 associate professors and lecturers, and a number of well-known think tank consultants at home and abroad.

Over the past five years, the Institute has undertaken 8 projects from the National Natural Science Foundation of China, 2 projects from the National Social Science Fund of China, 30 projects from such national ministries and commissions as the Ministry of Education, the Academy of Engineering and the Ministry of Science and Technology, and has provided over 100 high-quality consultation reports. It has established a wide network of international cooperation and holds international seminar on the development of science, technology and education policy annually for in-depth exchanges with scholars at home and abroad on hot issues of science, technology and education policy and engineering education in the frontier. So far, the seminar has been successfully held for five years.

Website: http://www.icstep.zju.edu.cn/

Email: icstep@zju.edu.cn

Tel: 0571 - 88981232

China Academy for Rural Development of Zhejiang University

China Academy for Rural Development of Zhejiang University (CARD) is one of the first national key bases for humanities and social sciences research approved by the Ministry of Education as well as the base for humanities and social sciences innovation of the national "985 Project". The core discipline of the CARD—"Management of Agriculture and Forestry Economy" got "A +" in the fourth round of national discipline evaluation, and was listed as a national "first-class" discipline.

Adhering to the idea of "based on Zhejiang, serving the country, going global", CARD combines theoretical research with the development and reform of China's agriculture, rural areas and farmers and actively provides consultation and suggestions for policymaking. It has put forward a series of innovative, forward-looking and operable policymaking reports on rural reform and development, more than 100 of which have received approval and comments from leaders at the national and provincial/ministerial levels and given full play to the role of a top think tank in serving agriculture, rural areas and farmers.

China Academy of West Region Development, Zhejiang University

Established in October 2006, China Academy of West Region Development

(CAWD) is a high-end think tank of China and a key new-type specialized think tank of Zhejiang Province.

Revolving around critical issues concerning the Great Western Development Strategy, the Belt and Road Initiative and regional coordinated development, CAWD has narrowed its research areas to the interplay between regional coordinated development and regional economic cooperation, humanized policy-making and ecology civilization construction, and focused its decision-making support on international regulation and risk control as well as data repository and policy evaluation. CAWD has submitted a number of key advisory reports that were approved by state's leaders, has been involved in drafting a series of major documents of the Central Committee of CPC and the State Council, and has completed more than 10 strategic plans issued or approved by the State Council.

Address: Building for China Academy of West Region Development, Zhejiang University (Zijingang Campus), Hangzhou, Zhejiang, China

Website: http://www.cawd.zju.edu.cn/

Tel: 0571 - 88981422

Institute of African Studies, Zhejiang Normal University (IASZNU)

Institute of African Studies of Zhejiang Normal University (IASZNU), founded in September 2007, is the first comprehensive institute specializing in African studies among China's universities. It is also a think tank integrating the functions of academic research, personnel training, policy consultation and international exchanges. So far, the Institute has undertaken 19 research projects sponsored by the National Social Science Fund of China and over 80 research projects commissioned by the Ministry of Education, the Ministry of Foreign Affairs and a variety of international cooperation projects. Among China's higher-learning institutions, IASZNU is the first institute to have founded the African Museum, Translation Center for African Studies, African Literature Library and Professional Database for African Studies, as well as a think tank website in five languages. The China-Africa Think Tanks Forum (CATTF) it founded in 2011 has become an influential high-end platform for China-Africa humanities exchanges and public diplomacy. Revolving around national strategy, the Institute has submitted a profusion of advisory reports based on in-depth investigation and research on Africa, among which several policy recommendations have been accepted or adopted by the state's leaders. As of now, IASZNU has become a center for public opinion guidance and public diplomacy serving China's African affairs.

Website: http://ias.zjnu.cn

Email: ias@zjnu.cn

Tel: 0579 - 82287076

China Business Working Capital Management Research Center, Ocean University of China

China Business Working Capital Management Research Center (CMTTC) was co-built by Ocean University of China and Accounting Society of China in the October of 2009. Supported by the Capital Efficiency and Financial Risk Analysis System developed by itself, CMTTC has been conducting investigation on the working capital management of listed companies in China, compiling and publishing *Annual Report on the Development of Working Capital Management*, as well as hosting Summit of Capital Management Think Tank of China and expanding Data Platform (http://cmttc.ouc.edu.cn/data). It serves as a think tank, literature library, information database and case pool in the field of capital management in China. Its research results have been accepted and adopted by renowned enterprises such as China National Petroleum Corporation (CNPC) and have won over 20 national, ministerial and provincial awards for its teaching and scientific researches.

National Academy of Development and Strategy, Renmin University of China

National Academy of Development and Strategy (NADS) was officially established in 2013 and was selected into the first batch of pilot China High-End Think Tanks in 2015. It is an independent nonprofit research entity integrating quality think tank research resources of Renmin University of China (RUC) that strives for mechanism and system innovations under the guidance of President Xi Jinping's governing thoughts. Following the research framework of the strategic blueprint of "Four Comprehensiveness", specializing in the study of modernized national governance, the Academy sticks to the goal of "national strategy, global vision, decision-making consultation, public opinion guidance", focuses on knowledge innovation and global future, strives to become a new-type Chinese think tank with international influence, and serves for national development strategy and social progress.

Tel: 010 - 62515049/0329

Website: http://nads.ruc.edu.cn

Email: nads_ruc@126.com (for administration);

nads04@ruc.edu.cn (for media)

Chongyang Institute for Financial Studies (RDCY), Renmin University of China

Chongyang Institute for Financial Studies (RDCY) of Renmin University of China was established on January 19th, 2013. It is the main program supported by an education fund from Mr Qiu Guogen, an alumni of Renmin University of China, and now the chairman of Shanghai Chongyang Investment Group Co., Ltd. As a new-style think tank with Chinese characteristics, it has invited dozens of former politicians, bankers, and preeminent scholars from over 10 countries as senior fellows, endeavoring to tackle social issues, provide suggestions and serve the people. At present, RDCY consists of seven departments and runs three research centers (the Center for Eco-Financial Studies, Global Governance Research Center, and the China-US People-to-People Exchange Research Center). The Institute has been highly recognized at home and abroad in financial development, global governance, relations among great powers, and macro policy studies.

Tel: 8610 - 62516805

Email: rdcy-info@ruc.edu.cn

Website: http://www.rdcy.org

Sina Weibo: @人大重阳 (RDCY)

WeChat Official Account: rdcy2013

Center for Capital Social Safety of People's Public Security University of China

Center for Capital Social Safety is one of the first bases for philosophy and social sciences research in Beijing. It is managed by the School of Public Order of People's

Public Security University of China, with over 40 full-time and part-time researchers and an annual research funding of more than 1.5 million yuan.

In recent years, the center has undertaken a series of major national issues in the field of social security, including projects of National Key R & D Program of China, major projects of the National Social Science Fund of China, and key philosophy and social sciences research projects of the Ministry of Education, of which such research achievements as "UAV control", "crime crackdown" and "subway anti-terrorism" have been commented by leaders at the national or provincial/ministerial levels. It published the blue book *Safe Beijing*, held the Forum on Capital Social Security, participated in the legislation of social security, formulated the security plan for Beijing-Zhangjiakou Winter Olympic Games in 2022, and worked out plans for the public security prevention and control system in Hainan, Wuhan, Dongguan, Karamay and other places. It has given full play to the role of a think tank.

Website: http://ccss.ppsuc.edu.cn/

Email: CCSS2004@126.com

Tel: 010 - 83903413

Collaborative Innovation Center of Industrial Upgrading and Regional Finance (Hubei)

Collaborative Innovation Center of Industrial Upgrading and Regional Finance (Hubei), founded in 2014, is one of the 15 second batch of Hubei collaborative innovation centers granted by Hubei's Innovation Development Plan for Project Institutions of Higher Education. It is also the first approved provincial collaborative innovation center of Zhongnan University of Economics and Law that studies regional development. Serving as a think tank, idea reservoir information base and talent pool for industry upgrading and regional finance, it mainly conducts researches on financial policy, industrial policy, market policy and so on with seven affiliates and 14 directly affiliated institutes. Since 2015, one of the Center's research achievements has been awarded with a national award while a number of others won provincial and ministerial awards.

Tel: 027 - 88386955

Email: chtl@zuel.edu.cn

The Co-Innovation Center for Social Management of Urban and Rural Communities in Hubei Province

The Co-Innovation Center for Social Management of Urban and Rural Communities in Hubei Province, founded in 2012, is a reformed think tank granted by CPC Hubei Provincial Committee and a research base for China's civil affairs policy granted by the Ministry of Civil Affairs. It has a provincial financial subsidy of three million yuan and an office space of over 400 square meters. The five research platforms of this Center studies social construction and social governance, ecological governance and green development, employment & entrepreneurship and social security, revitalization of rural areas and precision poverty alleviation, health and medical reform respectively.

The Center's efforts in fostering ecological citizenship has been commended by General Secretary Xi Jinping; its advisory reports have been approved by the national leaders and provincial leaders of Hubei; its research achievements have been awarded as outstanding, first-prized or second-prized consultation respectively on provincial and ministerial level.

Website: http://www.smjic.org

Tel: 027 - 88387563

Center for the Development of Rule of Law and Judicial Reform Research of Zhongnan University of Economics and Law

Center for the Development of Rule of Law and Judicial Reform Research of Zhongnan University of Economics and Law, a think tank specializing in strategic studies of legal development, was founded in November 2011 and currently combined with Hubei Institute for Strategic Studies of Legal Development. The Center was selected as the first research base for rule of law by China Law Society in 2015, a research base for applied theory research by the Supreme People's Procuratorate of PRC, and a key research base of humanities and social sciences in Hubei Province. Enjoying a high starting point, attaching great importance to progress, collaboration and system-building, it strives to provide the country with talents for social governance and rule of law and provide high-quality consulting services for the legislation and decision-making of central and local governments. It has also progressed by leaps and bounds in developing an academic system, discourse system, communication system and personnel training for social governance and rule of law by means of collaborative innovation and platforms such as Society with Rule of Law, Yangtze River Forum, Lecture on China's Rule of Law and 1000 Decision-Maker Service Plan of Action.

Center for Studies of Intellectual Property Rights, Zhongnan University of Economics and Law

Ten years since its establishment, the Center has been striving to solve problems, innovate theories, build a think tank and serve the society with the goal of building itself into a preeminent center at home and abroad. On the quest of developing a national think tank for intellectual property rights, it has set up a number of high-end research platforms for an all-round and collaborative innovation.

The Center has a research team composed of advanced talents well-structured in academic backgrounds and ages. It has undertaken more than 260 research projects commissioned by National Research Projects on Major Issues and Major Decisions, National Natural Science Foundation of China and National Social Sciences Fund of China. It has published more than 600 high-level academic papers in domestic and overseas journals such as *Social Sciences in China*, *Chinese Journal of Law*, *China Legal Science* and established key academic platforms such as the Nanhu Forum on Intellectual Property, contributing greatly to constructing China's intellectual property system.

China's Income Distribution Research Center (CIDRC)

China's Income Distribution Research Center (CIDRC) was founded in the November of 2010 aiming to develop into a world-class income distribution research center and a cradle for innovative talents, so as to carry out in-depth researches on the practice and theory of income distribution in China. CIDRC has held a number of international academic conferences and established cooperative relationships with many foreign universities. Since its inception, it has published many high-quality research findings, many of which have been reprinted by journals like *Chinese Social Sciences Digest* after their initial publishing and many others have won national and provincial awards. Research reports submitted by CIDRC have been approved and adopted by major provincial and ministerial leaders which cast positive influence on the society.

Tel: 027-88986475

Email: sunqunli@sina.com

Intellectual Property Research Institute of Central South University

The Institute of Intellectual Property of Central South University (IPRICSU) was established in 2011. It was jointly established by Central South University and Hunan Provincial Intellectual Property Office. It has the characteristics of "strategy, synergy and sharing" and has built a think tank operation mode of "college + government + enterprise + intermediary". It has formed a construction idea of "special characteristics, institutional innovation, leading development, and serving the society." The Institute is a provincial-level key think tank and professional characteristic think tank identified by the Propaganda Department of Hunan Provincial Party Committee. It is also the key research base of philosophy and social sciences of Hunan Province and the provincial-level Haizhi base of Hunan Science and Technology Association.

In 2013, the Institute became the national key link mechanism for patent protection; in 2012 and 2015, it was awarded with two advanced collectives for intellectual property talents in the national intellectual property system; in 2018, the Institute was inter-ministerial joint implementation of the intellectual property strategy implementation of the State Council. The conference office was selected as "the advanced collective of national intellectual property strategy implementation".

Email: hnipyiy@126.com

Tel: 0731-88660480

Website: http://law.csu.edu.cn/zscq/

Research Center of Chinese Village Culture, Central South University

Research Center of Chinese Village Culture is the earliest and largest innovation platform in China that revolves around the research and protection of Chinese traditional villages. It has introduced the conservation of Chinese village culture to China's cultural protection strategy, and introduced the research of Chinese village culture into China's humanities research; it's also the first to define "Chinese traditional villages". The Center has been commissioned with over 30 national, provincial and ministerial research projects, hosted a number of major academic activities such as the Chinese Village Culture Conservation Research Forum, and been conducting nationwide large-scale field investigations, the reports of which have been approved by the Party and state's leaders. Apart from the first *Blue Book of Chinese Traditional Villages* in China, the Center has also yielded a number of research achievements that were either listed as one of the Eight CTTI Outstanding Think Tank Achievements, or awarded with the First Prize of CTTI-BPA Think Tank Best Research Report and Top Ten Consultation of Hunan Think Tank Research.

Website: http://village.csu.edu.cn/

Email: village@csu.edu.cn

Tel: 0731-88877027

Institute of Guangdong, Hong Kong and Macao Development Studies, Sun Yat-Sen University

Institute of Guangdong, Hong Kong and Macao Development Studies of Sun Yat-Sen University, founded in 2015, is one of the first batch of national high-end pilot think tanks. The Institute consists of seven research centers, namely, Research

Center for One Country & Two Systems and Hong Kong and Macao Basic Law, Research Center for Hong Kong and Macao Political and Public Governance, Research Center for the Economy of Hong Kong and Macao, Research Center for Hong Kong and Macao Society, Research Center for the History, Culture and Values of Hong Kong and Macao, Research Center for the Cooperation between Hong Kong, Macao and Mainland China, as well as Research Center for Maritime Silk Road and Guangdong-HK-Macao International Cooperation. Focusing on major issues of the development and governance of Hong Kong and Macao as well as Guangdong-HK-Macao cooperation, the Institute strives to facilitate major decision-making of the Party and the government. The Institute has also established the Guangdong, Hong Kong and Macao Archives and Documentation Center, the Guangdong, Hong Kong and Macao Research Data Platform, and a number of thematic tracking databases on the economy and society of Hong Kong and Macao.

Website: http://ygafz.sysu.edu.cn

2017"CTTI智库最佳实践奖"评选活动报告

前 言

近年来,我国新型智库建设迎来了前所未有的发展机遇,也取得了一系列令人瞩目的成绩。无论是在智库研究、咨询实务,还是智库管理方面都涌现出了许多值得推广的典型。为宣传推广我国各级各类智库在研究、活动和管理方面的创新经验与独到做法,提升我国智库研究咨询和管理水平,推动新时代中国特色新型智库健康发展,南京大学中国智库研究与评价中心、光明日报智库研究与发布中心以"中国智库索引"(CTTI)数据为基础,开展2017年度"CTTI-BPA智库最佳实践奖"(以下简称"BPA三大奖")评选活动,以奖励和推广各级各类智库在研究咨询实务和管理方面的创新经验、独到做法。

1 智库最佳实践案例评选活动源起

1.1 最佳实践

最佳实践(Best Practice,BP)这一概念源于管理学领域,即"认为存在某种技术、方法、过程、活动或机制,可以使生产或管理时间的结果达到最优"。这一概念在软件设计、环境管理、人力资源管理、图书信息处理、公共政策分析等各个领域都有着广泛应用。

在企业管理中,最佳实践是指那些公认可以持续产生出色成果、并适用于不同情况的最佳做法。它是标杆管理的核心内容之一,是企业实现科学管理的关键所在。标杆管理(benchmarking),又称基准管理,是美国施乐公司于1979年首创的现代企业管理方法,与企业再造、战略联盟一起被西方管理学界并称为20世纪90年代三大管理方法。20世纪70年代末80年代初，一直保持着世界复印机市场垄断地位的美国施乐公司遭到了来自国内外尤其是日本的全方位挑战，市场份额锐减。为走出这一困境，施乐公司开始向日本企业学习，通过对比分析寻找差距，调整经营策略并重组流程，开展了广泛而深入的标杆管理，最终取得了优秀业绩。此后施乐公司开始大范围推广标杆管理法，选择同行业公司进行考察，通过对比找出自身症结所在，再采取相应解决措施。鉴于施乐公司的成功经验，IBM、杜邦、通用等公司纷纷效仿，寻找同行业内拥有管理方面最佳实践的公司，对标找差，优化企业实践。

具体来说，标杆管理就是企业将自身的产品、服务、生产流程等要素与行业中的领袖型企业进行比较，借鉴他人先进经验，改善自身不足，从而提高企业经营管理水平和核心竞争力。后来，美国生产力与质量中心对这一概念进行了系统化和规范化：标杆管理法是一个系统的、持续性的评估过程，通过不断地将企业流程与世界上居于领先地位的企业相比较，以获得帮助企业改善经营绩效的信息。

标杆管理的本质是一种面向实践、面向过程、以方法为主的管理方式，其基本思想就是系统优化、不断完善与持续改进，简单来说就是一个模仿、学习和创新的过程。这一过程中，作为"标杆"的"最佳实践"就尤为重要。如今标杆管理方法已经在各个领域得到了广泛应用，各行各业纷纷寻找本行业范围内的最佳实践，从中萃取先进工作经验并在本行业内宣传推广，从而促进行业共同进步。

图书馆领域使用"最佳管理"概念十分频繁。例如美国图书馆协会（ALA）的作用之一便是"制定各种标准与最佳实践模式"，协会及其分支机构会收集行业内典型项目与优秀案例，并进行系统整理，从中总结提炼出最佳做法，编制最佳实践指南加以推广，具体成果包括《信息素质计划最佳实践特征：指导方针》《研究图书馆协会EAD最佳实践指南》等。此外，ALA颁发的一系列专业认可奖中，就包括"学术/研究型图书馆最佳营销实践奖"，授予那些在市场营销方面拥有最佳实践的图书馆。

在医疗卫生领域，最佳实践的概念也得到了广泛使用。美国疾病预防控制中心（CDC）对于本领域内的最佳实践下了定义：最佳实践是为提高健康效果，使其产生公共卫生影响、符合证据质量项目实施的过程,并经过一系列同行反复评议取得最佳精确水平的实施结果。CDC 的做法是召集各级各地机构的流行病学、行为科学、项目设计与管理、评价及政策制定等领域的科学家、从业者、研究员、资金提供者和评价专家等相关人员,针对本领域内卫生问题,应用最佳实践的标准和不同类型的实践方法进行评议。这些专家先通过讨论将相关知识归类,再从多方面、多层次、不同等级开展持续性的评价和量化分析,并进行深入的对话交流,最终形成一个个最佳实践理论的案例模型,用于指导提高公共卫生项目实施的效果。

1.2 智库最佳实践

1.2.1 OTT 智库最佳实践系列

全球最大的智库专业网站 OTT(onthinktanks.org)2010 年成立于英国,旨在帮助智库以一种更具战略性的方式制定短期与长期决策。作为一个集合智库相关研究资源的数字平台,OTT 汇集了世界各地智库相关的最新数据、研究、分析、资源与特色,当前已成为全球政策研究领域的著名网站之一,为智库研究提供了大量服务、活动以及知识支撑。

2017 年,OTT 网站上发布了一个"OTT 最佳实践系列(OTT Best Practice Series)",其中包含了一系列智库最佳实践的相关介绍。系列内的每篇文章都根据不同的智库实践设立了不同主题,并以各种方式处理了信度问题,旨在通过这些管理、沟通、治理方面的最佳实践帮助智库提高声誉、提升效率与效益。

"OTT 最佳实践系列"认为,智库最佳实践是一种明确有效的任务执行方式,因为这些实践产生于那些业内公认的优秀智库中,且取得了良好成效。作者基于自身在智库研究领域的丰富经验,提炼了多个特定问题的实际策略与工作流程,并鼓励读者根据具体的使用环境进行调整。这一系列目前已经累积了 9 类最佳实践:智库研究项目文件与数据归档的最佳实践;智库研究人员招聘的最佳实践;资助者在资助智库方面的最佳财务实践;构建员工场外培训;智库研究项目管理顾问;智库的创新筹款策略;智库研究项目的成本监督;激励研究人员的专业发展基金;更大的政策影响力——智库项目结束后的跟踪交流。

1.2.2 智库最佳实践的内涵

从上述众多案例中可以看出,"最佳实践"可以是一项技能、一个方法、一种机制等。通过分析各行业对于"最佳实践"的定义,结合我国本土语境与智库发展状况,在此将智库最佳实践定义为:智库通过自我评估把人、财、物和项目管理等方面做事的最佳方式和最佳事项总结出来,形成组织管理的标杆案例。这些案例是智库管理活动成果的总结和提炼,具有较强的推广价值。但需要说明的是,智库最佳实践并非是绝对不变、放之四海而皆准的,对于不同类型、不同性质的智库来说,最佳实践的内涵也不尽相同。这些最佳实践只是给出了一个可供参考的标准,不同智库可以据此对标找差,结合自身战略规划与发展环境,实施适合本机构的最优方案。

1.2.3 智库最佳实践的要素

智库最佳实践的要素之一是来源。最佳实践必然是智库在日常运营管理过程中积极探索、不断尝试形成的,因而作为最佳实践的来源——智库本身,至关重要。首先智库工作者需要有主动性,在日常工作中不断思考、勇于实践,努力探索更优方案;其次智库的行动需要有目的性,无论是内部治理还是成果产出,都要秉持问题导向与目标导向的实事求是精神,在此基础上协调各方资源,集思广益;最后这些工作需要有持久性,即在实践过程中注重积累,详细记录例如管理心得、活动举办流程等内容,最大程度上使智库内部的隐性知识转化为其他机构都能够理解、更易传播的显性知识。

智库最佳实践的要素之二是主体。智库最佳实践具体表现为一份卓有成效的研究成果、一场极具影响力的活动,或是一项产生效用的管理方案等,而这些内容正是在智库实际运行管理过程中积累起来的。所以智库最佳实践的主体便是这些已被证明产生实际效用的经验总结。这些经验主要以两种形式存在,一种是存在于智库员工、专家头脑中的隐性知识,这些知识产生于长期的实践经验且依赖人的主观开发与认知,例如某位专家的研究报告撰写技巧。另一种是以书面形式存在的显性知识,这些知识产生于对本机构工作方法的总结与固化,包括智库的科研成果评价考核体系、新型人事管理制度等。

智库最佳实践的要素之三是过程。最佳实践中隐性与显性知识并存,这决定了智库最佳实践的提炼和传递过程都至关重要。最佳实践中隐性知识的提炼需要经历自我评估、自我总结、自我提炼等一系列过程;最佳实践的传递则需要有宣讲、交流、学习、付诸实施等过程。需要注意的是,最佳实践的学习过程具有互动性和动态性。动态性是指最佳实践的学习过程并非照本宣科,各类智库需要从自身实际出发,在反复学习、实践中探索出适合本机构的最佳方案。互动性是指最佳实践的传递需要通过交流沟通来达成更好的学习效果,传授者与学习者需要有机会面对面沟通交流,不但学习文字中的显性知识,而且交流头脑中的隐性知识。这也是我们在评选出 BPA 三大奖后召开智库最佳实践案例发布会的重要缘由。

1.3 中国智库需要寻觅适合自身发展的"最佳实践"

1.3.1 新型智库建设呼唤"最佳实践"

2015 年 1 月 20 日,中办和国办正式印发《关于加强中国特色新型智库建设的意见》,开启了新型智库发展的历史新阶段。全国出现了建智库与用智库的热潮,各地智库建设如火如荼。但当前现状与《意见》提出的新型智库建设的定位与目标相比,还存在一定差距,蓬勃发展的背后也隐藏着一系列问题,特别是不同级别、不同类型、不同地域的智库在发展过程中存在巨大差异。

习近平总书记在 2016 年哲学社会科学大会上指出:"近年来,哲学社会科学领域建设智库热情很高,成果也不少,为各级党政部门决策提供了有益帮助。同时,有的智库研究存在重数量、轻质量问题,有的存在重形式传播、轻内容创新问题,还有的流于搭台子、请名人、办论坛等形式主义的做法。"从中可以看出,虽然新型智库建设在推动国家治理体系和治理能力现代化的过程中发挥了积极作用,但也有部分智库被这场建设浪潮裹挟着前行,却始终无法解决发展过程中所面临的根本问题,在财务管理、人员激励、资源整合等方面依然面临很大掣肘。

另一方面,中外智库交流日益频繁,西方智库较为成熟的治理结构与运行机制传入国内,为我国智库的建设发展起到了良好的借鉴作用。然而国内外无论是智库发展的政治、经济、社会环境,还是智库建设的目标定位都不尽相同。我国智库建设不能照搬西方建设经验与发展模式,而是需要一批扎根中国智库本土实践、适应时代发展的中国特色新型智库探索出本土经验,起到带头引领作用。智库发展不平衡的现状迫切呼唤一批具有中国特色、典型的优秀智库"最佳实践",起到标杆与示范作用,带动中国特色新型智库建设整体发展。

1.3.2 新型智库建设过程中涌现"最佳实践"

2015年11月,习近平总书记主持召开中央全面深化改革领导小组第18次会议,审议通过了《国家高端智库建设试点工作方案》,强调要建设一批国家急需、特色鲜明、制度创新、引领发展的高端智库。2015年12月,随着国家高端智库建设试点工作会议召开,"实施国家高端智库建设规划"的宏伟构想迈出了实质性步伐。近些年来,国家高端智库在体制机制上寻求突破,积极探索完善智库内部治理结构与运行模式的新路径,在公共外交、决策咨询、舆论引导等方面都取得了重大进展,发挥的示范引领作用显著。同时,许多省市根据国家高端智库建设模式,开展省内重点智库建设试点,意在结合实际情况与行业特点探索本地区智库建设的新理念、新举措、新模式。在这个过程中,也涌现出了一批在研究、实务与管理方面初见成效的优秀专业智库。这些优秀智库产出了一系列具备前瞻性与针对性、内容创新的高质量研究成果,举办了一批在国内甚至国际产生重要影响力的活动,提供了众多最佳实践案例。

将这些有关深化体制机制改革、优化内部管理流程、提高智库成果质量和咨政能力的成功经验进行总结并加以推广,不仅是中国特色新型智库体系建设的要求,也是部分智库进行品牌宣传、提高自身影响力的需要,更是广大智库学习先进经验、结合自身实际进行对标管理、提高自身发展水平的迫切需求。

1.3.3 "最佳实践"为新型智库研究咨询赋能

一个相对封闭的智库组织的内部能量是有限的,在到达一定阶段后可能将难以满足组织继续发展的需求,此时就需要向外部寻找支援,即获得外部赋能。学习外部的最佳实践、借鉴其他智库的先进管理理念与实践经验,是智库获得外部赋能的一项有效手段。最佳实践案例反映了智库在具体环节中的流程和做法,对其进行剖析能够发现智库如何面对具体问题、通过什么方式来解决这些问题、最终取得了何种成效,从而从中提炼出具有推广价值与实操意义的运营与管理方法。

良好的智库内部运营与管理方法能够促进智库的健康高效运转,这是智库持续产生有竞争力研究成果的必要保障。本次智库最佳实践案例评选共分为最佳研究报告、最佳活动和最佳管理三类奖,其中研究报告是智库成果服务决策的典型代表,活动是智库输出观点、建设品牌与提高影响力的最重要途径,而管理则是智库成果有效产出与活动成功开展的必要支撑。

"他山之石,可以攻玉",智库学习最佳实践的过程,实际上是比较、模仿和创新的过程。将自身的成果产出、活动流程、管理模式等与各类最佳实践进行比较,借鉴其先进经验,重新思考与改进自身经营管理实践,从而提高运作效率,增强创新能力与竞争力,不仅有助于智库个体的进步,也有助于促进智库共同体内部的相互交流,从而推动中国特色新型智库治理体系的完善。

1.4 智库最佳实践案例评选活动的意义

南京大学中国智库研究与评价中心、光明日报智库研究与发布中心此次评选并发布 BPA 三大奖,意在进一步促进智库共同体的发展,发现优秀案例,给予各级各类优秀智库崭露头角的机会,并寄望 BPA 三大奖能够成为促进新型智库实践能力、选拔和表彰优秀智库的重要机制。

此次 BPA 三大奖评选活动的意义有以下几点:第一,通过智库最佳实践评选活动,进一步弘扬求真务实、理论联系实际的实践精神,进一步弘扬问题导向和目标导向的中国特色、中国风格、中国气派的中国智库实事求是精神。第二,通过智库最佳实践评选活动,发挥各智库的主动精神,按照"做中学"的方式,通过自我评估、自我总结、自我提炼贡献最佳案例,发掘发现推广一批能够引领新型智库人、财、物管理和项目管理的典型案例,通过宣传推广促进新型智库管理上的共同进步。第三,智库最佳实践评选本质上是一种标杆管理活动,智库的最佳实践案例评选活动促进了智库之间充分交流,促进了智库间的对标管理,可以较快地提升智库管理水平。

2 CTTI-BPA 最佳实践案例评选回顾

2.1 材料征集与审核

经过前期的论证与筹备环节,南京大学中国智库研究与评价中心和光明日报智库研究与发布中心于 2017 年 11 月发布了"中国智库索引智库最佳实践案例"(CTTI-BPA)评选启事,正式开始征集工作。2017 年度最佳实践案例涵盖 2015 年以来所有的智库成果,申报主体包括 CTTI 来源智库及非来源智库。智库最佳研究报告和最佳实践奖由智库主动申报,最佳管理由各省、自治区、直辖市智库主管部门提名。各机构申报文本需要负责人签字并加盖机构公章,一律通过邮箱提交扫描件,不接受印本。其他证明及辅助材料则需要通过邮寄方式提交纸质版本。

在收到申报材料后,工作人员对每份材料进行了仔细审查,针对其中不合规范或漏填、误填部分通过邮件、电话核实,保证其准确性与规范性。最终将所有申报材料分类、逐一编号,并针对每份申报材料制作专家评审表,为后续评选过程做好充分准备。

2.2 评选过程回顾

为提高奖项评选的科学性与专业性,评选过程本着公平、公正、公开的原则,主要采用专家组同行评议方法。专家组由智库负责人、智库主管机关领导和智库研究界专家组成。整个评选过程定性与定量方法相结合,以"中国智库索引"(CTTI)数据为重要参考依据,针对三类奖项各自特点分别制定了具体评选办法。

最佳研究报告奖和最佳活动奖采取机构主动申报、专家组审阅投票的方式决出入围名单。

最佳报告奖的评选过程中,主要考察参评研究报告的质量与影响力。报告的质量主要关注其针对性、前瞻性、科学性和学理性。高质量的研究报告必然是智库基于专业的理论基础,采用科学的研究方法、政策分析工具和技术手段,聚焦党和政府、社会民生亟待解决的实际问题而产出的,能够体现智库对所研究问题的整体把控力与科学预见能力。影响力包括报告的政策影响力、学术影响力及社会影响力。政策影响力主要关注研究报告对决策者产生的咨政建言作用;学术影响力考察报告衍生学术成果的学术价值;社会影响力不仅考察报告及其衍生品被各级各类媒体的报告情况,还强调报告所体现的人文关怀、社会责任等内容。

最佳活动奖则基于参评活动的宗旨、目的、方案和具体过程,考察活动的创新性与影响力。活动的创新性既包括活动内容创新,也包括形式创新;影响力不仅包括活动本身的影响力,还包括其衍生产品的影响力。活动的社会影响力除了关注媒体报道情况外,还着重考察活动对于社会热点问题及重大事件的关注度、活动的示范效应以及其中所体现的社会责任与人文关怀。国际影响力则侧重考察活动过程中的国际交流情况、智库在其中发挥的"二轨外交"作用等。

最佳管理奖采用各省市智库主管部门提名,专家组审阅投票形式决出入围名单。这一奖项主要针对被提名智库在管理方面的创新与成效,从组织架构、制度建设、运营管理等维度进行考察,具体包括智库的资金管理、人员管理、成果推广、对外合作等多项内容。力求评选出定位明晰、特征鲜明、机制完备、运作有序的中国特色新型智库。

2.3 评选内容分析

本次评选过程中,来自23个省、自治区、直辖市的智库机构共申报了441个项目,剔除其中不合规范、没有签字盖章的申报书,正式申报书共416份。其中"最佳研究报告奖"申报书216份,"最佳活动奖"申报书166份,各省市、自治区、直辖市推荐的"最佳管理奖"申报书34份。过去三年间中国特色新型智库建设的成效便能够在这些类型多样、内容翔实的申报材料中窥见一二:研究报告主题趋于多元化、专业化;智库活动蓬勃开展、品牌效应逐渐成形;体制机制建设有了新突破,涌现出一批在管理方面卓有成效的新型智库。

2.3.1 申报主体类型多样、分布广泛

一是申报主体类型多样，高校智库占主导，其他类型分布均衡。图1、图2、图3分别反映了三类奖项申报主体的类型分布情况。从中可以看出，高校智库在三类奖项的申报总数中分别占63%、74%、77%，数量上占据了绝对优势；此外，党校行政学院智库、社科院智库、科研院所智库等也是此次申报的重要参与者。从整体上看，除高校智库外，其他类型智库分布较为平均，未体现出明显差异。

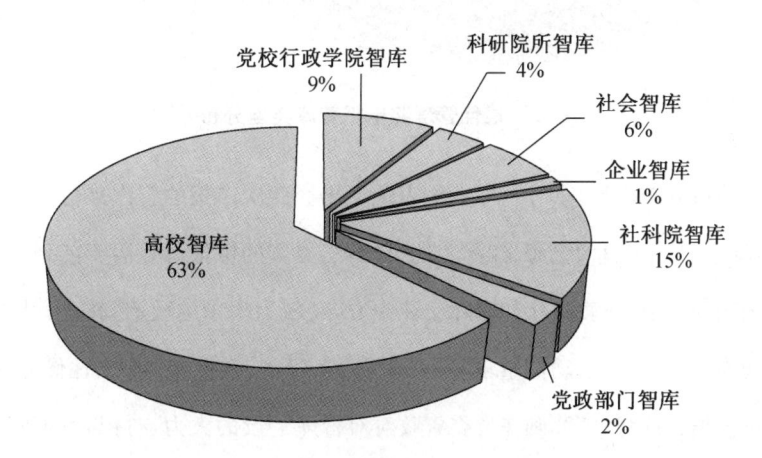

图1 最佳研究报告奖申报智库类型分布

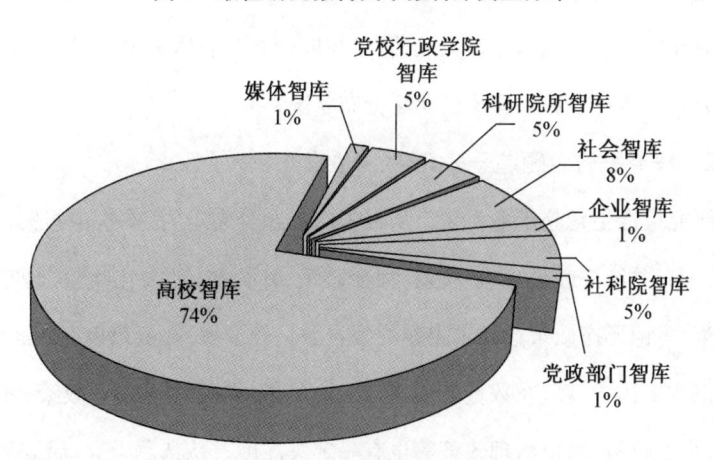

- 党校行政学院智库 9%
- 科研院所智库 4%
- 社会智库 6%
- 企业智库 1%
- 社科院智库 15%
- 党政部门智库 2%
- 高校智库 63%

图2 最佳活动奖申报智库类型分布

- 媒体智库 1%
- 党校行政学院智库 5%
- 科研院所智库 5%
- 社会智库 8%
- 企业智库 1%
- 社科院智库 5%
- 党政部门智库 1%
- 高校智库 74%

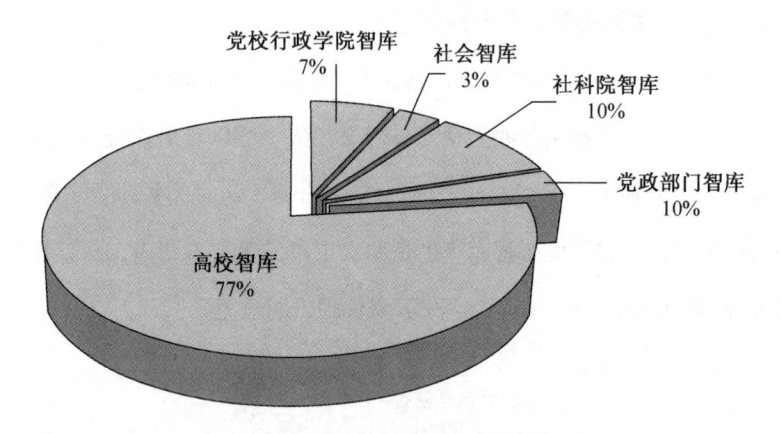

党校行政学院智库 7%
社会智库 3%
社科院智库 10%
党政部门智库 10%
高校智库 77%

图 3　最佳管理奖申报智库类型分布

二是地域分布广泛，京、沪、苏三地表现突出。此次申报的智库来自23个省、自治区、直辖市，其中北京、上海、江苏表现突出，三类奖的申报总数居于前列。其中北京作为全国的政治、科教文化和国际交往中心，有较为集中的政治、教育、科研优势，参选的智库研究报告、活动数量较多；上海凭借其经济、教育与国际交往优势，智库活动的数量占据了优势；江苏则在省委省政府对智库建设的大力支持与各智库的积极响应下，研究报告与智库活动的申报数量也跃居前列。此外，天津、内蒙古、云南、山东等地也对此次申报表现出了极大热情，参与度较高。总体来说，参与申报的智库类型和区域分布基本符合我国智库的实际分布状况。

2.3.2　研究报告主题趋于多元化、专业化

一是研究报告主题趋于多元化。从报告的主题分布上看，本次申报案例涉及32个主题，其中有关经济政策、产业政策、社会政策、外交政策、文化政策、政府治理、企业管理政策、意识形态政策这几个主题的报告数量较多，均在8篇以上。经济政策主题的参选报告多达46篇，在数量上遥遥领先。另外，各智库对农业政策、环境政策、教育政策、金融政策、城市治理政策等也有一定关注度。从选题上看，涵盖了"一带一路"建设、中国经济新常态、精准扶贫、供给侧结构性改革等过去三年中的热点问题。

二是报告主题趋于专业化。研究报告是智库的重要产出之一，其质量及专业化

水平很大程度上会影响智库在决策咨询过程中发挥的作用。此次申报的研究报告大部分都具有极强的专业性，都是立足本专业研究领域，结合党和政府、社会民生亟待解决的实际问题而形成的，具体涉及政治、经济、教育、电力、石油天然气等专业领域。同时，这些专业化的研究报告也是专业型智库核心能力的体现——即调查研究、数据采集与分析、建模计算以及规划评估的能力。例如江南大学食品安全风险治理研究院的系列《中国食品安全发展报告》，以食用农产品生产为起点，综合运用各种统计数据，结合大量的实证调查，研究我国生产、流通、消费等关键环节食品安全性（包括进口食品安全性）的演变轨迹，并对食品安全风险的现实状态与未来走势作出评估，体现了该智库极强的专业性，对客观、公正地反映中国食品安全风险治理体系与治理能力的现代化具有积极的作用。

2.3.3 智库活动蓬勃开展、品牌效应逐渐成形

一是智库活动蓬勃开展，内容丰富。智库活动是智库与各界增强交流，提高自身影响力的重要途径与有效手段。申报的166项活动内容丰富，形式多样，其中论坛和研讨会的数量位居前列，其次是调研、发布会、培训等形式。活动的内容既涉及国家面临的重大战略问题、社会热点问题，也涉及专业领域内的重点问题。智库通过这些活动扩大自身影响力的同时，也力求挖掘形成政策研究成果与产品，为相关领域的发展建言献策。例如全国经济综合竞争力研究中心福建师范大学分中心在服务厦门金砖会晤的活动中，围绕峰会主题和讨论议题，超前部署，深化研究，先后形成了高质量研究报告、一系列专著和文章，产生了积极的社会反响，为厦门会晤发出了"智库声音"，提供了"智库方案"。

二是智库活动形式创新。此次申报过程中，涌现出了一批形式创新、亮点突出的智库活动，这些活动或组织灵活、不受时空限制，或与互联网、新媒体紧密结合，是新型智库在建设过程中敢于创新、积极探索的生动体现。例如，浙江师范大学非洲研究院开展的《我从非洲来》纪录片的拍摄活动，利用影视手段发声，旨在通过智库研究的思想性和针对性，打破国内制作的同类题材在国际上传播力度有限的瓶颈，最终在国

内外都产生了积极反响。还有华东师范大学周边合作与发展协同创新中心分别在华盛顿、莫斯科成立了海外工作室,旨在通过这种形式打破国内外高校和研究机构、学科间的固化壁垒,充分利用国内外优质资源,打造高品质跨国工作平台,探索智库"走出去"的新模式。

三是注重政策传播推广和品牌建设。不少智库定期举办的学术论坛与研讨会,已经形成了品牌效应。这些活动多由智库精心策划,吸引了各界人士参与,进行思想交流与碰撞,逐渐成为本领域内极具影响力的交流合作平台。例如复旦发展研究院申报的"上海论坛",该论坛创始于2005年,迄今已成功举办了12届,是目前在上海举办的最具国际影响力的品牌论坛之一。还有南京师范大学中国法治现代化研究院的"年度十大法治影响力事件"评选发布活动,目前已持续发布了2015、2016、2017三个年度,以《法制日报》和法制网等媒体、网站、自媒体作为活动的发布与传播平台,在学术界、实务界和社会公众中产生了较大影响。

四是推动国际交流,开展二轨外交。深化国际交流与合作、提升国际影响力是中国特色新型智库建设过程中的重要一环。从本次申报材料中可以看出,不少智库特别是国家高端智库积极发挥公共外交的功能,主动开展国际交流活动,特别是在二轨外交中起到了关键作用。例如北京大学国家发展研究院与美国美中关系全国委员会联合主办的"中美经济二轨对话",活动每年举办两次,在纽约与北京交替进行,迄今已成功举办17次。对话成果上报中美两国相关部门,为中美双方政府决策提供参考,帮助两国学界、商界消化两国政府间对话的积极成果,增加两国民间的互相理解和信任。

2.3.4 智库体制机制建设有了新突破

此次报名参评最佳管理奖的智库共34家,其中经济与贸易领域、社会政策领域和综合研究领域的智库数量位居前三。经济与贸易领域主要包括财政、金融、收入分配、产业经济、企业营运、市场消费等研究方向,有9家智库主要从事该领域的相关研究,包括8家高校智库和1家社会智库。社会政策领域主要包括国家治理、社会管理、公共政策、城乡建设、住房、社会保障等研究方向,有5家智库主要从事该领域的相关研究,包括4家高校智库和1家党政部门智库。综合研究领域是指智库同时开展横跨多个领域的决策咨询工作,其中包括3家社科院智库和2家党校行政学院智库。此次被提名的智库均在管理方面积极探索,大胆创新,涌现出不少亮点。

一是完善治理结构,促进资源整合。例如清华大学应急管理研究基地,实行基地主任和首席专家制,设立了由来自各个相关领域专家学者组成的学术委员会,整合了各学科优势资源,同时该智库又重点加强与毕业生的广泛学术合作,形成了"小实体大联合"的超强高端研究团队。二是注重研究平台建设。例如华中师范大学中国农村研究院搭建的智库研究服务平台,充分体现了高度重视调查研究及其数据案例归档管理的特点,把智库的政策分析建立在了扎实的数据和事实基础之上。三是咨询成果转化机制创新。在咨询成果报送上,上海市高校智库研究和管理中心通过开办上海高校智库战略思想沙龙,成功实现了政府需求与专家成果的对接。

2.4 评选结果

2018年4月30日,经过专家在线通讯评审,共有78项申报入围,进入终审环节。5月8日,专家组举行终评会,最终评选出51件"2017CTTI-BPA最佳实践案例"。本着科学合理、数量适度、宁缺毋滥原则,本次评选最后共设立"智库最佳研究报告奖"、"智库最佳活动奖"和"智库最佳管理奖",三类奖分别设特等奖2名、一等奖5名、二等奖10名。表1、表2、表3分别为此次CTTI-BPA三大奖的获奖名单(同等级奖项内排名不分先后)。

表1 智库最佳研究报告奖

成果名称	申报单位	所获奖项
《社会矛盾指数研究》	北京市信访矛盾分析研究中心	特等奖
《重新认识和准确定义新时期我国社会的主要矛盾》	同济大学财经研究所	

（续表）

成果名称	申报单位	所获奖项
《谨防"限价房"变"福利房"和"腐败房"》	长江产业经济研究院（南京大学）	一等奖
系列《中国食品安全发展报告》	江南大学食品安全风险治理研究院	
读懂"一带一路"蓝图——《共建"一带一路"：理念、实践与中国的贡献》详解	中国人民大学重阳金融研究院	
《美欧智库对"一带一路"建设的态度发生积极变化》	中国社会科学院国家全球战略智库	
《中国传统村落蓝皮书·中国传统村落保护调查报告（2017）》	中南大学中国村落文化研究中心	
《独角兽企业发展报告》（系列研究）	北京市长城企业战略研究所	二等奖
《以"精准扶贫"实现"精准脱贫"》	福建社会科学院	
《关于服刑人员未成年子女的生存现状与救助建议的系列研究报告》	华南理工大学社会治理研究中心	
《中国绿色GDP绩效评估报告》	华中科技大学国家治理研究院	
《2016中国地方政府效率研究报告》	江西师范大学管理决策评价研究中心	
《经济发展新常态中的主要矛盾和供给侧结构性改革》	南开大学中国特色社会主义经济建设协同创新中心	
《关于推进丝绸之路经济带实施和区域合作共赢的调研报告》	陕西师范大学西北国土资源研究中心	
《京津沪深综合创新实力比较及对天津建设创新型城市的思考》	天津财经大学金融与保险研究中心	
《发展新一代人工智能面临的十大法律问题》	天津大学中国绿色发展研究院	
《贵州极贫乡镇"极贫"的现象解释与理性思辨——基于20个极贫乡镇调查研究的建议》	中共贵州省委党校贵州行政学院	

表 2 智库最佳活动奖获奖名单

成果名称	申报单位	所获奖项
中美经济二轨对话 & 国家发展论坛	北京大学国家发展研究院	特等奖
上海论坛	复旦发展研究院	
教育智库与教育治理高峰论坛	长江教育研究院	一等奖
当代中国智库服务科学决策的实践探索与路径选择——以福建师范大学竞争力研究中心服务厦门金砖会晤为例	全国经济综合竞争力研究中心福建师范大学分中心	
中国企业全球化论坛	全球化智库(CCG)(北京)	
《我从非洲来》(大型公共外交纪录片六集)	浙江师范大学非洲研究院	
年度中国十大法治影响力事件评选发布	中国法治现代化研究院(南京师范大学)	
出访东欧五国 构筑智库+复合外交政策网络对话机制	东中西部区域发展和改革研究院(北京)	二等奖
APEC背景下的新兴经济体和经济全球化工作坊	海国图智研究院	
中原智库论坛	河南省社会科学院	
设立海外工作室(美国威尔逊国际学者中心、俄罗斯高等经济大学)培养复合型智库精英人才	华东师范大学周边合作与发展协同创新中心	
长江经济带发展论坛	江苏长江经济带研究院	
中蒙俄智库国际论坛	内蒙古自治区发展研究中心	
环境与发展智库论坛	西部资源环境与区域发展智库(中国科学院兰州文献情报中心)	
云南大学对缅甸开展公共外交的创新实践	云南大学周边外交研究中心	
科教发展战略研讨会	浙江大学中国科教战略研究院	
"一带一路"安全研究高层论坛	中国-上海合作组织国际司法交流合作培训基地(上海政法学院)	

表 3　智库最佳管理奖获奖名单

智库名称	所获奖项
华中师范大学中国农村研究院	特等奖
山东社会科学院创新工程	
东南大学中国特色社会主义发展研究院	一等奖
南京大学应急管理研究中心	
清华大学应急管理研究基地	
上海市高校智库研究和管理中心	
云南财经大学印度洋地区研究中心	
北京交通发展研究基地(北京交通大学)	二等奖
重庆大学经略研究院	
重庆市生产力发展中心	
国家知识产权战略实施(天津大学)研究基地	
黑龙江省社会科学院	
湖南师范大学道德文化研究院	
江西师范大学苏区振兴研究院	
南开大学当代中国问题研究院	
陕西宏观经济与经济增长质量协同创新研究中心	
中国科学技术大学科技创新与区域发展研究中心	

2.5　会议回顾

2018年5月19日,2017 CTTI智库最佳实践案例(BPA)发布暨智库评价系统研讨会在南京召开。本次会议由光明日报智库研究与发布中心和南京大学中国智库研究与评价中心联合主办,旨在宣传和推广各级各类智库在研究咨询实务和管理方面的创新经验与独到做法、提升我国智库研究咨询和管理水平、推动新时代中国特色新型智库健康发展。有关省市智库主管领导、2017智库最佳实践案例单位代表、部分CTTI来源智库负责人、系统机构管理员及智库研究与评价领域学者等300余人参会。

光明日报副总编辑陆先高和时任南京大学党委副书记朱庆葆出席会议并发表致辞。复旦大学一带一路及全球治理研究院理事长、上海社科院智库研究中心常务副院长黄仁伟，北京大学国家发展研究院副院长、央行货币政策委员会委员黄益平，美国发展绩效研究所高级研究员雷蒙德·斯特鲁伊克博士，分别作大会主旨报告。

陆先高在致辞中提出："光明日报和南京大学深感智库实践的重要性，组织开展了'智库年度最佳实践奖'评选活动，包括最佳管理、最佳研究报告、最佳活动三个奖项。在此过程中，我们对中国智库体系的建设和组织管理有了日益深切的认识，当前智库应该从运营能力建设、研究能力建设、成果转化能力建设、传播能力建设和协同能力建设五个维度提升总体实力。"

朱庆葆指出："为推动建立具有中国特色和世界影响的中文学术成果和学术机构的评价体系，2017年，南京大学与光明日报在原中国智库索引——CTTI系统的基础上，又投入资源开发了CTTI Plus版，这是一项基于中国优势、凸显中国话语的自主创新，它摆脱了对西方产品的模仿，在设计理念、功能布局、数据采集机制、评价机制等方面都拥有自主知识产权。新系统上线后将有助于捍卫我国哲学社会科学的评价主导权。"

会上举行了2017"CTTI-BPA智库最佳实践案例"颁奖仪式。3大类、51个奖项在与会的智库界近300名专家学者的见证下，隆重揭晓。作为中国特色新型智库建设中涌现出的典型代表，他们用生动的实践证明了中国智库的蓬勃力量与无限生机。

同时，大会还发布了中英文版的《CTTI智库报告（2017）》，光明日报智库研究与发布中心副主任、光明日报智库版主编王斯敏指出，报告发布的"CTTI来源智库目录"是我国第一份用英文向全球发布的全国性智库目录，这将对世界了解中国智库、中国智库走向世界起到积极的促进作用。《CTTI智库报告（2017）》主要由两部分构成，分别是《2017年CTTI来源智库发展报告》和《2017年中国智库网络影响力评价报告》。第一部分《2017年CTTI来源智库发展报告》是针对来源智库整体发展状况的评价分析，首先回顾了中国特色新型智库建设政策议程设置的过程，其次介绍了

CTTI 二期平台和来源智库增补情况，在 2017 年度智库评价中，重点分析了社会智库和高校智库两类智库的 MRPA 测评数据结果。除了对社会智库和高校智库的测评分析，报告另外还分研究领域评价了 8 大类相关智库。第二部分是《2017 年中国智库网络影响力评价报告》。项目于 2017 年 3 月启动，至 2017 年 9 月完成。相较上一年度增加了 163 家智库研究的样本，这些智库样本主要来源于 CTTI，且类型更为复杂，网络表现力更为特殊，因此对智库的识别和异常数据清理显得格外重要。

南京大学中国智库研究与评价中心副主任、首席专家李刚教授主持了 CTTI Plus 系统发布及上线仪式。李刚指出，CTTI Plus 系统包含垂直搜索引擎，并开发了强大的智库信息管理系统，加上菜单式的智能化评价系统，形成了"三位一体"的新系统。同时，提供了云账号的模式。这两种方式使得 CTTI 系统本身可以为各省市的社科管理部门、智库管理部门服务，也可以提供给各高校的社科处管理本校的所有社科研究机构。同时，CTTI Plus 系统具备非常强大的数据管理功能，未来还有望在此系统上增加数据汇缴功能。

在主旨报告环节，上海社科院智库中心理事长黄仁伟总结了国内外智库发展的新趋势，认为中国特色新型智库建设呈现以下新特点：研究领域趋于专业性和专题性；智库向人工智能、大数据和云计算方向发展；智库的国际话语权功能在加强；智库媒体化和媒体智库化趋势明显；大学智库与民间智库蓬勃发展；资金来源正在发生变化，社会资金注入日益增多。北京大学国家发展研究院副院长、央行货币政策委员会委员黄益平结合北京大学国家发展研究院智库建设具体实践，提出独立性、专业性、有效性是智库"立身"的三大关键，强调智库建设的核心问题在于人，在于培养一批有家国情怀、以天下为己任的学者。美国绩效研究所高级研究员雷蒙德·斯特鲁伊克博士介绍了美国智库政策影响力的发展简史，并就人员聘用、质量监控等智库管理研究标准展开分析，指出中国智库在发展阶段应致力于建立良好的社会声誉，努力打造独立客观、技术过硬、政策建议高效的形象。

会议当天下午举行了智库最佳实践案例交流会，会上演示了上午正式上线的

CTTI Plus 新系统功能,并邀请复旦发展研究院、山东社会科学院、同济大学财经研究所、北京市信访矛盾分析研究中心等获奖单位就智库建设亮点、经验进行了介绍与分享。

此次会议更是得到了媒体的广泛关注,光明日报、光明网、新华网、中国社会科学网、扬子晚报等媒体都对会议进行了跟踪报道。

3 CTTI-BPA 最佳实践案例撷英

3.1 研究报告篇

3.1.1 北京市信访矛盾分析中心:《社会矛盾指数研究》——智库实证研究的佳作

北京市信访矛盾分析中心通过对"社会矛盾指数"的探索,构建了评价社会矛盾现状的规范标准,用量化的指标数据反映社会矛盾以及居民应对矛盾的各种行为分布,开启了政府部门量化检测社会矛盾的时代。

2011—2018 年,社会矛盾指数研究已连续开展 8 年,成果共计 100 余万字,年度连续性监测有助于政府站在客观理性的角度上观察社会民生、尊重社会民生与服务社会民生,使政府管理与体制改革更加具有科学性、回应性和前瞻性。

该项研究最大的成功之处在于构建了一个社会矛盾指数指标体系,这一体系包括物质性矛盾和价值性矛盾 2 个一级指标,11 项二级指标,29 项三级指标和 109 个具体问题。矛盾分析中心每年都会据此做公众社会调查,按照社会矛盾指数的基本逻辑框架计算出最终的社会矛盾指数,以此通过量化的指标数据客观地反映出社会矛盾的现状,填补相关领域的空白。除了构建指标之外,这一研究还创新性地引入"社会矛盾缓解机制"的概念,构建了社会矛盾与公共政策研究的关联点,重视从政策源头预防化解社会矛盾。通过对公共政策有效性的持续监测,推动公共政策制定、执行的科学化,从而实现社会矛盾的源头预防。除了物质性、价值性矛盾之外,北京市信访矛盾分析中心还专门针对不同阶段的社会热点问题做了调研报告,便于公众从不同领域和视角了解社会矛盾的现状和趋势,也为相关政府提供更多的决策参考。

从总体上来看,这项社会矛盾指数研究是基于扎实的理论基础与专家指导、在专业的数据支撑下,遵循科学的调研方法形成的,其创新价值在于凸显了对社会矛盾的预警、预测作用,重视从政策源头预防化解社会矛盾,体现了智库研究的战略性与前瞻性,对于新型智库开展基于数据的对策研究,并提高其精准性与实用性具有一定参考价值。

3.1.2 同济大学财经研究所：《重新认识和准确定义新时期我国社会的主要矛盾》——智库研究要抓重大现实问题,突出前瞻性

同济大学财经研究所的石建勋教授于2017年初撰写的报告《重新认识和准确定义新时期我国社会的主要矛盾》通过观察我国改革开放三十多年的快速发展以及时下现状,认为目前党章中关于社会主要矛盾的表述和定义已经很难准确反映现阶段我国社会主要矛盾的实际情况,最终提出我国社会主要矛盾表述的修改建议及修改理由。这一建议被十九大报告起草组参阅,最终被采纳写进了十九大报告。

这一研究报告的成功之处首先是基于对现实的深刻观察和思考。政策是历史的、具体的,应随着历史条件、社会主要问题的变化而转变,体现出历史起承转合的时代感、阶段性。对于社会主要矛盾的重新认识是对新时期我国生产力水平提高,人民日益增长、不断升级和个性化的物质、文化、精神、生态环境改善和社会保障需要的观察和思考。其次是紧跟中央智库建设战略部署,扎实推进服务治国理政咨政建言。从2012年十八大报告提出发挥思想库作用,同济大学即成立校属实体财经研究所。2016年根据中国特色新型智库建设的意见建立了同济大学国家创新发展研究院,把全校智库整合到这一平台,意在希望通过工科思维,将同济的传统优势转化成智库咨询成果。最后是坚持以专业性为基础的独立性。智库研究从报告、理论转化为政策不是一蹴而就的。我国社会主要矛盾变化的观点是在领导人强调主要矛盾没变的背景下提出的,经反复思考和坚持,通过内参、建议等多种方式历经两年得以在政策中体现,是基于智库专家的专业判断和智库的相对独立性的特点。

3.1.3 江南大学食品安全风险治理研究院:《中国食品安全发展报告》——在专业理论研究上凝练品牌成果;打造小而专、小而精、小而强,国际化视野的高校专业智库

《中国食品安全发展报告》系列迄今为止已连续出版六册,均以食用农产品生产为起点,综合运用各种统计数据,结合大量的实证调查,研究我国生产、流通、消费等关键环节食品安全性(包括进口食品安全性)的演变轨迹,并对食品安全风险的现实状态与未来走势作出评估。这套系列报告是江南大学食品安全风险治理研究院基于中国国情、中国问题、中国现实,思考食品安全风险中国特色的治理道路、实现食品安全风险治理的中国化创新探索的集中呈现,是高校专业智库建设的一项重要创新。

研究院的5点建设经验如下:一是依托学科优势与主管机构支持。研究院主要嫁接于一流学科和强势专业,江南大学的食品学科评估始终位居全国第一,在我国高校中最早设立了食品安全管理的二级博士点,形成了多学科交叉的新型学科。同时,智库作为江苏省首批重点培育智库,得到了国家和省级层面各级主管单位的支持。二是明确智库发展方向。研究院立足于国情和现实重大需求,在专注于食品安全风险治理的基础上不断扩大研究领域,着力打造行业特色,做专业智库。三是树立品牌成果,服务政府决策。研究院形成了"三位一体"的研究品牌,包括《中国食品安全发展报告》和《中国食品安全网络舆情发展报告》两份咨询报告及每年两版发行的《中国食品安全治理评论》,并积极将研究成果转化服务政府决策,其中许多建议得到了国家及其相关部门领导的批示。四是重视提升国际影响力。研究院积极开展国际交流合作,曾于2014年在美国出版了一本国际专著,用中国理论、中国语言、中国声音阐述中国食品安全风险的治理道路,参与国际话语体系。五是加强基础设施建设。研究院积极投入建设了江南大学第一个行为经济学实验室,同时开发了食品安全事件大数据挖掘与监测的平台,为中国食品安全治理提供了重要的数据基础。

3.2 管理篇

3.2.1 山东社会科学院创新工程：以创新工程为抓手，加速传统社科院迈向一流新型智库

山东社会科学院自2015年起正式实施创新工程，在3年的发展过程中成效卓著，探索出了一条"一个目标、双轮驱动、三项改革、四大支撑、五大功能、六大创新"的发展路径。

"一个目标"，即围绕"打造国内一流新型智库"的总体目标，努力建设马克思主义研究宣传的"思想理论高地"、省委省政府的重要思想库和智囊团、山东省哲学社会科学的高端学术殿堂、山东省情综合数据库和研究评价中心、服务经济文化强省建设的创新型团队。

"双轮驱动"，即实施基础理论研究和应用对策研究双轮驱动的发展战略，在增强理论学术话语权和影响力的同时，围绕山东经济社会发展亟待解决的重大现实问题进行全局性、前瞻性、战略性的研究，提升省委、省政府科学决策的能力和水平。

"三项改革"，是指深化科研管理、人事管理、经费管理改革。具体包括：打破原有的学术团队，建立新的研究创新团队，以创新团队的形式进入创新工程；打破原有的科研管理体制，依托创新工程，建立"能上能下，能进能出，竞争择优，灵活高效"的新型人事管理制度，实行严格的"准入"制度和"退出"制度；采取"开前门堵后门"的方法，优化资源配置，建立智力报偿制度。

"四大支撑"，包括强化体制机制、人才队伍、数字信息化以及精品成果的支撑，建立有利于优秀成果产出的科研组织管理体制机制，有利于创新人才选用的新型人事管理机制，有利于提升科研效率和水平的现代化信息支持系统，有利于持续创新的精品成果产出机制。

"五大功能"，即切实发挥好咨政建言、理论创新、舆论引导、社会服务、公共外交等新型智库的功能，加快传统社科院向新型智库迈进的步伐。

"六大创新"，具体涵盖建立准入、退出、报偿、配置、评价和资助等六大创新制度，

推出以科研组织运行方式、科研成果评价考核体系、科研辅助手段和方法、人事管理制度、人才培育方式、经费配置和使用管理改革创新的改革举措。

3.2.2 华中师范大学中国农村发展智库：三十年专注农村社会调查——从走村串户到构建大数据智库调查服务平台

华中师范大学中国农村发展智库是国内最早、最专业、最负盛名的农村综合性研究实体性机构之一，智库依托华中师范大学中国农村研究院成立，目前已形成了"五位一体"的建设机制，即：以服务国家农村决策为导向，以大型调查和大型数据为支撑，以海外农村调查和翻译为借鉴，以体制机制创新为平台，以一流的学术研究为目标建设高端农村发展智库。

首先，以服务国家农村决策为导向。研究院执行学院体制，长期跟踪和围绕的研究方向和发展领域是中国农村问题，智库建设紧紧围绕学科建设开展应用研究，立院之本便是"调查"。其次，以大型调查和大型数据为支撑。为支撑一流的咨询服务，中农智库建立了三大数据库系统：中国农村数据库系统、中国农村村情系统、中国农村智能决策系统。再次，以海外农村调查和翻译为借鉴。中农智库通过海外农村调查和农村资料翻译工程，开展中外基础与地方治理比较研究，与国际学术界对话。另外，以体制机制创新为平台。目前中农智库已经建立了"三天一报，五天一批"的机制，即每三天向党和国家有关部门呈送一份咨询报告，每五天能够获得中央领导或省部长批示的一份报告。最后，以一流的学术研究为目标建立建设高端农村发展智库。中农智库通过长时段跟踪调查、大样本定点调查、深层次挖掘调查、个案法惯行调查、综合性比较调查不断丰富调查方法，形成扎实的农村调查基本功。

3.3 活动篇

3.3.1 复旦发展研究院：上海论坛——始终坚持国际化路径，促进传统论坛转型为智库论坛

论坛与智库的结合，是上海论坛的重大创新与实践。"上海论坛"创始于2005年，由复旦大学和韩国高等教育财团主办，复旦发展研究院承办，迄今已成功举办了

十二届,是目前在上海举办的最具国际影响力的品牌论坛之一。论坛以"关注亚洲、聚焦热点、荟萃精英、推进互动、增强合作、谋求共识"为宗旨,以"全球治理与亚洲"为主题,经历了从单一到多元、从封闭到开放、从传统论坛形式到新型智库型论坛的发展过程。

上海论坛的特色之一在于其开放的理念。第一,复旦发展研究院秉承着开放办智库、开门办智库的理念,充分利用自己的国际合作网络和交流平台,积极引入国内外优秀资源,为智库及复旦大学的国际化战略提供服务。第二,论坛形成了一个规模庞大的国际顾问团,顾问团成员同时也是复旦发展研究院的国际顾问,这些顾问为论坛主题设置、议题建议出谋划策。第三,论坛吸引了一大批青年访问学者,尤其是来自"一带一路"沿线国家的青年访问学者。这些访问学者也成为论坛发展的生力军,为论坛贡献智慧和资源。特别是2015年以来开放了所有分论坛和圆桌会议的申报,紧密结合智库的建设发展,为国内外智库构建了一个共同发声和交流的平台,建立起了具有中国特色的智库生态圈。

上海论坛的另一大亮点在于智库成果的转化。通过挖掘与整合嘉宾观点和讨论成果,上海论坛形成了大量智库自身的研究成果,包括政策建议书、观点集萃、咨政报告等。同时,上海论坛也是各类智库成果的展示和发布平台,具体涉及金融科技、生态治理、网络理政等多个领域。

此外,上海论坛还承担着"二轨外交"的功能,其邀请到的大量国家前政要、退休官员、重要政府机构代表、非政府组织负责人等,对社会公众关心的热点话题或国家关注的重要议题进行公开或闭门讨论,表达观点、交流思想、加深沟通和理解,同时也让世界更加了解中国。通过这样的对话交流机制,论坛承担起了二轨外交的功能,逐渐成为中外高校交流、为中国智库成果转化发声、讲好中国故事、让世界理解中国的重要载体,让中国智库成果转化发声,也让世界更加了解中国。

3.3.2 浙江师范大学非洲研究院:"学科、智库、媒体三位一体"的发展路径

浙江师范大学非洲研究院近年来立足中非合作实践需要,成功探索出了一条"学

科、智库、媒体三位一体"的发展路径。

一是以学科建设为本体。非洲研究院从中国的非洲观、非洲战略，中非发展合作实践中，提炼出可以解释和促进中非共同发展和人类命运共同体的知识形态、理论体系、话语概念，奠定了知识与思想服务国家的学术基础，形成了"中国的非洲学"。二是以智库服务为功用。高校智库要坚持学科建设与智库建设二轮驱动，充分发挥战略研究、咨政建言、人才培养、舆论引导、公共外交五大功能。非洲研究院通过举办中非合作论坛、中非智库论坛等活动，成功突破了学术停留在小圈子内自说自话困境，形成了对国家社会实际影响力和服务功能。三是以媒体传播为手段。高校智库可以通过与媒体合作，推动中国学术走向世界，在核心对象国形成直接影响力，改变中国海外形象。非洲研究院通过举办中非媒体智库研讨会、与非洲主流媒体签订合作协议等形式，向非洲、世界传递"中国声音"。此次获奖的纪录片《我从非洲来》讲述了非洲人在中国的故事，旨在通过真实影像推动中非之间的相互了解。只有学科、智库、媒体融合发展，高校智库才能逐渐成为有国际影响力的学术机构与思想智库，推进国内外思想知识双向、平衡与互动。

院长刘鸿武总结了高校智库建设的五点体会：一是围绕国家战略做好总体布局与发展规划；二是发挥好学校在国家发展战略中特殊作用；三是按国家和地区期待建好本校发展研究院；四是组建好服务地方发展的学科创新群智库；五是将中国的本土经验话语转化为国际话语。

3.3.3 长江教育研究院：教育智库与教育治理高峰论坛——充分利用人大政协渠道，搭建一流专业论坛，十年如一日专注中国教育现代化

长江教育研究院主办的教育智库与教育治理高峰论坛以"与时代同行、为改革奉献"为主题，以"当今中国教育智库如何更好地参与和实施教育治理，提升公共服务能力，为教育行政部门建言献策，推进中国特色教育智库的建设"为主要内容，积极探索新形势下教育政策研究智库高效运转的体制与机制。

长江教育研究院是由湖北省教育厅、华中师范大学和长江出版传媒集团联合发

起的一所社会智库。该院自 2009 年起,连续十年于每年两会前在北京举办长江教育论坛,邀请全国人大代表、全国政协委员,以及教育部有关司局领导,共同探讨教育改革发展的话题,同时发布年度教育政策建议书、中国教育指数,以及年度十大教育关键词。在 2016 年 12 月 16 日于北京成功举办的"教育智库与教育治理高峰论坛"上,长江教育研究院荣获"教育建言卓越贡献奖"。

除此之外,长江教育研究院也十分重视与教育行政部门、科研机构与高校的战略合作。为逐步沟通全国教育资源渠道、实现研究成果共现、搭建一流的教育专业平台,研究院以湖北为中心,向南方、北方、西南进行扩散,与知名高校成立了合作智库共建,先后成立长江教育研究院北方教育智库,长江教育研究院南方教育智库、长江教育研究院华东教育智库、长江教育研究院西南教育智库。这些教育智库可以通过长江教育研究院向全国人大报送研究成果形成"咨询快报",充分利用人大、政协渠道,服务于中国教育现代化的改革和发展。

结 语

中国特色社会主义建设已经进入了伟大的新时代,党的十八大以来,中国特色新型智库建设涌现出许多研究、咨询、管理方面与时俱进、既兼具理论价值又有鲜明实践指导性的最佳研究、最佳活动以及最佳管理案例。本次 BPA 三大奖的评选活动充分挖掘了近年来我国智库在内部治理和运行模式上不断探索的最新成果,传播了智库建设的成功经验与先进理念,这些内容丰富、各有千秋的实践案例隐含了我国新型智库发展的脉络和未来方向。2017 CTTI 智库最佳实践案例(BPA)发布暨智库评价系统研讨会的召开,为各级各类智库提供了一个充分交流、学习借鉴先进经验的良好平台。

南京大学中国智库研究与评价中心、光明日报智库研究与发布中心联合开展 BPA 三大奖的评选与发布活动,意在进一步促进智库共同体的发展,发现优秀案例,给予各级各类优秀智库崭露头角的机会,并寄望 BPA 三大奖能够成为促进新型智库实践能力、选拔和表彰优秀智库的重要机制,也为中国特色新型智库建设提供生动例证。

2017 Report on the Best Practice Awards for CTTI Think Tanks

Preface

In recent years, the construction of new-type think tanks in China has ushered in unprecedented opportunities in development, and also made a series of remarkable achievements. Many examples emerged in think-tank research, consultation and management, are recommendable. Based on the data of the Chinese Think Tank Index (CTTI), both China Think Tank Research and Evaluation Center of Nanjing University and Think Tank Research and Release Center of *Guangming Daily* conducted the selection of "CTTI-BPA for Think Tanks" (hereinafter referred to as "three Awards for BPA") to publicize and spread the innovative experience and practices of various think tanks at all levels in research, events and management, and improve our management and consultation level as well as promote the sound development of new-type think tanks with Chinese characteristics in the new era.

1 The Origin of Best Practice Awards for Think Tanks

1.1 Best Practice

The concept of Best Practice (BP) comes from the field of management, i. e., "there is a sort of technology, method, process, event, or mechanism achieving optimal results of production or management time". Such a concept has been widely used in software design, environmental management, human resource management, book information processing, public policy analysis and other fields.

In business management, BP is recognized to constantly produce excellent results and applied in different cases. Among the core contents of benchmarking management, it is the key to scientific management for enterprises. Benchmarking or benchmark management, is a method of modern enterprise management created by Xerox in 1979. In the western management circle, it is also known as one of the "three management methods" including the other two, corporation reengineering and strategic alliance. In the late 1970s and early 1980s, Xerox, an American global corporation which had maintained a monopoly in the world photocopier market, was confronted with the gauntlet from home and abroad, especially from Japan and its market shares sharply shrank. In order to get out of this dilemma, Xerox began to learn from Japanese enterprises to find out the gap through comparative analysis, adjust the management strategy and reconstruct the business process, then widely and thoroughly carried out benchmarking management, and finally achieved excellent performance. Since then, Xerox widely promoted benchmarking management, visited companies in the same industry, found out its own problems by contrast and accordingly took appropriate measures. In view of Xerox's success, IBM, DuPont, General Motors and other companies followed it, so as to find out those with best management practice in the industry, making up their own disadvantages based on the good example to optimize enterprise practice.

Specifically, benchmarking means that enterprises compare with the leading ones in terms of elements such as products, services and production flow, learn from others' advanced experience, and overcome their own shortcomings so as to improve the level of business management and their core competitiveness. Later, such a concept is systematized and standardized by American Productivity & Quality Center

(APQC): benchmarking is a systematic, continuous evaluation process in which enterprises continually compare business processes with those of the world's leading ones to gain information that can help enterprises improve their management performance.

Benchmarking is naturally a method-based management style oriented by practice and process, and its basic ideas are system optimization and continuous improvement. This is simply a process of imitation, learning and innovation in which BP, as a benchmark, is particularly important. The methods of benchmarking are widely applied in every field at present, while various industries are looking for the best practice within their own industry from which they can absorb advanced work experience and make publicity and promotion, so as to achieve common progress of industries.

The concept of BP is frequently used in the field of library. One of the roles of the American Library Association (ALA), for example, is to "develop standards and models of best practice". The Association and its branches collect typical projects and good examples in the industry, and make a systematical arrangement in which they conclude the best practice. The guide of best practice is drawn up and extended, its outcomes including *Best Practice Features of Information Literacy Program: Guidelines*, *Best Practice Guide on Studying EAD of Library Association* and so on. In addition, a series of professionally recognized prizes given by ALA, including "Best Marketing Practice Award for Academic/Research Library", are awarded to libraries with best practices in marketing.

The concept of BP is also widely used in the field of health care. Centers for Disease Control and Prevention (CDC) makes a definition for it: best practice is the process of making effects on public health and implementing quality of evidence programs to improve health effectiveness, and the implementation result at the most accurate level repeatedly discussed by peers in the industry. The practice of CDC is to discuss and remark the health problems, standards of best practice application and different kinds of practice methods by scientists, practitioners, researchers, fund provider and evaluation experts of institutions at all levels in America in the areas, such as epidemiology, behavioral science, project design, management and evaluation and policy making. These experts first classify relevant knowledge through discussion, then carry out various sustainable evaluation and quantitative analysis in many aspects and levels, develop deep dialogues and communication, and finally form models of best practice theory to guide and improve the implementation of public health projects.

1.2 Best Practice of Think Tanks

1.2.1 OTT Best Practice Series

OTT (onthinktanks. org), the world's largest professional website of think tanks, was set up in the UK in 2010, aiming to help think tanks make short-and long-term decisions in a more strategic way. As a digital platform with research resources related to think tanks, OTT brings together the latest data, researches, analyses, resources and features associated with think tanks around the world, and now becomes one of the well-known websites in global policy research, providing a number of services, events and knowledge support for think-tank research.

OTT Best Practice Series was posted on the OTT website in 2017, including a series of introductions to best practices of think tanks. Each article in this series sets different topics for various think-tank practices and deals with the problem about reliability in a variety of ways to help think tanks enhance reputation, and improve efficiency and benefit through such best practices in management, communication and governance.

The "OTT Best Practice Series" is of the view that the best practices of think tanks are a clear, effective way to perform tasks, as such practices usually come from widely recognized think tanks and achieve good results. Based on the author's rich experience in think-tank research field, the actual strategies and workflows for many specific questions have been refined, and readers are encouraged to make adjustments under specific conditions. At present, nine kinds of best practices have been accumulated: best practice for archiving project documents and data of think-tank research; best practice for recruiting think-tank researchers; best financial practice for sponsors in funding think tanks; and other best practices, such as off-site training of staff, management consultants to think-tank research projects, innovative fund-raising strategies of think tanks, cost control of think-tank research projects, professional development funds to motivate researchers, and greater policy influence—further communication after think-tank projects.

1.2.2 Connotation of Think-Tank Best Practice

From all these examples, we can see that BP can be a skill, a method, a mechanism and so on. By analyzing the definition of BP in various industries, we combine the native context of China and the development of think tanks, and then define the best practice of think tanks as: think tanks sum up the best way and practice to make use of personnel, finance, material and project management by self-assessment, and bring benchmark cases of organization management. As the summary and extraction of the results of think-tank management events, these cases have much value to popularize. It should be pointed out that the best practice of think tanks is neither absolutely constant, nor universally true, while different types or levels of think tanks have different connotations of best practices. Such best practices are only regarded as a standard for reference, by which any think tank can find out the difference and combine their own strategic planning and development environment to implement the optimal scheme for their institutions.

1.2.3 Elements of Think-Tank Best Practice

Source is the first element of think-tank best practice. Best practice appears in the course of daily operation and management of think tanks by means of active exploration and endless attempts; therefore, think tanks themselves, as the source of the best practice, are of great importance. First, think-tank workers should have initiative to constantly think, to bravely practice, and to explore better schemes in their daily work. Second, the operation of think tanks should be objective that internal governance or achievements are consistent with the spirit of seeking truth oriented by problems and goals, and on the basis of it, the resources and brainstorming from all parties are coordinated. Third, these tasks should be persistent, that is, focusing on accumulation in practice and keeping detailed records, such as management reviews, the process of event organization, so as to achieve the greatest degree of transforming tacit knowledge inside think tanks to explicit knowledge that can be understood by other institutions and easily spread over.

Subject is the second element of think-tank best practice. The best practice of think tanks is embodied in a fruitful research, an influential event, or a practical management plan, all of which are accumulated in actual operation and management of think tanks. Thus, the subject of think-tank best practice is the lessons and conclusions that have proven to be effective in practice. These exist in two forms: one is the tacit knowledge in the mind of think-tank employees and experts, derived from long-term practical experience and relying on human subjective development and cognition, for example, an expert's writing skills research reports; the other is the explicit knowledge in written form, which comes from the summary and consolidation for working methods of their institutions, including think-tank evaluation system of scientific research achievements and new personnel management system.

Process is the third element of think-tank best practice. The juxtaposition of implicit and explicit knowledge in best practice determines the importance of extraction and transfer processes in think-tank best practice. The processes to extract tacit knowledge in best practice shall contain self-assessment, self-summary, self-refinement and so on, while the transfer shall include presentation, communication, learning, implementation. It should be noted that best practice has interactivity and dynamics in learning process. The former means learning, for all kinds of think tanks, should not go by the book, but proceed from actual conditions and explore the best scheme for themselves while repeatedly learning and practicing. The latter means the transmission of best practice requires communication to achieve better learning results in which both knowledge transmitters and learners need opportunities to communicate face to face, not only to learn the explicit knowledge in the text, but also to interchange the tacit knowledge in mind. It is also the important reason why we held the press conference of think-tank best practice cases after selecting the three Awards for BPA.

1.3 The Necessity of Chinese Think-Tank Development to Seek Best Practice

1.3.1 Calling for Best Practice to Develop New-Type Think Tanks

On January 20, 2015, the General Office of the CPC Central Committee and the General Office of the State Council officially issued "Opinions on Improving the Construction of a New Type of Think Tank with Chinese Characteristics" ("The Opinions"), starting a new phase for the development of new-type think tanks. It appears a tide of building and using think tanks in China, and their construction is in full swing. But there is still a gap between the current situation and the orientation and goal of the construction in "The Opinions". A series of problems are also hidden behind the vigorous development, especially the striking difference of different-type think tanks at different levels or in different regions in this process..

At the conference on philosophy and social sciences in 2016, President Xi Jinping pointed out, "In recent years, the construction of think tanks in philosophy and social sciences has been booming and also made many achievements, which help Party and government departments at all levels to make decisions. At the same time, some think tanks pay more attention to quantity than quality; some focus more on dissemination forms than content innovation; some still make formalistic practices, including inviting celebrities and hosting forums." It can be seen that, indeed, the development of new-type think tanks has played an active role in promoting the modernization of national governance system and capacity, but some think tanks may move forward with the wave of the construction, so that their underlying problems in development cannot be solved all the time, and they still stumble in financial management, staff incentives, resource integration and other aspects.

Moreover, the exchanges between Chinese and foreign think tanks are increasingly frequent, and western think tanks, with more mature governance structure and operation mechanism, have been introduced into China, which would provide a good reference to our development of think tanks. However, both political, economic, social environment and targets of think-tank construction are not the same at home and abroad. Our construction of think tanks should not copy western experience and development mode, while what we need is a batch of new-type think tanks with Chinese characteristics—their deep roots in practice of Chinese think tanks and strong adaption to the development of the age—which can sum up our own experience and take the lead. The current status of imbalance in think-tank development urgently calls for a group of typical, excellent think tanks with Chinese characteristics in Best Practice, playing an exemplary role as benchmarking to promote the overall development of new-type think tanks with Chinese characteristics.

1.3.2 Best Practice Emerging in the Construction of New-Type Think Tanks

"The Plan of Pilot Projects for China Top Think Tanks", adopted at the 18th session of the Central Leading Group for Deepening Reforms hosted by President Xi in November, 2015, focuses on developing a batch of top think tanks that the state is urgently need of, each being unique in its own way for institutional innovation and leadership in development. In December, 2015, with the work conferences of the pilot projects held, substantive progress was made for the grand idea to the "Implementation of the Construction Planning of National Top Think Tanks". In recent years, the high-end think tanks in China have sought breakthroughs in system and mechanism, actively explored a new path to improve the internal governance structure and operation model of think tanks, significantly advanced in public diplomacy, decision-making consultation and public opinion guidance and played an important role in leading and demonstration. Meanwhile, many provinces and cities, according to the construction model of national top think tanks, have launched pilots of key think tanks, which were intended to explore new ideas, measures and modes for think-tank development in the region combined with the actual situation and industry features. In this process, a series of outstanding specialized think tanks have also sprung in research, practice and management, and started to take effect. These excellent think tanks have produced a range of high-quality research results with foresightedness, pertinence and, innovative content, and organized various events with national, even international influence to provide numerous best practice cases.

It is necessary to sum up and extend the successful experience gained by deepening the reform of system and mechanism, optimizing the internal management process and improving the quality of think-tank results and consultation capacity, which is not only the requirement for building a new-type think tanks with Chinese characteristics, branding some think tanks and improving their influence, but also the urgent demand for think tanks to make benchmarking management and improve their own development by means of learning the advanced experience based on their conditions.

1.3.3 "Best Practice" Empowering Consultation to New Think-Tank Research

The internal energy in a relatively closed think tank is limited, and it may be difficult to meet the needs of the organization's continuing development after a certain period of time, at which we need to seek support from the outside, namely, obtaining external empowerment. Learning best practices from the outside and drawing on the advanced management ideas and practical experience of other think tanks are an effective means for a think tank to get external empowerment. The best practice cases reflect the process and practice of think tanks in the specific link, and we can find out how they deal with specific problems, how to solve these problems and what kind of results they have achieved in the end according to the analysis, so as to extract the operation and management methods with promotional value and strong practicability.

Benign internal operation and management approaches of think tanks can promote their normal and efficient operation, serving as the necessary guarantee to continue to produce competitive research results. The selection of the best practice awards is divided into three sorts: Best Research Report Award, Best Event Award and Best Management Award, in which study reports are a typical representative for think tanks' results, service and decisions; events are the most important way for think tanks to output thoughts, build brands and improve influence; management is necessary to produce effective outputs and carry out successful events.

It is going to say, "advice from others may help one overcome his shortcomings". For think tanks, learning from best practices is actually a process of comparison, imitation and innovation. By comparing their own achievements, event process, management mode with various best practices, think tanks can draw on these advanced experience, rethink and update their own management practice, so as to improve operation efficiency and enhance innovation ability and competitiveness, both not only helpful to the progress of the individual think tank, but also to the mutual exchange within think tank community, thus further promoting the perfection of the governance system of new-type of think tanks with Chinese characteristics.

1.4 Significance of BPA Selection for Think Tanks

Both China Think Tank Research and Evaluation Center of Nanjing University and Think Tank Research and Release Center of *Guangming Daily* have selected and released "three Awards for BPA" in order to further promote the development of think tank community, discover outstanding cases and offer an opportunity to all kinds of emerging excellent think tanks. It is hoped that the three Awards for BPA will become an important mechanism to boost the practical abilities of new-type think tanks and select and commend excellent ones.

The significance of this selection can be summarized as follows: First, through the best practice selection of think tanks, we can further carry forward the pragmatic spirit which apply theory to practice, and the down-to-earth spirit with Chinese characteristics, style and manner oriented by problems and goals. Second, this selection gives play to the initiative of all think tanks that in the process of "learning by doing", we can discover and promote a group of typical cases which can lead new think tanks in management of human, finance and property as well as project management by contributing the best cases through self-assessment, self-summary and self-refinement. We should advance common progress in management of new think tanks through publicity and promotion. Third, this selection is essentially a kind of benchmarking. The best practice cases selection of think tanks has facilitated full exchanges and benchmarking management among think tanks so as to improve their management level as quickly as possible.

2　Process Review of CTTI-BPA Cases Selection

2.1　Material Collection and Review

After the early argumentation and preparation, China Think Tank Research and Evaluation Center of Nanjing University and Think Tank Research and Release Center of *Guangming Daily* published a notice about selecting "China Think Tank Index-Best Practice Awards" (CTTI-BPA) in November 2017, and then the collection work began officially. The best practice cases in 2017 encompassed all achievements of think tanks since 2015, the declaration subjects including CTTI source think tanks and non-source think tanks. The Best Research Report Award and Best Activity Award should be voluntarily applied for by think tanks, while the Best Management Award is nominated by the competent departments of think tanks from provinces, autonomous regions and municipalities. Application materials of institutions at all levels should be signed by responsible persons and stamped by official seals, and all submitted through mailbox in the form of scanning documents, so the printed copies will not be accepted. Other certifications and supplementary materials need to be submitted in paper by mail.

After receiving the application materials, the staff will carefully examine one by one, and verify those with non-compliance or omission or incorrectness by mail or telephone to ensure their accuracy and normalization. Finally, full preparation for the later process are made by the means of classifying all application materials, numbering them in sequence and making expert review forms for each material.

2.2 Selection Process Review

In order to make the selection more scientific and professional, peer review of an expert group is mainly used in the process in line with the principle of fairness, impartiality and openness. The group consists of principals, directors or leaders and research experts of various think tanks. Combining the qualitative and quantitative methods, the whole selection process takes the data of CTTI as important reference, in which specific selection methods are formulated according to the respective characteristics of the three Awards.

The Best Research Report Award and Best Event Award are voluntarily applied for by institutions, and then reviewed and voted by the expert group to determine the shortlist.

The selection process of the Best Research Report Award is mainly about the quality and influence of the chosen research reports. The quality of reports focuses on their pertinence, foresight, scientificity and academic rationality. High-qualified research reports must be produced by think tanks on the basis of professional theories, using scientific research methods, policy analysis tools and technical means, focusing on the practical problems that need to be solved urgently for the Party, the government, the society and the people, and reflecting think tanks' overall control and scientific foresight on their research problems. Influence contains their policy influence, academic influence and social influence. Policy influence mainly is concentrated on the role of research reports playing in consultation and advice for policy makers; academic influence studies the academic value to generate academic results in these reports; social influence not only observes how these reports and their derivatives are reported by all kinds of media at all level, but also emphasizes the humanistic care and social responsibility reflected in the reports.

The Best Event Award is based on the aim, objective, scheme and process of these selective events, and studies their innovation and influence. The innovation of events includes both content innovation and form innovation, and their influence includes not only the influence of events themselves, but also the influence of their derivatives. Besides the media report, such influence also focuses on the concern of events about hot social issues and great events, their demonstration effect in which social responsibility and humanistic care are embodied. International influence gives special importance to the international exchanges in these events, the role of think tanks as "Two Track Diplomacy" and so on.

The Best Management Award is nominated by the competent departments of provincial and municipal think tanks, and then reviewed and voted by the expert group to determine the shortlist. This award is mainly aimed at the innovation and effectiveness of the nominated think tanks in management, considering them from those dimensions, such as organization structure, system construction and operational management.. Specifically, it includes fund management, personnel management, achievement promotion, external cooperation and so on, striving to select new-type think tanks with Chinese characteristics which are characterized by clear positioning, distinctive features, mature mechanisms and orderly operation.

2.3 Analysis of the Selection

In this selection process, think tanks from 23 provinces, autonomous regions and municipalities have applied for a total of 441 projects, and excluded non-standard, unsigned or sealed ones, finally there were 416 official applications, of which 216 were applied for "Best Research Report Award", 166 for "Best Event Award", and 34 for "Best Management Award" recommended by provinces, cities, autonomous regions and municipalities. The results of the construction of new-type think tanks with Chinese characteristics in the past three years can be partly reflected in the various and substantial application materials: the topics of research reports tend to be diversified and specialized; the activities of think tanks are developing vigorously and the brand effect is gradually taking shape; new breakthroughs have been made in the construction of institutions and mechanisms, and a batch of new think tanks that have achieved great success in management are springing up.

2.3.1 Diverse and Widely Distributed Subjects of Application

First, the types of application subjects are diverse, dominated by university think tanks, while other types of think tanks are distributed in balance. The three figures above respectively show the distribution of subjects applying for the three Awards. It

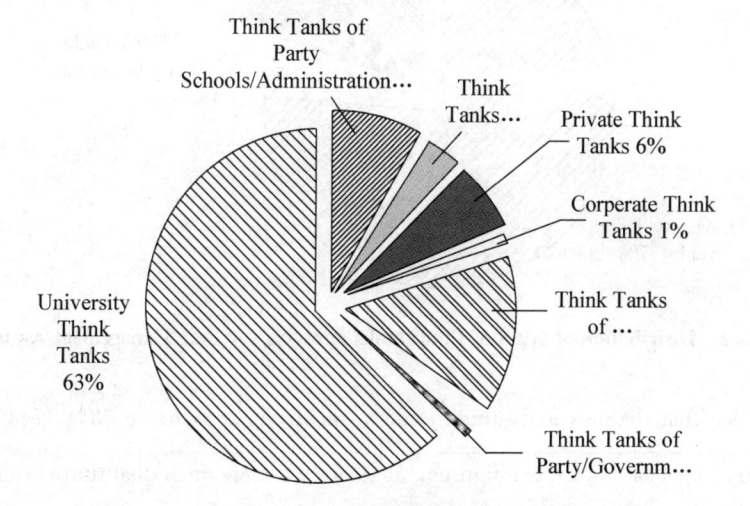

Fig. 1 Distribution of types of think tanks applying for Best Research Report Award

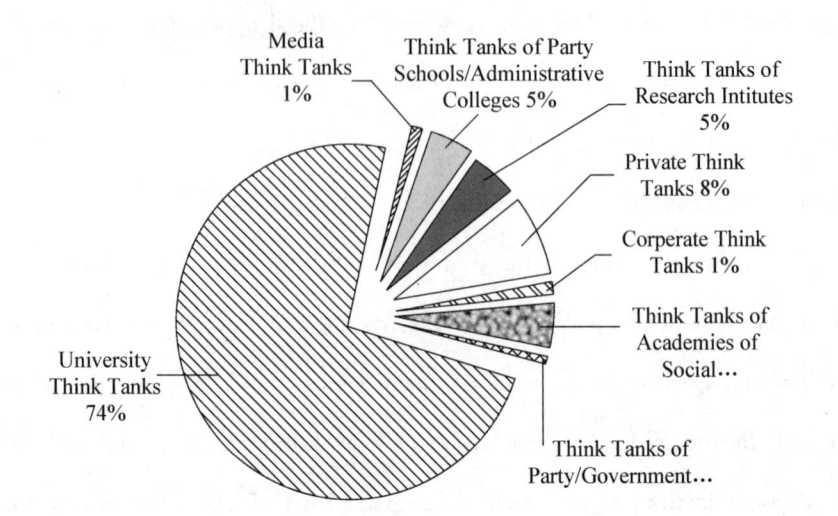

Fig. 2　Distribution of types of think tanks applying for Best Event Award

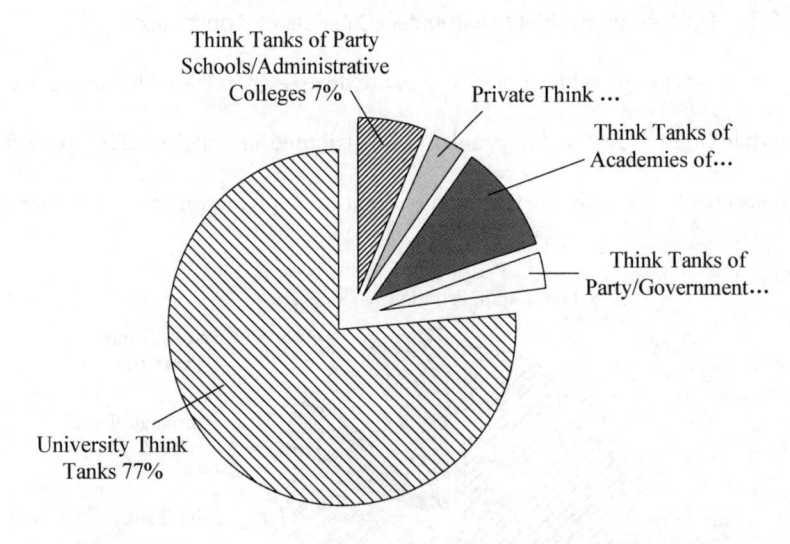

Fig. 3　Distribution of types of think tanks applying for Best Management Award

can be seen that the university think tanks respectively account for 63%, 74%, 77% of the total applicants in these figures, absolutely dominant in quantitative terms; in addition, the Party School or Administration Institute think tanks, think tanks of Academies of Social Sciences, and think tanks of research institutes are also important participants in application. On the whole, the distribution of think tanks is relatively average, without obvious difference, except for university think tanks.

Second, these application subjects are widely distributed, largely in Beijing, Shanghai and Jiangsu. The think tanks for this application come from 23 provinces, autonomous regions, municipalities, mainly in Beijing, Shanghai, Jiangsu, leading the total number of the three Awards for BPA. Beijing, as the center of politics, science, education, culture and international communication of the country, has more concentrated advantages of politics, education and scientific research so that these think tanks for application have more research reports and events; With the advantages of economy, education and international communication, Shanghai takes the lead of think-tank events in number; with the strong support of the provincial Party committee and government for think-tank construction and the positive response from various think tanks, the application number of research reports and events also leap to the front in Jiangsu. Moreover, Tianjin, Inner Mongolia, Yunnan, Shandong and other places have shown great enthusiasm for this application as well, with high participation. Generally speaking, such distributions of types and regions are basically in line with the actual distribution of think tanks in China.

2.3.2 Topics of Research Reports toward Diversification and Specialization

First, the topics of research reports tend to be diversified. According to the topic distribution, this application involves 32 topics in the research reports, many of them on economic policy, industrial policy, social policy, foreign policy, cultural policy, government governance policy, business management policy and ideological policy, all of which are more than 8 on average. As many as 46 application reports on economic policy are well ahead of the list. In addition, think tanks also pay attention to agricultural policy, environmental policy, education policy, financial policy, urban governance policy and so on. From the view of topic, it covers the hot issues in the past three years, such as the construction of the Belt and Road, the new normal of China's economy, targeted poverty alleviation and supply-side structural reform.

Second, the topics of the reports tends to be specialized. One of the important outputs of think tanks is research reports, whose quality and specialization level will largely affect the role of think tanks playing in the process of decision-making and consultation. Most of the research reports for this application are highly professional, all of which are based on their own research field, and combined with the practical problems of the Party and the government and the people's livelihood that need to be solved urgently, specifically involving politics, economy, education, electricity, oil, gas and other specialized fields. Meanwhile, these specialized research reports also reflect the core competence of professional think tanks as investigation research, data collection and analysis, modeling calculation, planning and evaluation. For example, *Report on China Food Safety Development*, a series of reports published by the Research Institute for Food Safety Risk Administration of Jiangnan University, starts with the production of edible agricultural products, and then synthetically applies various statistics, combined with a large number of empirical investigations to study the evolution of food safety of our country (including imported food safety) in key links, such as production, circulation and consumption, and makes the assessment of its current state and future trend, reflecting high specialization of the think tank and contributing to objectively showing the modernization of management system and governance capability of Chinese food safety risk.

2.3.3 Think Tank Events Booming and Brand Effects Taking Shape

First, the events of think tanks are vigorously developing, and rich in content. The events are an important and effective way for think tanks to strengthen communication with others and enhance their impact. The 166 applied events are rich in content and various in form, among which the number of forums and seminars come out on top, followed by research, press conferences, training and other forms. The content of the events involves not only the major strategic problems and social hot issues in China, but also the key issues in the professional fields. While extending their influence through these events, think tanks also strive to explore and produce policy research results and products, and make suggestions for the development of related fields. For example, the National Research Center for Economic Comprehensive Competitiveness of Fujian Normal University Branch, in serving the meeting of BRICS in Xiamen, focused on the topics of the summit and discussion, and deployed so advanced and researched so deep that successively formed high-quality research reports and a series of monographs and articles, which have produced positive social response, made the "voice of think tank" and provided the "plan of think tank" for this meeting.

Second, the forms of think-tank events are innovative. During this application, a batch of think-tank events with innovative forms and prominent highlights have sprung up. These events are either flexible in organization, regardless of time and space, or closely integrated with the Internet and new media, as a vivid illustration of new think tanks that dare to innovate and actively explore in the course of construction. For example, the filming of the documentary, *Africans in Yiwu*, carried out by the Institute of African Studies of Zhejiang Normal University and adopted the means of film and television, aims to break the limit of international dissemination of those videos with similar topics made at home based on the ideology and pertinence of think-tank research, which finally has produced a positive reaction at home and abroad. In addition, the Research Center for Co-development with

Neighboring Countries of East China Normal University has set up overseas studios in Washington, D. C. and Moscow respectively, aiming to break down the solidified barriers of universities and research institutions as well as disciplines at home and abroad, so as to make full use of domestic and foreign high-quality resources, build an excellent transnational work platform, and explore a new type for think tanks to "go out".

Third, think tanks pay attention to policy promotion and brand building. Many think tanks regularly hold academic forums and seminars, which have formed brand effects. Most of these events are well planned by think tanks, attract people from all walks of life to exchange thoughts, and gradually become influential platforms for exchanges and cooperation in their fields. For example, the "Shanghai Forum" applied by Fudan Development Institute, was founded in 2005 and has successfully held for 12 years so far, and has currently become one of the most internationally influential brands as a forum in Shanghai. Moreover, the "Top Ten Influential Legal Events" of the year, initiated by the Institute for Chinese Legal Modernization Studies of Nanjing Normal University, has been continuously released the selected events in 2015, 2016 and 2017, which were issued and spread on the platforms of media, websites and self-media like *Legal Daily* and its website, making great influence in academia, practice field and the public.

Fourth, think tanks promote international exchanges and carry out second-track diplomacy. Deepening international exchanges and cooperation and enhancing international influence are an important part in the construction of new types of think tanks with Chinese characteristics. It can be seen from the application materials that many think tanks, especially national top ones, actively function as public diplomacy and take the initiative to carry out international exchanges, especially play a key role in the second track diplomacy. For example, the China-US Economic Two-Track Dialogue, co-sponsored by the National School of Development of Peking University and the National Committee on United States-China Relations, is held twice a year in New York and Beijing by turns, and has been successfully organized 17 times so far. The results of the dialogue are reported to the relevant departments of China and the United States, which provide reference for the decision-making of the two governments, so as to help their academia and business circles digest the positive parts and improve the mutual understanding and trust between the two peoples.

2.3.4 New Breakthroughs in the Institutional Mechanisms of Think Tanks

A total of 34 think tanks have applied for the Best Management Award, with the number of top three think tanks in economy and trade, social policy and comprehensive research fields. The research of economy and trade filed is mainly oriented by fiscal, finance, income distribution, industrial economy, business operation, market consumption and so on. There are nine think tanks engaged in related research in this field, including eight university think tanks and one private think tank. The research of social policy filed is mainly oriented by state governance, social management, public policy, urban and rural construction, housing, social security and so on. There are five think tanks engaged in the relevant research in this field, including four university think tanks and one think tank of Party or government organizations. Comprehensive research field refers to thinks tanks participating in decision-making and consultation among multiple fields, including three think tanks of the Academy of Social Sciences and two think tanks of the Party school or administrative college. All nominated think tanks this time actively explored in management, boldly made innovation and emerged a lot of highlights.

The first breakthrough is the improvement of governance structure and the integration of resources. For example, the Center for Crisis Management Research of Tsinghua University, with the director and chief expert system, establishes an academic committee composed of experts and scholars in various related fields, and integrates the superior resources of different disciplines. At the same time, the think tank also focuses on strengthening extensive academic cooperation with graduates, forming a super-high-end research team of "small entities and large coalitions". The second is the construction of research platforms. For example, the think-tank research and service platform, set up by the Institute of China Rural Studies of Central China Normal University, is fully characterized by attaching great importance to investigation and research and the archival management of data cases, whose policy analysis is based on solid data and facts. The third is the innovation in the transformation mechanism of consultation results. In the report of consultation results, the Center for Think-tanks Research and Management in Shanghai has successfully realized the docking of government needs and expert achievements by holding the strategic thinking salon among university think tanks in Shanghai.

2.4 Selection Results

On April 30, 2018, a total of 78 applications enters the final session after the online communication and review of experts. On May 8, the expert group held a final evaluation meeting and selected 51 best practice cases for "2017 CTTI-BPA for Think Tanks". In accordance with the principle of scientific rationality, moderate amount, and putting quality before quantity, this selection finally set three Awards, for think tanks, "Best Research Report Award", "Best Event Award" and "Best Management Award", each of them involving two grand prizes, five first prizes and ten second prizes. The below Table 1, Table 2 and Table 3 list the winners of the three Awards for CTTI-BPA (no particular order for the award at the same level).

Table 1 List of Best Research Report Award for Think Tanks

Name of Report	Name of Think Tank	Prize
Research on the Social Contradictions Index	Beijing Institution of Letters to Government	Grand Prize
Rethinking and Accurately Defining the New-Era Principal Contradiction in Chinese Society	Institute of Finance and Economics of Tongji University	
Beware of the Changing from "Price-Limited Housing" to "Welfare Housing" and "Corrupted Housing"	Yangtze Industrial Economics Institution (Nanjing University)	First Prize
Series of Report on China Food Safety Development	Institute for Food Safety Risk Administration of Jiangnan University	
Understand the Blueprint of the Belt and Road——Detailed Annotation of "The Belt and Road": Concept, Practice and China's Contribution	Chongyang Institute of Financial Studies, Remin University	
Positive Changes in Attitude of American and European Think Tanks on the Construction of "Belt and Road"	National Institute of Global Strategy, Chinese Academy of Social Sciences	
Blue Book of Chinese Traditional Villages • Investigation Report on the Protection of Chinese Traditional Villages (2017)	Research Center of Chinese Village Culture, Central South University	
Development Report of Unicorn Enterprise (Series Research)	Beijing Greatwall Enterprise Institute	Second Prize
Realizing "Targeted Poverty Alleviation" by "Targeted Poverty Relief"	Academy of Social Sciences, Fujian	
A Series of Research Reports on the Survival Status and Relief Suggestions for Minor Children of Prisoners	Center of Social Governance Research, South China University of Technology	

Continued

Name of Report	Name of Think Tank	Prize
Appraisal Report on China Green GDP Performance	Institute of State Governance of Huazhong University of Science and Technology	
Research Report on the Efficiency of Local Government in China (2016)	Research Center of the Management-decision Evaluation of Jiangxi Normal University	
Principal Contradictions and Supply-Side Structural Reform in the New Normal of Economic Development	Collaborative Innovation Center for China Economy, Nankai University	
Research Report on Promoting the Implementation of the Silk Road Economic Belt and Win-Win Regional Cooperation	Northwest Land and Resources Research Center	
Comparison of Comprehensive Innovation Strength among Beijing, Tianjin and Shanghai and Shenzhen and Reflection on the Construction of Innovative City in Tianjin	China Center for Finance and Insurance, Tianjin University of Finance and Economics	
Ten legal Questions facing the Development of a New Generation of Artificial Intelligence	Research Institute of China Green Development of Tianjin University	
Explanation and Rational Thinking of the Phenomenon of "Extreme Poverty" in the Extremely Poor Township of Guizhou—Suggestions Based on Investigation and Research in 20 Towns of Extreme Poverty	Guizhou Provincial Party School of CPC, Guizhou Administration College	

Table 2　List of Best Event Award for Think Tanks

Name of Report	Name of Think Tank	Prize
Sino-US Economic Two-Track Dialogue & National Development Forum	National School of Development at Peking University	Grand Prize
Shanghai Forum	Fudan Development Institute	
Summit Forum on Education Think Tanks and Education Governance	Changjiang Educational Research Institute	First Prize
Practical Exploration and Path Choice for Service and Scientific Decision-Making of Contemporary Chinese Think Tanks—A Case Study of the Meeting of BRICS in Xiamen served by Fujian Normal University Competitiveness Research Center	National Research Center for Economic Comprehensive Competitiveness, Fujian Normal University Branch	
Globalization Forum of China Enterprise	Center for China and Globalization (Beijing)	
Africans in Yiwu (Six-Episode Documentary about Public Diplomacy)	Institute of African Studies of Zhejiang Normal University	
Selection and Issuing of China's Annual Top Ten Influential Legal Events	Institute for Chinese Legal Modernization Studies, Nanjing Normal University	
Visits to Five Eastern European Countries to Construct the Network Dialogue Mechanism of Think Tanks Plus Complex Foreign Policies	China Regional Development and Reform Institute (Beijing)	Second Prize
Emerging Economies and Economic Globalization Workshop in the Context of APEC	Intellisia Institute	
Hinterland Think-Tank Forum	Academy of Social Sciences, Henan	
Establishing Overseas Studios (Wilson Center for International Scholars, National Research University Higher School of Economics) to Train Compound Talents of Think Tanks	Research Center for Co-development with Neighboring Countries of East China Normal University	

Continued

Name of Report	Name of Think Tank	Prize
Research Institute of Jiangsu Yangtze River Economic Belt	Development Forum of Yangtze River Economic Belt	
International Forum of Sino-Mongolian-Russian Think Tanks	Development Research Center of Inner Mongolia Autonomous Region	
Think Tanks Forum of Environment and Development	Western China Think-tank on Resources, Environment and Development (Lanzhou Information Center, Chinese Academy of Sciences)	
The Innovative Practice of Yunnan University to Conduct Public Diplomacy in Myanmar	Centers for China's Neighbor Diplomacy Studies, Yunnan University	
Seminar on the Development of Science and Education Policy	Institute of China's Science, Technology and Education Policy, Zhejiang University	
High-level Forum on Security Research of the "Belt and Road"	China National Institute for SCO International Exchange and Judicial Cooperation (Shanghai University of Political Science and Law)	

Table 3 List of Best Management Award for Think Tanks

Name of Think Tank	Prize
Institute of China Rural Studies, Central China Normal University	Grand Prize
Innovation Project of Shandong Academy of Social Sciences	
Institute of the Development of Socialism with Chinese Characteristics, Southeast University	First Prize
Center for Crisis Management Research of Nanjing University	
Center for Crisis Management Research of Tsinghua University	
Centre for Think Tanks Research and Management in Shanghai	
Research Institute for Indian Ocean Economic, Yunnan University of Finance and Economics	

Continued

Name of Think Tank	Prize
Research Center for Beijing Transportation Development, Beijing Jiaotong University	Second Prize
Consilium Research Institute of Chongqing University	
Chongqing Center for Productivity Development	
Research Base for the Implementation of National Intellectual Property Strategy (Tianjin University)	
Heilongjiang Academy of Social Science	
Center for Studies in Moral Culture of Hunan Normal University	
Soviet Area Revitalization Institute of Jiangxi Normal University	
Research Institute of Issues in Contemporary China	
Center for Synergetic Innovation of Macroeconomic and Economic Growth Quality in Shaanxi	
Research Center of Anhui Science and Technology Innovation and Regional Development, University of Science and Technology of China	

2.5 Conference Review

On May 19, 2018, the Conference of announcing the results of 2017 CTTI-BPA for Think Tanks together with the Seminar of Think Tank Evaluation System was held in Nanjing. The conference, jointly hosted by the China Think Tank Research and Evaluation Center of Nanjing University and the Think Tank Research and Release Center of *Guangming Daily*, aimed to publicize and promote the innovative experience and unique practices of various types of think tanks at all levels in research, consultation, operation and management, improve our level of research, consultation and management and drive the healthy development of new-type think tanks with Chinese characteristics in the new era. More than 300 people attended the conference, including directors and leaders in charge of provincial and municipal think tanks, representatives of 2017 BPA for think tanks, heads of some CTTI source think tanks, administrators of systems and organizations, and scholars in the field of think-tank research and evaluation.

Lu Xiangao, deputy editor-in-chief of *Guangming Daily*, and Zhu Qingbao, deputy secretary of Party committee of Nanjing University attended and addressed the conference. The keynote speeches were made by Huang Renwei, president of Fudan Institute of "Belt and Road" & Global Governance and executive vice-president of CTTS of Shanghai Academy of Social Sciences, Huang Yiping, vice-president of National School of Development of Peking University and member of Monetary Policy Department of PBOC, Dr. Raymond Struyk, senior researcher of Results for Development Institute.

In his speech, Lu Xiankao said, "*Guangming Daily* and Nanjing University knew the importance of think-tank practice well so that we organized the selection of the "Annual Think-Tank Best Practice Awards", including Best Management Award, Best Research Report Award and Best Event Award. In the selection, we have increasingly deepened our understanding for the construction, organization and management of think-tank system in China. At present, we should enhance their overall strength in five dimensions by the means of developing the operational capacity, research capacity, the capacity to transform results, communication capacity and collaborative capacity."

Zhu Qingbao pointed out, "In order to promote the establishment of an evaluation system for Chinese academic achievements and institutions with Chinese characteristics and world influence, Nanjing University and *Guangming Daily*, on the basis of the original CTTI system, invested resources to develop the CTTI-Plus version in 2017, which is an independent innovation based on China's advantages and highlighting the Chinese discourse. It gets rid of the imitation for western products and shows our independent intellectual property rights in terms of design concept, functional layout, data collection mechanism, evaluation mechanism and other aspects. When the new system comes online, it will help to defend the power of evaluation of philosophy and social sciences in our country. "

The ceremony for 2017 CTTI-BPA for Think Tanks was held at the conference. Nearly 300 think-tank experts and scholars witnessed the announcement of three awards with a total of 51 prizes. As typical representatives in the construction of new types of think tanks with Chinese characteristics, the awarded ones proved the vigorous power and infinite vitality of the Chinese think tanks by their vivid practices.

At the same time, the conference also issued the Chinese-English version of *2017 CTTI Think Tank Report*. Wang Simin, deputy director of Think Tank Research and Release Center of *Guangming Daily* and chief editor of the think tank edition of *Guangming Daily*, pointed out that the "Think Tank Category of CTTI's Source", published in the report, is China's first national think-tank category in English to the world, which will greatly promote the world to know our think tanks and further drive them to the world. *2017 CTTI Think Tank Report* consists of *2017 CTTI Source Think Tank Development Report* and *2017 China's Think Tank Evaluation Report on the Network Influence*. The first part is an evaluation and analysis of the overall development of the source think tanks. It begins to review the process of setting the policy agenda for the construction of new-type think tanks with Chinese characteristics, and then introduces the platform of CTTI II and the supplement of the source think tanks. In the evaluation of think tanks in *2017*, it gives an emphasis to analyze the results of MRPA Assessment of social think tanks and university think tanks. In addition to these analyses, the report also evaluates the related think tanks of eight categories in research areas. The second part is *2017 China's Think Tank Evaluation Report on the Network Influence*. This project was launched in March 2017 and completed by September 2017. Compared with the previous year, it has increased 163 samples of think tanks, which are mainly from CTTI, with more complex types and more special network performance. Therefore, it is very important to identify think tanks and clean up abnormal data.

Professor Li Gang, deputy director and chief expert of China Think Tank Research and Evaluation Center of Nanjing University, presided over the publishing and launching ceremony of CTTI Plus system. Li pointed out that the CTTI Plus system contains a vertical search engine and develops a powerful information management system for think tanks, together with a menu-type intelligent evaluation system, forming a new system of "trinity". At the same time, it provides a pattern of cloud accounts. These two ways enable the CTTI system itself to serve the social sciences management departments of provinces and cities, think tanks management departments, and the social sciences departments of the universities to manage their all social sciences research institutions. Meanwhile, the CTTI Plus system is very powerful in data management, and it is expected to add the function of data transfer to this system in the future.

On the keynote presentation, Huang Renwei, president of CTTS of Shanghai Academy of Social Sciences, summarized the new trend in the development of think tanks at home and abroad, and suggested that the construction of new types of think tanks with Chinese characteristics presents the following new characteristics: the research field tends to be professional and thematic; think tanks are developing towards artificial intelligence, big data and cloud computing; the function of international discourse power of think tanks is being strengthened; the trend of the mutual integration between think tanks and media is obvious; University think tanks and private think tanks are booming; the sources of funding are changing, with increasing social capital. Huang Yiping, vice-president of the National School of Development of Peking University and member of the Monetary Policy Department of PBOC, combining the concrete practice in building the think tank at the National School of Development of Peking University, proposed that independence, specialization and effectiveness are the three keys to the "establishment" of think tanks. He emphasized that the core problem in the construction of think tanks lies in the cultivation of scholars who are committed to the country and concern about the world's affairs. Dr. Raymond Struyk, senior researcher of Results for Development Institute, introduced a brief history of the development of policy influence in the think tanks of the United States, and analyzed the management research standards of think tanks, such as personnel employment, quality control and so on. He pointed out that China's think tanks should strive to establish a good social reputation and seek to create an independent, objective and technical image with efficient policies and advice in the stage of development.

The conference held the exchange for think tank best practice cases in the afternoon, on which the new functions of the new CTTI Plus system, launched in the morning, were demonstrated. Some awarded institutions like Fudan Development Research Institute, Shandong Academy of Social Sciences, Tongji University Institute of Finance and Economics, Beijing Institution of Letters to Government were invited to introduce and share their distinctive features and experience in the construction of think tanks.

This conference has been paid more attention by the media. *Guangming Daily*, Guangming online, Xinhua Net, Chines Social Sciences Net, *Yangtse Evening Post* and other media have followed up on it.

3   Best Practice Examples of CTTI-BPA

3.1   Research report

3.1.1   Beijing Institution of Letters to Government: *Research on the Social Contradictions Index*—A Model Think-Tank Empirical Research

Through the exploration of the "social contradictions index", Beijing Institution of Letters to Government has standardized the evaluation of the current situation of social contradictions, and reflected the distribution of social contradictions and the beharviors of people in coping with them by the quantitative index data. It has ushered in a new era for government departments to quantitatively detect social contradictions.

From 2011 to 2018, the study on social contradictions index has been carried out for eight consecutive years, publishing works with a total of more than one million words. The annual continuous monitoring will help the government to observe, respect and serve people's livelihood from an objective and rational point of view, which makes the government management and system reform more scientific, responsive and forward-looking.

The greatest success of this study lies in the establishment of an indicator system of social contradictions index, which includes two first-level indicators, 11 second-level indicators, 29 third-level indicators and 109 specific problems of material contradictions and value contradictions. The Institution conducts public and social surveys every year based on the system, and calculates the final index of social contradictions according to the basic logical framework of the index, so as to objectively present the current situation of social contradictions through the quantitative indicator data and fill the blank in related areas. In addition to constructing indicators, this research also innovatively introduces the concept of "social contradiction mitigation mechanisms", constructs the connection points between social contradictions and the public policy researches, and pays attention to resolve the social contradictions at the policy source. Through continuously monitoring the effectiveness of public policies, we can promote their scientific formulation and implementation, so as to realize the prevention social contradictions at their source. Besides the material and value contradictions, Beijing Institution of Letters to Government has also made research reports on social hot issues at different stages for the public to understand the current situation and trend of social contradictions from different fields and perspectives, and also for the relevant governments to provide more decision-making reference.

On the whole, based on solid theoretical foundation and expert guidance, the study is made by scientific research methods with the support of professional data, whose innovative value lies in highlighting the early warning and prediction for social contradictions. The emphasis on the prevention and solution of social contradictions at the policy source embodies the strategic and forward-looking think tank research, which has certain reference value for new think tanks to carry out the data-based countermeasure research and improve its accuracy and practicability.

3.1.2 Institute of Finance and Economics of Tongji University: *Rethinking and Accurately Defining the New-Era Principal Contradiction in China's Society* —The Think Tanks Research Should Pay Attention to Major Practical Problems and Give Prominence to the Foresight

The report, *Rethinking and Accurately Defining the New-Era Principal Contradiction in China's Society*, was written in early 2017, by Shi Jianxun,

Professor of the Institute of Finance and Economics of Tongji University. Through observing the rapid development of China's reform and opening up for more than 30 years and the status quo, he considered that the expression and definition of the social principal contradiction in the Party Constitution at present is difficult to accurately reflect its actual situation in China, and finally put forward the suggestions and reasons for the modification of its expression. The proposal was referred to by the drafting group of the report of the 19th National Congress of the CPC and was eventually adopted in the report.

First, the success of this research report is based on deep observation and reflection on reality. Policies should be historical and concrete, with the change of historical conditions and main social problems, and should also reflect the phasing and up-to-date development in history. The rethinking of the main social contradiction is the observation and reflection on the people's ever-growing needs in material, culture, spirit, ecological environment improvement and social security with the development of productivity in China in the new era. Second, it closely follows the strategic deployment of the central think-tank construction, and solidly promotes services in governance and consultation. After the idea of seeking advice of think tanks was put forward in the report of the 18th National Congress of the CPC in 2012 Tongji University established the Institute of Finance and Economics as a school entity. Based on the opinion of building new-type think tanks with Chinese characteristics, the National Institute for Innovation and Development of Tongji University was set up in 2016, which integrates all think tanks of the university into this platform, and aims to transform its traditional advantages into think-tank consultation results through engineering way of thinking. Finally, it adheres to the independence based on professionalism. Transferring think tank research from reports and theories into policies cannot be done overnight. The view about the change of the principal contradiction in our society was presented in which our leader stressed that the principal contradiction has not changed, and it was embodied in policies through internal reference, suggestions and other ways after two years of repeatedly thinking and insisting, based on the professional judgment of think tank experts and the relative independence of think tanks.

3.1.3 Institute for Food Safety Risk Administration of Jiangnan University: *Report on China Food Safety Development*—Making Brand Achievements in Professional Theoretical Research; Building Small but Specialized, Fine and Strong Think Tanks with International Vision in Colleges and Universities

Up to now, the *Report on China Food Safety Development* series have been consecutively published six volumes, all of which start with the production of edible agricultural products, and then synthetically applies various statistic, combined with a large number of empirical investigations to study the food safety evolution of our country (including imported food safety) in key links, such as production, circulation and consumption, and makes the assessment of its current state and future trend. Based on China's national conditions, problems and reality, the series of reports, by the Institute for Food Safety Risk Administration of Jiangnan University, intensively show the exploration of Chinese innovation in thinking about and realizing the governance of food safety risk with Chinese characteristics, as an important innovation in the construction of specialized think tank of colleges and universities.

There are five points of construction experience of the Institute. First, It relies on the discipline advantages and the support of governing institutions. The Institute is mainly grafted with the first-class disciplines and dominant specialties. Food Science and Technology of Jiangnan University always ranks first in the discipline evaluation of China. It is the first to set up the second-level doctoral program of food safety and management among China's colleges and universities, and forms new interdisciplinary disciplines. At the same time, as one of the earliest key think tanks in Jiangsu Province, it is supported by national and provincial dominant units at all levels. Second, it clears about the direction of think-tank development. Based on the national conditions and major realistic demands, the Institute continues to expand its research fields on the basis of focusing on the governance of food safety risk and organically builds industry characteristics, so as to become a professional think tank. Third, it makes brand achievements and serves for government decision-making. The Institute forms a research brand of "trinity", including two consultation reports, *Report on China Food Safety Development* and *Report on China Online Public Opinion of Food Safety*, as well as *the China Food Safety Governance Review*, which is published in two editions each year, and actively promotes the research results to serve the government decision-making, many of whose advice have been instructed by the leaders of the state and its related departments. Fourth, it attaches importance to the promotion of international influence. The Institute actively carries out international exchanges and cooperation. It published an international treatise in the United States in 2014, in which the Chinese theory, Chinese language and Chinese voice were used to illustrate the governance of China food safety risk so that it could participate in the international discourse system. Fifth, it strengthens the infrastructure construction. The Institute actively invests in the construction of the first behavioral economics laboratory at Jiangnan University, and develops a platform for mining and monitoring big data of food safety incidents, which makes an important data foundation for food safety governance in China.

3.2 Management

3.2.1 Innovation Project of Shandong Academy of Social Sciences: Speed Up Transforming the Traditional Academy of Social Sciences to a First-Class New Think Tank Based on Innovative Projects

Shandong Academy of Social Sciences has carried out innovation projects since 2015, and has achieved remarkable results in the course of three years. It explored a development path with "one goal, two-wheel drive, three reforms, four supports, five functions and six innovations".

"One goal" is the overall objective to "build a first-class new type of think tank in China" and strive to develop the "ideological and theoretical highland" of studying and propagating Marxism, the important think tank of the provincial Party committee and government, the high-end academy of philosophy and social sciences of Shandong, the comprehensive database and research and evaluation center of Shandong, and the innovative team serving the construction of strong economy and rich culture in Shangdong.

"Two-wheel drive" means carrying out the strategy driven by basic theoretical research and applied countermeasure research. It can enhance the power of theoretical academic discourse and the influence, and at the same time, carries out overall, forward-looking and strategic researches on the major practical problems that need to be solved urgently in the economic and social development of Shandong, so as to improve the ability and level of scientific decision-making for the provincial Party committee and government.

"Three reforms" refers to deepening the reforms of scientific research management, personnel management and fund management at Shandong Academy of Social Sciences. The reform of scientific research management means it breaks the original academic teams and establishes a new research and innovation team to participate in the innovation project, breaking the original scientific research management system. The reform of personnel management means it, based on the innovation project, establishes a new type of personnel management system, which is "capable of promotion and demotion, entering and leaving, competitive and efficient", and implements strict "access" system and "exit" system. The reform of fund management means it applies the method of "making financing of local governments or not", optimizes the allocation of resources and establishes the compensation system of intelligence.

"Four supports" includes the strengthening of the institutional mechanisms, personnel force, digital informatization and fine outputs, so as to establish the system of scientific research organization and management for excellent achievements, the new personnel management mechanism for the employment of innovative talents, the modernized information support system for the improvement of the efficiency and level of scientific research, and the output mechanism for excellent achievements of continuous innovation.

"Five functions" means the new think tank should give full play to consultation and suggestions, theoretical innovation, public opinion guidance, social service, public diplomacy and soon, so as to speed up moving from the traditional academy of social sciences to the new type of think tank.

"Six innovations" specifically covers the establishment of six innovation systems, such as admission, withdrawal, reward, allocation, evaluation and financial support, and the introduction of reforms on the operating mode for scientific research organizations, the evaluation and assessment system for scientific research achievements, and the auxiliary means and methods of scientific research, personnel management system, talent cultivation, fund allocation and use of management, reform and innovation.

3.2.2 Institute of China Rural Studies of Central China Normal University: Rural Social Survey in Thirty Years—Developing from Village-to-Village Survey to Build the Investigation and Service Platform of Big-Data Think Tank

The Institute of China Rural Studies of Central China Normal University is one of the earliest, most professional and prestigious rural comprehensive research institutions in China. At present, a "five-in-one" construction mechanism has been formed to build a high-end rural development think tank, which is oriented by serving the national and rural decision-making, supported by large-scale surveys and data, mirrored by overseas rural survey and translation, based on the innovation of institutions and mechanism, and targeted at the first-class academic research.

First of all, it is oriented by serving the national and rural decision-making. The Institute adopts the system of schools. China's rural problem is the research direction and development field to follow and focus in the long term, and the think tank closely develops around the discipline construction to carry out applied researches, whose foundation is "survey". Second, it is supported by large-scale survey and data. In order to support the first-class consultation service, the think tank has set up three database systems: China rural database system, China rural villages system, and China rural intelligent decision-making system. Third, it takes example by overseas rural survey and translation. The Institute of China Rural Studies carries out a comparative study on the basic and local governance between China and foreign countries, and has a dialogue with international academies through overseas rural survey and the translation project. Fourth, it takes the innovation of institutions and mechanisms as the platform. At present, the Institute has set up the mechanism of "report every three days & instruction every five days", that is, to submit a consultation report to the relevant departments of the Party and state every three days, and a report that is instructed by central government leaders or provincial ministers every five days. Finally, it is targeted at the first-class academic research to build high-end rural development think tank. Through long follow-up investigation, large-scale sample survey in a fixed place, deep digging investigation, case-based habitual investigation and comprehensive comparative investigation, the Institute constantly enriches the investigation methods, and makes solid foundation of rural investigation.

3.3 Events

3.3.1 Fudan Development Institute: Shanghai Forum—Adhere to the International Path and Promote the Transformation of the Traditional Forum into a Think-Tank Forum

The combination of forum and think tank is an innovation and practice of the Shanghai Forum. "Shanghai Forum", founded in 2005, is co-hosted by Fudan University and Korean Foundation for Advanced Studies, and undertaken by Fudan Development Institute. Until now, it has been successfully held for 12 years, and become one of the most influential brand forums in Shanghai. By taking its mission to "Concentrate on Asia, Focus on Hot Issues, Congregate Elites, Promote Interactions, Enhance Cooperation and Seeking Consensus" and choosing the theme as "Global Governance and Asia" as the theme, the Forum has experienced the development process from single to plural, from closeness to openness, and from the traditional forum to the new think-tank forum.

One of the features of the Forum is its openness. First, with loosening the restriction of and opening to the construction of think tanks, Fudan Development

Institute fully utilizes its own international cooperation network and exchange platform and actively introduces excellent resources at home and abroad to provide services for the international strategy of think tanks and Fudan University. Second, the Forum has a large international advisory board. The members of the board are also the international consultants of Fudan Development Institute, who give suggestions to the setting of the theme and the discussion of topics. Third, the Forum attracts a large number of young visiting scholars, especially those from countries along the "Belt and Road". They also become the new force of the forum development, contributing their wisdom and resources to it. In particular, the Forum has opened the application of all sub-forums and round-table conferences and closely combined with the development of think tanks since 2015, to build a common exchange platform for domestic and foreign think tanks and form an ecological circle of think tanks with Chinese characteristics.

Another highlight of the Forum is the transformation of the results of think tanks. By mining and integrating guests' views and discussion results, Shanghai Forum has made a large number of its own research achievements, including policy recommendations, idea collection, consultation reports and so on. At the same time, it is also a platform for displaying and publishing the achievements of various think tanks, including fields of finance, science and technology, ecological governance and network governance.

In addition, the Shanghai Forum also develops the function of "two-track diplomacy". It invites a large number of former national dignitaries, retired officials, representatives of important government agencies and heads of non-governmental organizations to make public or private discussions on hot topics of concern to the public or important issues of national concern, express views, exchange ideas and deepen communication and understanding, while it can also make the world know China better. Through such dialogue and exchange mechanism, the Forum develops the function of "two-track diplomacy" and gradually became an important carrier for the exchange between Chinese and foreign universities, the transformation of Chinese think-tank achievements, the telling of Chinese stories, and the world's understanding toward China.

3.3.2 Institute of African Studies of Zhejiang Normal University: The Development Path as "Trinity of Disciplines, Think Tank and Media"

In recent years, the Institute of Africa Studies of Zhejiang Normal University has successfully explored a development path of "trinity of discipline, think tank and media", based on the practical demands of China-Africa cooperation.

First, the discipline construction is the main body. From China's view on Africa, the African Strategy and the practice of China-Africa cooperation, the Institute can extract knowledge forms, theoretical systems and discourse concepts to explain and promote common development between China and Africa and a community with a shared future for mankind, which establishes the academic foundation of knowledge and thought to serve the country and forms "African Studies in China". Second, the think-tank service is the function. The university think tanks should always be driven by discipline construction and think-tank construction, and give full play to the five functions of strategic research, consultation, talent training, public opinion guidance and public diplomacy. Through holding events like China-Africa Cooperation Forum and China-Africa Think Tank Forum, the Institute has successfully broken the academic dilemma of one-way conversation in the small circle and has made the practical influence and service to the state and society. Third, the media communication is the means. By virtue of the cooperation with the media, university think tanks can promote China's academic development toward the world, make the direct influence on the core targeted countries and change the overseas image of China. By hosting China-Africa media think tank seminars and signing cooperation agreements with the mainstream media in Africa, the Institute conveys the "Chinese voice" to Africa and the world. The awarded documentary, *African in Yiwu*, tells the story of Africans in China, which aims to promote mutual understanding between China and Africa by the means of real images. Only with the integration of discipline, think tank and media can the university think tanks gradually become influentially international academic institutions and ideological think tanks, and promote the bilateral balance and interaction of thought and knowledge at home and abroad.

Liu Hongwu, president of the Institute, summarized five reflections on the construction of university think tank. The first is to make a good overall layout and development plan around for the national strategy; the second is to give full play to the special role of universities in the national development strategies; the third is to build their own development research institute according to the expectation of the state and region; the fourth is to set up think tanks of discipline innovation to serve local development; the fifth is to transform China's native experiential discourse into international discourse.

3.3.3 Changjiang Education Research Institute: Summit Forum on Education Think Tanks and Education Governance—Make Full Use of the Channels of the CPPCC National People's Congress, Set Up the First-Class Professional Forum and Focus on the Modernization of China's Education All the Time

The Summit Forum on Education Think Tanks and Education Governance, hosted by Changjiang Education Research Institute, focuses on the theme of "Keeping Pace with Ages and Contributing to Reforms". It is mainly about "how to better participate in and implement education governance and enhance public service capabilities for today's education think tanks so as to provide suggestions for education administrative departments and promote the development of education think tans with Chinese characteristics", thus it explores actively the systems and mechanisms in efficient operation of the educational policy research think tank under the new situation.

Changjiang Education Research Institute is a social think tank, co-sponsored by Hubei Provincial Department of Education, Central China Normal University and Changjiang Publishing & Media Group. Since 2009, the Institute has held Changjiang Education Forum in Beijing for ten consecutive years before the two sessions, inviting representatives of the NPC, members of the CPPCC, and leaders of relevant departments of the Ministry of Education to jointly discuss the topic of education reform and development, and at the same time, published the annual policy recommendations on education, China education index, and the annual top 10 education keywords. At the Summit Forum on Education Think Tanks and Education Governance, held in Beijing on December 16, 2016, the Changjiang Education Research Institute was awarded the "Outstanding Contribution to Education Advice Award".

In addition, Changjiang Education Research Institute also attaches great importance to strategic cooperation with educational administrations, scientific research institutions and universities. In order to gradually communicate the channels of educational resources throughout the country, realize the co-realization of research results, and build a first-class education professional platform, the Institute takes Hubei as the center and spreads to the south, north and southwest, and then sets up a cooperative think tank with well-known colleges and universities. The Changjiang

Education Research Institute has successively established its Northern Education Think Tank, Southern Education Think Tank, East China Education Think Tank, and Southwest Education Think Tank. These education think tanks can submit their research to the NPC through Changjiang Education Research Institute and develop "consultation newsflash", and finally make full use of the channels of the NPC and the CPPCC to serve the reform and development of China's education modernization.

Conclusion

The construction of socialism with Chinese characteristics has entered a great new era. Since the 18th National People's Congress of the Communist Party of China, a lot of best practices with theoretical value and obvious practical guidance in research, event and management, keeping up with the development of research, consultation and management, have emerged in the construction of new types of think tanks with Chinese characteristics. This selection of the three Awards for BPA has fully exploited the latest achievements in the internal governance and operation mode of China's think tanks in recent years and spread the successful experience and advanced ideas of the construction of think tanks. These practices, rich in content, imply the vein of new types of think tank development in China and its future direction. The Conference of announcing the results of 2017 CTTI-BPA for Think Tanks together with the Seminar of Think Tank Evaluation System provides a good platform for all kinds of think tanks to fully exchange and learn from advanced experience.

The China Think Tank Research and Evaluation Center of Nanjing University and the Think Tank Research and Release Center of *Guangming Daily* jointly carried out the selection and release of the three Awards for BPA, in order to further promote the development of the think-tank community and discover more outstanding cases, which gives outstanding think tanks at all levels the opportunity to come to the fore. Moreover, it is hoped that the three Awards for BPA will become an important mechanism to boost the practical abilities of the new-type think tanks, to select and commend the excellent ones, and to provide a vivid example for the construction of new types of think tanks with Chinese characteristics.

图书在版编目(CIP)数据

CTTI智库报告. 2018 / 李刚, 王斯敏, 邹婧雅主编
．—南京：南京大学出版社, 2019.10
（南大智库文丛 / 李刚主编）
ISBN 978-7-305-22503-1

Ⅰ. ①C… Ⅱ. ①李… ②王… ③邹… Ⅲ. ①咨询机构—研究报告—中国—2018 Ⅳ. ①C932.82

中国版本图书馆CIP数据核字(2019)第149869号

出版发行	南京大学出版社
社　　址	南京市汉口路22号　　邮　编　210093
出 版 人	金鑫荣
丛 书 名	南大智库文丛
丛书主编	李　刚
书　　名	CTTI智库报告(2018)
主　　编	李　刚　王斯敏　邹婧雅
责任编辑	杨　博　张　静
照　　排	南京南琳图文制作有限公司
印　　刷	江苏凤凰通达印刷有限公司
开　　本	718×1000　1/16　印张36.25　字数527千
版　　次	2019年10月第1版　2019年10月第1次印刷
ISBN	978-7-305-22503-1
定　　价	98.00元

网　　址：http://www.njupco.com
官方微博：http://weibo.com/njupco
官方微信：njupress
销售咨询：(025) 83594756

* 版权所有，侵权必究
* 凡购买南大版图书，如有印装质量问题，请与所购
　图书销售部门联系调换